# CONTENTS

**PART TWO**    *Resolving Most Behavior Problems*    *77*

**CHAPTER 4**    *Problems and Who Owns Them*    *79*

# *PREFACE*

*Trouble-Free Teaching* is designed to provide pre-service educators with the classroom management skills they will require to maintain classroom environments that foster learning and enhance students' personal growth. The book suggests a three-stage approach to classroom management:

1. Because educators can avoid most behavior problems before they occur, the book begins by describing the management techniques that research indicates are helpful.

2. Unfortunately, even the best management techniques don't completely avoid behavior problems. For this reason *Trouble-Free Teaching* also includes techniques educators can use to solve behavior problems that occur even when they use good management techniques.

3. Since no technique works with all students, the book also provides teachers with the skills they require to individualize their approaches.

*Trouble-Free Teaching* acknowledges the fact that students who differ from their teachers in racial, ethnic, or socioeconomic background may come to class with learning and behavioral styles, values, interests, and goals that are acceptable to their families and communities but not necessarily to the schools. It recognizes the existence of sex-role stereotypes in schools and a generation gap between some students and some teachers and provides educators with suggestions for taking these cultural, generation, and gender differences into account when dealing with students' behavior problems.

*Trouble-Free Teaching* provides educators with both theoretical knowledge about the science of classroom management—the positions of well-known authors and the results of research investigations—and practical suggestions for implementing this knowledge in the classroom. However, the book doesn't leave readers with the impression that, having mastered its contents, they will be able to avoid or solve all classroom behavior problems. It acknowledges the limitations of the science of classroom management and discusses the factors beyond educators' control that affect their abilities to solve the behavior problems that confront them. To maximize readers' learning, research results which support suggestions in the text are listed in the reference sections of each chapter rather than described in detail in the text.

*Trouble-Free Teaching* includes a comprehensive view of classroom management that is wholistic and developmental. Instead of focusing on one age group such as elementary or secondary school students, it is designed to provide readers with an understanding of students as complete human beings who are at a specific stage in the developmental process. By explaining why some techniques are more or less effective with students at particular levels of psychological, intellectual, and moral development, the text will help educators select techniques that are developmentally appropriate for their students. For example, readers will be better able to determine the extent to which their students are ready to participate in the establishment of classroom rules and objectives, to settle disputes among themselves without guidance and supervision, to use self-management techniques, to exercise self-control for intrinsic rather than extrinsic rewards, and to behave appropriately because that is the reasonable and ethical thing to do rather than in order to obtain a positive consequence or avoid a negative one.

This text is also comprehensive in terms of the broad range of classroom management techniques it offers. Instead of describing a limited number of techniques in great detail, the book includes the wide range of techniques that are available to deal with behavior problems. Less experienced teachers can select those that best suit their personalities, philosophy of education, values, the circumstances in which they work, and the developmental levels of their students.

The information included in this book should empower educators to spend more time doing what they are supposed to do—teach, and their students should be able to spend more of their time doing what they are supposed to do—learn. The result should be measurable improvement in students' academic achievement and self-esteem.

The principles, concepts, strategies, and techniques included in the book come from my understanding of the writing and research of other professionals in the field, my training and experiences as a regular educator, special educator, clinical psychologist, and neuropsychologist as well as my experience living and working with different racial, ethnic, and socioeconomic groups. They have proven to be effective with regular education students, mainstreamed students, and students in special education programs at both the primary and secondary level. I sincerely hope they will be helpful to you.

## *Acknowledgments*

I am grateful to the following reviewers of the text for their many excellent suggestions: William J. Gnagey, Illinois State University; Thomas L. Good, University of Missouri, Columbia; Kristen D. Juul, Southern Illinois University at Carbondale; Janie Knight, Memphis State University; James Long, Appalachian State University; Ida Malian, San Diego State University; Tyrone Payne, Wright State University; and Richard Shepardson, University of Iowa.

I'm also grateful to my colleagues, Nancy Cloud, Susan Pellegrini, and Jeri Traub for their constructive criticisms of earlier versions of the manuscript and to Henry Fishel, Harry Krohn, and George Singfield, who taught me so much when I was a classroom teacher. I also thank my sponsoring editor, Frank Graham, who helped me give my best to this text.

# *INTRODUCTION TO CLASSROOM MANAGEMENT*

This introductory chapter begins by describing the components of an effective classroom management approach and the roles educators assume in order to manage their classrooms well. Then it discusses the value and importance of basing classroom management techniques on behavior research.

## *Components of an Effective Approach*

Since one picture is said to be worth a thousand words, let's begin by videotaping a typical day in the lives of certain teachers and their students to see if we can discover aspects essential to effective classroom management. We're in luck—the taping goes smoothly. Now it's time to review what we have recorded. Most teachers are doing an excellent job, but one seems less successful at maintaining order than her colleagues.

### *Avoiding Behavior Problems*

Ms. Tucker is a good instructor with a flare for the dramatic. She chooses interesting material, and her students like her. Despite this, she lost her students' attention a number of times, and a few were even disruptive.

Let's study some specific incidents. Here's one—seven or eight students are talking to each other; two are arguing over something. We rewind the tape to a few minutes earlier to see if we can discover why. Ms. Tucker is working with one student at her desk while the other students are working in their seats. Soon two students start talking, and then a few students near them look up to see what is going on. Ms. Tucker either doesn't hear them or chooses to ignore them. Pretty soon two more students start talking, then two more. By the time Ms. Tucker finally looks up, she has lost almost half the class. We can see from the tape that she should have intervened much earlier before the talking had spread.

We review the tape again to find another incident. Here, Ms. Tucker is standing in the front of the room talking to one student while most of the others are either looking around or talking to one another. We rewind from here, and everything looks fine. Ms. Tucker is in front of the room talking, and everyone is paying attention. Oh, oh! Joe just passed a note to someone, and Ms. Tucker sees it. She interrupts her presentation and starts lecturing Joe about how many times she has told him not to do this. Joe defends himself, and she chastises him some more. Meanwhile, she is losing the students, at least those who aren't interested in what she has to say about Joe, what Joe says back, or her response. Clearly Ms. Tucker would have been better off if she had handled the situation without stopping the lesson. From this review of Ms. Tucker's class, we can conclude that *classroom management includes the use of good group management techniques that keep the group on task and functioning smoothly without too many interruptions or disruptions.*

Now let's study certain students to see what we can learn about classroom management from them. Most seem to be doing just what they are supposed to be doing. They work at their task and look about as content as most students are in school. But a few are obviously behavior problems. Right off, Teresa attracts our attention because her behavior from one class to another is so inconsistent. In three classes she did fine, but her behavior left much to be desired in second period social studies. Let's study her behavior in that class more closely.

Teresa is whispering to the person next to her. Now she is getting up to sharpen her pencil. There she is looking around the room and doodling in her notebook. Oops, she has taken out a comic book. Oh! Oh! She's tapping the girl in front of her with a ruler, which starts another discussion. And so it goes.

Puzzled about why her behavior is so different in the social studies class, we study how each teacher works with her. This will help us figure out whether the way she behaves in social studies is related to the way her teacher, Mr. Garcia, deals with her or to other factors such as the time of day or her level of interest in the subject.

After watching all four teachers, we discover that Mr. Garcia doesn't do some of the things that Teresa's other teachers do. Specifically, each of Teresa's three other teachers keep a watchful eye on her. There, one goes to Teresa's desk to see how her work is coming along. Another has Teresa working with a peer tutor. Aha! The third teacher gives Teresa seatwork that is different from what most of the students are doing. Perhaps these teachers realize Teresa will stray if she doesn't get more help than the other students. Although we can't be sure from just viewing the video, it's beginning to look as if Mr. Garcia could have prevented Teresa's inattentive behavior by giving her the extra help she needed to stay on task. Studying the tape of Teresa has shown us that classroom management is more than just techniques for working with groups of students. *Classroom management includes using certain skills to keep individual students involved in productive work.*

*Students who aren't engaged by the classroom instruction can become restless and bored and may end up misbehaving; however, involved, interested students seldom misbehave.*

## Solving Behavior Problems

Now let's study another student, Hank, who is the most disruptive student on our tape. He calls out answers without being called on, forcibly takes material from other students, pushes someone on a swing during recess who doesn't want to be pushed, and leaves his lunch bag and garbage on the cafeteria table although the other students all clean up after themselves. In reviewing the tape to see if we can gain any insight into the problem, nothing that any of his teachers did seems to provoke his disruptive behavior. We also can't identify any early warning signs that his teachers might have used to intervene before he actually misbehaved. And, finally, we see no inconsistencies in his behavior with three different teachers in the classroom, during recess, or in the cafeteria. Hank is pretty much the same in all settings.

Although we can't be 100 percent sure, it looks as if something about Hank himself would have to explain why he misbehaves consistently even though his teachers use the kinds of group and individual management techniques that prevent most behavior problems. These classroom management techniques, which work for most students, don't work with Hank. This leads us to realize that classroom management involves more than just avoiding problems. *Effective classroom management includes techniques for solving the behavior problems of students who don't respond to techniques that generally keep the group functioning smoothly and most students involved in productive work.*

## Fostering Personal Growth

Finally, let's study one more teacher. Ms. Kelly has none of the problems we noticed in Ms. Tucker's tape. Her students almost always do what they are supposed to do without interruptions or disruptions. She clearly has much more control over students than Ms.

Tucker, but it is obvious that her students aren't happy. An example of their dissatisfaction is that while Ms. Kelly is talking, some students roll their eyes up, and others exchange knowing glances.

Let's rewind the tape to catch the beginning of this incident. Ms. Kelly is giving out homework. "I want all of you to put this assignment into your binders right now so no one loses it like the last one," she says in a clipped way. Some students begin to signal annoyance to each other. Three raise their hands, but Ms. Kelly continues without calling on them. "Do your own work. Follow the directions *exactly* as they are on the sheet, and remember what I said about no credit for assignments handed in late. No more excuses. You have two weeks to hand in your reports. That should be more than enough."

Now Ms. Kelly calls on one of the students, who asks, "Can we report on a book that isn't on the list if we . . .?" "No!" Ms. Kelly interrupts gruffly, without giving the student a chance to finish. "You may only report on books from the list." Ms. Kelly's students grimace, while another student raises his hand. Ms. Kelly calls on him. "But you said we would have a month to do our book reports." "I know I did," Ms. Kelly responds. "However, I changed my mind because of the class play." At that, a sea of hands shoots up, and most of the students look annoyed. "There's no sense wasting valuable time discussing it," Ms. Kelly continues without slowing down, "that's the way it has to be." Some students express their disagreement by sighing and murmuring. Ms. Kelly ends the discussion by telling everyone to put their binders away and to take out their math books.

In contrast to Ms. Tucker, Ms. Kelly is certainly in control of her class and can keep her students on task. But there is clearly room for improvement in the way she is managing her class. Ms. Kelly helps us see that classroom management is more than classroom control and merely avoiding or solving behavior problems—though these are important and necessary goals. *Classroom management includes creating a positive classroom environment that enhances students' personal growth.*

The videotapes showed us that educators need to have at least three types of competencies to manage their classroom effectively: (1) the ability to avoid problems by having the group function smoothly without too many interruptions or disruptions and by keeping individual students involved in productive work; (2) the ability to solve the behavior problems of students who don't respond to the management techniques that avoid most behavior problems; and (3) the ability to create classroom environments that enhance students' personal growth. The purpose of this book is to help educators acquire these abilities.

# *Three Aspects of the Educator's Role*

In addition to the three competencies just described, Kounin (1) suggests that there are also three aspects of a teacher's roles vis-à-vis his or her students: an instructor, a manager, and a person. Applying Kounin's categories to the videotape, we can see that Mr. Garcia might have been able to avoid Teresa's behavior problems by using more appropriate instructional techniques. Ms. Tucker's students would probably have behaved better if she had used more effective group-management techniques. And Ms. Kelly was too arbitrary and authoritarian as a person and in her personal relationships with her students.

In attending to all three aspects of the educator's role, this book describes instructional and managerial techniques teachers can use to avoid as many behavior problems as possible, solve those that do occur, and enhance their students' personal growth. Specific discussions will provide you with tools to gain insight into your personality and the way it is likely to affect the way you perceive and react to your students' behavior. These discussions include suggestions on how you can use your personality to maximum advantage in the classroom.

## *Limitations to the Educator's Role*

In this book I focus on what you can do as an individual to solve your students' behavior problems. But the effects of your efforts will also be influenced—and possibly limited—by the total school context (ecology). For example, if the previous teachers of your current second graders all allowed students to approach their desks when they were confused or unsure about their seatwork and go to the bathroom whenever the bathroom pass wasn't being used, students will have an easier time adjusting to your rules if they are the same than if you require them to raise their hands and ask permission to do such things. Likewise, even if you feel comfortable with occasionally expressing your pride in your seventh-grade students or your concern about their feelings by some kind of physical contact such as patting them on the back or placing an arm around their shoulders, you may hesitate to do this if your administrators frown on physical contact between teachers and students. Finally, even your best efforts to promote racial harmony among your students can fail if the rest of the faculty and school administration aren't working toward the same goal.

You may find it necessary, on occasion, to explain to students why some of your methods differ from those of your colleagues. In general, paying attention to the total school environment will help you become a better classroom manager, and you will see how the school environment limits or fosters your role. Since the total school ecology often affects the results of your individual efforts, you may want to take an active role in helping develop schoolwide policies, attitudes, and approaches that support your efforts with your students.

## *The Value of a Research-Based Approach*

Until fairly recently classroom management was an art, not a science, and some teachers excelled at this art. Today, as a result of considerable research, we know enough about the science of behavior to put classroom management on a scientific basis (although, as any experienced teacher will tell you, classroom management remains partially an art).

Behavior research has revealed the weakness in some basic assumptions about classroom management. For example, until recently, many educators believed that students' behavior could be managed by rewarding desirable behavior and ignoring and/or punishing undesirable behavior. Recent research into the effects of reward and punishment on classroom behavior, however, shows that the relationship between rewards and punishment and their subsequent behavior is much more complex than had been supposed. Chapters 2 and 3 discuss the implications of these results in detail. I mention these findings here as an example of the role that theory and research play in improving classroom management approaches.

The following are some of the findings on using positive and negative reinforcement to manage students' behavior. The references in parentheses refer you to more detailed accounts of the research. Contrary to popular myth, extrinsic positive reinforcement (a reward that comes from outside the student) doesn't always increase desired behavior (2,3). For example, praise from a teacher is likely to be ineffective if it's planned rather than spontaneous, is insincere, or is given effusively for trivial accomplishments. Under certain conditions, positive reinforcement can even have a detrimental effect on students' performance. In particular, students who are already motivated to learn and behave appropriately in the classroom may lose their intrinsic motivation to do so if they become too interested in earning extrinsic rewards (4–15). Positive reinforcement may increase students' learned helplessness and dependency if they come to rely excessively on their teachers' approval and opinion in place of their own motivation (16–18). And it can discourage creativity if students become more concerned about pleasing their teachers or conforming to their teachers' expectations than finding their own solutions to problems (19–22).

After reviewing the research on the effects of positive reinforcement, Deci concluded that "extrinsic rewards whether money, praise, good player rewards, or gold stars—under varying circumstances—have deleterious effects on the intrinsic motivation and performance of the rewardee . . . Many of the widespread practices and many of the widely espoused prescriptions for using extrinsic rewards to motivate people don't work the way practitioners and prescribers expect them to" (7, p. 193–94).

The other tactic, negative reinforcement, may not reduce the incidence of undesirable behavior either (2), especially negative reinforcement that is harsh, excessive, or unfair. Even when negative reinforcement does reduce undesirable behavior, it can have unwanted side effects, causing students to lose interest in learning, become anxious, drop out of school, lose respect for their teachers, or try to turn other students against the teacher (23–27). And withdrawing attention or ignoring students when they misbehave is ineffective if their misbehavior is maintained by peer attention or other environmental reinforcements beyond the teacher's control (2,3,27).

The use of consequences to control students can insulate teachers from important feedback. For example, students might hide the fact that they are bored, frustrated, or angry because of the consequences they incur when they show their true reactions. As a result, educators don't realize they might need more emphasis on positive classroom management approaches such as teacher-pupil relationships, instructional techniques, group management skills, and curriculum planning (28).

Students may also not experience consequences in the way their teachers intended. For example, praising students in front of their peers may be counterproductive with some students. And suspending students who want to avoid school may encourage, not discourage, them to misbehave. As Brophy and Putnam explain in their discussions of reinforcements:

Certain potential rewards, most notably teacher attention and praise and symbolic rewards, tend to be discussed as if they were universally rewarding. In fact, they are probably less rewarding than commonly believed. Many students find special attention or recognition from the teacher to be embarrassing or threatening rather than rewarding. (2, p. 53)

Findings show the effectiveness of positive and negative reinforcements as a classroom management technique varies with students' age, tending to be most effective with young children in kindergarten and first grade, somewhat less effective with older students, and least effective with secondary school students (2,29,30). Finally, no one has shown that behavioral change brought about by positive and negative reinforcements in one situation generalizes to other situations (classrooms, teachers, and so on) or is maintained when the extrinsic reinforcers are dropped (2,31).

Despite these research findings that question the widely held notion that positive and negative consequences are a fairly foolproof way of managing classrooms, the shelves of libraries and bookstores overflow with "how-to" books that describe how educators can solve behavior problems without citing any scientific bases for their suggestions. Even when such suggestions are helpful, without research it is difficult to determine under what conditions and with what types of students they are most and least likely to be effective. Research-based techniques are grounded in fact.

# *References*

THREE ASPECTS OF THE EDUCATOR'S ROLE

1. Kounin, J. S. (1970). *Discipline and Group Management in Classrooms*. New York: Holt, Rinehart & Winston.

LIMITED EFFECTIVENESS OF POSITIVE REINFORCEMENT

2. Brophy, J. E., & Putnam, J. C. (1978). *Classroom Management in the Elementary Grades*. ERIC ED 167, 537.

3. Skiba, R. J. (1983). *Classroom Behavior Management: A Review of the Literature*. ERIC ED 236 839.

CONTRADICTORY EFFECTS OF POSITIVE REINFORCEMENT

4. Condry, J., & Chambers, J. (1978). Intrinsic motivation and the process of learning. In M. R. Lepper & D. Greene (Eds.), *The Hidden Cost of Reward: New Perspectives on the Psychology of Human Motivation*. New York: Erlbaum.

5. De Charms, R. (1976). *Enhancing Motivation: Change in the Classroom*. New York: Irvington.

6. Deci, E. L. (1976). *Intrinsic Motivation*. New York: Plenum Press.

7. Deci, E. L. (1978). Applications of research on the effects of rewards. In M. R. Lepper & D. Greene (Eds.), *The Hidden Costs of Reward: New Perspectives on the Psychology of Human Motivation*. New York: Erlbaum.

8. Lepper, M. R., & Greene, D. (Eds.). (1978). *The Hidden Costs of Reward: New Perspectives on the Psychology of Human Motivation*. New York: Erlbaum.

9. Pittman, T., Boggiano, A., & Ruble, D. (1982). Intrinsic and extrinsic motivational orientations: Limiting conditions on the undermining and enhancing effects of reward on intrinsic motivation. In J. Levine & M. Wang (Eds.), *Teacher-Student Perceptions: Implications for Learning*. Morristown, NJ: Erlbaum.

10. Ross, M. (1976). The self-perception of intrinsic motivation. In J. H. Harvey, W. J. Ickes, & R. F. Kidd (Eds.), *New Directions in Attributional Research* (Vol. I). New York: Erlbaum.

DETRIMENTAL EFFECTS OF PRAISE ON LEARNING

11. Brophy, J. (1981). Teacher praise: A functional analysis. *Review of Educational Research, 51*, 5–32.

12. Condry, J. (1975). The role of initial interest and task performance on intrinsic motivation. In J. C. McCullers (Chair), *Hidden Costs of Reward*. A symposium presented at the American Psychological Association Convention, Chicago.

13. Good, T. L., & Grouws, D. A. (1977). Teaching effects: A process-product study in fourth grade mathematics classes. *Journal of Teacher Education, 28*, 45–50.

14. McGraw, K. (1978). The detrimental effects of rewards on performance: A literature review and a prediction model. In M. Lepper & D. Greene (Eds.), *The Hidden Costs of Reward: New Perspectives on the Psychology of Human Motivation*. New York: Erlbaum.

15. Miller, L. B., & Estes, B. W. (1961). Monetary rewards and motivation in discrimination learning. *Journal of Experimental Psychology, 61*, 501–504.

EFFECTS ON LEARNED HELPLESSNESS AND DEPENDENCY

16. Ginott, H. G. (1972). *Teacher and Child*. New York: Avon.

17. Kruglanski, A. W. (1978). Endogenous attribution and extrinsic motivation. In M. Lepper & D. Greene (Eds.), *The Hidden Costs of Reward: New Perspectives on the Psychology of Human Motivation*. New York: Erlbaum.

18. Weiner, B. (1979). A theory of motivation in some classroom experiences. *Journal of Educational Psychology, 71*, 3–25.

DETRIMENTAL EFFECTS ON CREATIVITY

19. Jenke, S., & Peck, D. (1976). Is immediate reinforcement appropriate? *Arithmetic Teacher, 23*, 32–33.

20. Johnson, D., & Johnson, R. (1975). *Learning Together and Alone: Cooperation, Competition, and Individualization*. Englewood Cliffs, NJ: Prentice-Hall.

21. Kruglanski, A. W., Friedman, I., & Zeevi, G. (1971). The effects of extrinsic incentive on some qualitative aspects of task performance. *Journal of Personality, 39,* 606–617.

22. Soar, R., & Soar, R. (1975). Classroom behavior, pupil characteristics, and pupil growth for the school year and summer. *JSAS Catalog of Selected Documents in Psychology, 5,* 873.

NEGATIVE REINFORCEMENT

23. Fisher, C. W., Berliner, D. C., Filby, N. N., Marliave, R., Cohen, L. S., & Dishaw, M. M. (1980). Teaching behaviors, academic learning time, and student achievement: An overview. In C. Denham & A. Lieberman (Eds.), *Time to Learn.* Washington, DC: National Institute of Education.

24. Masden, C. H., Becker, W. C., Thomas, D. R., Koser, L., & Plager, E. (1968). An analysis of the reinforcing function of 'sit down' commands. In R. K. Parker (Ed.), *Readings in Educational Psychology.* Boston: Allyn & Bacon.

25. Meacham, M. L., & Wiesen, A. E. (1969). *Changing Classroom Behavior: A Manual for Precision Teaching.* Scranton, PA: International Textbook Company.

26. Saunders, M. (1979). *Class Control and Behavior Problems.* Berkshire, England: McGraw-Hill.

IGNORING BEHAVIOR

27. Jones, F. H., & Miller, W. H. (1974). The effective use of negative attention for reducing group disruption in special elementary school classrooms. *Psychological Record, 24,* 435–458.

ELIMINATING FEEDBACK

28. Ryan, B. (1979). A case against behavior modification in the "ordinary classroom." *Journal of School Psychology, 17* (2), 131–136.

REINFORCEMENT AND STUDENTS' AGE

29. Forness, S. R. (1973). The reinforcement hierarchy. *Psychology in the Schools, 10,* 168–177.

30. Stallings, J. (1975). Implementation and child effects of teaching practices in Follow Through classrooms. *Monographs of the Society for Research in Child Development, 40,* 7–8.

GENERALIZATION

31. Emery, R., & Marholin, D. (1977). An applied behavior analysis of delinquency: The irrelevancy of relevant behavior. *American Psychologist, 32,* 860–873.

# PART ONE

# AVOIDING BEHAVIOR PROBLEMS

# *Introduction*

As we noted in Chapter 1, the first stage of an effective classroom management approach is to use techniques that avoid as many behavior problems as possible and to do this in ways that enhance the students' personal growth. In many instances, the same techniques educators use to prevent behavior problems also enhance their students' personal development, and then these two goals are complementary. An example of this occurs when helping students to be more responsible for their own behavior, to be more empathic about how their actions affect others, and to be more patient also helps them control their own behavior. But sometimes teachers use classroom management techniques that interfere with their students' personal growth. By using ridicule and sarcasm to control the students, for example, the teacher may lower their self-esteem. Or teachers may be so dominating and controlling that they stunt the development of their students' self-confidence, judgment, and initiative. Because certain techniques that help avoid behavior problems can also interfere with students' personal growth, it is important to be selective in the techniques you choose.

Enhancing students' personal growth can mean different things to different people. For purposes of this book, enhancing your students' personal growth will stand for fostering the development of the following ten characteristics:

1. Self-esteem: self-acceptance, a healthy self-image, and a perception of self-worth that are reflected in personal, academic, and social behaviors
2. Self-confidence: confidence regarding personal and social skill development
3. Responsibility: reliability and investment of self in personal and social commitments
4. Initiative: the ability to undertake and sustain independent effort
5. Honesty/Trust: the ability to express feelings honestly and openly to others
6. Empathy: the ability to respond to others with objectivity and understanding
7. Judgment: the ability to make appropriate decisions independently and to adapt behavior to the demands of a situation
8. Flexibility: the ability to adjust to change and to alter behavior constructively
9. Patience: the ability to accept differences during interaction with others; the ability to delay personal need gratification; the ability to handle frustration.
10. Humor: the ability to employ humor appropriately, both in general and in situations involving conflict, to maintain perspective and release stress (1, p. 7).

This part introduces a four-step approach to avoid most behavior problems. You start by motivating students to want to behave appropriately because it's the right thing to do. Then you establish procedures for handling potentially disruptive situations. Next you establish rules that clarify how students are expected to behave. Finally you convince students that it is necessary for them to comply with classroom rules and procedures.

Although all four steps contribute to avoiding behavior problems, motivating students to want to behave is the most important in a democratic society. Autocratic societies can rely on coercion and consequences to keep their citizens in line, but a democratic nation requires citizens who voluntarily sacrifice their personal desires for the benefit of the group when necessary, accept the will of the majority, and respect the rights of others. This doesn't mean that enforcing the cost of misbehavior, the fourth step, is unnecessary—just that it should not be the most important or receive the most emphasis in a classroom management approach. To have classrooms approximate the real world and to prepare students for that world, educators should stress internal, not external, control and intrinsic, not extrinsic, motivation.

When students want to behave appropriately, they are more willing to exercise their self-control and improve their relationships with others by helping them to more willingly accept the rights of others, sacrifice their desires for others' benefit, and accept group goals. These motivational techniques also make students more able to assume responsibility for their own actions and accept the role their actions play in provoking responses from others.

With respect to their own goals, such techniques aid students in exercising more self-discipline and enable them to sacrifice a less important satisfaction of the moment to achieve a more important future satisfaction. They also prepare students to endure the difficult, frustrating, and distasteful but necessary aspects of life that we can't avoid if we want to accomplish worthwhile goals.

Students who have developed such self-control have many of the personal qualities needed to behave appropriately in school. Educators can use a number of techniques to foster this type of self-discipline in their students, including satisfying their students' basic needs, relating to their students in ways that enhance the development of their self-control, modeling appropriate behavior, promoting group cohesiveness, and rewarding students when they exercise self-discipline. Chapter 2 describes techniques educators can use to motivate their students to want to behave properly.

Chapter 3 explores techniques that manage such potentially disruptive situations as start-ups, transitions, obtaining permission, distributing materials, and so forth. The chapter describes how to lessen the likelihood that students will misbehave. Finally, for students still tempted to misbehave, they will be less likely to do so if the teacher enforces the cost of misbehaving. The chapter outlines techniques for convincing students that misbehaving would not be to their advantage, including making the rules explicit, making the rules acceptable to them, convincing students that they will be caught if they break the rules, and convincing students that, once caught, they will experience the consequences of their actions.

# CHAPTER 2

# *MOTIVATING STUDENTS TO WANT TO BEHAVE APPROPRIATELY*

Educators can avoid many behavior problems by motivating students to want to behave appropriately. You can accomplish this by satisfying students' basic needs so they can attend to academic matters, maintaining positive student-teacher relationships, modeling the behavior that students should emulate, promoting group cohesiveness, and—when necessary—rewarding students for behavior appropriately.

## *Satisfying Students' Basic Needs*

All people have basic needs that they strive to fulfill, and students are more likely to behave appropriately when these needs are satisfied (2). This is because human needs are organized in a hierarchical way so that people primarily concerned with getting their basic needs met are less likely to take care of higher level needs. Below is a hierarchically ordered list of human needs starting with basic survival needs and working up from there.

1. Physiological satisfaction—taking care of hunger, thirst, rest.

2. Safety—avoiding injury, physical attack, pain, extreme temperatures, disease, psychological abuse.

3. Love and acceptance from others and a feeling of belonging to a group.

4. Self-esteem, self-confidence, and a sense of purpose and empowerment.

5. Self-actualization. (3,4)

When students are preoccupied with their physical well-being, safety, or pain, chances are they will be too concerned with these basic issues to care much about learning arithmetic skills or American history. In the classroom, they may act out their anger, resentment, and frustration at not having their basic needs fulfilled. And they may be jealous of their more fortunate peers and show this in a variety of ways.

Because, like all people, students have the right to have their basic needs satisfied and they can't be expected to function adequately in school if these needs aren't satisfied, educators should place the highest priority on seeing that their students' basic needs are being met. But educators don't have primary responsibility for assuring that students' basic needs are satisfied. They do, though, play an important role in this area of concern.

To play your part in seeing that your students' basic needs are met, be on the lookout for signs that your students aren't being fed, clothed, or cared for adequately or that they are the victims of physical, sexual, or psychological abuse. You can't solve these problems on your own, but you can—and are legally obligated to in most states—report your observations to those who can do something about the situation.

On a personal level, you can provide students with some of the love, acceptance, and feeling of belonging we all require, and you can encourage other students to do the same. Enhance your students' sense of personal power by allowing them a role in the decision-making process in class. Improve their self-esteem and self-confidence by providing them with opportunities to solve their own problems, resolve their own conflicts with others, and experience success in activities they choose. Protect students who are ethnically, racially, religiously, economically, physically, or intellectually different from their peers from being laughed at, teased, or rejected. And avoid using sarcasm, ridicule, and harmfully frank statements to control your students. Specific techniques for accomplishing the goals of meeting students' basic needs are described in subsequent chapters.

## Positive Teacher-Student Relationships

The ways in which you choose to relate to your students in the three aspects of your role—as instructor, manager, and person—can increase their willingness to cooperate, learn, and behave appropriately and can motivate them to use you as a role model (5,6). The following suggestions for establishing a positive teacher-student relationship appear commonly in the literature on classroom management. Research has not yet determined whether all of these suggestions always work, but experts have been virtually unanimous in recommending them.

### Instructor

A well-planned curriculum implemented by a well-prepared teacher who presents a study topic so that it holds the interest of the students has traditionally been considered a deterrent to disruptive behavior (9, p. 21).

This assertion in one form or another is shared by many writers on classroom management (10–16) and has been supported by research (7,8). Although curriculum development and instructional techniques are not covered in a class on behavior problems, any discussion of how you can motivate students to want to behave has to involve the importance of your role as instructor—it's a key to unlocking your students' desire to behave.

## *Manager*

*Being in Charge*    Teachers seen by their students as being in charge of their classes have fewer behavior problems to contend with than those students seen as not being in charge. The critical distinction is that the teacher act as an authority and not as an authoritarian.

Educators seen as not in charge of their classrooms are described as noninterventionists (28) and even nonentities (29). They experience more behavior problems, possibly because their lack of classroom leadership tempts students to misbehave (18,30,38,39).

In contrast, authoritative teachers maintain their authority and leadership, but they also provide students with a role in the decision-making process, seek consensus, and make sure that the students understand the rationale behind their decisions. Authoritarian teachers do just the opposite; they keep all the power to themselves and deny their students a role in the decision-making process.

Goss and Ingersoll describe the difference between authoritarian and authoritative teachers in the following way.

> The authoritarian teacher exercises firm, rigid, autocratic control. The teacher dominates, but the domination is aloof and not directed at the positive personal growth of students. Students' self-esteem or self-concept is of little consequence. Because order and control are ends in and of themselves, control becomes repressive.

> The authoritative teacher also exercises firm control, but the control is paired with warmth and genuine concern for the well-being of the students. Order and control are seen as a means to an end. The teacher views classroom control as an element in providing an atmosphere in which students may experience positive personal growth.

> The authoritative teacher, as we define this person, establishes a degree of control and structure within the classroom that offers a sense of stability and security. Limits of acceptable behavior are clearly specified and the ramifications of violating limits are understood. The limits are not arbitrary and dogmatic; they are fair and reasonable (32, p. 10).

Gnagey offers the following explanation for why some teachers are too authoritarian.

> Their primary concern is maintaining order. They tend to stereotype students in terms of their appearance, behavior, and parents' socioeconomic status. Despots perceive students as irresponsible, undisciplined people who must be controlled through punishment. These teachers view misbehavior in moralistic terms and take each violation as a personal affront. They maintain impersonal relationships with their students and expect them to accept the despot's decision without question (29, p. 25).

*Educators who maintain positive relationships with their students tend to have few problems with them.*

If you have had experience managing groups of students, your answers to the following questions will help you determine whether you would be comfortable permitting your students to play a role in the decision-making process. If you find you would not be, you might want to look into developing this capacity.

---

## Self-Quiz: Students and Decision Making

Do you or would you include your students in the following processes if they were sufficiently mature?

  Establishing classroom rules

  Determining the consequences of not following classroom rules

Setting up classroom routines

Deciding what should be included in the curriculum

Selecting teaching materials

Choosing class outings, trips, etc.

*Self-Quiz:*
*On Student Questions*

Would you encourage students to question you about these topics?

Is a rule necessary?

Is a punishment fair?

Is a homework assignment excessive?

Is seatwork just busy work?

Is some aspect of the curriculum irrelevant or boring?

Is a grade fair?

Is the amount of time allotted for certain assignments too short?

Should students who finish their work before the others be allowed to use their free time doing what they want?

*Being Fair*    Good managers are fair. They don't prejudge students based on ethnic, cultural, gender, socioeconomic, physical, or intellectual factors. They may consult their students' cumulative records or previous teachers about them, but they maintain an open mind and draw their own conclusions. (Chapter 12 discusses cultural differences in greater detail.)

Good managers also have realistic expectations for their students. They don't overestimate what outstanding students can accomplish or how well their model students

*Self-Quiz: On Fairness*

Once you have had experience working with groups of students, your answers to the following questions will help you assess how free of bias your perceptions and expectations of your students are in the classroom.

- Are the behavior problems you identify always, or almost always, attributed to one group? Is it always boys who are most troublesome, Black children, girls, or Chicano children?
- Are your children divided in their seating, with the girls all on one side and the boys all on the other? Or the Black children all on one side and the white all on the other?
- Do you spend more time with one group than another? That is, do you stand and

teach on the side of the room where one group sits? Do you direct your comments to and make pleasant eye contact with one group more than the other? Do you actually work more often with one group rather than the other?
- Have you indignantly dismissed, without serious consideration of the possibility that it may be true, an accusation by a child that you are prejudiced against a particular group?
- Do you teach literature to the children without including the work of minority writers?
- Do you teach history from the adopted textbook without making corrections and filling in omissions about minority groups?
- Do you use, without commenting about this to the children, reading books that do not include stories with minority-group characters? (27, pp. 91–92).

can behave. They also avoid underestimating the potential achievements of students with learning problems.

Research indicates that educators tend to treat high achievers and low achievers differently. Specifically, teachers usually call on high achievers more often (19,22,31); give them more positive attention, feedback, praise, and approval (21,23,25,33,36); and both prompt them and wait longer for them to answer questions (35,37). Educators also tend to seat high-achieving students closer to their desks (17,24,34), and research shows that students who sit closer to their teachers learn more (17,24,26,40). To be a fair manager, try to avoid these tendencies and treat all students equally.

---

## Self-Quiz: Working with Low Achievers

Your answers to the following questions about low achievers will help you evaluate how fair you are being in your work with them. Do you:

1. Call on low achievers less frequently to answer questions or demonstrate something?
2. Wait less time for them to answer?
3. Give them less encouragement or assistance after you have called on them?
4. Give them less praise when they answer correctly?
5. Praise them for answers that really aren't correct?
6. Criticize them more for incorrect answers?
7. Give them less feedback?
8. Interrupt them more often when they are reciting?
9. Maintain less eye contact with them when you lecture?
10. Allow them to do less work than others are expected to complete in order to receive credit?
11. Seat them far from you? (20,22).

---

## Person

Kounin (6) and other researchers (7) have demonstrated that students who like their teachers learn more and behave better than students who don't. While evidence does not support a particular list of personality traits that characterize popular and well-respected teachers, researchers suggest that students are more likely to have positive feelings toward teachers who listen to their students and encourage them to express themselves; are genuine, honest, and sincere; are friendly; communicate understanding, acceptance, and empathy; and maintain a sense of humor (29,41–54).

*Active Listening*    Teachers who are good classroom managers know how to listen—and listen actively—to their students. Gordon defines active listening in the following way.

> Active listening, as opposed to passive listening (silence), involves interaction with the student, and it also provides the student with proof (feedback) of the teacher's understanding (45,66).

*Sometimes active listening may require you to encourage students to talk about things that you may not want to hear about or deal with.*

According to Gordon, active listening involves (1) encouraging your students to communicate whatever is troubling them, (2) trying to discover the true meaning of what they have communicated if it isn't clear, (3) checking with them to determine whether your understanding is correct, and (4) communicating your understanding to them. Gordon cites seven attitudes or mental sets that characterize an effective listener.

1. Have confidence in your students' abilities to solve their own problems.

2. Accept whatever feelings or ideas students express regardless of whether you agree with them—otherwise students may be reluctant to express themselves.

3. Realize that these feelings are often transitory and that expression defuses them.

4. Try to help students, and provide time in your teaching schedule to do so.

5. Empathize with your students' feelings without becoming too upset by them to be helpful.

6. Work toward becoming comfortable about hearing the real-life problems of your students.

7. Maintain the privacy and confidentiality of whatever your students reveal about themselves unless the law requires you to do otherwise as in the case of suspected child abuse.

## THEORY FOCUS: GORDON ON TEACHER EFFECTIVENESS

Thomas Gordon's approach to classroom management is based on the assumption that students can, in most instances, solve their own behavior problems with guidance from their teachers. In his book *Teacher Effectiveness Training*, Gordon describes a nondirective approach. This strategy helps students become aware of the inappropriateness of their behavior and its effects on others and to identify specific ways they can improve their behavior on their own.

Gordon advises educators to avoid power struggles with students. He believes that if a teacher wins, the result is that the students resent their teacher. But if educators give in to their students, this encourages more misbehavior. Instead of power struggles, he suggests that educators should aim for no-win exchanges in which they use active listening techniques to help students identify solutions to a problem that both teacher and student can agree on. Although Gordon is against the use of consequences to convince students to behave, he does feel that dangerous or disruptive situations call on educators to take a more directive role.

Compare the following conversations between teachers and students. Can you see how the first teacher discouraged and the second teacher encouraged the student from sharing his thoughts and feelings?

STUDENT:  I have a cousin staying over my house that's real weird.

TEACHER:  He is?

STUDENT:  Yeah! He does all kinds of drugs.

TEACHER:  Like what?

STUDENT:  Reefer and crack.

TEACHER:  What do you think of him?

STUDENT:  He's real chilly.

TEACHER:  Really?

STUDENT:  Sure.

TEACHER:  You're kidding me, aren't you?

STUDENT:  Yeah.

STUDENT:  I have a cousin staying over my house that's real weird.

TEACHER:  He is?

STUDENT:  Yeah! He does all kinds of drugs.

TEACHER:  Like what?

STUDENT:  Reefer and crack.

TEACHER:    What do you think of him?

STUDENT:    He's real chilly.

TEACHER:    You think he's chilly?

STUDENT:    Yeah. Everyone likes him. He's a big shot.

TEACHER:    Are you chilly too?

STUDENT:    Yeah!

TEACHER:    You mean you do drugs too?

STUDENT:    What do you think, I'm crazy?

TEACHER:    Do you think you're crazy?

STUDENT:    Sometimes.

TEACHER:    Why?

STUDENT:    Because of what it says on TV about crack kills.

TEACHER:    It sounds like you're worried about doing drugs.

STUDENT:    Yeah.

*Being Genuine*    Almost everyone responds to a person who is genuine. Teachers are genuine when their words and actions express their true feelings and opinions. And when teachers are genuine, their students know they can trust what the teacher tells them.

Teachers have two basic reasons for not always being genuine. They may not be able to admit to themselves that they have certain feelings, or they may not be able to express their feelings to the students. Certain teachers may even hide their positive feelings from their students, but more often teachers are uncomfortable about expressing—or even feeling—their negative emotions.

If your answers to the questions in the box suggest that you might have difficulty being genuine with your students, Chernow and Chernow (42) suggest that accepting the following three basic truths will help you be more honest with them.

1. In the natural course of events students will sometimes make you uncomfortable, angry, and even furious.
2. You are entitled to have these feelings without also experiencing guilt or shame because they are natural.
3. You are entitled to express your feelings as long as you do so in a way that doesn't harm your students.

To constantly "stuff your feelings"—that is, try to act as if nothing bothers you—can quickly lead to teacher burnout. The goal here is to express your real feelings in ways that help, not harm, your students. For example, suppose you are explaining to Tom why he shouldn't have picked on a younger student during recess. But instead of listening to you, Tom is looking around the yard and making it clear that he has no interest in what you're

*Self-Quiz: Communication with Students*

Ask yourself whether you think you would be able to communicate the following to your students in an appropriate way.

Disapproval of a student's behavior

Anger at the way the student relates to the opposite sex

Anger at the way the student treats other students

Anger at the way the student treats you

Disappointment that the student didn't keep a promise to you

Discouragement or frustration about your inability to motivate the student

Rage over your inability to control the student

Mistrust of the student's motives

Disbelief in what the student says

Which of the following do you think you would have trouble admitting even to yourself?

Dislike for a student as a person

Revulsion for a student's handicap

Preconceived notions about the student's honesty, motivation, potential, and the like based on the student's ethnic or socio-economic background

Disappointment that the student doesn't appear to like you despite your efforts

saying. You tell him that he isn't listening, but he keeps looking around. You feel frustrated and more than a little upset. You tell yourself that he is just being defensive, that he isn't purposely trying to get you angry. But that doesn't change your feelings, though, and a rage starts building inside of you. You recall that the last time you felt like this you walked away rather than express your feelings, but that only made you angrier because it seemed like that was what Tom wanted. Just remembering this makes you even angrier now. What should you do?

First, you need not feel guilty or think you are a poor teacher for being angry. Most people would get angry in that situation. Second, you shouldn't try to mask your feelings behind a smile and walk away. Instead, tell Tom how you feel but in a way that doesn't attack him personally. You can do this by focusing on his behavior, not on him as a person. "Tom, I'm getting angry. I feel you're not paying attention to what I'm saying, and that upsets me." This would be one acceptable way of expressing your feelings. Another good way would be to say, "Tom, when I see you looking everywhere but at me when I'm trying to tell you something important, it seems like you're not listening and don't care. That upsets me." Then a good follow-up, after expressing your feelings, is to set clear expectations for future behavior: "I'd like you to listen when I talk to you so we can get back to the business of you being a good student and me doing my job, too." "What's the matter with you, didn't anyone ever teach you to look at people when they talk to you?" and "Look at me when I'm talking to you" are two inappropriate ways of expressing yourself because they belittle him as a person.

*Being Friendly:*   Friendly teachers are effective managers. They are open, approachable, and available rather than closed, distant, and aloof. They are also interested in their students as people and are willing to listen to things that aren't directly related to their students' education. In turn, they reveal their interests and the kind of people they are by sharing their feelings, values, and opinions. This makes them "come alive" for their students. Though no teacher can actually be a friend of thirty students or six classes of thirty students, teachers can be friendly.

Shumsky (51) has identified two types of friendly teachers, one effective, the other ineffective. The first develop friendly relationships with students based on strength, respect, and trust while they maintain their role as the person in charge. The second type, motivated by a need to be accepted by students in order to build up their own self-esteem, reject taking charge and choose a weak role for themselves. The first type of friendly relationship with students is positive; the second is destructive, leaving the class lacking strong leadership.

*Communicating Acceptance and Empathy*   Accepting, empathic people feel good to be around. Teachers who are accepting treat all students with respect regardless of the way they behave or their achievement level. They accept their students, but not necessarily their students' behaviors. And when they disapprove of or reject certain behavior, they don't disapprove of or reject the students who acted inappropriately.

Notice the difference between the following statements. The first column describes students' *behavior* in nonjudgmental ways. The second describes the *student* in judgmental terms. The first column rejects behavior. The second rejects the person.

| | |
|---|---|
| You're interrupting. | You don't have any manners. |
| You're late again. | You're irresponsible. |
| You didn't hand in your work three times in the past two weeks. | You're lazy. |
| You are not contributing to your group by making suggestions. | You're selfish. |
| You're not paying attention to Latanya. | You're too self-centered. |

Empathic educators try to understand their students from the students' points of view, and they often can appreciate the how and why of their students' thoughts and feelings. They understand that, given the circumstances and their students' developmental levels, their thoughts and feelings are both natural and normal. Empathic teachers can communicate their understanding of what their students are experiencing and their appreciation of why they feel and think as they do. But they don't always agree that their students should act on their thoughts and feelings. The following are some examples of empathic statements.

"I can appreciate how nervous you feel about performing the play in the auditorium today after forgetting your lines in practice yesterday. And I can understand that you don't want to participate. I remember how I felt when something like that happened to me.

But I think you will do fine today since you remembered all your lines this morning when Steve cued you."

"You look like you're ready to kill Harry for what he said about your mother. I don't blame you for being angry. But let's see if we can handle the situation in another way."

"I guess you feel pretty bad about breaking Aretha's project. Even though it really wasn't your fault, it still doesn't work anymore. But let's see what you can do to make it up to her. Okay?"

## *Modeling Desirable Behavior*

The conventional view of teachers is that they stand in front of their students and teach them by telling them things. It may seem easier for teachers to tell students how to behave than to actually behave that way themselves, but students—especially younger ones— usually learn more from what their teachers do than from what they say (55–61). Here are alternative ways educators can handle problems in their classrooms. Which ones serve as more positive models for students?

- Harry starts a conversation while the teacher is explaining something to the class. The teacher:
    a. writes his name on the board, calling everyone's attention to his misbehavior.
    b. catches his eye and frowns slightly, conveying disapproval without calling attention to him.

- When the teacher calls on Cecilia, she says she can't answer because the teacher's directions weren't clear. The teacher:
    a. tells her to pay attention next time so she won't need to make excuses.
    b. asks her what part she didn't understand and goes over it again.

- Larry, the class clown, does something really funny. The teacher:
    a. laughs at his antics along with the other students in the class.
    b. ignores his behavior and suppresses a smile.

- Thomas, the class bully, pushes Jake. The teacher:
    a. steps in, separates them, and tells Thomas to stay in during recess so they can have a talk.
    b. yells at Thomas to stop, separates them, and scolds Thomas for his behavior.

- Rose has come to class without her homework for the third time in one week. When the teacher asks her to read the assignment, she says she left it home. The teacher:
    a. says she doesn't believe her.
    b. says they will have to talk about the problem later in the morning.

- When the teacher tells Steve what his punishment will be for doing something wrong, Steve complains that the teacher isn't being fair. The teacher:
    a. stops the lesson for a while longer and asks Steve why he thinks he is being treated unfairly.
    b. tells Steve that the teacher, not he, is in charge so there is no point in discussing it.

## *Promoting Group Cohesiveness*

Research indicates that students will behave better if the class forms a cohesive group and adheres to positive group norms, such as we don't laugh when someone makes a mistake; we don't make fun of each other; everyone—even poor players—gets a chance to play on a team during recess (62–64). Students form a cohesive group when they have a feeling of unity among them; they think in terms of "we" as well as "I"; they experience a sense of oneness with the group; and they are willing to accept some frustration, pain, and sacrifice of personal goals to help achieve group goals.

Group cohesiveness among students can reduce or eliminate many potential behavior problems that might otherwise arise if students feel less positive toward each other. Group cohesiveness decreases: arguments between cliques; scapegoating of out-groups, minority students, and weaker students by in-groups, majority students, and dominant students; conflicts between males and females; disputes among students over minor issues; tattling and name calling (62). Group cohesiveness also makes students more willing to work cooperatively and put the group's goals ahead of personal goals. It increases students' willingness to conform to group norms and expectations as well. For all these reasons, a cohesive group that has accepted positive group norms exerts a strong influence on its members to behave appropriately out of loyalty and solidarity with the group. Thus, promoting group cohesiveness and the group's acceptance of positive norms will help you motivate your students to want to behave.

## *Working Together Cooperatively*

The more groups of students cooperate by working together and the more they communicate with each other in class, the more likely they are to form cohesive groups. So, despite the fact that competition is often the norm both inside and outside of school, include and stress cooperative-learning experiences and group projects in your curriculum.

You can involve students in the decision-making process to the degree that they are developmentally ready. This gives them opportunities to interact and work together as a group. If you work with younger students, instead of establishing classroom rules and selecting group activities by yourself, give your students chances to work together by assign-

*A creative teacher can devise many ways to involve students in cooperative activities.*

ing them a role in the process. With older students, establish the general objective and let them figure out how to reach it and organize the process under your supervision and guidance. For example, inform them that the class will take an outing or perform a play, but allow them to choose where to go or which play to perform from a list of alternatives you prepare in advance. In another example, advise them that they will be required to take a test on a particular topic within a specified period of time, but allow them to decide how much time they need to prepare for it. Finally, don't automatically intervene when students have disputes or differences of opinion if they are mature enough to settle their own disputes. Instead, encourage them to resolve the conflicts on their own with your assistance when it is possible for them to do so.

## *Minimizing Subgroup Formation*

It's natural for some students to be attracted to one another and to want to work and play together, but make sure your students also work with students they may not select on their own. This helps them to perceive the larger "we" of the whole class as well as maintain loyalty to just their friends. Achieving this may mean playing an especially active role in getting younger boys and girls to work and play together, ensuring that the groups you assign students to are racially, ethnically, and socioeconomically heterogeneous and providing low-status students opportunities to work cooperatively with high-status students.

Another technique that helps minimize subgroups among your students is to de-emphasize ability grouping. Grouping by ability levels can be a devisive influence in the classroom. You can also make sure that all students participate in group activities so there aren't participants and nonparticipants. For example, when selecting the list of plays for the class to choose from, make sure all of them have a large number of parts and assign two or more students to share the main roles. And when students are playing during lunch or recess, encourage girls and boys to play group games such as kick ball, punch ball, jump rope, and other games together to discourage them from forming all male or all female groups.

Create a climate of acceptance for individual differences in interests, abilities, opinions, cultural characteristics, and lifestyles in your classroom. Encourage your students to value diversity. Let them know that everyone can do something well, no one can do everything well, and by working together they can do great things. This will discourage the formation of subgroups based on differences. Teaching students to accept and value individual differences will prepare them to be better people and better citizens. It will also decrease the likelihood that individuals will be picked on or rejected because they are different.

## Increase the Value of the Group

Making the group more appealing and valuable in your students' eyes will increase cohesiveness. You can accomplish this by highlighting the positive aspects of the group. Tell them how much *they* have achieved, how well *they* are doing, and what *they* can achieve by *their* efforts. Plan appealing group activities, outings, challenges, and explorations. Assist the group to accomplish things that will be a credit to all its members such as performing for other classes, raising money for good causes, developing a class project together, or creating a celebration for the entire class.

## Maintaining Cohesiveness

Once achieved, you have to maintain group cohesiveness for it to continue. Conflicts among students are bound to occur, and so will group failures that make membership in the group less attractive. Fielding these challenges well maintains the group unity.

*Settling Disputes*   When conflicts develop, they should be resolved quickly with as much group participation as possible. Allow time in your schedule for students to solve the problems and conflicts that arise among them. Class time is not only for learning academic subjects; it is also for discovering how to resolve problems, which is a critical lifelong skill.

*Maintaining Faith in the Group*   When your class fails to achieve its own or others' expectations, you can help your students put their lack of success in proper perspective. Instead of expressing disapproval, disappointment, or blame, ask students to investigate with you what the cause of the problem was. Did you or the group set expectations that were too high? Did you neglect to drill your students on the material they didn't do well on

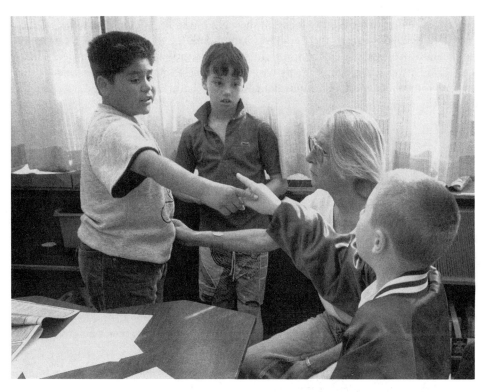

*Group cohesiveness may suffer if conflicts among students aren't resolved.*

during the exam? Did your students allow themselves less time to complete a project or prepare for an exam than they actually needed? Did you wait too long before telling them to put the laboratory equipment away? Instead of lecturing the group about what they did wrong and urging or pressuring them to work harder or to be more cooperative, try to turn the problem into a learning experience. Help them discover what their mistakes were, to learn that mistakes are a natural part of the learning process, and to decide what they can do to succeed next time.

## *Rewarding Appropriate Behavior*

Motivating students to want to behave appropriately and getting students to behave in a desired way for the moment are not the same thing. Motivating students toward appropriate behavior is a broad-based goal that involves influencing their intrinsic motivation and enhancing their personal growth over time. Managing students to achieve the right behavior right now is a short-term goal that involves extrinsic motivation. Rewarding students who are behaving well can keep them on the right track (65–70), but research described later in this chapter suggests that certain uses of rewards for good behavior at the moment can actually decrease students' intrinsic motivation toward appropriate behavior. Therefore, to be an effective classroom manager, place a higher priority on techniques that increase your students' intrinsic motivation over those that achieve their compliance for the moment.

## *Two Kinds of Appropriate Behavior*

For individual students to learn, they must attend, concentrate, tolerate frustration, stay on task, and participate actively. But for entire classes to function smoothly, students must be good group members. They must learn to wait their turn, wait to be called on, share, cooperate, respect the property of others, listen to others, and so on. To date, research about the effects of rewarding desirable behavior has focused primarily on students as learners, not on students as members of a group. Therefore, it's possible to base on research decisions about when to reward students who are fulfilling their roles as learners, but not about when to reward them for fulfilling their roles as members of a group.

*Students as Learners*    The available evidence indicates that rewarding desirable behavior such as staying on task, completing seatwork, and the like when the work is unattractive, boring, repetitive, and involves practicing skills that have already been partially learned does indeed improve student behavior. But when the work is new, interesting, challenging, or not yet learned, rewarding desirable behavior has a detrimental effect on students' behavior (71–77).

The fact that rewarding students increases their motivation to do boring work but not work that is interesting and challenging is common sense. Students probably have little intrinsic motivation to do work that is boring and repetitive, whereas they are much more likely to be self-motivated to master new and challenging information. For example, young children who have already learned how to tie their shoelaces, although poorly, and older students who have partially mastered the basics of multiplication may not be particularly motivated to practice these skills without some extrinsic motivation.

Excessively rewarding students for behaving appropriately even when the work is repetitive, boring, and unattractive may have its shortcomings, too. Even if it does improve students' behavior for the moment, it may not change the students' attitudes. For example, this practice might encourage students to expect extrinsic rewards when they cope with the less pleasant aspects of learning instead of learning to accept these as part of any job, in school or out. Perhaps most important, when students are praised and attended to for doing what is expected of them, they can experience this as controlling and manipulative. They may come to feel that they are accepted and cared for only when they fulfill their teachers' expectations and not their own. This can cause them to feel resentful and angry.

What doesn't at first make sense is why rewarding students who behave appropriately when the work is new, challenging, and as-yet unlearned should encourage poor behavior. A number of reasons have been suggested for why this occurs.

First, superfluous rewards can influence intrinsically motivated students to shift to extrinsic motivation. Then, instead of trying to master the task for its own sake, they become more interested in the reward. Also, when students become so satiated with teacher praise, stickers, smiling faces, and so on that they lose interest or outgrow them (78–80) and when such rewards just aren't available, students are less motivated to attend, concentrate, or tolerate frustration without the expectation of an extrinsic reward for doing so.

Second, superfluous rewards can make generally independent students lose their ability to function independently by causing them to rely on their teachers' feedback and approval. Teacher rewards can also decrease students' self-confidence if students attribute their success to their teachers' input rather than to their own efforts (81–83).

Finally, research indicates that extrinsic rewards can decrease students' creativity (84–87). Perhaps this happens because extrinsic rewards motivate students to accomplish what they think their teachers want them to accomplish in the way they think their teachers want them to accomplish it rather than to follow their own creative inclinations.

*Students as Group Members*    Although no direct evidence shows that rewarding students for being good group members can have a detrimental effect on their behavior, the results of the studies cited above regarding the effects of rewards on their learning does raise that possibility. The results to date suggest that rewarding students who are already intrinsically motivated to be good group members may train them to do so for extrinsic rewards. Certain well-behaved students may also experience superfluous rewards as controlling and manipulative. Until we know more about these possibilities, educators may be wise to reward students for being good group members sparingly rather than routinely.

# How to Reward Appropriate Behavior

Rewarding students is most likely to be effective when you meet certain conditions. *Reward students for behavior you believe deserves to be rewarded, not because they seek it.* Research indicates that some students elicit rewards from their teachers by bringing their completed work up to be praised or by smiling profusely when teachers compliment them to encourage more praise (88–90). No evidence suggests that students who are so dependent on teacher feedback actually benefit from this praise as they are already behaving appropriately—perhaps even "too" appropriately.

A second condition is that *the students be aware of the specific behavior that is being rewarded* (91–92). For example, complimenting a student for working for 40 minutes straight is a much clearer message than praising her for being a "good student" because the feedback focuses the student's attention on the specific behavior that is being rewarded.

Another condition is that *the students agree that the behavior they are being rewarded for deserves to be rewarded.* Some educators praise low-achieving students not only when they succeed, but also when they merely try to succeed, perform well, or give the right answer (93–99). Brophy (88) points out that this may actually worsen, not improve, students' functioning. Students may doubt their own ability or lose confidence in their teachers if they think: "She must really think I'm hopeless if she praises me for that!" or

"What's the matter with her? How could she think that was good work?" Similarly, if students are praised, given stickers, stars, or checks every time they sit up straight, wait in line, listen quietly to a story, or engage in any other routine behavior, they may experience the reward as insincere, silly, or simply irrelevant and not credible.

For a reward to work, *your words and actions must be congruent.* Some educators give students verbal rewards for things that they don't truly believe should be rewarded, but they reveal their true feelings by tone of voice, gesture, or body language. Research indicates that students can respond negatively to such confusing double messages (88).

Another key condition is that *the students actually experience the reward as rewarding.* Same-age students don't respond equally to the same rewards. For some, teacher praise can exert a powerful influence on their behavior; others may respond better to more material-istic forms of reward such as stickers, candy, toys, and so on. Students at different develop-mental levels also experience rewards in different ways. For example, by the time students are in intermediate schools, they usually care more about what their peers think of them than about their teachers' opinions. (See the section on motivational development in this chapter for a more detailed discussion of this topic.)

Students and teachers often have different ideas about what is rewarding. What some teachers think are effective rewards students experience as irrelevant and vice versa. Sec-ondary teachers, for example, often overrate the rewarding influence of recognizing stu-dents for behaving appropriately by mentioning their names in the school newspaper or over the loudspeaker or giving them a chance at special privileges and having contests that they can win. In turn, they tend to underrate the rewarding influence of providing students with the opportunity to achieve their own goals, to be accepted as a person in their own right, and to gain peer approval (100).

*Students must understand that the accomplishments for which they are being rewarded were the result of their own intrinsic motivation, efforts, and abilities and not the extrinsic reward.* This will increase the likelihood that they will attribute their success to themselves rather than to others (101–105).

*For rewards to work they must be timely.* The longer teachers wait before rewarding students for behaving appropriately, the less likely it is that the student will connect the reward with the desirable behavior. Thus, rewarding students, especially younger ones, at the end of the day or before lunch for their earlier behavior may be much less effective than rewarding them right at the moment.

*A final condition is that the rewards are offered sparingly.* This helps ensure that re-wards don't lose their effectiveness because students lose interest in them.

## *Destructive Rewards*

We have already noted that rewards used improperly can cause students to become more dependent and less creative or to feel manipulated and change their behavior for the worse. The inappropriate use of rewards can create other problems as well.

*Rewarding Undesirable Behavior*    Educators sometimes unintentionally reward undesirable behavior. For example, when teachers reward students for completing seatwork assignments, students may conclude that their teachers are more interested in speed and quantity than in the quality of work. But when teachers reward students only *after* evaluating the students' work, the message students receive is quite different. Then they see that quality also counts.

*Using Undesirable Rewards*  Rewarding students by allowing them to go on errands while others are working at their desks or by excusing them from doing part of their homework may increase appropriate behavior, but it also gives students the message that seatwork and homework are onerous and unnecessary chores that they should avoid if possible.

*Creating Competition and Jealousy*  If teachers reward students only when they behave appropriately, those who don't receive an equal share of recognition and acceptance may become jealous. Rewarding students for good behavior in hopes that other students will improve the way they behave to get these rewards can also engender resentment and jealousy in the left-out students. Statements intended to motivate students to copy their peers' behavior, such as "Look how well Cecilia is doing her math" may backfire, causing some students to misbehave even more and interfere with group cohesiveness, an important goal in its own right.

## Proper Use of Rewards

This discussion on the pitfalls of using rewards improperly is not meant to imply that you avoid all rewards. Some praise and recognition probably does most of us a lot of good. The point was to encourage you to avoid the superfluous or routine use of rewards.

### Self-Quiz: On Appropriate Use of Rewards

Your answers to the following questions will help you decide when and how to reward students for behaving appropriately. Rather than asking yourself these questions every time you are inclined to reward a student, which is unnecessary and could destroy your spontaneity, think about them from time to time when the situation warrants.

1. Is the student already motivated? Would a reward be unnecessary and superfluous?
2. Is my goal at the moment to get the student to continue to behave appropriately or to motivate the student to want to behave appropriately?
3. Would rewarding the student further my goal if my objective is to increase his or her intrinsic motivation?
4. Does the student's behavior really merit a reward, or would the reward lack credibility right now?
5. How will the student perceive my attempts to reward her or him—as controlling or manipulative, embarrassing, an indication that I don't expect as much from her or him as I do other students, or as welcomed signs of my acceptance and recognition of worth, ability, and effort?
6. What kinds of things does the student experience as rewarding—public praise, peer approval, special privileges?

| EFFECTIVE REWARDS | INEFFECTIVE REWARDS |
| --- | --- |
| 1. Students rewarded for specific behaviors | Students routinely rewarded |
| 2. Reward increases students' intrinsic motivation | Reward increases students' extrinsic motivation |
| 3. All students have adequate opportunity to earn rewards | Some students have little opportunity to earn rewards |
| 4. Students rewarded for specific behaviors | Students rewarded for being good and well-behaved in general |
| 5. Students aware of specific behavior being rewarded | Students unaware of behavior being rewarded |
| 6. Students agree that the behavior deserves to be rewarded | Students don't perceive behavior as meriting award |
| 7. Students aware that they earned reward through own efforts and achievement | Students attribute effort and success to reward |
| 8. Teachers' words and actions are congruent | Students receive inconsistent message |
| 9. Students rewarded for significant effort and achievement | Reward based on lowered standards and expectations |
| 10. Students experience rewards as positive | Students experience rewards as negative |
| 11. Rewards personalized to students' interests, desires, and developmental level | Students experience reward as irrelevant |
| 12. Reward is timely | Reward is delayed |
| 13. Students rewarded only for desirable behavior | Undesirable behavior inadvertently rewarded |

## Motivational Development

What motivates students to behave appropriately in school depends to some extent on their ages (106–109). Preschoolers, kindergarteners, and students in the primary grades are usually willing to comply with rules just because teachers say so. They will tend to do what they are told in order to obtain smiles, attention, and praise from their teachers as well and to avoid their teachers' disapproval and lectures. They find such things as candy, stickers, checks, and stars rewarding. At this age, students need immediate reinforcement and gratification.

As they get older, students are less willing to do things just because their teachers say so. This makes their teachers' attention and approval less influential in motivating them, and peer approval becomes more important. Other kinds of material rewards such as trips, food, and special events replace stickers, checks, and smiling faces as effective rewards. They are also better able to accept symbolic rewards that they can turn in for the real thing in the future.

*Students tend to be most responsive to approval and disapproval in the primary grades.*

By adolescence, some students may question any rule that seems arbitrary to them. Their teachers' approval can be totally irrelevant compared to the approval of their peers. Rewards that were effective when they were younger may play a much smaller role in motivating them than graduating from school, preparing for a job, or earning the grades necessary to be accepted by the college of their choice.

Hartner (107) provides a theoretical explanation for these observations. According to her, students' motivational systems develop in an orderly way. She suggests that preschool and primary school students are externally oriented; they respond to adult approval of their behavior and use feedback from adults to judge their successes and failures. As a result, they respond positively to being told that they are good students because they raise their hands, wait their turn, and so on. Because of this perspective, they also want to know that their teachers think well of their drawings, paintings, stories, and other efforts.

By the time students are in the upper elementary grades, though, they can reward themselves for behaving appropriately. Now they tell themselves that they are good students because they raise their hands and wait their turn. Thus, while preschool and primary teachers should praise their students for behaving well, upper elementary and secondary teachers should encourage students to reward themselves for "good" behavior. This means focusing comments more on providing students with factual feedback about how they are doing—their strengths and weaknesses, successes and failures.

Hartner claims that by the time students are in secondary school, they have internalized standards they can use to evaluate their own accomplishments. As a result, teachers should reduce the amount of feedback they provide their students and instead encourage students to evaluate themselves. In other words, as students mature, teachers can prompt them to function independently in order to foster their personal growth.

Examples of Age-Appropriate Praise

| PRIMARY GRADES | UPPER ELEMENTARY GRADES | SECONDARY SCHOOL |
| --- | --- | --- |
| That's a beautiful picture. | You should be proud of your picture. | Your picture has great perspective. |
| You did an outstanding (great) job on the test. | How do you feel about getting almost everything right on the test? | Your reading comprehension score was a little lower than your vocabulary score. Why do you think that is? |

Teachers should also emphasize intrinsic motivation instead of using extrinsic rewards. Hartner has described four kinds of intrinsic motivation that keeps students interested. According to Hartner, students are intrinsically motivated to respond to their environments in new and varied ways; they also have a natural curiosity about the new and different; they look forward to achieving competency; and they prefer challenging, rather than routine, tasks.

## Self-Quiz: How You Use Rewards

Your answers to the following questions will help you evaluate the way you intend to reward desirable behavior when you are in the classroom.

1. Is your goal in rewarding students to gain their compliance for the moment or to increase their intrinsic motivation?
2. Do you overemphasize extrinsic rewards rather than techniques that foster intrinsic motivation?
3. How often do you reward students for behaving appropriately—too often, not often enough, about right?
4. Do you reward students routinely out of habit or only when you think the situation calls for it?
5. Do students have other ways of obtaining your acceptance and recognition besides behaving appropriately?
6. Do all of your students get their fair share of acceptance and recognition?
7. Do you individualize feedback by selecting rewards that your students will actually experience as positive, by anticipating how they will react to being rewarded, and by choosing the best way to reward them?
8. Do you reward students merely for completing work and making contributions, or do you reward them for the quality of their efforts, or both?
9. When rewarding students, do you make sure they understand that they have earned the reward through their own efforts?
10. Do you avoid using rewards destructively?
11. Do you reward students for behaving appropriately so others will follow their example?
12. Do you reward students when their work and behavior actually don't merit it with positive statements in order to balance out the occasions when you criticize them for misbehaving?
13. Do you reward students who seek your praise?

An effective classroom manager adjusts motivational techniques to match the students' developmental levels. Not praising youngsters who need praise or expecting too much of younger students can create disappointment and cause unnecessary behavior problems. Equally ineffective is trying to motivate older students in ways that make them feel like children. A course in developmental psychology, included in almost all teacher preparation programs, will help you understand students' different developmental levels and needs.

## Summary

You can increase students' desire to behave appropriately by satisfying their basic needs, maintaining positive relationships with them, modeling the behavior you expect from them, and promoting group cohesiveness. Rewarding desirable behavior also encourages students to behave appropriately if the rewards match your students' motivational development levels. Using rewards excessively or inappropriately can stifle students' creativity, cause competition among them, and make them overly dependent on the opinions of others.

## Activities

I. In each of the following examples, think of an alternative statement that rejects the student's behavior and not the student.

| REJECTS BEHAVIOR | REJECTS STUDENT |
|---|---|
| A student refuses to allow another student to have a turn. | Nice boys and girls allow others to have their turns. |
| A student doesn't clean up after himself. | Don't be lazy. |
| A student talks while someone else is reciting. | Don't be impolite. |
| A student doesn't complete her part of a group assignment. | You haven't been a very good group member. |
| A student teases another student about being overweight. | Can't you think about other people's feelings? |
| A student takes more than her share at snack time. | Don't be selfish. |

II.  Think of an empathic response to each of the following situations.

 1.  A second grader refuses to sit at a table with three classmates of the opposite sex.

 2.  A student becomes frustrated during seatwork, crumples her paper noisily, and throws it on the floor, attracting everyone's attention.

 3.  A student storms out of the room, slamming the door behind him, after some classmates laugh at the mistakes he makes during oral reading.

 4.  A student throws his snack at another student who teased him about the "exotic" food he brought from home.

 5.  A student sulks because she wasn't called on in class during sharing time, and she had something special to tell her classmates.

III.  Complete the following chart about motivational differences at different developmental levels.

| | PRIMARY GRADES | MIDDLE SCHOOL | HIGH SCHOOL |
|---|---|---|---|
| Why students comply with rules | | | |
| The forms of positive rewards they respond to | | | |
| The roles of extrinsic versus intrinsic rewards | | | |
| How much delay students can tolerate before they are rewarded | | | |
| The extent to which students can evaluate their behavior and achievements and reward themselves | | | |

# References

PERSONAL GROWTH

 1.  Ontario Department of Education. (1986). *Behavior: Resource Guide*. ERIC ED 284 386.

SATISFYING BASIC NEEDS

2. Braun, C. (1976). Teacher expectations: Socio-psychological dynamics. *Review of Educational Research, 46* (2), 185–213.

3. Maslow, A. H. (1960). Some basic propositions of a growth and self-actualization psychology. *Association of Supervision and Curriculum Development Yearbook.* Alexandria, VA: Association of Supervision and Curriculum Development.

4. Maslow, A. H. (1970). *Motivation and Personality* (2nd ed.). New York: Harper & Row.


TEACHER-STUDENT RELATIONSHIPS

5. Brophy, J. E., & Putnam, J. G. (1978). *Classroom Management in the Elementary Grades.* ERIC ED 167 537.

6. Kounin, J. S. (1970). *Discipline and Group Management in Classrooms.* New York: Holt, Rinehart & Winston.


EDUCATOR AS INSTRUCTOR

7. Anderson, L. M., Evertson, C. M., & Emmer, E. T. (1979). *Dimensions in Classroom Management Derived from Recent Research.* ERIC ED 175 860.

8. Coker, H., Medley, D. M., & Soar, R. S. (1980). How valid are expert opinions about effective teaching? *Phi Delta Kappan, 62* (2), 131–134.

9. Davis, J. E. (1974). *Coping with Disruptive Behavior.* Washington, DC: National Education Association.

10. Jones, F. (1987). *Positive Classroom Discipline.* New York: McGraw-Hill.

11. Jones, V. F., & Jones, L. S. (1986). *Comprehensive Classroom Management: Creating Positive Learning Environments* (2nd ed.). Boston: Allyn & Bacon.

12. Mauer, R. F. (1985). *Elementary Discipline Handbook: Solutions for the K–8 Teacher.* West Nyack, NY: Center for Applied Research in Education.

13. Sabatino, D. A., Sabatino, A. C., & Mann, L. (1983). *Discipline and Behavior Management: A Handbook of Tactics, Strategies, and Programs.* Rockville, MD: Aspen.

14. Tanner, L. N. (1978). *Classroom Discipline for Effective Teaching and Learning.* New York: Holt, Rinehart & Winston.

15. Tobin, K. G., & Capie, W. (1980). *Student Engagement in Middle School Science Classrooms.* ERIC ED 194 522.

16. Unruh, A. (1977). Teachers and classroom discipline. *NASSP Bulletin, 61* (406), 84–87.

EDUCATOR AS MANAGER

17. Adams, R., & Biddle, B. (1970). *Realities of Teaching: Explorations with Video Tape.* New York: Holt, Rinehart & Winston.

18. Anderson, L. H., Evertson, C. M., & Emmer, E. T. (1979). *Dimensions in Classroom Management Derived from Recent Research.* ERIC ED 175 860.

19. Brophy, J. E., & Good, T. L. (1970). Teachers' communication of differential expectations for children's classroom performance: Some behavioral data. *Journal of Education Psychology, 61,* 365–374.

20. Brophy, J. E., & Good, T. L. (1974). *Teacher-Student Relationships: Causes and Consequences.* New York: Holt, Rinehart & Winston.

21. Chaikin, A., Sigler, E., & Derlega, V. (1974). Nonverbal mediators of teacher expectancy effects. *Journal of Personality and Social Psychology, 30,* 144–149.

22. Cooper, H., & Good, T. L. (1983). *Pygmalion Grows Up.* White Plains, NY: Longman.

23. Cornbleth, C., David, O. L., Jr., & Button, C. (1974). Expectations for pupil achievement and teacher-pupil interaction. *Social Education, 38,* 54–58.

24. Daum, J. (1972). *Proxemics in the Classroom: Speaker-Subject Distance and Educational Performance.* Paper presented at the annual meeting of the Southeastern Psychological Association.

25. de Groat, A., & Thompson, G. A. (1949). A study of the distribution of teacher approval and disapproval among sixth-grade pupils. *Journal of Experimental Education, 18,* 57–75.

26. Delefes, P., & Jackson, B. (1972). Teacher-pupil interaction as a function of location in the classroom. *Psychology in the Schools, 9,* 119–123.

27. Epstein, C. (1979). *Classroom Management and Teaching: Persistent Problems and Rational Solutions.* Reston, VA: Reston Publishing.

28. Glickman, C. D., & Wolfgang, C. H. (1979). Dealing with student misbehavior: An eclectic review. *Journal of Teacher Education, 30* (3), 7–13.

29. Gnagey, W. J. (1981). *Motivating Classroom Discipline.* New York: Macmillan.

30. Goldstein, J. M., & Weber, W. A. (1979). *Managerial Behaviors of Elementary School Teachers and Student On-Task Behavior.* Paper presented at the American Education Research Association, San Francisco.

31. Good, T. L. (1970). Which pupils do teachers call on? *Elementary School Journal, 70,* 190–198.

32. Goss, S. S., & Ingersoll, G. M. (1981, February). *Management of Disruptive and Off-Task Behaviors: Selected Resources.* Washington, DC: ERIC Clearinghouse on Teacher Education, Sp. 017 373.

33. Hoen, A. (1954). A study of social class differentiation in the classroom behavior of nineteen third grade teachers. *Journal of Social Psychology, 39,* 269–292.

34. Rist, R. (1970). Student social class and teacher expectations: The self-fulfilling prophesy in ghetto education. *Howard Educational Review, 40,* 411–451.

35. Rosenthal, R. (1973). The Pygmalion effect lives. *Psychology Today, 7,* 56–63.

36. Rothbart, M., Dalfren, S., & Barrett, R. (1971). Effects of teachers' expectancy on student-teacher interaction. *Journal of Educational Psychology, 62,* 49–54.

37. Rowe, M. (1974). Wait-time and rewards as instructional variables, their influence on language, logic and fate control: Part one, wait-time. *Journal of Research in Science Teaching, 11,* 81–94.

38. Ryans, D. G. (1952). A study of criterion data. *Educational and Psychological Measurements, 12,* 333–344.

39. Thompson, G. G. (1944). The social and emotional development of preschool children under two types of educational programs. *Psychological Monograph, 56* (5), Whole No. 258, 1–29.

40. Schwebel, A., & Cherlin, D. (1972). Physical and social distancing in teacher-pupil relationships. *Journal of Educational Psychology, 63,* 543–550.

EDUCATOR AS A PERSON

41. Aspy, D. N., & Roebuck, F. N. (1977). *Kids Don't Learn from People They Don't Like.* Amherst, MA: Human Resource Development Press.

42. Chernow, F. B., & Chernow, C. (1981). *Classroom Discipline and Control: 101 Practical Techniques.* West Nyack, NY: Parker.

43. Ginott, H. G. (1972). *Teacher and Child: A Book for Parents and Teachers.* New York: Macmillan.

44. Glasser, W. (1969). *Schools Without Failure.* New York: Harper and Row.

45. Gordon, T. (1974). *Teacher Effectiveness Training.* New York: Wyden.

46. Kleinfeld, J. (1972). *Instructional Style and the Intellectual Performance of Indian and Eskimo Students.* Final Report, Project No. 1-J-027. Office of Education, U.S. Department of Health, Education, and Welfare.

47. Kohut, S., Jr., & Range, D. G. (1979). *Classroom Discipline: Case Studies and Viewpoints.* Washington, DC: National Education Association.

48. Norman, J., & Harris, H. (1981). *The Private Life of the American Teenager.* New York: Rawson, Wade.

49. Rogers, C. R. (1969). *Freedom to Learn.* Columbus, OH: Charles E. Merrill.

50. Schmuck, R., & Schmuck, P. A. (1979). *Group Processes in the Classroom.* Dubuque, IA: William C. Brown.

51. Shumsky, A. (1968). *In Search of Teaching Style.* New York: Appleton Century Croft.

52. Weber, W. A. (1982). *The Classroom Management Project: A Technical Report.* Princeton: Educational Testing Services.

53. Weber, W. A., Roff, L. A., Crawford, J., & Robinson, C. (1983). *Classroom Management: Reviews of the Teacher Education and Research Literature.* Princeton: Education Testing Services.

54. Wolfgang, C. H., & Glickman, C. D. (1986). *Solving Discipline Problems: Strategies for Classroom Teachers* (2nd ed.). Boston: Allyn & Bacon.

MODELING APPROPRIATE BEHAVIOR

55. Bryan, J., & Walbek, N. (1970). Preaching and practicing generosity: Children's actions and reactions. *Child Development, 41,* 329–353.

56. Charles, C. M. (1981). *Building Classroom Discipline.* White Plains, NY: Longman.

57. Clarizio, H. F., & Yelon, L. S. L. (1976). Learning theory approaches to classroom management: Rational and intervention techniques. *Journal of Special Education, 1,* 267–274.

58. Cullinan, D. A., Kauffman, J. M., & La Fleur, N. K. (1975). Modeling: Research with implications for special education. *Journal of Special Education, 9,* 209–221.

59. Good, T., & Brophy, J. (1984). *Looking in Classrooms* (3rd ed.). New York: Harper and Row.

60. Prentice, N. M. (1972). The influence of live and symbolic modeling on prompting moral judgment of adolescent delinquents. *Journal of Abnormal Psychology, 80,* 157–161.

61. Scheiderer, E. G., & O'Connor, R. D. (1973). Effects of modeling and expectancy of reward on cheating behavior. *Journal of Abnormal Child Psychology, 1,* 257–266.

GROUP COHESIVENESS

62. Johnson, L. V., & Bany, M. A. (1970). *Classroom Management: Theory and Skill Training.* New York: Macmillan.

63. Schmuck, R. A., & Schmuck, P. A. (1975). *Group Processes in the Classroom.* Dubuque, IA: William C. Brown.

64. Stanford, G. (1980). *Developing Effective Classroom Groups.* New York: A & W Visual Library.

POSITIVE EFFECTS OF REWARDS

65. Becker, W., Engelmann, S., & Thomas, D. (1975). *Teaching 1: Classroom Management.* Chicago: Research Press.

66. Becker, W. C., Masden, C. H., Arnold, C. R., & Thomas, D. R. (1967). The contingent use of teacher attention and praise in reducing classroom behavior problems. *Journal of Special Education, 1* (3), 287–307.

67. Brophy, J. E., & Putnam, J. G. (1978). *Classroom Management in the Elementary Grades.* ERIC ED 167 537.

68. Hall, R. V., Lund, D., & Jackson, D. (1968). Effects of teacher attention on study behavior. *Journal of Applied Behavior Analysis, 1,* 1–2.

69. Masden, C. H., Becker, W. C., & Thomas, D. R. (1968). Rules, praise, and ignoring: Elements of elementary classroom control. *Journal of Applied Behavior Analysis, 1* (2), 139–150.

70. Zimmerman, E. H., & Zimmerman, J. (1962). Alteration of behavior in a special classroom situation. *Journal of the Experimental Analysis of Behavior, 5,* 59–60.

DETRIMENTAL EFFECTS OF REWARD

71. Condry, J., & Chambers, J. (1978). Intrinsic motivation and the process of learning. In M. R. Lepper & D. Greene (Eds.), *The Hidden Costs of Reward: New Perspectives on the Psychology of Human Motivation.* New York: Erlbaum.

72. De Charms, R. (1976). *Enhancing Motivation: Change in the Classroom.* New York: Irvington.

73. Deci, E. L. (1976). *Intrinsic Motivation.* New York: Plenum Press.

74. Deci, E. L. (1978). Applications of research on the effects of rewards. In M. R. Lepper & D. Greene (Eds.), *The Hidden Costs of Reward: New Perspectives on the Psychology of Human Motivation.* New York: Erlbaum.

75. McGraw, K. G. (1978). The detrimental effects of reward on performance: A literature review and a prediction model. In M. R. Lepper & D. Greene (Eds.), *The Hidden Costs of Reward: New Perspectives on the Psychology of Human Motivation.* New York: Erlbaum.

76. Pittman, T., Boggiano, A., & Ruble, D. (1982). Intrinsic and extrinsic motivational orientations: Limiting conditions on the undermining and enhancing effects of reward on intrinsic motivation. In J. Levine & M. Wang (Eds.), *Teacher-Student Perceptions: Implications for Learning.* Morristown, NJ: Erlbaum.

77. Ross, M. (1976). The self-perception of intrinsic motivation. In J. H. Harvey, W. J. Ickes, & R. F. Kidd (Eds.), *New Directions in Attributional Research* (Vol. I). New York: Erlbaum.

DECREASE EFFECTIVENESS OF REWARDS

78. Safer, F., & Allen, R. *Hyperactive Children: Diagnosis and Management.* Baltimore: University Park Press, 1976.

DEVELOPMENTAL DIFFERENCES

79. Forness, S. R. (1973). The reinforcement hierarchy. *Psychology in the Schools, 10,* 168–177.

80. Stallings, J. (1975). Implementation and child effects of teaching practices in Follow-Through classrooms. *Monograph of the Society for Research in Child Development, 40,* 7–8.

LEARNED HELPLESSNESS AND DEPENDENCY

81. Ginott, H. G. (1972). *Teacher and Child*. New York: Avon.

82. Kruglanski, A. W. (1978). Endogenous attribution and extrinsic motivation. In M. R. Lepper & D. Greene (Eds.), *The Hidden Costs of Reward: New Perspectives on the Psychology of Human Motivation*. New York: Erlbaum.

83. Weiner, B. (1979). A theory of motivation in some classroom experiences. *Journal of Educational Psychology, 71*, 3–25.

DECREASED CREATIVITY

84. Jenke, S., & Peck, D. (1976). Is immediate reinforcement appropriate? *Arithmetic Teacher, 23*, 32–33.

85. Johnson, D., & Johnson, R. (1975). *Learning Together and Alone: Cooperation, Competition and Individualization*. Englewood Cliffs, NJ: Prentice-Hall.

86. Kruglanski, A. W., Friedman, I., & Zeevi, G. (1971). The effects of extrinsic incentive on some qualitative aspects of task performance. *Journal of Personality, 39*, 606–617.

87. Soar, R., & Soar, R. (1975). Classroom behavior, pupil characteristics, and pupil growth for the school year and summer. *JSAS Catalog of Selected Documents in Psychology, 5*, 873.

RECRUITING PRAISE

88. Brophy, J. (1981). Teacher praise: A functional analysis. *Review of Educational Research, 51* (1), 5–32.

89. Stokes, T., Fowler, S., & Baer, D. (1978). Training preschool children to recruit material communities of reinforcement. *Journal of Applied Behavior Analysis, 68*, 488–500.

90. Yarrow, M., Waxler, C., & Scott, P. (1971). Child effects on adult behavior. *Developmental Psychology, 5*, 300–311.

IDENTIFYING THE BEHAVIOR BEING REWARDED

91. Harris, A., & Kapiche, R. (1978). Problems of quality control in the development and the use of behavior change technology in public school settings. *Education and Treatment of Children, 1*, 43–51.

92. Sharpley, C. F., & Sharpley, A. M. (1978). Contingent vs. noncontingent rewards in the classroom: A review of the literature. *Journal of School Psychology, 19* (3), 250–259.

INAPPROPRIATE PRAISE

93. Amato, J. (1975). *Effect of Pupils' Social Class on Teachers' Expectations and Behavior*. Paper presented at the annual meeting of the American Psychological Association, Chicago.

94. Brookover, W., Schweitzer, J., Schneider, J., Beady, C., Flood, P., & Weisen-backer, J. (1978). Elementary school social climate and school achievement. *American Journal of Educational Research, 15,* 301–318.

95. Cooper, H. M. (1979). *Communication of Teacher Expectations to Students.* Paper presented at the conference on Teacher and Student Perceptions of Success and Failure and Applications for Learning and Instruction, University of Pittsburgh, Pittsburgh, PA.

96. Fernandez, C., Espinosa, R., & Dornbusch, S. (1975). *Factors Perpetuating the Low Academic Status of Chicano High School Students* (Memorandum No. 138). Palo Alto, CA: Stanford University, Center for Research and Development in Teaching.

97. Kleinfeld, J. (1975). Effective teachers of Eskimo and Indian students. *School Review, 82,* 301–344.

98. Rowe, M. (1972). *Wait-Time and Rewards as Instructional Variables: Their Influence on Language, Logic and Fate Control.* Paper presented at the annual meeting of the National Association for Research in Science Teaching.

99. Weinstein, R. (1976). Reading group membership in first grade: Teacher behavior and pupil experience over time. *Journal of Educational Psychology, 68,* 103–116.

PERCEIVING REWARDS DIFFERENTLY

100. Ware, B. (1978). What rewards do students want? *Phi Delta Kappan, 59,* 355–356.

ATTRIBUTION OF CAUSE OF SUCCESS

101. Anderson, L., & Prawat, R. (1983). Responsibility in the classroom: A synthesis of research on self-control. *Educational Leadership,* 62–66.

102. Andrews, G., & Debus, R. (1978). Persistence and the causal perception of failure: Modifying cognitive attributions. *Journal of Educational Psychology, 70,* 154–166.

103. Chapin, M., & Dyck, D. (1975). Persistence in children's reading behavior as a function of N length and attribution training. *Journal of Abnormal Psychology, 85,* 511–515.

104. Dweck, C. (1975). The role of expectation and attribution in the alleviation of learned helplessness. *Journal of Personal and Social Psychology, 31,* 674–685.

105. Weiner, B. C. (1979). A theory of motivation for some classroom experiences. *Journal of Educational Psychology, 71,* 3–25.

MOTIVATIONAL DEVELOPMENT

106. Brophy, J. E. (1981). Teacher praise: A functional analysis. *Review of Educational Research, 51* (1), 5–32.

107. Hartner, S. (1978). Effectance motivation reconsidered: Toward a developmental model. *Human Development, 21,* 34–64.

108. Meyer, W. U., Bachmann, M., Bierman, U., Hempelmann, M., Plager, F. O., & Spiller, H. (1979). The information value of evaluative behavior: Influences of praise and blame on perceptions of ability. *Journal of Educational Psychology, 79,* 259–268.

109. Walker, H. (1979). *The Acting Out Child: Coping With Classroom Disruption.* Boston: Allyn & Bacon.

# *HANDLING POTENTIAL DISRUPTIONS*

This chapter describes techniques to handle potentially disruptive situations—such as start-ups, transitions, and obtaining permission—in ways that avoid behavior problems. It also suggests techniques you can use to reduce the potential for disruption inherent in certain instructional methods. The chapter offers effective procedures for establishing rules and helping students comply with them. It also includes exercises to help you gain insight into how your personality will influence the ways in which you will try to manage potentially disruptive situations.

If not handled well, some situations could tempt generally well-behaved students to misbehave. Examples of such potentially disruptive situations include:

Beginning class at the start of the day or period, after recess, or after lunch

Transition times between activities

When students are waiting to request permission for certain activities

Times when students are called from class by the office or leave early for medical appointments

Late arrivals

Fire drills

Handing in late assignments

Informing students about what was covered and the homework they missed during an absence

Unanticipated schedule changes due to bad weather, audiovisual equipment breakdown, teacher work days, standardized testing, and so on

The discussion begins by focusing on three typical potentially disruptive situations: starting up the class, transitions between activities, and obtaining permission. These three serve as examples of how valuable it is to establish procedures before disruptions occur.

## *Start-Ups*

The first few minutes of class as the day begins, right after recess, or following lunch at the elementary or intermediate level can be a waiting time for students who arrive early or settle down quickly. Having optional work on the board for them to do can keep them busy until everyone is ready. Options include new vocabulary words, map research for social studies, an interesting puzzle, or a special "stumper problem." You can also let students work on their journals, get a head start in silent reading, or select a learning center to work at for the first few minutes.

## *Transitions*

Transitions—the times when students are finishing one activity and preparing for and actually starting the next activity—often find students not actively engaged in productive work. When transitions aren't smooth—and students are waiting to be told what to do, are confused about what to do next, don't have enough time to end one activity and prepare for the next, or their teachers are attending to distributing or putting away things rather than to the people in the class—disruptive behavior problems are more likely to occur (1–4). Transitions can be especially disruptive if they occur without any warning or when the bell for recess, lunch, or dismissal sounds while students are still working. At such times, students are ready and eager to leave and reluctant to delay their departure to put things away, to hear what the homework assignment is, and so on.

When, in contrast, transitions are smooth, students switch from one activity to another quickly and without disruptions. They will also have more time for learning. Paying attention to transitions is classroom management time well spent.

### *Four Common Mistakes*

Kounin (3) identified four common mistakes teachers make during transitions. He named these *thrusts*, *dangles*, *flip-flops*, and *fragmentations*.

*Thrusts*    These occur when the teacher suddenly interrupts an activity with no warning: "Time's up," "Everyone stop working," "Close your books," "It's recess time." When teachers end activities without warning, students in the middle of their work may interfere with the transition by expressing their reluctance to end what they were busy doing. In some instances, they may continue working on the earlier activity and not hear the directions that they will need to do the next activity well.

You can avoid such situations by giving your students advanced notice that an activity will end soon. Telling your students they will have to stop in five minutes or advising them not to start another problem if they won't be able to finish it in the next two minutes are simple ways of avoiding thrusts.

*Students often welcome the opportunity to help out during transitions.*

*Dangles*    Educators leave students "dangling" when they get too involved in setting up materials, reviewing lesson plans, conversing with a student who needs extra attention, and making students wait too long for the next activity. The students are ready, but they have nothing to do except wait patiently or "get into trouble."

Sidestep having students dangle during transitions by having the materials you will need to use or to distribute handy so you won't have to look for them. Use transparencies and an overhead projector instead of having students wait while you write things on the board. Establish automatic routines with your students for putting things away, collecting and distributing materials, and other classroom activities to reduce students' waiting time during transitions.

Another option instead of giving out all of the laboratory equipment, athletic equipment, or art supplies yourself is to assign two or three monitors to help if your students are old enough to assume that kind of responsibility. Establishing automatic routines using students' assistance will reduce waiting time and free you to attend to the students rather than to housekeeping chores.

Another strategy is to avoid bottlenecks during transitions by putting materials in an easy-to-reach spot and by having more than one distribution point where students can pick up or check out what they need. Also arrange the furniture and equipment in the classroom so it doesn't block traffic when transitions mean that students have to move from one place to another.

Stainback, Stainback, and Froyen suggest testing out the traffic pattern:

> Teachers can identify major traffic routes by "walking through" the activities that are likely to occur during the course of a school day. They may find that furniture and equipment placed in close proximity to storage areas, the cloakroom, or the classroom door must be relocated to allow for smooth, unobstructed travel. Likewise, traffic pattern testing may suggest a classroom plan or rule that can eliminate some congestion or disruption, for example, "No more than three students are allowed in the cloakroom at one time," "Enter the cloakroom from the left and exit from the right." (4, p. 13)

If you are working with younger students, arrange their cubbies, coat hangers, lockers, and other access areas so that groups of them can get to these areas at the same time without having to wait too long for turns. You can help kindergarteners and students in early elementary grades by identifying storage locations with color codes or pictures.

*Flip-Flops*   These occur when educators direct their students' attention back to a previous activity after they have started a new one. Examples of flip-flops include stopping a lecture about Indians to give the math homework after math has ended or interrupting a lesson to answer questions from students who don't know what they should be doing because they weren't paying attention while the class was being prepared for the activities. Such flip-flops readily interfere with the momentum of the lesson and can make it difficult to get the class back on track.

To avoid flip-flops, make sure you complete all aspects of one activity before moving to the next one. Check that all students are paying attention while you are preparing them for the next activity, and double check that all of them know what they are supposed to do. Whenever you discover that you have omitted something after you have changed activities, ask yourself if you really need to deal with it at the moment or if you can wait for a less disruptive time.

*Fragmentations*   Fragmentation refers to moving the group along piecemeal instead of together. Educators can fragment the group by having the class start a new activity one row at a time or by preparing the Robins for their reading assignment while having the Blue

## THEORY FOCUS: KOUNIN ON CLASSROOM MANAGEMENT

Jacob Kounin investigated how teachers' behavior affects the ways their students behave. He introduced the practice of videotaping classrooms to study how students reacted to different types of classroom management techniques. He discovered that effective classroom management was characterized by four factors he labeled "with-it-ness," overlapping, smoothness, and momentum. These increase students' on-task behavior. In contrast, classroom management characterized by dangles. flip-flops, bottlenecks, fragmentations, and desist orders that are rough, unclear, and untimely lead to off-task and disruptive behavior. His book, *Discipline and Group Management in Classrooms*, is considered by many to have initiated the scientific study of classroom management.

Jays wait their turns to be told what to do. Again, when students are waiting with nothing to do, they may be tempted to pass the time doing things that they wouldn't ordinarily do if they were actively engaged in learning activities.

You can avoid fragmentations by preparing your whole class simultaneously for a new activity. If you have to work with different groups separately before they can start, have the Blue Jays engage in a self-directed activity while you are giving the Robins their instructions and/or materials.

## *Timing*

Determining when to end an activity and begin another one is just as important as determining how to make the transition between two activities. Because students' attention spans differ, they won't all be capable of working efficiently and cooperatively for the same

| TRANSITIONS | |
|---|---|
| *Effective Management Techniques* | *Ineffective Management Techniques* |
| Warning students that an activity will end shortly—five-minute warning | Ending an activity abruptly without warning |
| Shortening transition time by having materials ready in advance, using transparencies, and so forth | Poor housekeeping procedures or stopping to write things on the board |
| Using several distributors and distribution points | Bottlenecks caused by students waiting to receive materials |
| Arranging the room to facilitate student movement, providing easy access to cubicles or lockers, color coding storage areas | Traffic jams |
| Completing all aspects of an activity before beginning a new one; making sure everyone is attending before giving directions or initiating an activity | Interrupting one activity to return to an earlier one |
| Preparing all students for an activity simultaneously; assigning self-directed activities if students have to wait | Moving the group along piecemeal |
| Monitoring students' attention span | Requiring students to continue an activity they can't concentrate on |
| Providing self-directed activities for students who finish early | Requiring faster students to wait idly |
| Providing slow workers other chances to complete their work | Penalizing slow workers for incomplete assignments |

amount of time. Thus, whether students are working individually at their seats or in small or large groups, it's important to end the activity before they are no longer able to cooperate and start misbehaving.

One way to determine when students "have had it" with an activity is to identify a "steering criterion group" (5–7)—that is, a few students who represent those with the shortest attention span—and monitor them. Another way is to monitor the group as a whole for signs that some of them are fading. Signs that would indicate this are fidgeting, looking around, combing their hair, talking to others, writing or exchanging notes, and so on.

It is just as important to give your fast-working students self-directed activities to engage in while they wait for their less speedy peers to complete seat assignments. (See Chapter 11.) Slow workers, who are unable to complete seatwork in the allotted time, may be more willing to proceed to the next activity without resisting if you give them an opportunity to complete their assignments at a later, more convenient time. (See Chapter 11.)

In circumstances when the whole group requires more time to work at an activity than they are able to devote to it without becoming restless, you might try boosting their interest. Helpful comments include: "I know you guys must be almost pooped, but we can finish this in a few more minutes" or "We're almost done—let's try to finish up before we quit." If this doesn't help, you can give the groups a short break and then return to the activity if your schedule permits.

## *Obtaining Permission*

When teachers are busily involved with helping a student, working with a group of students, or doing work at their desks, they may not notice that a student is waiting to ask for permission to sharpen a pencil, get a drink, go to the bathroom, and the like. Young students with low frustration tolerances or strong needs (to use the bathroom) may not be able to wait very long before interrupting their teachers or expressing their frustration in disruptive ways.

One way you can handle such situations is to allow students to attend to certain needs without obtaining your permission. This will cut down on your students' waiting time and the potential for associated disruptions. But because some students may abuse the freedom to move around the room without consulting you, you may prefer to have students obtain your permission in these situations. If you do, establish routines that enable them to gain your attention as quickly and unobtrusively as possible. This will cut down on their waiting time and maintain your control over their movements. You can also establish routines that make it unnecessary for students to leave their seats in some situations by handing out sharpened pencils at the beginning of the class and meeting other anticipated needs before they arise.

Which of these three approaches will work best for you depends in part on your personal style. Whichever you emphasize, though, the following suggestions should help.

1. Make a conscious choice—ahead of time—about how you wish to handle each of the situations just described. You may decide to allow students to get up without permission to do certain things in the room but not others or allow students to move around the room freely but not leave the room without permission.

2. Whatever choice you make, organize the classroom environment to minimize disruptions. For example, select pencil sharpeners that don't make a lot of noise and locate several so students can reach them easily. Follow the same principle with movable storage cabinets, wastepaper baskets, and so on.

3. Maximize activities in which students can be self-directed. Minimize those for which students must obtain permission. This gives you more time for important things and also fosters your students' personal growth.

4. If you want to allow students to do some things without asking permission, make sure they are mature enough to handle this privilege. Younger children may be able to use the pencil sharpener without any problem, but allowing them to get materials from storage cabinets could cause difficulties. Monitor students closely, especially at the beginning of the school year, to make sure they can handle the privilege and don't abuse it.

In general, students shouldn't be permitted to pester others while moving around, nor should they be allowed to absent themselves from the classroom by repeated trips or long visits to the water fountain or bathroom. One way of supervising when, how often, and how long students leave the room is to locate one or two larger passes for the drinking fountain and the bathroom in a place you can monitor. If students don't abide by the rules you have set up, employ the techniques in Chapter 4 that you think will solve the problem.

## *Teaching Students Procedures*

As noted in the previous sections, you can avoid many potentially disruptive problems by establishing procedures for doing such things as starting activities, distributing materials, moving from place to place, obtaining permission, and so on. However, just telling students about certain procedures is not enough. The younger they are, the more you need to teach them how to follow procedures and give them opportunities to practice. Typical procedures include where students line up for a fire drill, how materials are distributed, what students do when they come late, and so on. The best time to teach such procedures is during the first few days of the school year. It may seem that having students practice the procedures you want them to follow uses up time at the beginning of the year and is less interesting and more tedious than other activities, but doing this will make your class more trouble free for the rest of the year. Techniques for assisting students to follow procedures and rules are discussed in more detail in the section on "Establishing Rules" below.

# *Three Instructional Approaches*

Each of the methods teachers use for instruction has certain inherent characteristics that may stimulate behavior problems if not handled properly. Three of the most common approaches educators typically use to instruct students are: assigning students seatwork to be done individually; lecturing students interspersed with question-and-answer periods (direct instruction); and stimulating student interaction through group discussions, debates, group projects, cooperative learning, and the like. (This latter is high student involvement instruction.)

The following discussion is designed to help you use these instructional strategies in ways that maximize their effectiveness while minimizing their potential for disruptiveness.

## *Seatwork*

Students who can't continue working on their own because they need help with a particularly difficult problem or a step in a process or need to have their work checked before going on to another activity may not always wait patiently for their teachers to notice and attend to them. The following suggestions can help you avoid any problems this might create (8–11).

1. Establish routines that enable students to gain your attention as quickly as possible.

2. Instead of requiring students to keep their hands raised while waiting for you to notice, establish an alternative signal, for example, a small cardboard stand they can place on their desks. If you know that a number of students will require your assistance with a particular project or assignment, use a take-a-number system or have them add their names to a list in a prominent place so you can attend to them in order.

3. Give students feedback about their work efficiently. Checking students' work before permitting them to go on may be educationally sound as you can determine if they have mastered a particular skill and can move ahead. But this approach uses up a lot of class time that you could spend teaching, and it means students have to wait for you if you can't respond to them immediately. As an alternative, allow them to place completed work that doesn't require your immediate feedback in a to-be-checked folder for you to review at a more convenient time.

To handle fast-working students who may get into trouble if they have nothing to do but wait, you can instruct students to proceed to the next group of problems or questions when they finish if the assignment allows for this. If that isn't feasible, you can permit them to select an acceptable activity at their desks or at a learning center of their choice. The latter can create more problems than it solves if it motivates students to be more interested in finishing fast to gain free time than in doing their work well. To avoid this possibility, you will have to monitor the quality of your fast-working students' work.

Sometimes you can give students who work at a slower rate than their peers a little extra time to finish. If not, you might allow these students to complete some of their work at home or excuse them from having to complete every single problem in an assignment. In particular, slow readers may require a head start if they are going to finish something that the whole group will be discussing. (See Chapter 11 for additional suggestions on managing fast- and slow-working students.)

## Direct Instruction

Most behavior problems occur during times when the teacher is lecturing or other students are reciting, and students' thoughts drift. Instead of listening to what is being said, students can become management problems by daydreaming, scribbling, engaging in side conversations, writing, passing notes, and so forth (12–14).

The following techniques will help you maintain your students' attention when you lecture.

- Select topics and materials that are interesting and relevant to your students.

- Adjust your method of presentation to your students' developmental levels.

*Why are the students whispering? Is the lecture boring? Do they already know the work? Does one of them have some news that can't wait?*

- Use proper pacing and timing (see the section on this later in the chapter).

- Actively involve your students in the learning process by encouraging them to react to your presentation, directing them to query you when they are confused or in doubt, and by asking questions periodically to evaluate the effectiveness of your presentation.

The techniques described below will enable you to maintain the group's attention during question-and-answer periods.

- Vary the procedure you follow to select students to call on: ask for volunteers at times, call on students randomly at other times, or call them in order. Calling students randomly maintains their attention since they won't know if they will be asked to recite. This also keeps them actively thinking because they can't just sit back and passively wait to hear what the volunteers have to say.

- Ask the question first, give students a few moments to think about it, and then call on someone. This will maintain your students' attention better than calling on someone and then asking the question because the students won't know whether they will be the one you call on.

- Call on students in order only when a question has many possible answers, for example, naming the fifty states, the thirteen colonies, the ten reasons why, and so on. Then ask your students not to repeat any of the states, colonies, or reasons given by other students.

- Intersperse group recitation with individual recitations. Have everyone in class express his or her opinions or vote on a decision by a show of hands.

## Group Discussion

Probably the most challenging instructional strategies for classroom management are those that have students working together, but these are also highly engaging for the students. This group of techniques will assist you in maintaining the group's attention when students are interacting with each other.

Teach students to talk to the rest of the class, not only to you when they recite.

Have them face the other students, not you.

Make sure they wait until everyone is paying attention before beginning.

Check to see whether everyone can hear and whether they understand what their peers have said. Students have no reason to pay attention when their peers recite if they can't hear or understand them.

Have students comment about what the other students have said.

# *Establishing Rules*

Like procedures, rules are expectations for how students should or will behave. But procedures describe routines that students should follow in carrying out certain tasks that are basically functional and may vary considerably from school to school and teacher to teacher. Rules, on the other hand, describe appropriate behavior. Examples of rules are: students should wait their turn, work independently during tests, and respect the property of others. Rules typically describe how students should relate to each other and to their

---

## THEORY FOCUS: THE CANTERS ON ASSERTIVE DISCIPLINE

In their book, *Assertive Discipline,* Lee and Marlene Canter propose an approach to classroom management that includes the following principles:

- Teachers have the right to determine the environment, structure, routines, and rules that will facilitate learning in their classrooms.
- Teachers have a right to expect and insist that students will conform to their standards.
- Teachers should prepare a discipline plan in advance that includes explicit statements of their expectations, routines, and rules and the intervention approach to be used if and when students misbehave.
- Students don't have the right to interfere with the rights of others or to impede their learning.
- When students don't conform to teachers' expectations, teachers can respond in several ways: They can react nonassertively—passively surrendering to their students; hostilely—responding angrily and vindictively; or assertively—calmly insisting and assuming that students will fulfill their expectations.
- Since students who misbehave know the rules and so choose to behave inappropriately, with very few exceptions teachers should not accept the excuses students

offer for their misbehavior. To do so only encourages students to misbehave more.
- Teachers should use consequences—positive if possible, negative if necessary—to convince students that it is to their benefit to behave appropriately.
- Teachers shouldn't feel guilty about asserting their rights and using harsh negative consequences when necessary. They should keep in mind that students want their teachers to help them control themselves.
- When necessary, teachers also have the right to ask for and receive help from parents and school administrators in order to handle students' behavior problems.

The Canters describe their work in the following way: "We developed Assertive Discipline to give classroom teachers a systematic plan for dealing with student misbehavior. When a plan is in place, students know exactly what behaviors are expected in the classroom, and they can make a choice: to behave and enjoy the rewards or to misbehave and pay the consequences. . . . As teachers become more skilled at managing their classrooms, they can then provide better instruction and home in on the individual needs of their students." (Lee and Marlene Canter, personal communication, April 14, 1989.)

teachers or how they should behave in certain situations. Cangelosi (22) suggests that rules serve four purposes: to maximize on-task behavior and minimize off-task behavior; to provide students with a safe and comfortable learning environment; to prevent students from disturbing other students in the school; and to maintain acceptable standards of decorum.

## Necessary Rules

Experts in the field agree that rules are necessary (15–20). Without rules, students wouldn't know how to behave appropriately because to some degree expectations of acceptable behavior in and outside of school differ (17). For example, outside of school it may be totally appropriate for students to move around and take breaks whenever they want to while doing their homework, for more than one person to speak at a time, or for students to express themselves in four-letter words. But in school, these behaviors are likely to be unacceptable.

## Effective Rules

Experts tend to agree that to be effective, rules should be reasonable, observable, positive, and few in number (21– 26).

*Reasonable Rules*    Rules are reasonable if they are necessary and not arbitrary. For example, it is necessary for students to be silent during fire drills, keep their hands off other students during class, and respect the property of others. But is it reasonable to prohibit students from chewing gum, from wearing clothes in class that may make teachers uncomfortable, or from swearing? Educators disagree about the reasonableness of such prohibitions. See Chapter 6 for a more detailed discussion of how and why educators disagree about whether certain behaviors should or should not be permitted in school.

*Observable Rules*    Some authors (23,24,26) suggest that certain rules—such as students should be polite, respectful, responsible, and the like—are difficult for students to conform to because ideas about what polite, respectful, and responsible mean vary widely. For example, people disagree about whether one must always say please and thank you to be polite or always hand in homework on time to be responsible. The authors cited believe that because students may be unclear about exactly what to do and not do when they are told to be polite, be responsible, and so on, rules should be observable. Examples of observable rules are, "Walk, don't run, in the hallways" and "Do your own work on tests." Brophy and Putnam (21) and others, however, suggest that more general rules applicable to many situations, such as, "Keep the classroom neat" and "Treat others with courtesy and respect," are preferable because they avoid a long and unnecessary list of specific things to do and not do.

*Positive Rules*    To the extent possible, rules should state what students are to do and not what they shouldn't do. The value of this approach is that it will provide students with guidelines on how to behave correctly. For example, "Raise your hand and wait to be called on" is preferable to "Don't call out" because it teaches a procedure. In certain cases, though, negative statements are necessary: for example, "Don't spit" versus "Keep your saliva in your mouth."

*Few Rules*   Most experts suggest that a few good rules are better than many detailed rules. First, students may experience a long list of rules as oppressive. Also, they may not be able to remember and follow them, especially in the primary grades.

---

## THEORY FOCUS: BROPHY RESEARCHES PRACTICE

Jere Brophy has authored or coauthored a dozen books about classroom management and instruction, including *Looking into Classrooms, Student Characteristics and Teaching, Teacher Behavior and Its Effects, Teachers Make a Difference, Teachers' General Strategies for Dealing with Problem Students, Recent Research on Teaching*, and *Learning from Teaching: A Developmental Prospective*. He and his coauthors have probably conducted, reported on, and evaluated more research on classroom management than any other group of individuals in the field.

Brophy's books are designed to enable teachers to base their decisions about classroom management strategies and techniques on scientific knowledge. Following the path cut out by Jacob Kounin, Brophy and his coauthors have contributed much toward our present understanding of effective classroom management and have helped bridge the gap between what theorists claim are good management techniques and what research indicates actually works in practice. For example, he has led the way in establishing developmentally appropriate expectations and classroom management techniques for students at different grade levels, and he has also helped to establish the limitations of such techniques as using consequences and ignoring students to modify students' behavior.

---

# Who Should Establish Rules?

Many educational theorists suggest that students should participate in developing classroom rules (27–31). To support their approach, these authors typically cite one or more of the following reasons. First, participating in the development of rules teaches students how to function in a democratic society. Such participation also helps students understand why specific rules are necessary, which in turn makes them more willing to abide by them. And then students, like all people, are more willing to accept rules they help formulate. They point out that teacher-formulated rules can engender hostility and rebellion in some students who have difficulty obeying authority.

Other authors believe that educators should formulate rules on their own and explain them to their students (32–37). The reasons these authors give to support their position include the idea that educators can't achieve their educational goals unless they possess the power to maintain classroom environments that suit them as individuals. Thus, educators have the right to establish the conditions necessary for them to succeed. In addition, they believe that teachers, not students, know what behaviors and standards have to be enforced so students can learn. They suggest as well that teachers, not students, are responsible for the classroom. Thus, allowing students to help set standards of behavior abrogates their responsibility.

These theorists also point out that by the time students have been attending school for a while, they realize a schoolwide set of norms exists for almost all aspects of their behavior. To pretend that they are actually helping formulate such classroom rules is hypocritical, and students readily perceive that they are merely being manipulated and subtly coerced into stating their agreement with already-established rules. Students go along with the pretense of agreeing to the rules, but their acquiescence to the process doesn't necessarily affect their behavior.

Another point is that while it may be feasible to involve students in developing rules in elementary schools, secondary school teachers can't function adequately with a different set of rules each period of the day. And, finally, students in a democratic society have to learn to abide by rules that are formulated by others.

Unfortunately, very little research exists regarding these conflicting opinions. The research that has been done indicates that classroom rules help students behave appropriately regardless of how they are formulated (30–40). Some research indicates that, at least in the lower grades, student participation in developing classroom rules increases the likelihood that they will abide by them (133,135,136). But no evidence shows that teacher-formulated rules don't work, too.

## *When to Establish Rules*

More theorists suggest that classroom rules should be established and taught as early as possible in the school year (41). For example, Brophy and Putnam state:

> Rules need to be stressed on the first day of school and again periodically during the next few weeks, as necessary, until they are working satisfactorily. There is no need for a teacher to be artificially strict or threatening (there is no support for the "don't smile until Christmas" notion), but students should be clear about what the rules are and should receive assistance in remembering and following them, if necessary. Especially in the early grades, getting the year off to a good start may require the teacher to show students what to do and give them practice in doing it rather than just telling them. (46, p. 37)

Four reasons are typically cited for establishing classroom rules early. The first is that establishing rules early could avoid some misbehavior that occurs simply because students don't know what is expected of them. Second, the sooner students know the rules, the sooner they will start following them. Third, students are more receptive to learning rules at the beginning of the year. And finally, criticizing students' behavior before they have been told what is expected of them is unfair.

In contrast to this approach, a few authors suggest that the teacher should establish rules during the year as the occasion arises because students are more likely to see and understand the reason for a rule that is set up in response to a real, current problem. A second reason for this is that students may feel oppressed by being given a long list of rules at the beginning of the school year. The limited research evidence that exists regarding these two positions favors establishing rules at the outset rather than intermittently as the occasion arises.

---

### THEORY FOCUS: GLASSER'S REALITY THERAPY

William Glasser believes that students are in control of their own behavior and choose whether to behave appropriately or not. Since students misbehave when they make poor choices, Glasser's approach, as described in his book *Reality Therapy*, is designed to help students make better choices. Like the Canters, he advises educators not to accept students' excuses for their behavior. Instead, he provides educators with a ten-step process for helping students focus on the results, not the causes, of their actions. This process may or may not involve consequences. For example, students who are unaware of how their behavior affects others may agree to change their behavior once they know the results of their actions. Students who already know that their behavior is unacceptable and are unwilling to modify it may require increasingly severe consequences to motivate them toward change.

One of the many techniques Glasser suggests for giving students insight into their behavior and applying pressure to change is the class meeting. Glasser feels that a regular class meeting, conducted weekly or even more often, can provide students with feedback about how their behavior affects others, a variety of ideas and plans to select from for improving their behavior, and the peer support and pressure that could help them to make significant changes. Whichever technique the teacher uses, the key to successful behavioral change, as Glasser sees it, is for students to accept responsibility for their behavior and to develop a written plan that indicates the behavior to be modified and the consequences that will result from following or not following the agreed-upon plan.

---

## Teaching Rules

Experts in the education field agree that students in the primary grades need to be taught how to abide by class rules. Recommended activities include practicing acceptable behavior, discussing rules, and role playing (42,43). They also suggest that young students need to be reminded of the more important rules by having them posted conspicuously. But it seems unlikely that older students would need to be taught rules they have probably been exposed to many times in their educational careers.

## Achieving Compliance

For rules to be effective, teachers have to enforce them. As Carson and Carson have said:

Even if rules are short, positively stated, conspicuously posted, and are reasonable expectations of behavior, rules are ineffective if they cannot be enforced with appropriate consequences. Effective teachers therefore have rules that specify both behavior and the consequences for compliance with or violation of rules. (23, p. 135)

Not all students, though, will require the same amount of enforcement to get them to comply with rules. Certain students have to expect that they will be caught if they break the rules and will also have to pay consequences for their transgressions for them to follow the rules. But many other students will obey school rules without close supervision simply because they are motivated to do so—unless there are extenuating circumstances. Teachers who believe that most students can be encouraged to want to behave appropriately emphasize techniques that motivate students toward appropriate behavior and deemphasize enforcement. Teachers who perceive students as less than willing to abide by the school rules stress the expectation that the rules will be enforced. The point of view espoused in this book is that enforcement (extrinsic motivation) plays an essential role in classroom management, but increasing students' motivation to want to behave (intrinsic motivation) should take precedence as essential preparation for life in a democratic society.

Rule enforcement involves two steps: monitoring students' behavior and intervening when they misbehave. The sections that follow discuss these two key aspects of rule enforcement.

## *Monitoring Behavior*

Kounin (3) and others (44–49) have demonstrated that students are more likely to abide by classroom rules if they believe that their teachers will notice when they misbehave. In Kounin's work, students who believe their teacher knows what is going on in their classes are described as being "with-it." Teachers who have "with-it-ness" seem to have eyes in the back of their heads. They can attend to more than one thing at a time. And even while working with one student or a small group, they notice what other students are doing. When something starts to go wrong, they intervene right away before things get out of hand and the problem spreads. If more than one student is involved, the teacher focuses on the instigator or initiator, not the followers. In all these ways, with-it teachers convince their students that it is pointless to try to get away with things.

The following suggestions are aimed at helping you convince students of two important points: you will catch them if they misbehave, and you will intervene quickly and effectively.

1. Arrange the classroom furniture and your desk so you can see and hear what is going on.

2. Maintain eye contact with your students and move around the room to use your physical presence as a way of discouraging misbehaving.

3. Keep your eyes and ears open and periodically scan the class while you are working with individuals or small groups.

4. Be on the lookout for signs of impending trouble such as scowls and frowns, students looking around the room, or a small flurry of energy, and intervene *before* anything actually happens.

5. As soon as a disruptive incident occurs, intervene before it becomes serious or spreads to other students.

*The closer students are, the easier it is to monitor their behavior and intervene in a timely fashion when they misbehave.*

6. When you intervene, focus your attention on the instigator of the problem, not an innocent victim if there is one. Specifically, intervene with the student who actually passed a note, asked to see someone's answers during an exam, or made a remark about a student's mother, not with the unwitting recipient, the student who says, "Do your own work," or the one who says, "Don't say anything about my mother or else."

7. When two disruptive events occur simultaneously—a student reading a comic in one part of the room and two students teasing a third elsewhere—attend to the more serious misbehavior first.

## Intervening With Consequences

Although research shows that students are less likely to behave inappropriately when their teachers observe them and intervene appropriately, educators differ on what form such interventions should take. Many authors take the position that the cause of the infraction is irrelevant (50–54). They maintain that regardless of the cause, teachers should handle misbehavior by immediate, automatic, and consistent consequences. Here are some representative examples of this point of view:

> There must be consistent *consequences* for rule fulfillment or infraction . . . Bending the rules for specific pupils or situations should be avoided unless this has been planned with students in advance. (53, p. 92)

> Peer pressure, inadequate parenting, learning disabilities, personal stress, and poor health are just some of the factors that make it more difficult for some students to be on-task than it is for other students. However, it is a fallacy that the presence of such factors excuses students from being responsible for their own behavior. (50, p. 31)

> There is no excuse for bad behavior. All students, except for some with known brain dysfunction, can behave acceptably. Behavior is a matter of choice. Students choose to behave the way they do. Consequences are not arbitrary punishment. They are results that students choose just as they choose their behavior. (52, p. 211, 213)

Other authors disagree; they argue that teachers should match their intervention techniques to the causes of their students' misbehavior (55–57). Goss and Ingersoll have stated:

> The teacher must be aware of the underlying causes of behavior. For example, aggression that results from trouble at home should be treated differently from aggression resulting from boredom. Teacher control and interventions are alerted in relation to the interpretation of the reasons for a behavior. Intervention is neither arbitrary nor capricious. (55, p. 11)

At present, no research evidence indicates which of these two approaches is the more effective. Thus, the choice of whether you use consequences routinely or match intervention techniques to the causes of your students' misbehavior will probably depend on your personality and your perception of how best to manage students' disruptive behavior.

The point of view of this book is that educators should select intervention techniques that are appropriate for the causes of their students' problems (see Part Three). It is true that the application of immediate, routine, and consistent consequences is a useful and necessary technique for students who need to be discouraged from misbehaving because they haven't yet acquired the intrinsic motivation necessary to abide by rules. But it's equally if not more important to motivate these students to want to behave even in the absence of consequences. (How to do this is the subject of Chapter 9.) This idea is well expressed in the following statement by Jones and Jones:

> Behavior that violates accepted rules should be dealt with by discussing the matter with the child. This does not mean that reasonable punishments should not be employed, but when dealing with unproductive behavior we must help children examine both their motivations and the consequences of their actions . . . In a very real sense, a punishment orientation reinforces a low level of moral development and does not help children develop a higher, more socially valuable level of morality. (26, p. 195–196)

# Moral Development

The importance of adapting your techniques to your students' motivational developmental levels was discussed in the previous chapter, noting that younger and older students respond differently to teachers' praise, attribute the reasons for their successes to different factors, and require different amounts of instruction about what is expected of them and how to abide by classroom rules at the outset of the school year. This section covers how you can adapt your classroom management techniques to the moral development of students. (See Chapter 9 for additional information.)

## Three Stages

Piaget (67), Kohlberg (66), and others (58–73) have researched and described the stages children go through in relation to the reasons for conforming to societal expectations. Although these authors disagree on certain points, in general their work indicates that children's moral development includes at least three stages. (Keep in mind, though, that just as children learn to walk and talk at somewhat different ages, the ages at which they pass through these stages also vary with each individual.)

---

### THEORY FOCUS: KOHLBERG ON MORAL DEVELOPMENT

Lawrence Kohlberg is one of the world's foremost researchers on moral development throughout the life span. In such books as *The Psychology of Moral Development, The Stages of Ethical Development: From Childhood through Old Age, The Measurement of Moral Judgment,* and *Moral Education, Justice and Community: A Study of Three Democratic Schools,* he has contributed much to our understanding of the different types of moral thinking individuals are capable of at various stages of their development. He has also studied the evaluation of moral development and how to foster moral growth. Although the process of moral development now appears to be more influenced by cultural factors and is less universal than Kohlberg had originally thought, his work has contributed a great deal to our understanding of how to improve youngsters' moral functioning.

---

*First Stage: Extrinsic Consequences*    Children are in the first stage of moral development until the age of seven or eight. Able to see the world from their own perspective only, they cannot control their behavior by "putting themselves in the other person's shoes," by empathizing with others, or by accepting the idea that others also have rights. Their level of morality, called moral realism, is based on the question, What will adults do to me if I do such and such? In this stage children do what is expected of them because adults have authority over them, and positive consequences follow "good" behavior and negative consequences follow "bad" behavior.

**Toddlers:** Even this preliminary kind of morality takes a period of years to develop in children. Infants do whatever they want, but by the toddler age, youngsters have to submit to authority. Toddlers control themselves for three basic reasons. First and perhaps foremost, adults force their will on them. By taking things out of their hands, putting things beyond their reach, dressing them in certain clothing, holding onto them firmly in public buildings, and so on, adults teach toddlers they can both keep them from doing things and force them to do things. When children realize this, they are less likely to engage in power struggles that they know they can't win. Second, adults teach toddlers that when they do what they are told, they get such positive reinforcements as smiles, hugs, praise, sweets, and the like. But when they don't do as they are told, they are scolded, smacked on the hand, deprived of their toys, or given "time out" away from the others. Finally, adults model the way they want toddlers to behave and give them enough attention, nurturance, and love to motivate them to want to copy adults.

**Preschool students:** Educators use the same three techniques with preschoolers. They teach children that they must submit to authority; they model the behavior they want the students to copy and motivate them to want to copy it. Though preschoolers have a greater capacity to control themselves, the type of self-control they are capable of is still very much like the self-control of toddlers. That is, when they are told not to do something—especially if they are told repeatedly—they generally respond appropriately. But they still can't be relied on to exercise self-control without others there to tell them what to do and what not to do.

The words adults use with toddlers are almost invariably the command type: "don't," "stop," "no." Preschoolers are ready for two other types of command words: "wait," "just a minute," "later," and "do it," "pick it up," "you do it." Thus, toddlers can begin to learn that they can't do everything they want, but preschoolers can also learn to wait and to do things for themselves or to at least help out a little.

**Primary grade children:** When students are in kindergarten and first grade, typical self-control issues they struggle with include waiting to be called on, taking turns, not interrupting others, listening when other students are reciting, sharing materials, and so on. Fortunately, by this time they can remember the consequences of their previous behavior. As a result, teachers have a fourth method they can use to teach these students to behave appropriately: They can remind them what happened the last time they did the wrong thing or didn't wait.

Primary grade students can also understand, although at a basic level, such ideas as people can't all fit through one door at the same time and no one can be heard if everyone talks at once. This gives educators a fifth technique: They can explain the reasons why certain rules and procedures are necessary. Lacking experience and maturity, these youngsters have only a limited capacity to understand and recall the reasons their teachers give them for certain behaviors. But explaining the why's and wherefore's to them in a way they can understand may still be helpful. Such explanations can help them to progress to the next stage since submitting to authority is only a basic beginning in a democratic society that calls for citizens with a higher level of moral development.

*Second Stage: Natural Consequences*    Students who are between 7 and 11 are usually in the second stage of moral development, sometimes referred to as the cooperative, reciprocal, or constructive stage. In this stage students are much more able to understand why rules are necessary. They can readily see that they have to be quiet so their classmates can hear the speaker or that they must put things back where they belong so they can find them the next time they need them. But once students can appreciate why some rules are necessary, they may question the necessity for other rules that seem arbitrary to them. For example, they may want to know why they can't chew gum in class or dress the way they want to if it doesn't hurt or interfere with anyone else. During this stage, they want to be told why they should or shouldn't do certain things, and they are less willing to do things just because their teachers say so. Educators who rely too often on power to control students who have progressed beyond moral realism may find that their techniques spark dissatis-faction or outright rebellion in students who want to be treated more maturely.

Because students at this stage can appreciate why rules are necessary, they are able to distinguish between necessary and arbitrary rules and can see other people's points of view and empathize with their feelings. They can also understand concepts of justice, fair play, and so on and so are able to participate in making classroom rules and determining the consequences when students don't abide by them. As we will see in the next chapter, this kind of experience can help prepare students to function fully in a democratic society.

*Third Stage: Intrinsic Consequences*    When students enter the final stage of moral development (usually when they enter junior high school), they begin to behave appro-priately because it's the "right" or "good" thing to do. Instead of conforming just because of what teachers will do to them and what other students will think about them, they begin to exercise self-control and behave appropriately even if no one will know what they do or no one rewards or punishes them. As a result, at this stage educators can place greater em-phasis on rational discussion and appeals to social responsibility instead of positive and negative consequences when attempting to motivate their students. They can now encour-age their students to behave appropriately for the good of the class or because it's the "right" way to behave.

A democratic society can't function properly unless its citizens have reached this stage of development, and so one goal of education should be to help students attain this level of morality. Overreliance on consequence and failure to provide students with the oppor-tunity to exercise this type of moral self-control may stunt their development. Involvement in class discussions about moral issues and taking part in projects that right injustices and reduce inequality such as feeding the poor and confronting prejudices can foster their moral development (see Chapter 9).

# *Adapting to Students' Moral Development*

Very little research has studied the effects of adapting management techniques to stu-dents' stages of moral development. Yet so many authors have suggested these adaptations and so many teachers have reported that they seem to work that using them until research either supports or refutes them seems reasonable. This section discusses using and adapting management techniques that correspond to the three stages of moral development.

Students in the first stage of moral development—preschool and primary grade students—respond to consequences. Rewarding them for behaving appropriately and applying negative consequences when they misbehave helps teach them about the real world. Thus, although consequences shouldn't be the teacher's main approach to classroom management, they do play an important role with young students.

Older students who haven't been exposed to life's lessons at home or elsewhere and come to school believing they can "get away with" doing whatever they please also need to learn that, at least in school, they have to abide by rules. But such students are only a small fraction of the school population. These students also need to develop intrinsic motivation so they won't want to get away with things. Knowing that there will be consequences if one misbehaves is also needed to keep many well-behaved students on track, just as knowing that the IRS may audit one's taxes or the parking meter attendant may ticket one's car helps citizens abide by the laws.

This means that the use of consequences, especially negative ones, should be limited to these three situations. Thus, except for use with a small percentage of students, negative consequences should play only an extremely minor, insignificant, and primarily deterrent role with upper elementary and secondary school students. Educators who punish older students excessively or who rely heavily on the threat of punishment for control risk making students resentful and rebellious about being treated like "babies" or "criminals." Such educators also neglect their responsibility to help students develop the intrinsic motivation needed to function as true citizens in a democratic society.

Because upper elementary and secondary students can understand why it's necessary to behave appropriately, follow rules, and be good group members, they should be approached—at least in part—as rational people capable of managing their own behavior once they know how they should behave and why it's necessary for them to behave that way. Secondary school teachers in particular should foster their students' intrinsic motivation. This isn't meant to imply that secondary school teachers and administrators can dispense with consequences. Consequences are a fact of life. What it means, once again, is that after the primary grades, consequences should play a minor, deterrent role.

## *The Educator's Personality*

Research indicates that educators' personalities, values, beliefs, and so on help determine the ways they manage their classrooms (74–76). Specifically, educators differ in terms of how much movement and talking they allow in their classes, the kinds of activities students can engage in without obtaining their permission, the types of instructional approaches they use, how much they emphasize acquiring basic skills and knowledge or improving interpersonal skills, whether they use authoritative or authoritarian classroom management techniques, the relative emphasis they place on fostering students' intrinsic motivation to behave appropriately as opposed to using extrinsic consequences, the roles they assign students in developing classroom rules, and whether they emphasize cooperation or competition to motivate their students.

# Self-Quiz:
# Student Feedback

The following are sample types of questions you can use to find out how your students perceive you when you are student teaching or have your own class. The actual questions you ask and the way you word them would depend on what you are interested in learning from your students as well as on their developmental level. For example, you might ask older students to rate you on a scale of one to ten, one to five, or as excellent, good, fair, poor, or very poor. But younger students might relate better to single, double, triple, home run, or always, usually, sometimes, and never.

I am friendly.

I am polite and respectful.

I don't lose my temper.

I am fair.

I make you feel good about yourself.

I am not sarcastic.

I don't embarrass you in front of your classmates.

I listen to your complaints, discuss them, and tell you whether I agree with you or not and why.

I call on you as often as I call on other students.

I listen to your answers and comments and give you my honest reactions to them.

I give you permission to do the things you want to do when you want to do them.

I allow you to participate in making decisions that affect you, help decide when tests will be given, and choose where we will go on class trips.

I encourage you to talk to me about whatever is on your mind even if it isn't related to school.

I do my best to make time before, during, or after class for you to discuss whatever you want with me.

I give you my honest opinions when we discuss things.

I understand how you feel about things.

I act the way I expect you to act.

I encourage everyone in class to get along and to cooperate with each other.

I encourage students to solve the conflicts between them on their own.

I praise and criticize you only when you deserve it.

I make sure the class knows what to do when they come in at the start of the day, at the beginning of the period, after lunch, and after recess.

I give you enough time to complete your work.

I don't require you to ask for permission to do certain things you can do on your own.

I don't make you wait too long when you need help with difficult work or want permission to do something.

I allow you to help decide the class rules and the consequences for breaking them.

Classroom rules are clear.

Classroom rules are fair.

I am in charge of the class.

I know who is doing what in class.

I don't expect too little or too much from you.

I expect you to act your age, not younger or older.

I treat you like someone your age should be treated.

## *Self-Evaluation*

You can gain insight into the way your personality, values, opinions, assumptions, and other qualities could be influencing how you manage or would manage your classroom by examining the choices you would make in each of the areas mentioned above. In addition to reviewing your own responses, you have other resources available to help you learn more about your own personal style.

## *Feedback from Students*

The various self-evaluation activities in this chapter will aid you in discovering both the way your personality affects your choice of classroom managing techniques and the effectiveness of how you employ them. Feedback from students is another important source of information about how effective your classroom management techniques are.

## *Summary*

By handling such potentially disruptive situations as start-ups, transitions, and obtaining permission properly, it's possible to sidestep many potential classroom behavior problems. Establishing procedures and rules can also help you eliminate problems. In order to ensure that students will comply with established procedures and rules, it's necessary to monitor the students' behavior and intervene when they misbehave. Such intervention techniques should be suited to students' levels of moral development.

## *Activities*

I. List some activities you could assign students at the beginning of the school day, after recess, or after lunch that would help avoid potential problems during start-ups. Use the class or program you plan to work in to establish the students' ages.

II. Review the arguments for and against each of the following controversial practices. Formulate your opinion, and state the reasons for your decision.

Including versus not including students in developing classroom rules

Establishing rules at the beginning of the school year versus later in the term

Intervening immediately, automatically, and consistently when students misbehave versus taking the causes of students' misbehavior into consideration

III. List the management techniques that you can use to be effective with students at each of the following levels of moral development to help them behave appropriately: stage one—extrinsic consequences, stage two—natural consequences, stage three—intrinsic consequences.

# *References*

TRANSITIONS

1. Anderson, L. M., Evertson, C. M., & Brophy, J. E. (1979). An experimental study of effective teaching in first grade reading groups. *Elementary School Journal, 79* (4), *1*, 193–223.

2. Arlin, M. (1979). Teacher transitions can disrupt time flow in classrooms. *American Educational Research Journal, 16* (1), 42–56.

3. Kounin, J. (1970). *Discipline and Group Management in Classrooms.* New York: Holt, Rinehart & Winston.

4. Stainback, W., Stainback, S., & Froyen, L. (1987). Structuring class to prevent disruptive behaviors. *Teaching Exceptional Children, 19* (4), 12–16.

The references below deal with steering criterion groups.

5. Arlin, M., & Westbury, I. (1976). The leveling effect of teacher pacing on science content mastery. *Journal of Research in Science Teaching, 13*, 213–219.

6. Dahloff, U. (1971). *Ability Grouping, Content Validity and Curriculum Planning Analysis.* New York: Teachers College Press.

7. Lundgren, U. P. (1977). *Model Analysis of Pedagogical Process.* Stockholm: CWK Gleerup.

These articles discuss managing waiting time.

8. Berliner, D. (1978). *Changing Academic Learning Time: Clinical Intervention in Four Classrooms.* Paper presented at the annual meeting of the American Educational Research Association, Toronto, Canada.

9. Brophy, J. E. , & Evertson, C. M. (1976). *Learning from Teaching: A Developmental Perspective*. Boston: Allyn & Bacon.

10. Brophy, J. E., & Putnam, J. G. (1978). *Classroom Management in the Elementary Grades*. ERIC ED 167 537.

11. Yinger, R. (1979). Routines in teacher planning. *Theory into Practice*, 18, 163–169.

The following articles cover maintaining group focus.

12. Good, T. (1978). *The Missouri Mathematics Effectiveness Project: A Program of Naturalistic and Experimental Research*. Paper presented at the annual meeting of the American Educational Research Association, Toronto, Canada.

13. Kounin, J. S. (1970). *Discipline and Group Management in Classrooms*. New York: Holt, Rinehart & Winston.

14. Kounin, J. S., & Doyle, P. H. (1975). Degrees of continuity of a lesson's signal system and the task involvement of children. *Journal of Educational Psychology*, 67, 159–164.

NECESSARY RULES

15. Canter, L., & Canter, M. (1976). *Assertive Discipline*. Seal Beach, CA: Canter & Associates.

16. Dreikurs, R., & Grey, L. (1968). *A New Approach to Discipline: Logical Consequences*. New York: Hawthorne Books.

17. Gnagey, W. J. (1981). *Motivating Classroom Discipline*. New York: Macmillan.

18. Masden, C., & Masden, C. (1970). *Teaching/Discipline*. Boston: Allyn & Bacon.

19. Morgan, D. P., & Jenson, W. R. (1988). *Teaching Behaviorally Disordered Students: Preferred Practices*. Columbus, OH: Charles E. Merrill.

20. Tikunoff, W. J., Word, B., & Dasho, S. (1978). *Three Case Studies*. (Report A78–7). San Francisco: Far West Laboratory for Educational Research and Development.

EFFECTIVE RULES

21. Brophy, J. E., & Putnam, J. G. (1978). *Classroom Management in the Elementary Grades*. ERIC ED 167 537.

22. Cangelosi, J. S. (1986). *Cooperation in the Classroom: Students and Teachers Together*. Washington, DC: National Education Association.

23. Carson, J. C., & Carson, P. (1984). *Any Teacher Can: Practical Strategies for Effective Classroom Management*. Springfield, IL: CC Thomas.

24. Charles, G. M. (1981). *Building Classroom Discipline: From Models to Practice*. White Plains, NY: Longman.

25.  Gnagey, W. J. (1981). *Motivating Classroom Discipline*. New York: Macmillan.

26.  Jones, V. F., & Jones, L. S. (1986). *Comprehensive Classroom Management: Creating Positive Learning Environments*. Boston: Allyn & Bacon.

ESTABLISHING RULES WITH STUDENTS

27.  Glasser, W. (1969). *Schools Without Failure*. New York: Harper & Row.

28.  Guarnaccia, V. J. (1972). The effectiveness of school rule codes in reducing misbehavior in elementary school classes. *Dissertation Abstracts International 33* (6–B) 2810 (Order No. 72–31–955).

29.  Jensen, R. E. (1975). Cooperative relations between secondary teachers and students: Some behavioral strategies. *Adolescence, 10*, 469–482.

30.  Schmuck, R., & Schmuck, P. A. (1979). *Group Processes in the Classroom*. Dubuque, IA: W. C. Brown.

31.  Tjosvold, D. (1980). Control, conflict, and collaboration in the classroom. *Education Digest, 45* (8), 17–20.

The articles that follow describe establishing rules without student participation.

32.  Bloom, R. B. (1980). Teachers and students in conflict. The CREED Approach. *Phi Delta Kappan, 61*, 624–626.

33.  Canter, L., & Canter, M. (1976). *Assertive Discipline*. Seal Beach, CA: Canter & Associates.

34.  Dobson, J. (1970). *Dare to Discipline*. Wheaton, IL: Tyndale House.

35.  Englander, M. E. (1986). *Strategies for Classroom Discipline*. New York: Praeger.

36.  Johnson, L. V., & Bany, M. A. (1970). *Classroom Management Theory and Skill Training*. New York: Macmillan.

37.  McDaniel, T. R. (1982). How to be an effective authoritarian: A back to basics approach to classroom discipline. *Clearing House, 55*, 245–247.

These references discuss the efficacy of rules.

38.  Masden, C. H., Jr., Becker, W. C., & Thomas, D. R. (1986). Rules, praise and ignoring: Elements of elementary classroom control. *Journal of Applied Behavior Analyses, 1*, 139–150.

39.  O'Leary, K. D., Becker, W. C., Evans, M. B., & Sudargas, R. A. (1969). A token reinforcement program in a public school: A replication and systems analysis. *Journal of Applied Behavior Analyses, 2*, 3–13.

40.  Walker, H. M. (1979). *The Acting-Out Child: Coping with Classroom Disruption*. Boston: Allyn & Bacon.

The citation below focuses on establishing rules early.

41.  Emmer, E., Evertson, C., & Anderson, L. (1980). Effective management at the beginning of the school year. *Elementary School Journal, 80*, 219–231.

These articles are on the topic of communicating expectations and rules.

42. Anderson, L., Evertson, C., & Emmer, E. (1980). Dimensions in classroom management derived from recent research. *Journal of Curriculum Studies, 12,* 343–356.

43. Evertson, C. M., & Emmer, E. T. (1982). Effective management at the beginning of the school year in junior high classes. *Journal of Educational Psychology, 74* (4), 485–498.

## MONITORING BEHAVIOR

44. Borg, W. R., & Ascione, F. R. (1982). Classroom management in elementary mainstreaming classrooms. *Journal of Educational Psychology, 74,* 85–95.

45. Brophy, J. E., & Evertson, C. M. (1976). *Learning from Teaching: A Developmental Perspective.* Boston: Allyn & Bacon.

46. Brophy, J., & Putnam, J. (1978). *Classroom Management in the Elementary Grades.* Research Series Number 32. East Lansing, MI: Institute for Research on Teaching, Michigan State University.

47. Crawford, J., Gage, N., Corno, L., Stayrook, N., & Mitman, A. (1978). *An Experiment on Teacher Effectiveness and Parent-Assisted Instruction in Third Grade* (preliminary draft). Stanford, CA: Center for Research at Stanford, Stanford University.

48. Emmer, E., & Evertson, C. (1981). Synthesis of research on classroom leadership. *Educational Leadership, 38,* 342–347.

49. Evertson, C. M., & Emmer, E. T. (1982). Effective management at the beginning of the school year in junior high classes. *Journal of Educational Psychology, 74* (4), 485–498.

## INTERVENING WITH CONSEQUENCES

50. Cangelosi, J. S. (1988). *Classroom Management Strategies: Gaining and Maintaining Students' Cooperation.* New York: Longman.

51. Carson, J. C., & Carson, P. (1984). *Any Teacher Can: Practical Strategies for Effective Classroom Management.* Springfield, IL: CC Thomas.

52. Charles, C. M. (1981). *Building Classroom Discipline: From Models to Practice.* White Plains, NY: Longman.

53. Kerr, M. M., & Nelson, C. M. (1983). *Strategies for Managing Behavior Problems in the Classroom.* Columbus, OH: Charles E. Merrill.

54. Masden, C. H., Jr., & Masden, C. K. (1970). *Teaching/Discipline.* Boston: Allyn & Bacon.

These references deal with matching causes and interventions.

55. Goss, S. S., & Ingersoll, G. M. (1981). *Management of Disruptive and Off-Task Behaviors: Selected Resources.* Washington, DC: ERIC Clearinghouse on Teacher Education.

56. Johnson, L. V., & Bany, M. A. (1970). *Classroom Management: Theory and Skill Training.* New York: Macmillan.

57. Redl, F. (1975). Disruptive behavior in the classroom. *School Review, 83* (4), 569–594.

MORAL DEVELOPMENT

58. Aronfreed, J. M. (1968). *Conduct and Conscience: The Socialization of Internalized Control over Behavior.* New York: Academic Press.

59. Bear, G. B., & Richards, H. C. (1981). Moral reasoning and conduct problems in the classroom. *Journal of Educational Psychology, 73,* 664–670.

60. Brockman, J. et al. (1978). *The Developmental Relationship Among Moral Judgment, Moral Conduct, and a Rationale for Appropriate Behavior.* ERIC ED 165 051.

61. DePalma, D. J., & Foley, J. M. (Eds.). (1975). *Moral Development: Current Theory and Research.* New York: Erlbaum.

62. Edelman, E. M., & Goldstein, A. P. (1981). Moral education. In A. P. Goldstein, E. G. Carr, W. S. Davidson, & P. Wehr (Eds.), *In Response to Aggression.* New York: Pergamon.

63. Freeman, S. J. M., & Biebink, J. W. (1979). Moral judgment as a function of age, sex and stimulus. *Journal of Psychology, 102,* 43–47.

64. Gibbs, J. C., Arnold, K. D., Ahlborn, H. H., & Cheesman, F. L. (1984). Facilitation of sociomoral reasoning in delinquents. *Journal of Consulting and Clinical Psychology, 52,* 37–45.

65. Hoffman, M. L. (1970). Moral development. In P. H. Mussen (Ed.), *Manual of Child Psychology, Vol. 2* (3rd ed.). New York: John Wiley.

66. Kohlberg, L. (1984). *The Psychology of Moral Development.* San Francisco: Harper & Row.

67. Piaget, J. (1965). *The Moral Judgment of the Child.* New York: Free Press.

68. Rest, J. R. (1983). *Morality.* In P. H. Mussen (Ed.), *Handbook of Child Psychology* (4th ed.). New York: John Wiley.

69. Rothman, G. (1972). The influence of moral reasoning on behavioral choice. *Child Development, 43,* 397–406.

70. Staub, E. (1979). *Positive Social Behavior and Morality*. New York: Academic Press.

71. Tanner, L. N. (1978). *Classroom Discipline for Effective Teaching and Learning*. New York: Holt, Rinehart & Winston.

72. Turiel, E. (1974). Conflict and transition in adolescent moral development. *Child Development, 45*, 14–29.

73. Zimmerman, D. (1983). Moral education. In A. P. Goldstein (Ed.), *Prevention and Control of Aggression*. New York: Pergamon.

THE EDUCATOR'S PERSONALITY

74. Dobson, J. E., & Campbell, N. J. (1979). The relationships of teachers' philosophy of human nature and perception and treatment of behavioral problems. *Humanist Educator, 18* (1), 23–31.

75. Jury, L. E., Willower, D. J., & Delacy, W. J. (1975). Teacher self-actualization and pupil control ideology. *Alberta Journal of Educational Research, 21* (4), 295–301.

76. Rohrkemper, M. M., & Brophy, J. E. (1979). *Classroom Strategy Study: Investigating Teacher Strategies With Problem Students*. ERIC ED 175 857.

# PART TWO

# RESOLVING MOST BEHAVIOR PROBLEMS

# *Introduction*

This part focuses on behavior problems that occur in your classroom even when you're doing a great job of managing your class. You may be following all of the principles already discussed, and one, two, or a few students still call out, talk when they should be listening, refuse to do what you ask of them, scribble and doodle instead of write, get into arguments with other students, "challenge your authority," pay attention for only 30 to 40 percent of the time allotted, and so forth.

When students misbehave despite your best efforts to avoid behavior problems, you can use four questions to help you decide on a good course of action.

1. *Whose problem is it?* Is it the student's problem or yours?

2. *Should I intervene?* Should you tolerate the behavior or attempt to deal with it?

3. *If so, when?* When would be the most effective time to intervene—as soon as you notice the behavior problem or at some other time?

4. *How should I intervene?* Which of the many strategies would be most likely to work in this particular situation?

This part will help you answer these questions so that you can solve most of your classroom behavior problems as quickly and as effectively as possible.

# *PROBLEMS AND*
# *WHO OWNS THEM*

This chapter will help you become a better observer and evaluator of students' behavior. It explains why teachers sometimes misperceive or misunderstand their students' behavior or interpret behavior differently. Most importantly, the chapter contains exercises that will provide you with insight into your own particular and subjective ways of viewing your students' problems. This will enable you to do a better job of determining if there is a problem and, if so, whose it is.

At first glance, the question of whether a behavior problem exists and, if so, whose it is may seem superfluous to you. You may believe that educators should be able to tell when a problem exists in their own classrooms and who is causing it. These questions, though, are not as straightforward as they may seem (1–12). Sometimes, whether a particular behavior is a "problem" or not depends on the eye of the beholder. For example, some teachers think it's okay for students to converse while doing their seatwork so long as they don't disrupt other students and stop after a brief exchange. Other teachers would intervene immediately. Certain teachers allow students to call out a question without raising their hands so long as they don't do so habitually and don't take other students' turns. Other teachers do not allow any calling out in their classes. Some teachers intervene just as soon as students begin to be disruptive to make sure things don't get out of hand. Other teachers wait to see if the students will get back on the straight and narrow on their own. Even the strictest teachers don't attend to every infraction of the rules, especially if they think it will be more trouble than it's worth or they are doing something they feel is more important (13–19).

Lawrence, Steed, and Young (15) describe the variables involved in whether certain behaviors will be considered disruptive.

> Behavior only becomes disruptive at certain times and in certain places; it is disruptive to wander about in a French lesson but not in Drama, in the corridors at certain hours but not in the craft room; it is disruptive to keep silent in English discussion but not in Mathematics. What is seen as disruption by A may be welcomed as creativity by B and for both the same behavior may change its significance depending on the time of the day or week. . . . There seems to be no easy way of categorizing the precipitating

circumstances although in many, the element of teacher stress seems important. Descriptive studies reveal an unending series of circumstances in which the teacher's patience will be exhausted and it is difficult to move from the specific to the general. Time of day, time of the year (especially when examinations make heavy demands on teachers' time), poor health, overwork, domestic upset, previous experience, age, sex, class—all may contribute to explanations of why particular forms of behavior in individuals are sometimes allowed, sometimes stigmatized. (15, p. 17)

While Lawrence, Steed, and Young emphasize that the specific situation as well as the mood of the teacher at the time help determine whether a certain behavior is regarded as disruptive, Gordon (14) stresses a third contributing factor: Some teachers are generally more accepting than others and have shorter lists of what they consider unacceptable behavior.

## Two Kinds of Behavior Problems

Student behaviors that educators typically want to change fall into two groups: (1) those that almost all educators agree are problems, and (2) those about which they disagree. For example, virtually all educators would agree on the importance of trying to change the following behaviors: rarely staying on-task for more than five minutes, cheating during exams, teasing and hitting younger students, coming to school "high" on drugs, constantly calling out answers, and avoiding new or difficult tasks. On the other hand, not all educators would agree that they should necessarily try to change such behaviors as chewing gum in class, boasting to others about one's accomplishments or grades, making extremely frank comments to others about their mistakes or shortcomings, being extremely passive and submissive, or being extremely assertive and competitive.

Behavior that everyone agrees is a problem should definitely be addressed. Educators not only have the right to try to change such behavior, they also have an obligation to do so. But teachers' rights and obligations to try changing behavior are less clear when educators do not agree that a problem exists. Thus teachers need to consider whether their perceptions of students' behavior are influenced by their own values, priorities, personal likes and dislikes, and life experiences before deciding whether or not to intervene. Learning how to distinguish between the two kinds of behavior problems and what to do about the second kind of behavior are two main themes of this chapter.

## Self-Defeating or Harmful Behaviors

Examples of behaviors that harm the students who commit them include provoking rejection by pestering, teasing, or annoying other students; avoiding new or difficult tasks or challenges because of a poor self-concept; being so dependent on the assistance, opinions, or praise of others that this interferes with learning to do things for oneself, to think for oneself, and to decide for oneself; being so cocky, rebellious, defensive, and the like that the suggestions and criticisms of others are automatically rejected out of hand; coming to school on drugs. Examples of behaviors that infringe on the rights of others are interrupting what is going on instead of waiting; pushing ahead of others, and calling out when it is someone else's turn to answer; taking things that belong to other students, refusing to share, and not returning things that have been borrowed; hitting others, breaking their things, calling them names, and purposefully doing things to make them feel bad or to upset them.

## Behaviors That Challenge Values or Expectations

Behaviors that may not conform to educators' expectations and values include being more assertive or passive than some educators feel is okay, working at a pace that makes some educators uncomfortable, and being more competitive than some educators think students should be. You can tell that qualities like assertiveness, work speed, and competitiveness are vague and subject to individual judgments.

The uncertainty about the right and obligation to intervene with behavior that doesn't conform to teachers' personal expectations and values or that distresses or disturbs them doesn't mean that educators must accept such behavior just because it isn't harmful or doesn't interfere with the rights of other students. Educators aren't superhuman, perfect beings. If you try to endure too much, the resentment, anger, and frustration that are bound to build up inside could impede your ability to teach your classes. It could also interfere in your relationship with both the students who prompted these feelings and with other students in the class as well. But this also doesn't mean that educators should always try to change behavior that they disapprove of or that bothers them. What it does mean is that educators should examine their reasons for wanting to change behavior before deciding whether or not to intervene.

## Differing Perceptions of Behavior

Educators may perceive students' behavior differently because they have different cultural backgrounds, values, or personalities. Each of these can radically affect how they "see" certain behavior.

### Cultural Differences

One reason educators may disapprove of or be upset by behavior that neither harms nor interferes with the rights of others is that cultural differences can affect whether or not a student's behavior seems appropriate, polite, fair, or moral. The teacher's cultural back-

*Teachers may find that their perceptions of students may be different from the perceptions of their colleagues.*

ground can make a big difference. For example, in some cultures, people are brought up to be *considerate* of others: "Don't play the stereo too loudly," "Don't make noise too early, you will wake the people in the next campsite," and "Play outside with your friends so your brother can study." In other cultures, youngsters are brought up to be *tolerant* of others: "Don't let the radio bother you," "You better go to sleep early—you know campers make noise in the morning," and "Learn not to be distracted by other people—the world can't stop just because you have to do your homework."

Teachers from cultures that bring up children to be considerate of others are more likely to perceive students as interfering with the rights of others or as unwilling to share, conform, or go along with the group. As a result, they may intervene in situations that other educators would accept as reasonable behavior.

Some of the many areas of behavior influenced by cultural factors include cooperation, competition, sharing, waiting one's turn, apologizing for mistakes or errors, and expressing feelings. Cultural factors play such an important role in the classroom that a separate chapter, Chapter 12, is devoted to them.

## Values Differences

Values are our ideas and feelings about what is good, proper, worthwhile, and desirable and what is bad, improper, worthless, and undesirable. We can state, explain, and justify our values. In that sense they are rational and intellectual.

All individuals from the same cultural background do not have the same values because they are brought up by different parents in different neighborhoods and schools, belong to different socioeconomic classes, and so on. As a result, educators with similar cultural backgrounds may react very differently to their students' behavior when values are brought into play. For example, educators differ in terms of what they consider appropriate student-teacher relationships. Some expect students to be acquiescent because their teachers are adults—students are to take in what they are taught, speak when spoken to, and raise questions only about what they don't understand but not about their teachers' beliefs or the way their teachers instruct them. Other educators want their students to play a more active role in what they learn, to question them, and to help determine the way the class is run.

Teachers place different values on the rights of the individual vis-à-vis the rights of the group. In some situations, when a conflict arises between the wishes or needs of the individual and the group, certain teachers expect the group to be more tolerant of the individual, while others may prefer the individual to be more group oriented. Educators also have differing ideas about how assertively students should seek to obtain what they want and how straightforward and frank students should be about their opinions and feelings when these don't agree with those of other students. Finally, educators often differ about the best way for students to resolve arguments and disagreements among themselves.

Educators place different values on punctuality and promptness. Some will take credit off for assignments that are turned in late, while others don't consider promptness at all. Educators also disagree about the relative importance of academic subjects, extracurricular activities, sports, the arts, and family activities. As a result, what some educators consider acceptable reasons for not completing an assignment or missing school, others consider a poor or no excuse.

Because many differences exist among educators' values, whether a student's behavior is considered a problem will largely depend on who his or her teacher is. This means that educators should be aware of when their personal values and expectations influence their perceptions of their students' behavior. They can then take this added information into account when deciding whether or not to treat the behavior as a problem.

## Psychological Differences

All people, educators included, are upset by some things that other people can take in stride. Thus, a student's behavior can be seen and treated as a problem in one case and ignored in another depending on the personality of the educator in charge. For example, imagine you are an eighth-grade teacher on recess duty. You emerge from the building and spy a large crowd of students in a corner of the school yard. Pushing and elbowing your way through the crowd, you see the school bully beating up on the school scapegoat. Now ask yourself who upsets you more—the bully who is constantly taking advantage of weaker students or the scapegoat who is forever allowing himself to be taken advantage of? Stop reading now until you have given yourself time to find an honest answer to the question. *Don't* answer that you are equally upset by both. When you have your answer, read on.

"What's the matter with you? How many times have you been told not to pick on the other children? You ought to be ashamed of yourself! I'm taking you to the principal's office. Let's go," you tell the bully, while trying to control your anger—that is, providing the bully is the one who upsets you most. "What's the matter with you?" you ask the scapegoat—if it's the scapegoat that upsets you—frustration clearly evident in your voice. "How many times are you going to allow yourself to be beaten up before you learn to stand up for yourself? You and I have to have a talk about this," you continue, disregarding the bully for the moment.

Compared to values that we can state, explain, and justify, psychological factors are less intellectual and rational. An individual may experience intense reactions but often without knowing why. When people say things like, "I just can't stand her when she does that" or "That kind of thing drives me up the wall" or when they lose control or explode about some incident that objectively doesn't merit such a strong response, they are often in the dark about why they react the way they do.

Many reasons explain why people's psychological makeups affect the way they see things and react to them. To begin with, people are usually comfortable when others act the same way they do and uncomfortable when they behave differently. Educators who are assertive and competitive are likely to accept such behavior from their students, but educators who are more passive and cooperative may react negatively to the same behavior. Likewise, educators who have a very high energy level and are very active may be more accepting of students who have difficulty sitting still in class than educators who are more sedentary.

Educators who strive to be sensitive to the feelings of others may think that students who boast about their talents, grades, achievements, and so on or are extremely critical of other students should be taught to be more concerned about others' feelings in response to their behavior. Other educators who are more straightforward in the way they express their feelings and less concerned about their effects on others may think that these "boastful" and "critical" students are merely proud of their accomplishments and honest about how they see their peers. Instead of wanting to change these students, such educators may believe the other students should learn to be less sensitive and less insecure about themselves.

Educators who are slow and careful workers may be unable to abide students who work fast because their "frenetic" pace makes them nervous. Other educators may react poorly to students who seem to be working so slowly and meticulously they will never finish anything on time.

Second, people are comfortable when others behave in ways that complement—or complete—their behavior and uncomfortable when they don't. For example, educators who enjoy helping and supporting others are complemented by students who seek and react positively to their help, approval, and support. But if these same students seek help and approval from educators who prefer to maintain a more aloof, distant, or so-called "professional" relationship with their students, these teachers may see the students as whining, dependent, insecure, and in need of developing more self-confidence and learning to function more independently.

A third explanation for why people see things a certain way is that they often react defensively when confronted with some aspect of their personalities they prefer to deny. Educators, for example, may create unnecessary conflicts between themselves and their students if they can't admit the truth about themselves. "Don't ask any more questions," they tell their students, but what they can't admit to themselves is that they don't know something. "Are you questioning my integrity," they ask their students when they can't face the fact that they acted arbitrarily or unfairly.

An associated problem is that educators may avoid seeing their students' problems if the students' behavior requires a response that would be too confronting. Those who have difficulty being disciplinarians may inadvertently permit students to do things they should not be allowed to do in order to avoid having to discipline them. Those who have difficulty accepting their natural inclinations to sometimes place their own desires ahead of those of others may give in to students more than they should in order to protect themselves from thinking that they are selfish. A few well-chosen words from students such as, "That's not fair, don't you like us? The other teachers don't make us do that," are often all that is necessary to manipulate these educators because they are ready to do almost anything to defend themselves against thinking they are selfish.

Another explanation for some responses is that people who are insecure about some aspects of their personalities may be highly sensitive to possible challenges or slights. For example, educators unsure of their ability to maintain order in the class may misperceive students who are unable to adhere to certain rules as being unwilling to do so and purposely challenging the teacher's authority. Those who are unsure of their teaching ability may believe that students who are talking or laughing about something are making fun of them or something they have said or done. Those who are insecure about their self-worth or how people perceive them may be quick to interpret their students' behavior as disrespectful. And educators who can't admit that they have a short fuse may believe that students behave in ways that upset them *in order to upset them.*

An additional factor is that people's perceptions of the present are highly colored by their past experiences in similar situations or with similar people. Thus, educators could be predisposed against certain students because of their experiences with the students' older brothers or sisters or with other students of the same ethnic or racial background.

Finally, some people are more understanding of other people's problems or mistakes if they have gone through similar experiences themselves. In particular, educators who suffered academic or social problems as students or who got into trouble for delinquent behavior yet succeeded despite their problems may be less worried about or threatened by students undergoing similar experiences. As a result, they may be less likely to treat these students' behavior as problems to be corrected or changed even though the students may actually need their help.

## *Evaluating Your Perceptions*

As the examples indicate, to be human is to be subjective, to make mistakes, to overreact, to deny, to evaluate others in terms of one's own values, and to misperceive and misinterpret others' behavior. Educators are not exempt from this pattern of behavior. When you are an experienced teacher or have completed student teaching, the following section will help you identify when your personal reactions are affecting the way you perceive and experience your students' behavior. Since all teachers are also human beings, it would be surprising if you never experienced any of the problems listed below.

## Self-Quiz: Perceptions of Student Behavior

"Yes" answers to the following questions can indicate that your values and personality *may be* causing you to overreact to an existing problem or to perceive a problem where, in fact, none exists.

1. Do you have the same difficulty with many students?
2. Do you feel a lot of anger or resentment toward a particular student?
3. Do you have less control over your actions with certain students?
4. Is the problem something you can't tolerate in anyone including yourself?
5. Do you think your students act the way they do in order to bother or upset you?
6. Do you interpret your students' misconduct as rebellious or disrespectful?
7. Do you resent the freedom and opportunity your students have that were forbidden to you?
8. At times are you moody, tense, edgy, or irritable because things your students do, which shouldn't bother you, do bother you?
9. Are you often concerned about who is really in control—you or your students?
10. Do you vacillate between two extemes such as permissiveness and strictness?
11. Do you react negatively when students make critical comments about your instructional or management techniques or imply that you are wrong or don't know something?
12. Do you find yourself thinking that some of your students are just like their siblings or others who belong to the same racial, ethnic, or socioeconomic group?

"Yes" answers to the questions listed below *can* indicate that you *may be* underestimating the severity of a problem or perhaps denying that a problem exists.

13. Do you find you are particularly solicitous or understanding about a particular student's behavior?
14. Do you believe your colleagues are too strict?
15. Do you have difficulty admitting that your students have behavior problems because deep down you are afraid you may not be able to help them?
16. Are you so worn out by your own problems that you can't deal with the possibility that your students may also need your help?
17. Do you tell yourself that your students will soon stop doing what they are doing because you are the kind of person who tries to avoid conflicts with others or who has difficulty admitting that real problems exist?

While "yes" answers to any of the questions above can indicate that you may be misperceiving or misinterpreting your students' behavior, it's also possible that your perceptions are correct. One or more of your students may indeed be purposefully trying to annoy you. Some of your students could in fact be disrespectful or rebellious. You may have legitimate reasons for feeling angry or resentful about a particular student. Students can indeed be just like their siblings in some respects. Some parents really do fail in their responsibilities to teach their youngsters the society's values and morals. But there are times when students need understanding and patience, and sometimes we can help a student better by not making an issue of his or her behavior.

*A second opinion can often confirm a teacher's perceptions and feelings about students.*

## Obtaining a Second Opinion

If, after thinking through your answers to the questions above, you are undecided about whether your values and personality are influencing your perceptions of students' behavior, you might consider seeking a second opinion and asking your colleagues what they think. Sometimes a more objective opinion from someone who knows what is going on in your class or who has had the same students can be extremely helpful.

### Self-Quiz: Evaluating Your Perceptions

Your answers to the following questions can provide you with the additional information you need to evaluate your perceptions of and reactions to your students, using comparisons between yourself and other teachers.

1. Do your colleagues have fewer problems than you do with some of your students?

2. Do your colleagues think you overreact to certain problems or students?
3. Do you insist more than your colleagues do that your students' behavior must always conform to your expectations?
4. Do you try to teach your students values that your colleagues don't agree are part of an educator's responsibility?
5. Do your colleagues think you are too lenient with one or more of your students?
6. Do your colleagues disagree with some of your perceptions about your students?

Keep in mind that a "yes" answer to one or more of these questions doesn't necessarily mean that you are misperceiving or misinterpreting your students' behavior. That is, though, one possible explanation for the fact that you and your colleagues disagree.

If your answers to these questions indicate that a student of yours does have a problem that you have been avoiding or overlooking, you may feel badly that you haven't provided the needed help. Try to go easy on yourself. The realization that your student has the problem is the first step in doing something about it.

If, in contrast, your answers indicate that you have been overreacting to minor problems or seeing problems where none exists, you may be unhappy about what you have been doing and judge yourself harshly. But your current and more accurate perception of your students' behavior will go a long way toward eliminating the "problem" and along with it your need to continue to try to solve it.

# Using Formal Assessments

Most educators rely on their own subjective observations to decide whether their students' behavior is unacceptable and requires their intervention. A few prefer to supplement their personal observations with formal instruments (20–30). Teachers who know their students well may find that formal instruments provide very little additional information, and they may value their perceptions more than the results of a test with a small number of items that aren't designed to suit their particular needs. Formal instruments, however, do have the advantage of objectivity. Plus, when the results they produce agree with a teacher's perceptions, they serve as supportive evidence. When results disagree, they may be an essential check on the teacher's subjective, incorrect perceptions.

Age Appropriate Objective Instruments

| INSTRUMENT | GRADE/AGE RANGE |
| --- | --- |
| Behavior Checklist | Kindergarten–second grade |
| Behavior Evaluation Scale | Kindergarten–twelfth grade |
| Revised Behavior Problems Checklist | Five years–adolescence |
| Child Behavior Profile | Six–eleven years |
| Child Behavior Rating Scale | Kindergarten–third grade |
| Devereux Adolescent Behavior Rating Scale | Thirteen–eighteen years |
| Devereux Elementary School Behavior Rating Scale | Kindergarten–sixth grade |
| School Behavior Checklist | Four–thirteen years |
| Walker Problem Behavior Identification Checklist | Preschool–sixth grade |

# Summary

There are two kinds of behavior problems: (1) behavior that is self-defeating or harmful to the student who commits it or infringes on the rights of others, and (2) behavior that doesn't conform to an educator's personal expectations or values but isn't self-defeating or harmful and doesn't interfere with the rights of others. Educators have the right and obligation to try to change the first kind of behavior. Their right to intervene with the second kind of behavior, however, is less clear. Educators may react personally to their students' behavior because of differing cultural backgrounds, values, and personalities. Therefore, the first step in dealing with behavior problems is to determine whose problems they are. While most educators rely on their observations to decide whether their students' behavior requires their intervention, some prefer to supplement such observations with formal instruments.

# Activities

Review the following report written by a biology teacher about Joan, a fifteen-year-old student with many problems. State which problems are likely to be hers and which may be the teacher's personal reactions to Joan's behavior.

*Initial report: January.* At the beginning of the term, Joan was attentive, cooperative, and motivated. She seemed to be genuinely interested in the work. However, by the end of September, she seemed to be exploiting the class and the teacher. It was as if she had been spending the first few weeks developing a good relationship with me that she could exploit at a later date. She began to act as if I were her medical adviser. Three or four times a week she would ask me about minor lacerations on her hands or arms. After a few weeks I began to tell her to see the nurse about them. When I did this, she stopped having accidental injuries to show me.

Joan constantly chews and cracks gum in class in order to get a reaction from me. I told her quite often that although I realized she might need to chew gum, I could not accept the cracking that went along with it. I told her that I had gone halfway by allowing her to chew gum in class and asked her to meet me halfway by not cracking her gum.

I believe that Joan needs structure. This is especially necessary when she refuses to listen to my requests that she start working, open a book, take an examination, and so on. She needs direction and firmness tempered by understanding. Therefore, on these occasions I demand that she work, place a pencil in her hand, open her book for her, and tell her that if she does not begin working I will send her to the principal.

Joan has a great many self-doubts. She is constantly asking me questions about heredity, mental illness, amnesia, and various diseases. She appears to be quite worried about this. During one class period, when we were discussing cancer, she began to cry. Suddenly she was screaming and demanding that I stop the discussion. I explained to her why I could not do this and suggested that she stay outside until she had regained control of herself. She left but returned shortly before the end of the period and explained that her mother had died from cancer. Since then, she has never displayed such outbursts when the topic has been discussed.

Biology is probably difficult for Joan because many of the topics upset her. When we begin such a topic, she refuses to attend to the subject matter. This is especially true when we are studying the nervous system. She uses these occasions as excuses for becoming disturbed. Her friend Deborah does the same thing, and then they both use it as an opportunity to ruin the period.

Sometimes the work in class is too difficult for her. This is usually when we are starting a new topic. At these times she becomes agitated, claims that she does not understand the work, and gives up attempting to succeed. When this happens, I point out to her that it is normal for anyone, including her, to be apprehensive about work that is new, and I try to encourage her to overcome her apprehensiveness. In order to build up her self-confidence, I point out her successes in previous units that were just as difficult for her at first. In fact, I have continually complimented her wherever possible about a nice dress or a new hairdo in order to help her feel better about herself.

Joan often compares herself to Deborah, whom she thinks is the incarnation of perfection. This, of course, adds to her self-doubts because she is not as good a student as Deborah is. She also joins in whenever Deborah behaves disruptively.

Joan wants sympathy from adults. She believes that no one cares for her. When she feels this way during class, she is extremely melancholy and apathetic. I feel that Joan can certainly be helped. She needs even more acceptance, help, care, and attention than she has been receiving. Unfortunately, Joan has learned that those who make the most noise and cause the greatest disturbance often receive the most attention. This is probably a major reason for her recent outbursts. This is especially bad for her because it does not help her learn self-control.

*Report card comment.* Joan is doing well. With a little more effort, she should earn an even better grade.

*Spring report: April.* At the beginning of the second term, Joan attempted to do her work and control her behavior. She attended class and completed most of her assignments. Recently events outside of school have interfered with her classroom functioning because she brings all her difficulties into the classroom with her. For example, today she was upset when she came to school. She refused to work, tore papers, broke pencils, paced the floor, stared out of the window, and screamed, "Leave me alone!" when I asked her to sit down.

The other day she walked into the classroom and sat in the back of the room instead of in her own seat. I knew that she was disheartened by something. However, I also knew that we must not continue to allow her to withdraw into herself and not function. Hoping to involve her in the work, I asked her if she had a pencil. She said that she was not going to do any work and did not need one. I told her that if she did not want to work in the class she would have to sit in the principal's office. She refused to work, and I placed her name on the misbehavior list. She stated that she was not going to work or leave the room. After I had spent five minutes of the class time attempting to reason with her, I had to walk up to her and gradually nudge her to the door. She began to scream, curse, and threaten me. Then I told her and the class that the term was drawing to a close, and we no longer could afford to devote class time to her disruptions. I stated very strongly to her and the rest of the class that I would not surrender to her demands just because she was persistent in them. I also let her know that she had better begin to help herself because if she did not make an attempt to improve her habits, she would not pass the course.

*Final report: June.* Joan made a tremendous amount of progress during the past three months. Now she is able to read through the chapter before she asks questions about the work. She has been able to control her behavior even when emotionally upset. Although she is still somewhat disturbed by discussions of disease, she no longer loses control of herself. In the past few weeks, I have heard her compliment her peers, giving them recognition for their accomplishments. This also is a very positive area for her. I have noticed that she no longer looks up to Deborah, who she thought was completely perfect and therefore vastly superior to her. For the past month or so, she has dressed conservatively, using her makeup with extreme reservation.

Biology was a difficult and challenging subject for her. She tried her best to succeed and in doing so has become confident that she can succeed academically. She has also learned to relate to her peers. I believe that she has made a tremendous change for the better.

# *References*

IS THERE A PROBLEM?

The following references discuss the process of identifying students with behavior problems and the difficulties inherent in this process.

1. Baker, E. H., & Thomas, T. F. (1980). The use of observational procedures in school psychological services. *School Psychology Monographs, 4,* 25–45.

2. Cosper, M. R., & Erickson, M. T. (1984). Relationships among observed classroom behavior and three types of teacher ratings. *Behavior Disorders, 9* (3), 189–194.

3. Epstein, M. H., Cullinan, H. D., & Sabatino, D. A. (1977). State definitions of behavior disorders. *Journal of Special Education, 11,* 417–423.

4. Hartman, D. P. (1982). Using observers to study behavior. *New Directions for Methodology of Social and Behavioral Science, Publication No. 14.* San Francisco: Jossey-Bass.

5. Koppitz, E. M. (1977). Strategies for diagnosis and identification of children with behavior and learning problems. *Behavior Disorders, 2* (3), 136–140.

6. Marcus, S. D., Fox, D., & Brown, D. (1982). Identifying school children with behavior disorders. *Community Mental Health Journal, 18* (4), 249–256.

7. McAuley, R., & McAuley, P. (1977). *Child Behavior Problems.* New York: Free Press.

8. Ollendick, T. H., & Meador, A. E. (1984). Behavioral assessment of children. In G. Goldstein & M. Hersen (Eds.), *Handbook of Psychological Assessment*. New York: Pergamon.

9. Smith, C. R. (1977). *Identification of Youngsters Who Are Chronically Disruptive.* Department of Public Instruction, Special Education Division, Des Moines, IA. Mimeo.

10. Spivack, G., & Swift, M. (1973). The classroom behavior of children: A critical review of teacher administered rating scales. *Journal of Special Education*, 7, 55–89.

11. Walker, H. (1978). Observing and recording child behavior in the classroom: Skills for professionals. *Iowa Perspective*, 4, 1–9.

12. Walls, R. T., Werner, T. J., Bacon, A., & Zane, T. (1977). Behavior checklists. In J. D. Cone & R. P. Hawkins (Eds.), *Behavioral Assessment*. New York: Brunner/Mazel.

## IF SO, WHOSE IS IT?

The articles below deal with the possibility that the problem may be in the eyes of the beholder.

13. Algozzine, B. (1980). The disturbing child: A matter of opinion. *Behavior Disorders*, 5 (2), 112–115.

14. Gordon, T. (1974). *Teacher Effectiveness Training*. New York: Wyden.

15. Lawrence, J., Steed, D., & Young, P. (1984). *Disruptive Children: Disruptive Schools*. New York: Nichols.

16. Marlin, R., & Lauridsen, D. (1974). *Developing Student Discipline and Motivation: A Series for Teacher In-Service Training*. Champaign, IL: Research Press.

17. Mour, S. (1977). Teaching behaviors and ecological balance. *Behavior Disorders*, 3 (1), 55–58.

18. Swick, K., & Howard, R. (1975). Disruptive behavior: Causes, effects, solutions. *Instructional Psychology*. Summer.

19. Thompson, G. (1976). Discipline and the high school teacher. *The Clearing House*, 49, 408–413.

## FORMAL ASSESSMENT INSTRUMENTS

Although an informal approach to evaluating students' behavior problems is recommended in this chapter, many educators prefer to supplement teacher observations with formal instruments. Some of the published instruments currently available are listed below.

## THE BEHAVIOR CHECKLIST

20. Rubin, E., Simpson, C., & Betwee, M. (1966). *Emotionally Handicapped Children and the Elementary School*. Detroit, MI: Wayne State University Press.

THE BEHAVIOR EVALUATION SCALE

21. McCarney, S. B., Leigh, J. E., & Cornbleet, J. (1983). *Behavior Evaluation Scale.* Columbia, MO: Educational Services.

THE BEHAVIOR PROBLEM CHECKLIST

22. Quay, H. C. (1977). Measuring dimensions of deviant behavior: The Behavior Problem Checklist. *Journal of Abnormal Child Psychology, 5,* 277–289.

23. Quay, H. C., & Peterson, D. R. (1983). *Revised Behavior Problem Checklist.* Coral Gables, FL: University of Miami.

24. Von Isser, A., Quay, H. C., & Love, C. T. (1980). Interrelationships among three measures of deviant behavior. *Exceptional Children, 46,* 272–276.

THE CHILD BEHAVIOR PROFILE

25. Edelbrock, C. S., & Ackenbach, T. M. (1984). The Teacher Version of the Child Behavior Profile. I. Boys 6–11. *Journal of Consulting and Clinical Psychology, 52,* 207–217.

THE CHILD BEHAVIOR RATING SCALE

26. Cassell, R. (1962). *The Child Behavior Rating Scale.* Los Angeles: Western Psychological Services.

THE DEVEREUX ADOLESCENT BEHAVIOR RATING SCALE

27. Spivack, G., Spotts, J., & Haines, P. E. (1967). *The Devereux Adolescent Behavior Rating Scale.* Devon, PA: Devereux Foundation.

THE DEVEREUX ELEMENTARY SCHOOL BEHAVIOR RATING SCALE

28. Spivack, G., & Swift, M. (1967). *Devereux Elementary School Behavior Rating Scale Manual.* Devon, PA: Devereux Foundation.

THE SCHOOL BEHAVIOR CHECKLIST

29. Miller, L. C. (1977). *School Behavior Checklist.* Los Angeles: Western Psychological Services.

THE WALKER PROBLEM BEHAVIOR IDENTIFICATION CHECKLIST

30. Walker, H. (1976). *Walker Problem Behavior Identification Manual.* Los Angeles: Western Psychological Services.

# WHETHER, WHEN, AND HOW TO INTERVENE

## To Intervene or Not

In the real world, people don't follow the rules 100 percent of the time. At times adults call out without waiting to be called on during a meeting in the urgency to speak. Sometimes they cut in and out of traffic lanes on the highway when they are in a hurry. They also "make up" a more socially acceptable reason for not going to work, canceling an appointment, or not accepting an invitation because, for one reason or another, they don't feel comfortable telling the truth.

The same things happen in school. Very few students follow all the rules all the time. At some point in their educational careers—at least once in a while—most students will call out, whisper to their neighbors, run in the hall, lie about why they couldn't do their homework, pass notes, tease someone, pretend they have to go to the bathroom, or do something else that breaks a rule or standard of behavior. Teachers who intervene every time their students don't fulfill the school's behavioral objectives would develop a reputation among students for being overly strict, dominating, inflexible nags. Worse, they would waste considerable precious time dealing with behavior that could and should be overlooked. Below are some guidelines that may help you decide whether or not to intervene when your students don't behave appropriately. These suggestions are based on the experience and opinions of many educators, not on research-derived information.

## Unnecessary Intervention

It may come as a surprise in a book on classroom management that some situations are better left alone. The following paragraphs characterize circumstances when it may be either unnecessary or undesirable to intervene.

*Minor infractions:* Intervening when behavior is only a minor infraction and isn't disruptive or contagious may be counterproductive. You might be better off overlooking an occasional incident of calling out an answer, whispering to a neighbor, looking out the window, making an innocuous side remark, and so on than to make an issue of it. The key is that you can do this so long as overlooking it doesn't encourage students to "get into the habit" of doing such things. Experiences in the classroom will enable you to make this kind of judgment with a reasonable degree of accuracy.

*Accidental, unintentional misbehavior:* When students spill things, bump into others, call out answers, accidentally take the wrong book or coat, it may not be necessary to intervene unless the students need your help in learning how to avoid accidents. The same principle applies when students say things in the heat of the moment that they quickly regret having said.

*Extenuating circumstances:* Misbehavior caused by special conditions should be tolerated. For example, when a normally well behaved student gets argumentative because she has done poorly on an exam for the first time during the school year or she is in a bad mood due to a cold, or when your students can't settle down because some good news is announced over the public address system or the fire alarm bell goes off accidentally or they will soon be taking standardized tests or a fun trip has been canceled due to inclement weather, it may be more prudent to overlook their atypical behavior than to confront them about it.

*Unrealistic expectations:* As we noted in Chapter 4, some inappropriate behavior may *only* be inappropriate in the eyes of a particular educator. "Behavior problems" that are problems only because teachers unrealistically expect young students to behave like older students and older students to behave like adults or because educators' personalities and values make them uncomfortable with certain behaviors don't require intervention with students. Instead the teacher may need to work on changing perceptions or instructional methods. For example, when many or most of the second-grade class begins to look around the room, talk to each other, and fidget in their seats, it may be time for the teacher to readjust the length of the lesson to their attention spans and to give up on trying to get them to concentrate for longer than they are able to.

*Two Kinds of Flexibility*    The preceding discussions of times when it might be better to overlook certain behaviors rather than to intervene show how important flexibility is in applying rules and expectations. But being flexible in situations that require adaptability is one thing; yielding to the temptation to lower your standards in order to avoid necessary hassles when you are tired, overworked, trying to cover a lot of material in a short time, or being pressured by students trying to intimidate you is another. The first kind of flexibility (adaptability) is helpful to students; the second kind (inconsistency) may encourage your students to misbehave even more. The first kind can help you avoid unnecessary and fruitless confrontations; the second kind will only postpone necessary conflicts until later when students can become even more difficult to deal with. Learning to distinguish between being inconsistent or being adaptable takes experience and practice.

## Necessary Intervention

Some situations pretty clearly call for a response. The following are examples of circumstances that usually require some form of intervention by teachers.

1. *Harmful behavior:* Students should not be allowed to harm themselves or bully, tease, slander, insult, hit, or provoke other students. Students who are the victims of bullying, insults, and the like have the right to expect you to intervene quickly and effectively.

2. *Distracting behavior:* Behavior that distracts other students or seriously interferes with their ability to achieve your instructional objectives such as attention-seeking clowning, note passing, humming aloud requires your intervention.

3. *Testing behavior:* Students who are testing you in order to find out what they can and can't get away with by challenging your authority, refusing to follow directions, and so on should be shown by your behavior that you will intervene whenever it's necessary to do so. This is especially important when other students are waiting to see how you will handle the problem.

4. *Contagious behavior:* Disruptive behavior that is likely to be copied by other students in your class should be dealt with before other students become involved.

5. *Consistent misbehavior:* Intervene regularly whenever students' misbehavior represents a consistent regular behavior pattern that requires a consistent response from you.

6. *Contractual behavior:* Behavior that represents a failure to abide by a commitment from a student when that student has promised not to act in a particular way should not be overlooked (see discussion of contingency contracting in Chapter 9).

## When to Intervene

Once you decide that your students' behavior does indeed require you to intervene, the next challenge you face is deciding when the most effective time is to do so. Some situations require you to intervene immediately, but in others a short delay might prove helpful.

### Immediate Intervention

Certain guidelines can help you determine when it is important to step in right away to stop what is happening. The following examples indicate the types of behavior that require immediate intervention.

1. *Dangerous and harmful behavior:* Intervene instantly when students' behavior is potentially dangerous or harmful to themselves or others. Stop young students if they start toward the street on their own during a class trip. Prevent older students from hurting themselves or others by misusing science equipment in the laboratories.

Even if the situation isn't clearly dangerous, in circumstances with so much potential for harm, it's better to be safe than sorry. You should also intervene as quickly as possible when students hit, pick on, bully, or victimize others. Finally, despite the saying "sticks and stones will break my bones but names will never harm me," verbal abuse can hurt almost if not just as much as physical abuse, and it requires your immediate intervention.

2. *Destructive behavior*: Students shouldn't be allowed to damage things that are expensive, hard to replace, or belong to or are used by other students. Your immediate intervention at the first sign of trouble can discourage—or, if necessary, prevent—students from intentionally or unintentionally completing such destructive acts.

3. *Behavior that can get worse*: Nip behavior problems that are likely to intensify if not corrected in the bud. Stop an argument between two students that appears about to lead to a real fight immediately. Students who are backing themselves into corners should be given face-saving ways out of the predicaments they are creating for themselves. Students who are testing you to see just how much you will let them get away with should also be stopped before they get themselves into serious trouble.

4. *Contagious behavior*: Stop misbehavior that is potentially "catching" before it spreads and other students get involved.

5. *Self-perpetuating behavior*: Misbehavior that is intrinsically rewarding—such as cutting ahead in line, taking others' things or money, or teasing—should be stopped before students receive any reinforcement for their actions. Otherwise the reinforcement they receive could strengthen their motivation to continue to misbehave despite any negative consequences you apply.

## Delayed Intervention

In some cases it is better to delay intervention than to respond immediately to students' misbehavior. Because students wind up getting blamed for things they haven't done, the intervention causes more disruption than it avoids. The following are some examples of situations in which immediate intervention can be counterproductive.

1. *When you don't have all the facts*: When you aren't sure of the facts, it might be better to hold off responding to what appears to be a problem until you know enough to intervene appropriately. In our society we generally follow the principle that it's better to let a guilty person go free than to punish an innocent one. If you aren't certain that students who seem to have started down the path of misbehaving will actually misbehave, it may be a good idea to give them the opportunity to control themselves so long as the situation isn't likely to be dangerous, destructive, or contagious. For example, if—after handing out test papers to your class—you notice that a student has some notes left on her desk, it might be better to see what she will do instead of intervening right away. Perhaps she wasn't paying attention when you told the class to clear their desks, and she will put her notes away before she

looks at the test questions. In another example, if you overhear someone say something nasty to another student, you may get angry, but perhaps the other student provoked the response. It may be better not to correct the first student on the basis of an incomplete understanding of the situation; wait until you have found out all the circumstances.

2. *When the timing is wrong:* It may be better to postpone dealing with a problem until a more convenient time if the immediate circumstances will not permit you to deal with it effectively. The following are examples of when it may not be the right time to intervene.

- *Insufficient time:* If a student misbehaves at dismissasl time, you may have to wait if you want to discuss your student's behavior with her at length. A simple statement such as "Libby, we'll have to discuss what you just did during your lunch break," is all you need to let her know that you are aware of what she did and plan to handle it.

- *Disruptive effects of intervening:* If you are at a point in a lesson when it would be unwise to stop to handle a behavior problem as you would like to, it may be better to briefly signal your disapproval to the student and deal with it in a more constructive manner at a less disruptive time.

- *When students are too sensitive to expose themselves publicly:* If dealing with students' behavior in public would embarrass them, consider waiting until you can talk to them privately.

- *When students are too upset to deal with their behavior rationally:* When students are extremely angry, jealous, or resentful, it may be more prudent to discuss their behavior with them after they have calmed down.

## *Weighing the Choices*

Unfortunately, in many classroom situations the choices aren't as clear as they are in the examples just described. For instance, a student may be doing something that you think will get worse if you don't intervene, but based on your past experience with this student you also believe he will respond angrily if you call the class's attention to his behavior. What do you do: allow the situation to get worse or risk the student's ire? What should be your response if a student who reacts defensively to public criticism has said something insulting to you, and other students are attentively waiting to see how you will handle the situation?

When such situations occur, you should weigh the pros and cons of intervening immediately and make a decision that reflects your best judgment. If it works out well, great! If it doesn't, change your approach the next time, and try again. Teaching is an art. We all have to learn from experience. When you make a mistake, try to understand where you went wrong. Ask a colleague for feedback, if necessary. Whether what you tried worked or not, you are certain to learn something from each experience.

# How to Intervene

Once you choose to intervene, your next move is to intervene effectively.

## Five Strategies

Redl (3) and others (1,4) have identified five strategies educators can use to handle their students' behavior problems: changing, managing, tolerating, preventing, and accommodating.

---

### THEORY FOCUS: REDL ON MANAGING BEHAVIOR PROBLEMS

Fritz Redl founded Pioneer House, a residential program for middle-school-age boys with emotional problems. He also coauthored *The Aggressive Child*, which describes the techniques staff at Pioneer House used to rehabilitate these youngsters. Many of the techniques described in Chapter 6 for managing students' behavior without consequences were first described by Redl. He is also responsible for the introduction of the life-space interview described in Chapter 10. In his other books, *Mental Hygiene in Teaching*, *When We Deal with Children*, and *Understanding Children's Behavior*, Redl has adapted the techniques from Pioneer House for use in regular classrooms. These techniques include accommodating classroom environments to students' emotional needs, managing their surface behavior without resorting to negative consequences, and preventing dangerous or disruptive behavior in nonpunitive ways. Though his books describe an eclectic approach, in comparison to many educators he stresses taking students' conscious and unconscious motivation into consideration when handling their disruptive behavior. In doing so, he was one of the first educators to suggest how certain Freudian insights could be applied in the classroom.

---

*Changing*   Techniques in the area of changing try to modify the attitudes, values, motives, beliefs, expectations, self-concepts, and so on of students so that they won't have to behave in the same inappropriate way in given situations. Helping a ten-year-old afraid to stand up to boys who pick on him to overcome his fears is an example of changing. Helping a student who is inappropriately insecure about her abilities and talents to perceive herself more accurately is another.

*Managing*   Since it takes a while to change students and sometimes educators do not have the power, influence, or time to do this, they usually have to manage their students' behavior problems. Managing refers to techniques that modify a situation enough to make it less likely that a student will exhibit a behavior problem. Managing techniques aren't designed to change a student; rather their effect is to help the students exert more self-control over their behavior until changing techniques can do their job. In the case of the student who is inappropriately insecure about her abilities, an educator would certainly want to change her emotional reaction to the subjects and situations that make her insecure, but until the educator can do this, he might try managing the situation by telling the student that he will give her all the help she needs, that he won't grade her work, or that she can take a makeup exam if she does poorly on a test. These techniques won't change the student's feelings about herself, but they may help her manage her insecurity so it doesn't affect how she functions in school as much.

Educators can also use managing techniques with students who have physiological problems that cannot be changed. For example, a teacher may not be able to change highly active or overactive students, but she can help them manage their behavior by allowing them to release some of their energy when they are restless and fidgety. While this may not make these students any less active overall, it may enable them to avoid problem behaviors for the moment, which can be a blessing for all concerned.

*Two kinds of managing techniques:* Educators can use two kinds of management techniques—those that involve consequences and those that don't. When educators use consequences to manage their students' behavior, they are using power to convince students to control themselves. To do this, they remind students what will happen if they do such and such, or they reward students for behaving the way they want them to behave and punish them for behaving in inappropriate ways. When educators manage students' behavior without consequences, they don't use power. Examples of this approach are diverting students' attention from things that are upsetting them to something unrelated, making a joke out of something they are taking too seriously, and speaking softly and calmly to them when they are nervous or frightened. None of these techniques involves the use of consequences or power.

*Managing and Changing Compared*    Managing techniques handle misbehavior for the moment. Changing techniques try to modify students' attitudes, motives, self-concepts, and the like so they will not misbehave in the future. Convincing students likely to misbehave that they have to behave or they will be caught and punished is an example of managing students. But motivating these students to want to behave appropriately even when they won't be caught is changing them. Ignoring the attention-seeking behavior of students who play the clown until they stop clowning is managing their behavior because they may play the clown elsewhere and receive attention for doing so. Teaching them how to obtain attention in more acceptable ways is changing them.

*Tolerating*    Because changing techniques don't change students' overnight, and management techniques don't always work, despite educators' best efforts, their students will sometimes do just what they are trying to get them not to do. Adults are the same. When adults resolve not to take their bad moods out on their families, not to complain about some aspect of their spouse's personality, or to make some other behavior change, they often do pretty well for a while, but then they slip. Students generally have less maturity, wisdom, and experience than adults have. If adults can't be perfect and they slip occasionally, students will probably slip more often. When this happens, educators should tolerate their behavior so long as it isn't too self-defeating, unfair, harmful, or dangerous.

To tolerate problem behavior means to accept it temporarily. This is an appropriate strategy when students can't control *all* their behavior *all* the time, when it will take time for educators and others to eliminate the cause of the problem, or when management techniques won't do the job. When educators tolerate students' behavior problems, they allow students to misbehave, give up too soon, withdraw from the group, pout or cry over nothing, and so on because the educators know that the students can't help themselves for the moment. But they tolerate the behavior only temporarily until they can manage it or until changing techniques affect the students so that they no longer misbehave. It might also be appropriate to tolerate misbehavior due to extenuating circumstances or the heat of the moment if you believe that students are unlikely to repeat this behavior problem.

*Preventing*   Sometimes it's necessary to prevent students from doing things that will harm them or others or infringe on their rights. Specifically, you cannot let depressed or guilt-ridden students harm themselves. Do not let students who behave destructively with temper tantrums disrupt the class for too long or break things that don't belong to them. Preventing students from harming themselves, disrupting the class, or destroying other people's property by removing them from the area, placing yourself between the students and their intended victims, and so on doesn't change what is causing their problem. But when an educator's managing techniques don't work, prevention is certainly a necessary strategy while trying to deal with the causes.

*Accommodating*   The final strategy is accommodating. When educators accept the fact that some of the physiological causes of their students' behaviors are unchangeable, that in some respects students are who they are, educators can help by accommodating demands, expectations, routines, disciplinary techniques, and so on to the unchangeable aspects of their students. Educators may also want to accommodate their behavioral expectations to their students' culturally determined behavior patterns so long as their behavior is effective and doesn't interfere with the rights of others.

*Accommodating and Tolerating Compared*   Superficially, accommodating and tolerating look similar. In both cases educators permit their students to behave in ways that differ from how the majority of students behave. The difference between the two is that educators accommodate permanently to the unchangeable aspects of their students' personalities or their cultural behavior patterns but tolerate only temporarily their changeable yet presently unmanageable, and unacceptable, behavior. For example, one might accommodate the length of in-seat reading assignments to the shorter attention span of a student, but only temporarily tolerate the moodiness of a student who lost a fight during lunch.

# *Idealistic and Realistic Choices*

Ideally it may be desirable to change students so they no longer need to behave as they do; realistically this is a tough goal to achieve. The typical classroom teacher has little time to devote to changing students with behavior problems, and administrators tend to give more priority to managing students with behavior problems than to changing them (often with justification). In addition, the more students an educator has, the less likely he is to have time for the individual attention necessary to eliminate the causes of these behavior problems. Thus, secondary teachers with many classes of different students will have to depend more on managing than on changing techniques. Elementary teachers will be somewhat less dependent on these techniques. But special educators, resource specialists, and teachers in private schools with small classes will have more opportunity to attempt to *change* students who misbehave.

Class size also affects an educator's ability to accommodate her demands and expectations to the unchangeable aspects of a student's personality and to tolerate certain kinds of disruptive behavior. Thus secondary schoolteachers may have to resort to preventing some behavior that elementary schoolteachers might be able to tolerate. Again, special educators, resource specialists, and private schoolteachers may be able to be more flexible—to tolerate more behavior and accommodate their expectations and routines to their students' individual differences.

Because educators find themselves in different teaching situations, this book includes a variety of techniques for dealing with a given behavior problem. This wide-ranging approach to handling problem behaviors will enable educators to select the techniques that suit their particular situations. Including techniques that are appropriate for different settings provides other benefits as well. It helps regular education teachers to identify students whose behavior problems may require more individual attention than they can provide, and it enables them to work more cooperatively with resource specialists and others in a team approach to provide the services that mainstreamed students with behavior problems require.

## *Educators' Response Patterns*

Although educators should select techniques and strategies that are appropriate for their particular students and teaching situations, every educator has a personal way of reacting to behavior problems. Clinical experience indicates that most educators follow one or another of five typical patterns discussed below in responding to students who are misbehaving.

The first pattern is to use all five strategies. Educators who fall into this group try to understand why their students behave as they do, and then they select strategies that fit the causes of the problems. They generally make the right decisions, but—like everyone else—they sometimes make mistakes.

The second group of educators relies a great deal on changing and managing without consequences. They tend to believe they can change students by reasoning with them. Thus, they try to find out why students behave as they do, often asking them what the matter is, what's bothering them, why they don't want to do something, and other similar questions. They are usually good at reasoning with, persuading, and cajoling students, but they avoid using negative consequences either because they don't believe it's a good idea to punish students or they are uncomfortable with being disciplinarians.

A third group uses a lot of preventing and managing without consequences. If these techniques don't work, they tend to tolerate students' behavior problems rather than try to change them. Many of these teachers also have difficulty being authoritative.

The fourth group of educators uses managing with consequences as a primary strategy. They may be behaviorists who believe this is the best strategy, or they may believe in the philosophy of "spare the rod and spoil the child." Some are perhaps uncomfortable unless they feel themselves to be in control of their students. Finally, they may be so angry and resentful that they have very little patience for their students.

The last group tends to tolerate and accommodate to students' behavior problems. Some of these educators believe that students' behavior problems are just their unique ways of responding to the world and should be accepted as such. Others defensively fool themselves into believing that the students' behavior problems are acceptable. And still others realize that their students have behavior problems, but they do very little to try to change them. This may be because they are so overwhelmed by the behavior that they give up, or else they are so involved in their own problems they are unable to devote the time and energy needed to deal with their students' problems.

---

## Self-Quiz: How You Handle Behavior Problems

Although it's natural to have your own ways of reacting to students' problems that reflect your own unique personality, at certain times your habitual responses will not be the most effective ones. Self-insight and awareness about your preferred or usual ways of responding to your students' behavior can enable you to choose consciously instead of reacting automatically. If you are an experienced teacher or have worked with children or teenagers, this activity may give you some insight into how you typically react to behavior problems. First, list all of the behaviors that you find unacceptable in your students for whatever reason. Second, list the techniques you usually use to handle these behaviors. Third, categorize each of these techniques in terms of the five strategies discussed in this chapter; then count up the number of techniques in each category. Finally, compare the totals to determine which strategies you use most and least often.

---

Gordon (2) identifies eight myths about "Good Teachers" that inhibit teachers who believe in them from using the full range of strategies and techniques available to them when dealing with students' behavior problems. Do you believe in any of them? If you do, can you understand how your beliefs might limit your ability to respond appropriately to your students' behavior problems?

1. Good Teachers are calm, unflappable, always even-tempered. They never lose their "cool," never show strong emotions.
2. Good Teachers have no biases or prejudices. Blacks, whites, Chicanos, dumb kids, smart kids, girls and boys all look alike to a Good Teacher. Good Teachers are neither racists nor sexists.

3. Good Teachers can and do hide their real feelings from students.
4. Good Teachers have the same degree of acceptance for all students. They never have "favorites."
5. Good Teachers provide a learning environment that is exciting, stimulating, and free, yet quiet and orderly at all times.
6. Good Teachers, above all, are consistent. They never vary, show partiality, forget, feel high or low, or make mistakes.
7. Good Teachers know the answers. They have greater wisdom than students.
8. Good Teachers support each other, present a "united front" to the students regardless of personal feelings, values, or convictions. (2, p. 22)

---

## Self-Quiz: Unnecessary Limits

Here are some additional questions to ask yourself so you can determine whether your habitual patterns or personal style may limit your range of options.

1. Are you much more concerned than most adults about what others think about you? If you are, do you find that you are reluctant to use certain management techniques that you would like to because you are concerned that they will change how your students feel about you?

2. Are you much less concerned than most adults about the opinion of others? If so, do you disregard your students' complaints about some of the management techniques you use and their suggestions of alternative ways of handling their problems?

3. Are you comfortable with your role as leader of the class, or does your desire to be your students' equal make it difficult for you to use certain techniques?

4. Are you comfortable with your role as an authority figure, or do you have difficulty setting limits and using consequences to help your students control their behavior?

5. Do you enjoy helping others to the point that you would rather have your students dependent on you for your assistance than work independently?

---

## Summary

When students misbehave, educators should determine whether, when, and how to intervene before deciding on a response. Sometimes it's unnecessary or undesirable to intervene; at other times it's essential to do so. In some situations immediate intervention is imperative; in other situations it's more prudent to delay.

Educators can use five strategies in responding to their students' behavior problems: changing, managing, tolerating, preventing, and accommodating. Which strategies and techniques are successful depends in part on the educator's teaching situation. Although educators should select strategies and techniques that are appropriate for both their students' problems and their teaching situations, many educators tend to react to their students' behavior partly out of habit.

# *Activities*

I. The exercises that follow should help you apply the concepts just reviewed to practical situations. For each of the incidents below, decide whether you would accept the behavior or intervene. Then, if you feel you would intervene, decide whether you would do so immediately or later.

1. While the class is collecting laboratory equipment, Tina, a 14-year-old, purposely pushes another girl who accidentally bumped her, causing the girl to drop a glass flask.

2. After you have told Steven, an eight-year-old, not to read comic books, you notice him with his head down, apparently reading something in his lap. The last time he disregarded your instructions, you told him he had to let you hold his comic books until dismissal, which caused a long drawn-out argument.

3. Although the rest of the class has begun to work on an exam you have just handed out, Tony and Jeff, two ten-year-olds, are still talking with their tests unopened and unread.

4. While you are dictating words during a spelling quiz, Alissa, a 12-year-old, returns to class after spending more than ten minutes in the bathroom despite promising you that she would be back in time to do the spelling.

5. Loretta, a six-year-old, spills paint all over the table and begins to cry.

6. You see Bob, a 13-year-old, open a switchblade knife on the playground during recess.

7. Jim, a 16-year-old known to have a bad temper and to get into fights, suddenly spins around, tells the person behind him that he better shut his mouth or he will shut it for him, and then goes back to work.

8. Carlos, a seven-year-old who hasn't learned to wait until he is called on to answer, calls out an answer, then puts his hand over his mouth in a way that indicates he realizes his mistake.

9. Alice, a five-year-old, pushes David off a tricycle when he refuses to let her have a turn.

10. At dismissal time you overhear Ronnie, a 16-year-old, say to Frank, "Now I's gonna beat the shit out of you."

11. Tim, a 17-year-old you know is extremely concerned about not calling attention to himself or his academic problems, is looking at the test of the person next to him.

12. Chris, an eight-year-old, is entertaining the students near him by pretending to put his finger in his nose and then in his mouth.

13. On your way to class late, you notice Jason, a 17-year-old, kissing his girlfriend in the hall just out of sight of anyone in the room.

14. You think that Ralph, a 13-year-old, might be selling drugs when you see him and another student exchange some small objects during recess.

15. Sonia, a six-year-old, gives one of her usual, seemingly on-purpose, ridiculously incorrect answers to your question, which delights the rest of the class.

II. State whether each of the alternative techniques for dealing with the following behavior problems is an example of changing, managing with consequences, managing without consequences, tolerating, preventing, accommodating, or a combination of these strategies.

1. A preschool student is unwilling to share materials, give someone else a turn on the swing, and the like without a struggle. The teacher:
   a. explains why children have to share and allow others to have turns.
   b. punishes the student when he refuses to share.
   c. makes sure he doesn't get the toy, swing, or whatever first so that others do not have to wait for him to give them up.
   d. purposely makes him wait extra long so he experiences what others feel when he makes them wait and then discusses his feelings with him.

2. A kindergarten teacher is about to read a story to his class. During story time, he has the group sit around him. One of his students is immature for her age and cannot attend to oral reading for as long as her peers. The teacher:
   a. sits the student up front so he can keep an eye on her and catch her attention if it wanders.
   b. places the student on the periphery of the group so that if her attention wanders, she won't distract the other students as easily.
   c. takes her aside before having the students change their seats and tells her she will get a reward if she listens to the whole story.

3. A second grader starts teasing a girl working in his group whom he delights in teasing almost any chance he can. The teacher:
   a. tells him to stop.
   b. tells him to stop and punishes him for his behavior.
   c. tells him to stop and describes what will happen if he does it again.
   d. switches him to another group.
   e. takes him aside and explains why he should not tease other children.

4. While a class of second graders is working in a small group, a student comes up to the desk and complains that another student is teasing her. This student has complained about the same boy and various other students many times before. The teacher:

    a.  listens to what she has to say and then suggests that she join a different group.

    b.  listens to the student and then asks her if she has any idea why the boy teased her.

    c.  tells her that the other children will continue to tease her until she changes the way she reacts to their teasing.

5. While she is taking an arithmetic test, a fourth grader stretches forward to read what the student in front of her has written. The teacher:

    a.  stands near her for a minute or two to indicate that she is being observed.

    b.  confiscates her paper and gives her a zero.

    c.  calls her up to the desk and explains to her why students should do their own work on tests.

    d.  changes her seat so she cannot copy.

    e.  calls her up to the desk and tells her to do her own work.

6. A fifth grader does everything including her seatwork so slowly that she is seldom able to complete an assignment within the time allotted. The teacher:

    a.  talks to her about the importance of working faster.

    b.  offers her a reward if she finishes the work in time.

    c.  takes off credit for incomplete items.

    d.  allows her to start before the others so she can finish on time.

    e.  allows her to finish her class assignments after school.

    f.  accepts what she can do within the time allotted without taking off credit.

    g.  reminds her periodically to work faster.

7. A seventh-grade student who has been a good student until recently drags himself into class looking like he has no energy, sits down, puts his head on his desk, and appears to be tuning out everything around him. When this happens, the teacher:

    a.  calls on him to bring his attention to the work at hand.

    b.  allows him to withdraw because he is obviously upset about something.

    c.  walks up to him, taps him on the back, and tells him he has to pay attention even if he is upset or go to the office.

8. A ninth-grade student who has only been in this country for two years says she wasn't able to do her homework because she had to translate during a meeting her parents had with a community agency. She has made similar statements four or five times in the two months she has been in the class. The teacher:

    a.  tells her that her excuse isn't acceptable and gives her a zero for the assignment.

    b.  gives her extra time to complete the assignment but takes off credit for lateness.

    c.  gives her extra time without any penalty.

    d.  explains that schoolwork should come before other obligations and suggests she should explain that to her parents.

9. An eleventh-grade student glares at another student and threatens to punch him if he doesn't shut up. The teacher:

    a.  sends them to the office.

    b.  tells them to cool it and describes the consequences if they don't.

    c.  tells them there are better ways of dealing with disagreements and asks them to stay after class for a few minutes to discuss it.

10. A twelfth-grade student resists doing almost anything he is asked to do. The teacher:
    a. asks him if he saw the basketball playoffs on TV the previous night in order to begin to develop a better relationship with him so he can convince him to be less resistive.
    b. tells him he can earn a reward if he agrees to do what he is asked to do.
    c. asks him why he often refuses to do what is asked of him.
    d. allows him to get away with it.

# *References*

1. Fine, M. J., & Walkenshaw, M. R. (1977). *The Teacher's Role in Classroom Management: Humanistic-Behavioral Strategies for Promoting Constructive Classroom Behavior.* Dubuque, IA: Kendall/Hunt.

2. Gordon, T. (1974). *Teacher Effectiveness Training.* New York: Wyden.

3. Redl, F. (1966). *When We Deal With Children.* New York: Free Press.

4. Shirley, R. L. (1979). Strategies in classroom management. *Educational Digest, 45* (4), 7–10.

# *HELPING STUDENTS BEHAVE APPROPRIATELY*

This chapter describes intervention techniques for working with students who are willing to behave appropriately. The techniques discussed here don't require an in-depth knowledge of what causes students' behavior problems, and they don't involve a great deal of time or effort that might better be spent teaching. For the most part, they are designed to deal with the problem at the moment through managing, accommodating, and preventing; they are not concerned with changing students. Part Three describes approaches you can use with students who don't respond to these techniques because the causes of their behavior problems require more individualized, time-consuming, or change-oriented techniques.

The techniques described here are divided into different groups according to the kinds of problems they are designed to handle. They include techniques for:

- Dealing with behavior problems that are partly the result of classroom environmental factors.

- Helping students who can't conform to classroom rules due to lack of practice.

- Aiding students who can't stop themselves from acting out strong feelings appropriately.

- Providing additional external control to students who want to behave appropriately but can't because they lack self-control in some situations.

- Helping students realize when and how often they misbehave.

- Issuing desist orders.

- Convincing students open to reason that it would be right for them to behave appropriately.

# *Eliminating Environmental Causes of Misbehavior*

Chapter 3 described several techniques good managers can use to eliminate potentially disruptive factors from their classroom environments. This section includes additional suggestions for dealing with behavior problems caused by environmental factors that occur when the techniques listed in Chapter 3 don't work. A few examples of how you can make additional modifications in your classroom to handle these problems are described below (1). (Chapters 10 and 11 include added suggestions for dealing with environmental factors that require a more in-depth understanding of individual students.)

## *Restructuring*

When students are unable to comply with what you planned for them because they are upset by such unanticipated events as good or bad news announced over the intercom, a fight between two students during recess that brings to the surface racial or ethnic tensions, a conflict between class members, a substitute teacher the previous period, or something equally upsetting, it may be necessary to restructure your plans for the day. Instead of trying to get them to settle down and get to work despite what is bothering them, you may find it more effective to "go with the flow." This might involve adapting your expectations, teaching style, or lesson plan to their mood or taking out one of the emergency lessons you have prepared for just such occasions. In certain cases it might be even better to depart from the content of your course and deal with whatever is upsetting them in an open and honest way.

## *Dealing With Competing Diversions*

Sometimes events in the classroom can rivet everyone's attention and disrupt the best planned and executed lesson. Rabbits mating in the middle of your lecture, a suggestive description in a novel, a picture from the *National Enquirer*, a joke from a recent comic book, or a drawing by the class cartoonist being passed around can make competing for your students' attention a tough challenge. In such cases, it would be best to remove whatever is diverting their attention. But in cases where the disruptive influence is a fire engine or ambulance across the street, you might allow your students to satisfy their curiosity by looking out the window; then lower the shades and get back to work. Or if the class is excitedly buzzing about something that happened during recess, an event soon to be held in the auditorium, or a program they saw on television, let them get it out of their system by discussing it for a few minutes and then get back to work.

## *Providing Hurdle Help*

Although most students can cope with the normal day-to-day frustrations and delays of school life, some act out because they want help with their work and can't wait for it. No matter what system you devise to ensure that students who need your help to keep working will get it as soon as possible, chances are that you will sometimes have one or two students who cannot tolerate any significant delay in obtaining your assistance. The frustration they experience may cause them to demand your attention and/or express their feelings in disruptive ways. One effective way to manage this problem is to provide the help such students need to get over the hurdle that is blocking them as quickly as possible. While boosting them over won't help the students learn to cope with normal delays, it does let you manage their disruptive influence while you are using one or more of the changing techniques described in Chapters 7 and 8. But if you find yourself having the same problem with a number of students, it may be that the system you have devised or the lesson plan you are following is at fault and not the students' inabilty to cope with delay. The solution in that case would be to modify your system or lesson plan.

# *Helping Students Follow Rules*

Since, as we noted, major differences exist between how youngsters are allowed and even encouraged to behave outside of school and the way they are required to behave in school, students in the primary grades need time to learn exactly what they are supposed to do and to give them practice in doing it. Students who have attended schools in other countries where expectations for behavior are different from our expectations and students who move from one part of the United States to another or are bused from one ethnic neighborhood to another also require time and practice to learn how to conform to the new expectations. (See Chapter 10.) The same applies to students faced with new teachers whose standards and expectations differ significantly from those of their previous teachers or to new situations in school that call for new ways of behaving. For example, going from a permissive teacher to a strict disciplinarian or from an unstructured approach that calls for a lot of student interactions, free choice of activities, and free movement between learning centers to an approach that is primarily seatwork and lecture or vice versa can require new ways of behaving that take time to master.

Fine and Walkenshaw (2) have suggested that students who misbehave because they are still in the process of learning how to behave appropriately should be given "learner's leeway." This involves treating them as students who need to be taught how to follow rules and expectations, not as students who resist doing so since their "misbehavior" is caused by lack of skill, not lack of motivation.

The following six-step approach is especially appropriate when students—especially young ones who need learner's leeway—misbehave.

1. Make students aware that they aren't behaving appropriately. Statements such as, "That's not the way to do it," "You're breaking the rule," or "You've forgotten the fourth rule," delivered in a noncritical, supportive tone of voice are examples that inform students they have *inadvertently* behaved inappropriately. But saying the same thing in a complaining, critical, or threatening tone of voice can easily change the message your students receive. Instead of simply hearing that they have made a mistake—which they can correct next time—they may hear that you are dissatisfied with them, that you believe they could have behaved more appropriately, or else that they had better behave more appropriately. Any of these would be both an inaccurate and unfair message to give them.

2. Tell students exactly what it was that they did wrong and, if necessary, explain why it was inappropriate—again in a noncritical, nonjudgmental way.

3. Provide students with examples of the right behavior by modeling it yourself or by pointing out when other students are behaving in the appropriate way.

4. Give students additional opportunities to practice the correct behavior.

5. Offer students feedback about how they are doing, but don't praise or reward them for behaving appropriately. (They don't have a motivational problem.) For example, "That's the way to do it," "Now you're on the right track," or "That's much better."

6. If, despite your best effort to be nonjudgmental and uncritical, students act as if they felt criticized or threatened because they had misbehaved, explain that you understand it wasn't their fault and that you realize it will take time for them to get used to your particular way of running the classroom.

## *Helping Students Handle Strong Feelings*

When students experience especially strong feelings, they sometimes lose control of themselves. The intensity of their emotions gets the better of them, and they do things they wouldn't normally do. The following are some techniques you can try when students express strong feelings in unacceptable ways (3–9).

## *Tolerating Inappropriate Behavior*

Some things students do in the heat of the moment that they wouldn't ordinarily do are so minor you can overlook them since this won't increase the chances that students will behave that way when they aren't upset. While educators would certainly disagree about which behaviors are minor or major transgressions, such things as a slammed book, a stomped foot, or an angry look might be included in most of their lists as minor infractions.

Students who on occasion overreact impulsively to strong feelings often realize their mistakes as soon as they have made them or when they calm down. Overlooking their behavior for the moment may give them the opportunity to correct themselves, apologize, or make amends for what they said or did without your intervention.

## Managing Strong Feelings

When the expression of strong feelings would be too disruptive to be tolerated, educators can use a number of techniques to help students manage how they express their feelings.

*Active Listening*    At times merely listening to students and allowing them to express their feelings can help them regain self-control. Active listening discussed in Chapter 2 can be an effective first step when students are upset.

*Acknowledging Feelings*    One way to help students manage strong emotions is to acknowledge their feelings and to validate their right to feel the way they do while suggesting alternative ways for them to express themselves (3). Acknowledging their feelings can calm them down somewhat, and then providing them with more desirable ways of acting out their feelings, still gives them acceptable ways of expressing themselves. For example, if a student has just used a string of four-letter words to express her reaction to what another student has said about her sister, avoid reprimanding or punishing the student. Instead, it may be more effective to tell her you understand how hurt and angry she must feel about what the other student said but that you hope she can express her anger in language that is more acceptable in school. This approach may get your point across in a way that is less likely to provoke a defensive reaction when the student feels she was in the right and shouldn't be reprimanded or punished for retaliating against the other student.

*Discharging Feelings*    You can help students who are too upset to control themselves discharge (get rid of) their feelings in nondisruptive or harmless ways. The idea is to allow them to "let off a little steam" so that the pressure doesn't make them explode. Running errands, cleaning up work areas, and rearranging storage cabinets are activities that might help angry students work off some tension.

*Relaxing Students*    Helping students to relax by allowing them to eat something they like, talking to them in a calm manner, allowing them to listen to music with earphones, or even giving them a back rub if you are comfortable doing so can reduce their need to act out their feelings.

*Providing Escape*    Sometimes merely giving students the chance to postpone or escape a difficult situation by allowing them to use a computer, work at a learning center, or play a game in a free-time area can help them regain control over themselves in a few minutes.

*Students who are upset may benefit from some time alone.*

## Preventing Problem Behavior

You must prevent students with the potential to react to strong feelings in disruptive, dangerous, or destructive ways from doing so if you can't help them manage their feelings. Occasionally you may have to remove students from your classroom until they have calmed down enough to regain their self-control or else protect them from hurting themselves or others, damaging property, or getting into serious trouble.

*Minor Problems*   Just how flexible educators can be in handling their students' expression of strong feelings depends on how disruptive or dangerous they are. For example, when students say things in the heat of the moment that they wouldn't ordinarily say, you can use any of the techniques described above. You could, for example, overlook their statements if you think it's possible to do so without repercussions. But if you can't, you could—before intervening—give them the opportunity to correct themselves, apologize, or make amends for what they did once they are calm and have had a chance to reflect. If Harriet says something insulting about your racial, ethnic, or religious background after seeing her failing grade at the top of a test paper you have just handed back, give her a chance to apologize when she has calmed down. If Sammy walks through the door calling another student four-letter words because of what he said about Sammy's mother in the hall, give him a chance to correct himself by saying something like, "What?" "What did you say?" or "I couldn't hear you."

If that doesn't work, you could acknowledge their feelings and suggest alternative ways of expressing them. You could, for example, tell Harriet that you understand how badly she feels about failing the test and why she might blame you for failing her. Then, if that defuses the situation a little, you might suggest other more acceptable ways of expressing her feelings about her grade, such as saying she thinks you made a mistake, she believes she deserved a better grade, or she feels you were unfair. Applying the same principle to Sammy, you could say that you understand why he is angry and remind him that he could use other language to express himself while in school. If Harriet and Sammy are still unable to control themselves, you could provide them with an escape valve—the opportunity to work at a learning center or in a free-play area until they calm down while telling them that you will deal with their behavior later.

As you read these suggestions, you may have felt they didn't address the real problem. Perhaps you believe it would be more effective to help Harriet accept the responsibility for her failing grade and Sammy to understand that being angry is not an excuse for cursing in class. The problem is that the intensity of their feelings may override their ability to deal with situations rationally, or they may be too angry to be able to appreciate your point of view or too resentful or defensive to admit that they deserve to pay the consequences for their behavior. Later, when they aren't so emotionaly upset, they may be more receptive to your intervention techniques. So long as they won't disrupt the class, harm anyone, or destroy something, it may be wise to postpone further action until they have calmed down.

You might also have thought of using consequences to help Harriet and Sammy control themselves or of offering them a reward if they exercised self-control and/or informing them of the consequences if they continued to behave as they did. Using consequences was purposely omitted here. Although no research evidence supports or refutes this approach, the position taken here is that when students are too upset to control their actions, positive and negative consequences usually have little effect on their behavior. (See Chapter 10 for a more detailed discussion of this point of view.)

*Serious Problems*    Students who react to their strong emotions in dangerous, destructive, or very disruptive ways, or who have the potential to do so, leave educators with little flexibility since they have to choose techniques that will work immediately. If Harriet were to throw a disruptive temper tantrum or Sammy were to attempt to hit a student he was angry at, your options would be limited because you couldn't tolerate their behavior. It's also unlikely that they would correct their behavior on their own. In addition, they would probably be too upset to respond to your acknowledgment of their feelings and to your suggestions of alternative ways of expressing themselves. Eventually, they might react favorably to being allowed to escape the situation by spending time in another section of the room until they calmed down, but you would still have to do something immediately to interfere with their disruptive behavior. (See the next section for suggestions on dealing specifically with these kinds of behavior problems.) Considering the intensity of emotion needed to incite students who normally don't throw temper tantrums or hit other students in class to do so, you might have to excuse them from class until they regain enough of their composure to be able to control themselves.

Students don't always "act out" when they are overwhelmed by strong emotions. Sometimes they withdraw psychologically and/or physically from situations that overwhelm them. They are especially likely to withdraw when they are too depressed to relate to external demands or too anxious to confront situations directly. (Chapters 8 and 10 describe techniques you can use with students who are too depressed or anxious to conform to the normal demands of school or to relate to the group.)

# Providing External Control

This section describes several techniques you can use to provide students who are unable to resist the temptation to misbehave in certain situations with the additional external control they need. These techniques include distracting students, signaling awareness and disapproval of their misbehavior, proximity control, using space and grouping, and issuing mild desist orders and warnings.

## Distracting Students

Sometimes you can manage students about to lose control by distracting their attention from whatever is overstimulating them. Distracting them doesn't help them learn self-control, but it does avoid the impending loss of self-control and the immediate problems that could create. For example, you may be able to help a preschooler who comes to class almost in tears because she has difficulty separating from her mother to forget her troubles by asking her to look at a picture with you or to help decorate a page in the booklet the class is preparing. In another example, you may be able to distract a student on the verge of escalating a minor disagreement into a major confrontation with another student by asking him to help you do something or run an errand.

## Signaling Awareness and Disapproval

Because of your personality, you may prefer to call your students' attention to their misbehavior rather than distract them from it. Signaling you have noticed that a student is reading a comic book, moving toward off limits material, or dipping into something in a cooking class before it is time to, and making it clear that you disapprove of his behavior by a frown or a movement of your hand or head may be all that's needed to help the student control himself (10).

## *Proximity Control*

When signaling your awareness and disapproval isn't enough, positioning yourself close to the students may do the trick (12). For example, you may have signaled your awareness that a student's eyes are roaming in the general direction of her neighbor's papers during an exam, but the student still doesn't control her behavior; standing closer to her for a few moments may do the job. Your own calm physical presence can help settle students who are upset so that they don't act out their strong emotions. Seating the preschooler on the verge of tears next to you or moving close to the two students arguing about what each said to the other could be a simple, effective intervention technique.

## *Using Space and Grouping*

You can use the physical space in the classroom to provide students with additional external control (11, 12). The most straightforward example is to separate students who can't seem to stop talking to each other and seat each of them with nondisruptive students. That decreases the negative effect they have on each other and increases the positive effects the nondisruptive students can have on them. Again, separating two students who are arguing may be more effective than either signaling disapproval or standing near them if they are too upset to control themselves when they are so close together. Finally, placing distractible students where there are few distractions or behind a screen or in a cubicle may help them concentrate better.

## *Self-Monitoring*

Sometimes helping students realize how often, how long, and in what situations they misbehave can give them enough self-insight to control themselves if they are motivated to behave appropriately (14–17). In certain cases, just learning what they are doing, when they are doing it, and how often is enough to help students modify their behavior. This parallels the cases of those lucky individuals who, once they start counting calories and learn which foods are fattening and how many calories they are consuming, are able to cut down sufficiently to lose weight or people who, having been told that what they are doing bothers others, are able to stop almost immediately.

Because insight alone can sometimes be sufficient, particularly with older students, it might be a good idea to start with seeing if merely helping students discover how often they call out, get up, talk to their neighbors, and so on will enable them to modify their behavior. To do this, have your students tally the number of times they do a specific, countable behavior such as interrupting, chatting with neighbors, bringing comic books to class, and the like. Or have them keep track of the amount of time they spend in the bathroom, drawing, talking to their neighbors, or carrying on other inappropriate behavior. Hopefully, when they see the total picture, some of them, at least, will change their behavior.

## *Issuing Desist Orders*

At times, a more direct approach may be called for, and you might want to tell students directly to stop doing whatever it is they are doing wrong (10, 13). For example, when it's urgent to get a student to put something fragile down, to not misuse a complex piece of equipment, to stop provoking a student about to explode, you may have to issue a direct order so that it gets your student's immediate attention and compliance. When you find yourself in such a situation, your desist orders are more likely to be effective if you follow the following guidelines (10, 18, 22).

1. Clearly identify what it is that you want students to stop. Statements such as, "Don't do that" and "John, behave yourself" are too vague and less desirable than, "Close the closet door," "Don't call out," and "Don't write on your desk."

2. Suggest appropriate alternatives. When you tell a student to close the closet door, add, "Ask me if you need something inside." When you tell students not to call out, say, "Raise your hand, and I will call on you when it's your turn."

3. When you tell students what to do, your voice and gestures should let them know that you are serious and mean business.

4. Use mild desist orders. While your attitude should be firm and businesslike, it shouldn't be harsh. Don't yell or use sarcasm or ridicule to pressure the student to obey you. And don't express surprise, shock, or disappointment about their behavior. Statements such as, "That's a stupid thing to do," "Don't you know better than that?" or "I'm surprised at you" tend to backfire. Even if they work for the moment, they can lower students' self-esteem and increase their resentment.

5. If possible, speak to students privately, not publicly. For example, if a student is drawing something instead of doing her work, walk up to her and whisper your instructions. This would probably be less embarrassing to her and less disruptive to the other students than calling out her name from your desk and ordering her to stop drawing.

6. Focus on your students' behavior, not on them. "Don't tap your foot or your pencil" and "Don't ask again once you have been told no" are better than, "Why are you always tapping your foot?" and "Don't be a pest."

7. Avoid challenging or confronting statements that can place you in a win-lose, battle-of-wills situation with your students. "You aren't supposed to go to the restroom without permission" may be less challenging to a teenager than, "You *can't* leave the room." And, "Give Mary back her book and see me after class" may be a more acceptable order than, "Give Mary back her book and apologize to her right now."

8. If you believe that merely telling students to stop won't be enough, remind them of the consequences if they don't comply with your orders.

9. Make sure students are aware that you will follow through on what you have said by watching and waiting to make sure the students comply before turning your attention elsewhere and by reminding them of the consequences they incurred the last time they didn't comply.

# *Reasoning with Students*

## *Explaining Why Rules Are Necessary*

Students who don't understand why certain rules are necessary may be more willing to comply with your expectations if you explain why they should do so. While no research evidence either supports or refutes this commonsense notion (13), it seems to be a sensible approach with students who don't understand the reasons for particular rules. When dealing with such students, after telling them that they shouldn't do something, explain why their behavior is unacceptable and why another way of behaving is more appropriate. For example, if the student who opened the door to the storage closet doesn't understand why you told him to close it, don't leave him thinking he has to close it only because you said so. Instead, explain that some of the equipment inside can break or hurt someone if not handled properly. Or when you tell young students not to talk while someone else is reciting, remind them how hard it is to understand what the speaker is saying when they don't pay attention and for the other students to hear when more than one person is speaking.

This doesn't mean, however, that you should regularly explain the reasons why rules are necessary every time students break them. That would be unnecessary, too time-consuming, disruptive, and counterproductive. But when students truly don't understand why certain rules are needed, explanations can change students' attitudes about them.

## *Active Listening*

If students disagree with a rule they think is unnecessary or they believe that they haven't done anything inappropriate—and they aren't the kind of students who habitually challenge your authority whenever they are caught misbehaving—hearing them out and then explaining your perception should increase the likelihood that they will behave appropriately (20). They may be more willing to cooperate because you have listened to their side of the story, which makes them feel more positive toward you. And they may also accept your perception of why the rules really are fair or their behavior really was inappropriate. (See Chapter 2.)

## *Correcting Misunderstandings*

Students who misbehave because they misunderstand situations are likely to correct their behavior once they perceive the situation accurately. With a student who is acting up because she thinks another student unfairly marked one of her answers on a test wrong, explaining that her answer really was incorrect can short-circuit her angry response. Helping a student understand that the reason she wasn't chosen for a team, part, or group was to give others who are less able a chance and not because she wasn't good enough or wasn't wanted, can also avoid a potentially disruptive response.

*Adolescents can often resolve issues and disagreements among see themselves with only minimal supervision.*

## Appealing to Values

When mature students who have been brought up to behave ethically, usually identify with the group, and want to behave appropriately misbehave, you can sometimes control them by appealing to the ethical and moral values they already accept. According to Fine and Walkenshaw:

> Some of the values that teachers can appeal to include: (a) an appeal to the mutual respect between teacher and child, as, "You are treating me rudely. Do you think that I have been unfair to you?" (b) an appeal to reality consequences or cause and effect relationships, as, "If you continue to talk, we will not have time to work on our Christmas gifts," (c) an appeal to the child's group code and awareness of peer reactions, as, "If you continue to spoil their fun, you can't expect the other boys and girls to be your friends," and (d) an appeal to the teacher's power of authority, as, "As your teacher, it is my job to see that nobody gets hurt; I cannot allow this behavior to continue and still take good care of you." (25, p. 80)

## Role Playing

When students' misbehavior adversely affects others, role playing can be an effective intervention with students old enough to put themselves in other people's shoes (23–26). Having students play the role of the students who lost their turns, were excluded from a game during recess, or didn't get a chance to talk, and asking them how they feel and think can help them appreciate the negative effects of their behavior.

# Realistic Thinking Development

Most of the techniques for reasoning with students described above are more appropriate for older rather than younger students. As Piaget (27) and others have demonstrated, students become more rational as they mature. The thinking of toddlers and preschoolers, for example, is extremely unrealistic; toddlers will hide themselves from others by closing their eyes because they believe others can't see them since they can't see others. And preschoolers believe in Santa Claus and the Tooth Fairy. By the time children are ready for kindergarten or first grade, their thought processes are more logical. They begin to understand that the world around them and the things that happen to them usually have logical explanations. This helps them overcome their fears of ghosts and monsters, but it also prevents them from continung to believe in the Tooth Fairy and Santa Claus.

During elementary school, children's logical thinking improves. But they are still prone to blame other people and circumstances for the problems they create for themselves. And they still tend to mistakenly think their teachers and others treat them unfairly because they cannot yet appreciate other people's preferences and points of view. Youngsters at this age have a better understanding of time, but they still underestimate how long it will take them to do certain things like their homework, and they overestimate the time they spend doing unpleasant things like practicing the piano.

## Self-Quiz: On Techniques to Help Students

Below are some techniques that don't involve consequences you can use to help students behave better. Which of these techniques have you used? Which ones would you feel comfortable using? Which ones would you be reluctant to use? Why?

Helping students follow rules:

- Providing learners leeway
- Informing students that their behavior is unacceptable
- Explaining to students why their behavior is unacceptable
- Providing models of appropriate behavior
- Providing students with opportunities to practice acceptable behavior

Helping students cope with strong feelings:

- Overlooking behavior done in the heat of the moment
- Acknowledging students' feelings
- Providing students with opportunities to discharge their feelings
- Relaxing students
- Providing escape

Providing external control:

- Distracting students
- Signaling awareness and disapproval
- Using proximity control
- Using space and grouping
- Teaching students self-monitoring skills
- Using desist orders

Reasoning with students:

- Explaining the "whys" of rules
- Active listening
- Appealing to values
- Role playing

Adolescents' thinking processes are much more advanced than students in elementary or intermediate school. To begin with, they are more realistic about time. They are also more able to distinguish among the impossible, the possible, and the probable. They can recognize their own role in the problems they encounter with people, and they are more able to admit when they are the cause of their own difficulties. Though they may not always act like it, adolescents are capable of dealing with issues that arise in the classroom in a much more realistic manner.

To be effective as a classroom manager, you should adjust your techniques to the kind of thinking that characterizes your students. You can do this by spending more time listening to older students' points of view and explaining your perceptions to them and less time bribing, cajoling, insisting, and demanding.

## *Summary*

You can help many students who misbehave despite your best efforts to avoid behavior problems in your classroom without resorting to consequences. You can solve their problems by eliminating the environmental causes of their behavior, teaching them how to follow rules, helping them to cope with strong feelings, providing external controls, teaching them how to monitor their behavior, issuing desist orders, and reasoning with them.

## *Activities*

Each of the incidents described below is followed by a number of techniques that could be used to help students modify their behavior. Determine which would be effective solutions to the problem, and describe how you would use them.

1. Van, a 13-year-old student who was exposed to a great deal of trauma during the war in Cambodia before emigrating two years ago, becomes very upset whenever wars are discussed in his social studies class. (Eliminating environmental causes of students' behavior, helping students cope with strong emotions, reasoning with students, correcting misunderstandings.)

2. Jeff, an 11-year-old who often copies on tests, is allowing his eyes to wander in the direction of another student's paper during an examination. (Providing external control, teaching students to monitor their behavior, issuing desist orders, reasoning with students.)

3. Jane, an immature 5-year-old with a short attention span, starts to talk to the student next to her while you are reading a story to a group of students seated on the floor in front of you. (Eliminating environmental causes of students' behavior, teaching students how to follow rules, issuing desist orders.)

4. Warren, a 7-year-old who is a poor sharer, refuses to share some art materials with another student in his group. (Teaching students how to follow rules, providing external control, issuing desist orders, reasoning with students.)

5. Francis, a 12-year-old with a bad temper, pushes a student and threatens to hit him in the nose if he doesn't take back what he said. (Helping students cope with strong feelings, providing external control, issuing desist orders, reasoning with students.)

6. When you call on Michael, a 14-year-old who is functioning three years below grade level, to recite, he answers angrily that he didn't do his homework because it was boring. (Eliminating environmental causes of students' behavior, helping students cope with strong feelings, reasoning with students.)

7. You have observed Karen, a 6-year-old, take Carlotta's paintbrush, and Carlotta tries to pull it out of her hands. When you tell Karen to return it to her, Karen says it's hers, not Carlotta's. (Teaching students how to follow rules, issuing desist orders, reasoning with students.)

8. Eddie and Carl, two 16-year-olds, hand in virtually identical book reports. When you tell them that, they deny that they worked together or copied. (Using desist orders, reasoning with students.)

9. As she often does, Bertha, an 8-year-old, calls out the answer without waiting to be called on. (Teaching students how to follow rules, teaching students how to monitor their behavior, issuing desist orders, reasoning with students.)

10. Enrique, a 10-year-old who is limited in his English proficiency because he has only been in the United States for a year and a half, stays in the bathroom for almost 15 minutes while the class is working on oral reading. This is not the first time he has gone to the bathroom to avoid reading aloud. (Eliminating the environmental causes of students' behavior, helping students cope with strong feelings, teaching students to monitor their behavior, issuing desist orders, reasoning with students.)

# *References*

ELIMINATING ENVIRONMENTAL CAUSES OF MISBEHAVIOR

1. Long, N. T., Morse, W. C., & Newman, R. G. (1965). *Conflict in the Classroom: The Education of Emotionally Disturbed Children.* Belmont, CA: Wadsworth.

HELPING STUDENTS FOLLOW RULES

2. Fine, M. J., & Walkenshaw, M. R. (1977). *The Teacher's Role in Classroom Management* (2nd ed.). Dubuque, IA: Kendall/Hunt.

HELPING STUDENTS HANDLE STRONG FEELINGS

3. Axline, V. M. (1947). *Play Therapy*. New York: Houghton.

4. Bloom, R. B. (1977). Therapeutic management of children's profanity. *Behavior Disorders*, 2 (4), 205–221.

5. Grossman, H. (1965). *Teaching the Emotionally Disturbed: A Casebook*. New York: Holt, Rinehart & Winston.

6. Grossman, H. (1972). *Nine Rotten Lousy Kids*. New York: Holt, Rinehart & Winston.

7. Marshall, H. H. (1972). *Positive Discipline and Classroom Interaction: A Part of the Teaching-Learning Process*. Springfield, IL: CC Thomas.

8. Morse, W. C. (1985). *The Education and Treatment of Socio-Emotionally Disturbed Children and Youth*. Syracuse, NY: Syracuse University Press.

9. Redl, F., & Wineman, D. (1957). *The Aggressive Child*. New York: Free Press.

PROVIDING EXTERNAL CONTROL

10. Kounin, J. S. (1970). *Discipline and Group Management in Classroom*. New York: Holt, Rinehart & Winston.

11. Stainback, W., Stainback, S., Etscheidt, S., & Doud, J. (1986). A nonintrusive intervention for acting out behavior. *Teaching Exceptional Children*, 19 (1), 38–41.

12. Stainback, W., Stainback, S., & Froyen, L. (1987). Structuring the class to prevent disruptive behavior. *Teaching Exceptional Children*, 19 (4), 12–16.

13. Weber, W. A., Roff, L. A., Crawford, J., & Robinson, C. (1983). *Classroom Management: Reviews of the Teacher Education and Research Literature*. Princeton, NJ: Educational Testing Service.

SELF-MONITORING

14. Broden, M., Hall, R., & Mitts, B. (1971). The effects of self-recording on the classroom behavior of two eighth-grade students. *Journal of Applied Behavior Analysis*, 4, 191–199.

15. Johnson, S. M., & White, G. (1971). Self-observation as an agent of behavioral change. *Behavior Therapy*, 2, 488–497.

16. McKenzie, T., & Rushall, B. (1974). Effects of self-recording on attendance and performance in a competitive swimming training program. *Journal of Applied Behavior Analysis*, 7, 199–206.

17. Sagotsky, G., Patterson, C. J., & Lepper, M. R. (1978). Training children's self-control: A field experiment in self-monitoring and goal setting in the classroom. *Journal of Experimental Child Psychology, 25,* 242–253.

ISSUING DESIST ORDERS

18. Bordeaux, D. B. (1952). How to get kids to do what's expected of them in the classroom. *Clearing House, 55,* 273–278.

19. Jones, F. H. (1987). *Positive Classroom Discipline.* New York: McGraw-Hill.

20. Lasley, T. J. (1981). Classroom behavior: Some field observations. *High School Journal, 64* (4), 142–149.

21. Masden, C. H., Becker, W. C., Thomas, D. R., Koser, L., & Plager, E. (1968). An analysis of the reinforcing function of 'sit down' commands. In R. K. Parker (Ed.), *Readings in Educational Psychology.* Boston: Allyn & Bacon.

22. O'Leary, K. D., & O'Leary, S. G. (Eds.) (1977). *Classroom Management: The Successful Use of Behavior Modification.* New York: Pergamon Press.

REASONING WITH STUDENTS

The references below can help you learn how to increase students' intrinsic motivation.

23. Blackham, G. J., Silberman, A. (1971). *Modification of Child Behavior.* Belmont, CA: Wadsworth.

24. Brophy, J., & Rohrkemper, M. (1980). *Teachers' Specific Strategies for Dealing with Hostile and Aggressive Students.* Research Series No. 86. East Lansing, MI: Institute on Research in Teaching, Michigan State University.

25. Fine, M. J., & Walkenshaw, M. R. (1977). *The Teacher's Role in Classroom Management* (2nd ed.). Dubuque, IA: Kendall/Hunt.

26. Schmuck, R., & Schmuck, P. A. (1979). *Group Processes in the Classroom.* Dubuque, IA: W. C. Brown.

REALISTIC THINKING DEVELOPMENT

27. Piaget, J. (1950). *The Psychology of Intelligence.* New York: Harcourt.

# *OBTAINING STUDENTS' COMPLIANCE BY USING CONSEQUENCES*

As we noted in Chapter 3, teachers who use effective instructional techniques, satisfy students' basic needs, maintain good relations with them, model desirable behavior, promote group cohesiveness, reward appropriate behavior, handle potentially disruptive situations, and establish and enforce procedures and rules can avoid most behavior problems. Chapter 6 pointed out how many students who misbehave even when their teachers are doing as much as possible to avoid behavior problems can be helped to behave appropriately by eliminating the environmental causes of their misbehavior, teaching them how to follow rules, helping them cope with strong feelings, providing them with additional external controls, and reasoning with them. As we will see in this chapter, a few students, especially young ones still in the first stage of moral development and older ones who are overly playful, a little mischievous, interested in seeing what they can get away with, and the like need to be shown that it's to their advantage to behave appropriately through the use of extrinsic consequences. This chapter describes how you can use such consequences to convince these students to behave appropriately.

## *Positive Consequences— Rewards*

All things being equal (which they seldom are), students are more likely to do things they will be rewarded for than punished for. Thus, even though the effects of rewarding as a technique are limited, and one can never know ahead of time whether a particular student will or will not change his behavior to obtain a reward, providing and withdrawing positive consequences can be an effective way of handling *some* students' behavior problems. (You may want to review the information about the effectiveness of praise and other forms of reward on students' behavior included in Chapter 2.)

The classroom management literature details a variety of techniques for using rewards to modify students' behavior. In addition to those discussed in Chapter 2, three are especially practical in regular education settings. (Other techniques that require a more individualized, in-depth approach are covered in Chapter 9.)

## Rewarding Incompatible Behavior

It's sometimes possible to modify students' unacceptable behavior by rewarding them for behaving appropriately in ways that are incompatible with their undesirable behavior (1–5). For example, if students know they can earn rewards for on-task behavior, they may resist the temptation to talk to their neighbors, get up to sharpen their pencils, or write notes to their friends. You can apply this same principle to reduce talking in line by rewarding students for standing quietly; to handle calling out answers by rewarding students for raising their hands; and to discourage lying when being truthful is painful by rewarding telling the truth.

Rewarding students to behave appropriately in ways that are incompatible with their unacceptable behavior often means you can avoid punishing students for misbehaving. Research indicates that positive consequences are more effective than negative consequences and have fewer undesirable side effects.

To use these techniques effectively, you should let students know exactly what they have to do in order to be rewarded. Also make sure they understand you will be observing them periodically on an unpredictable, random schedule so they can't anticipate when their behavior will be evaluated. Finally, consistently reward students only when they are behaving appropriately.

Although no current research provides evidence about the circumstances under which rewarding incompatible behavior is most likely to be effective, experience indicates that the cause of the students' misbehavior plays an important role. Rewarding students for standing quietly in line would probably be more effective with students who talk out of boredom than with students who want to show their peers that they don't care about school rules. Rewarding students for raising their hands to reduce calling out is more likely to work with students who want to give the right answer and please their teachers than with students who want others to appreciate how smart they are. And rewarding students for on-task behavior to decrease talking may be more effective with students who are talking because they need a short break from their work than with students who are talking because the work is too difficult for them.

## Rewarding Improvement

A somewhat similar technique, but one that focuses on the unacceptable behavior not the incompatible acceptable behavior, is to reward students for improvement (6, 7). You can apply this approach in a number of ways. If a student calls out repeatedly on the average of eight or nine times per day, you can:

1. Reward the student for calling out fewer times a day.

2. Give the student increasing numbers of points, tokens, or other recognition for fewer misbehaviors—for example, one point for calling out five times, two points for calling out only four times, three points for calling out only three times.

3. Reward the student for spending increasing amounts of time in class without calling out, starting with a half hour, then three quarters of an hour, then an hour, and so on.

4. Give the student increasing numbers of points or other rewards depending on the lapse of time between incidents of calling out—four points if he doesn't call out again for an hour, five points if he doesn't call out for two hours, and so forth.

To use this technique effectively, follow the guidelines listed below.

1. Determine the baseline—the average number of times the student behaves inappropriately during a given period of time or the average interval between incidents of inappropriate behavior.

2. Decide on how much improvement you can realistically expect from the student. Can you expect her to halve the number of times she calls out or gets up from her seat or only reduce it by 20 percent during the first few days of using this technique?

3. Make sure the student knows exactly which behavior or behaviors he is not supposed to do and what the reward schedule will be for each degree of improvement.

4. Suggest alternative appropriate ways for the student to behave if possible.

5. Reward the student for improvement in his behavior according to the schedule.

6. Modify your schedule so the student has to demonstrate greater and greater degrees of improvement in order to receive a reward until you feel that her behavior is acceptable.

7. Eliminate the extrinsic rewards and encourage the student to behave appropriately for intrinsic rather than extrinsic reasons.

## Using Peers as Models

Students sometimes change their behavior when they observe their prestigious peers behaving in more appropriate ways if they value them and want to be like them. Assigning a student to work with a partner who has a lot of prestige and who stays busy and productive for the whole time can encourage her to put more effort into class assignments. Reminding another student that the other members of the football team come to class on time and don't "horse around" might help him control his behavior. Also, rewarding (praising) peer models for behaving appropriately may motivate another student to modify her behavior in order to receive the same reward (10, 11, 13).

Sabatino suggests the following procedure for using peers as models of appropriate behavior:

1. Specify the behaviors to be modeled.
2. Provide situations in which students are likely to observe peers engaged in these specified behaviors.
3. Label target behaviors and draw the students' attention to them, thereby directing behavior toward a desired goal.
4. Identify appropriate behaviors, using peer pressure to recognize and reinforce them.
5. Provide a variety of models and settings so students can practice appropriate behaviors.
6. Identify high-status models (older, same sex) who have a positive influence on student behavior.
7. Remedy situations where students might see other students winning positive consequences by disruptive or inappropriate behavior.
8. Emphasize to students their role as models of appropriate behaviors. (13, p. 11)

Several advantages have been cited for using peers as models. First, students can observe exactly how they are expected to behave. Students can also see that the behavior can be performed and is, in fact, performed by their peers. In addition, students observe other students receiving rewards they themselves might want. Finally, the prestige of the students serving as models may encourage other students to change their behavior even in the absence of any extrinsic reward.

*Students can consider peer models as examples to emulate, but they may also consider them as simply teacher's pets.*

Although using peers as models can be effective with some students (8), it could back-fire with others (9, 12). With these students, instead of motivating them to behave appropriately, it can make them resentful and jealous of the student models who are the recipients of their teachers' praise and attention. It can also lead others to label the model students as "teacher's pets" and to abuse and ridicule them. These reasons make using peers as models open to question as a highly effective way to change students' behavior.

## Planned Ignoring

Planned ignoring is a technique for managing behavior problems that involves eliminating the attention students receive from their teachers and other students for misbehaving. The assumption underlying this approach is that when the students no longer get the attention that motivates their inappropriate behavior, they will have no reason to continue to misbehave.

The kinds of attention students seek from others varies from student to student. Some just want to know they are being noticed. Others are seeking acceptance and recognition from their peers. Still others hope to gain tokens of love and concern from their teachers. Finally, there are those who are rewarded by signs that they have provoked hostility and rejection from others.

In the past many authors were overly optimistic about the extent to which planned ignoring could change students' behavior (19, 23). Now, though considerable evidence shows that ignoring behavior can work in certain situations (14–16, 18– 20, 22–24), it is also clear that many classroom behavior problems are unaffected or even grow worse when ignored (17, 21). This is because ignoring misbehavior that isn't designed to have an effect or to provoke a reaction may encourage future misbehavior once students learn they can misbehave with impunity.

Although planned ignoring can be an effective technique for temporarily managing certain attention-seeking behavior, it still doesn't teach students how to gain the attention they want in appropriate ways. It also doesn't address the causes of their misbehavior. While looking into these causes may not be necessary in every case, students who purposely try to be rejected or laughed at, who curry favor from their peers because they can't make and keep friends without doing so, or who are overly dependent on teacher praise need help with the emotional problems causing their actions. (See Chapter 10.)

*Using Planned Ignoring Effectively*   Keeping in mind the fact that planned ignoring is sometimes only a start in working with students who seek inappropriate forms of attention, the following steps will assist you in deciding when and how to use it effectively.

1. *Determine whether students' misbehavior is attention-seeking.* Some of the unacceptable ways students may seek attention include: whining or crying; acting delinquently by refusing to follow rules, using foul language, and so on; playing the fool (clowning); bragging; pulling practical jokes on others, telling jokes, and making wisecracks; asking teachers to help them when they really don't need help or to check their work when it's obviously correct; asking to have directions repeated; purposely making careless mistakes; pretending to be sick, hurt, frightened, or upset;

making self-derogatory statements; tattling on other students; asking for permission that obviously won't be given.

Students often behave in these ways to have an effect on others. But they may have other reasons as well. When young students whine or cry, they may behave that way because they haven't adjusted to the structure and demands of school and the expectations of their teachers. Students may sometimes ask for help they don't need or feedback because they lack confidence in their ability and not just to get attention. Likewise, students who consistently ask to have instructions and explanations repeated may have hearing problems, or they may be so distractible that their attention is elsewhere when the class is being told what to do and how to do it. And some students may actually believe they are sick or hurt and actually feel frightened even though no "apparent reason" exists for them to feel this way.

Thus, before deciding to manage a behavior problem by ignoring it, be fairly certain that it's actually designed to elicit a reaction from you or your students. Sometimes it's better to give students attention even though you think they don't need it than to deny them the attention they require. It may also be more prudent to provide students more help than they seem to need when they ask for assistance, to give them more attention than you think they require when they appear to be feigning illness, and to repeat directions that they should have understood than to erroneously ignore their solicitations when they actually need what they are seeking.

2. *Make sure students know what behavior you want them to change, why the behavior is inappropriate, and why you and/or the other students will be ignoring it.* Students who understand why you and/or their peers are ignoring them may be less likely to misinterpret being ignored as rejection of them rather than their behavior. When they know what you are doing and why you are doing it, they may be less inclined to resist your efforts. (See step five.)

3. *Obtain the cooperation of the other students in the class if their reactions to the behavior you want to manage is reinforcing it.* Attention-seeking behaviors such as asking for unnecessary help, tattling on others in private, and feigning illness are probably done to obtain a reaction from adults, but acting like a delinquent, playing the fool, making wisecracks, or passing gas as loudly as possible are typically done to get a reaction from other students. When students misbehave to get peer attention, whether or not you ignore the behavior is less important than getting the students to ignore it.

Before soliciting your students' cooperation, determine whether it would be wise to identify the student in question since some students may feel embarrassed or resentful if their problems are dealt with publicly, and they could then resist your efforts to modify their behavior and even behave worse.

If you think the student can handle it and if the student agrees to be identified, you can explain to the class why they should ignore the student when she makes a wisecrack, clowns around, and so on. Then monitor the group's reaction to the student's behavior. Finally, praise and give credit to the group when the student's behavior begins to change.

If you think it would be unwise to identify the student, you still have options. You can select a convenient occasion to meet with your class that is not close in time to any attention-seeking attempts by the student and have a general discussion about why certain kinds of class reactions encourage students to behave inappropriately without mentioning specific students. Make an effort to help your students understand why ignoring attention-seeking behavior is more desirable, and then monitor the group's reaction to the student's behavior. You can also conduct additional discussions as needed.

4. *Eliminate all reinforcement of the attention-seeking behavior.* Make sure you and the other students in the class consistently ignore the students' inappropriate behavior. If you only reduce, instead of eliminate, the attention your students receive, they may still get enough attention to maintain their behavior. Their attention-seeking behavior may even increase because they believe if they try harder, it will only be a matter of time before they succeed in getting the attention they want.

5. *Expect an initial worsening of the behavior, substitution of other forms of attention-seeking behavior, or spontaneous recovery of the behavior after it has ceased.* When students stop receiving the attention they were used to getting for their misbehavior, they may try harder or switch to some other form of misbehavior to get it before finally giving up. Even after they have given up, they may occasionally try again to see if with the passage of time you or the group have weakened in your resolve.

6. *Evaluate your efforts.* If, after a reasonable period of time, your students' attention-seeking behavior persists even though you and/or the other students in the class have ignored it, determine whether you may be overlooking some other source of reinforcement either in or out of class. If you can't discover any, it may be that the behavior in question isn't attention-seeking and requires another type of intervention.

---

## Self-Quiz: Choosing Techniques

While you can use the techniques described in this section successfully to handle behavior problems, some are more effective with certain kinds of problems than others. For example, the attention-seeking antics of the class clown may be improved by planned ignoring; however, if the same student took the things she wanted to play with from other students instead of waiting her turn, planned ignoring would probably make the situation worse. Rewarding incompatible behavior would probably be a more effective technique to use.

The following exercise is designed to help you apply the ideas in this section to some typical classroom behavior problems. For each example, decide which of the following techniques (rewarding incompatible behavior, rewarding improvement, using peers as models, or planned ignoring) you would choose. Justify your choice and describe in detail how you would use the technique.

1. A 10-year-old leaves his lunch bag, orange peels, tray, and other lunch remains at the table when he leaves to play.
2. A 15-year-old, seemingly on purpose, gives obviously ridiculous answers when called on.
3. A 13-year-old complains whenever a less-skilled student is chosen for his team during recess and lunch.
4. A 7-year-old pushes and hits other students when she is angry at them.
5. An 8-year-old wanders around the room when she is supposed to be doing her seatwork, especially during math.

It is not always easy to get students to ignore attention seekers especially when they behave in obnoxious, disgusting, or provocative ways. In such cases, you may find it necessary to use other techniques to work with the students. (See Chapter 8.) It's also difficult to get older students who derive pleasure from the problems of other students, who build themselves up by putting others down, or who are opposed to what school stands for because they are doing poorly or have delinquent attitudes to cooperate with you. In such cases, you may have to change their attitudes about school or their motivation so that they will be more willing to cooperate. (See Chapters 7 and 8.) It's also difficult to use planned ignoring with primary grade students because many of them are too immature to either understand why they should ignore their classmates' behavior or to control their natural spontaneous reactions.

# Negative Consequences— Punishment

The previous sections described techniques for dealing with behavior problems without using negative consequences to modify students' behavior. Some educators take the position that teachers can handle almost all classroom behavior problems adequately without resorting to negative consequences. Others believe that punishment—or at least the anticipation of punishment—is needed to deal with some students in certain situations. The position taken in this book is that although punishment is an unpleasant and distasteful technique, it is often necessary to use it in combination with other techniques with young students who are still in the first stage of moral development and with older students who think they can get away with things. But when students misbehave because they are immature, distractible, anxious, upset, confused, scapegoated, and so on, you should deal with their misbehavior by means of other, nonpunitive techniques.

## Defining Punishment

Educators use the term *punishment* in two different ways. Some educators distinguish between mild consequences such as private statements of disapproval, loss of free time, and so on and harsher consequences such as corporal punishment or ridicule. They use the term *negative consequences* for mild consequences and *punishment* for harsh consequences. Others define punishment as the purposeful application of negative consequences of any kind in order to decrease the frequency of a behavior. According to this definition, mild desist orders and signaling teacher disapproval wouldn't be considered punitive because although they may be distasteful and disagreeable to students, they are intended to provide students with feedback about their behavior and not to add noxious consequences to that behavior. On the other hand, any extrinsic consequences, whether mild or harsh, intended to be disagreeable do fit the definition. As you can see from the organization of this book, the second definition, treating the terms *negative consequences* and *punishment* synonymously, is the one used here. This is because educators and students often perceive the severity/intensity of a particular negative consequence differently. Thus, while educators may think they are using mild negative consequences, students may experience them as harsh.

## Using Punishment Effectively

The following factors will influence the effectiveness of your efforts when you use negative consequences to modify your students' behavior.

*Students' Perceptions of Consequences*    Students must experience negative consequences as distasteful, noxious, or disagreeable for them to work. You may, for example, decide to punish a student by sending her to the office or to a time-out area in the classroom, but if the student is uncomfortable in class because she isn't prepared and doesn't want to be called on or because she thinks she can't do the work, she may experience the time-out as rewarding, not punitive. In the same vein, a student attempting to prove to his delinquent peers that he doesn't care about school may be encouraged, not discouraged, to misbehave when you reprimand him in front of his classmates. In fact, research has indicated that just about any noxious consequences can be rewarding to certain students (25–28).

Therefore, in order to use negative consequences effectively, you should select consequences that you believe will be experienced as disagreeable by the particular student you plan to use them with. And once you have applied them, you should check to determine whether they actually have the desired effect on the student.

*Providing a Rational Cognitive Structure*    Your efforts will be more successful if your students know the specific targeted behavior, why it was inappropriate, why you intend to use punishment rather than another technique to correct the problem, and why you think the particular punishment you have selected is fair before you actually use it (20–32). Identifying the behavior that they need to eliminate helps them comply with your expectations if they decide to do so. Convincing them that their behavior is inappropriate, that punishment is the appropriate way of dealing with the problem, and that this particular punishment is fair may decrease their resistance to your efforts. On the other hand, if they blame you rather than their behavior for the negative consequences they incur, and if they believe you are treating them unfairly, they may overtly resist your efforts to modify their behavior. As an alternative, they may acquiesce overtly but then covertly act out their resentment by trying to undermine your authority with other students or trying to get away with other things when your attention is directed elsewhere.

*Alternative Behaviors*    Students who use unacceptable means of satisfying their desires may be more willing to stop behaving inappropriately if they are offered acceptable ways of obtaining satisfaction (33–36). You may not always be able to suggest alternative ways for students to attain their goals, but when you can, students will be able to both avoid being punished and fulfill their desires. No acceptable alternative behavior may exist for a student who steals other students' possessions, but you can certainly teach the class clown how to get attention in more appropriate ways, and you can teach a young student who grabs things from other students how to ask others to share.

*Intensity*    Because certain students can experience a public reprimand as positive when they want to impress their peers with their willingness to stand up to their teacher and a period of time-out or a trip to the office can reward students who want to avoid participating in the activity at hand, it's essential to choose consequences that the students in question will actually experience as punishment (25–28). If the students don't perceive a cost, they won't feel a need to change their behavior. Even when students experience consequences as negative, the intensity (severity) of the punishments they receive affects their reactions to them. Punishments that involve very little cost to students compared to the positive reinforcement they receive from misbehaving can have little or no effect on their behavior in comparison to punishments that involve considerable cost (37–39, 41, 43). This may be one reason some authors conclude that punishments should be as intense (severe) as possible so long as the punishment is not unethical or abusive (38). But research also indicates that harsh punishments can backfire and have serious undesirable side effects.

Most authors who believe that a role exists for punishment in classroom management suggest that they should be only as intense as necessary to motivate students to modify their behavior (40, 42). One of the policies some educators follow to achieve this is to use milder forms of punishment first and then gradually increase the intensity until the desired effect is reached. This is the approach favored here because it helps educators avoid being more punitive than necessary. Some authors, though, feel it's a mistake to gradually escalate the intensity of punishment. For example, according to Morgan and Jenson:

> Erring on the conservative side by using a weak intensity or short duration may be a disservice to the child. Although all educational and clinical procedures should use the least restrictive approach to punishment, we may be doing children great harm by slowly adapting them to greater intensities or duration of a punishing stimulus. For example, to begin by using one minute of time-out and increasing the requirement gradually up to an hour teaches the child to withstand intense punishment, not to change misbehavior. The least restrictive punishing stimulus is one that will not be constantly increased and is effective in reducing an inappropriate behavior. The best strategy is to be familiar with the educational and clinical literature and know what intensities have been successfully used with students in different populations. (42, p. 137)

Another policy educators often follow to avoid being overly punitive is to never decide on students' punishment when they are angry or upset with them. Postponing such decisions until you are calm, relaxed, and rational can help keep you from saying and doing things that both you and your student will soon regret.

*Consistency*    Many theorists advise educators to be consistent in their use of punishment. In doing so they refer to three types of consistency—among teachers, in handling of different students, and in responses to the same student. Authors who believe educators should use punishments consistently cite the following reasons for their opinion.

They feel that consistency among teachers is essential because when some teachers permit students to do what other teachers forbid them to do, students can become confused. Students are then unsure whether it's really inappropriate for them to behave in those ways. They may ask themselves why it's not okay to do something in science that it is okay to do in social studies. When teachers apply punishments of varying intensities for the same infractions, students may question the fairness of a given punishment. A student may

*Reprimanding students privately, in the hall or elsewhere out of sight of the rest of the class, can make a bitter pill a little easier to swallow.*

protest that since one of his teachers only holds him back from recess for five minutes and only if he calls out more than twice during the period, it's not fair for him to miss the whole recess just because he called out only once in another classroom.

Consistency in handling different students is also essential. Specifically, if some students can get away with doing something, other students may be tempted to try getting away with it as well. Students may also think they are being punished unfairly if they receive consequences for doing what other students do with impunity—and they may be right.

Consistent responses to the same student are also necessary because if students are punished for doing something one time but not the next time they commit the same infraction, they may not understand, and they may be tempted to take a gamble and misbehave again.

While research indicates that consistent punishment is more effective than inconsistent punishment (32, 44–51), and some consistency is essential to avoid arbitrary punishment, the position of this book is that a certain amount of flexibility is also necessary. First, as individuals, educators have their own personalities, cultural backgrounds, values, and philosophies of education, and these variations make it impossible for all educators to feel comfortable handling behavior problems in the same way. Thus, it is both impractical and unfair to expect everyone on a particular teaching staff to agree 100 percent about what behaviors should be punished, which students should be punished, under what circumstances students should be punished, and which punishments are fair and reasonable.

Second, since different students may break the same rule for different reasons, it's neither fair nor efficient to treat all students alike. It may be appropriate to use punishment to convince students who aren't intrinsically motivated to abide by the rules. This lets them know it's necessary for them to do so or else. But students who break rules out of ignorance, in the heat of the moment, in response to a prior provocation, or because of some personal problems at home shouldn't be punished for their transgressions.

Finally, you shouldn't punish students who have made a real effort to improve their behavior and have done so if these students give in to temptation after a significant period of good behavior. A reminder or a warning delivered in a nonthreatening way may be more appropriate—and more effective.

The reasons just presented support rational, planned, justifiable flexibility, not inconsistency, in the use of negative consequences. Although it's understandable that teachers' moods, burnout, or stress may cause them to react one way to certain behavior on one day and another way the next day, nothing justifies such inconsistency. Nor does anything justify teachers relating differently to different students due to prejudice or personal likes and dislikes. Because justifiable flexibility in the use of punishment can seem like inconsistency to students when they see others handled in nonpunitive ways for doing just what they are punished for, it's imperative to explain to students why they are being treated differently. They may not accept the difference at first, but if you explain your reasons each time you punish students, a good likelihood exists that they will eventually accept your reasoning.

*Timing*   Many authors suggest that punishing students as soon as they start to misbehave keeps them from gaining the potential satisfaction of completing the misbehavior—satisfaction that could counteract the negative effects of the punishment. They also argue that the sooner educators intervene, the less likely it is that students' behavior will grow worse because they think they can get away with even more.

> A punishing stimulus should be delivered immediately with as little delay as possible. For optimal effectiveness a punishing stimulus should be presented in the early stages of a misbehavior instead of at its conclusion. Many misbehaviors are linked together like a chain, with less severe responses leading to more intense responses until, at the end of the chain, the child is totally out of control. For example, time-out would be more effective at the beginning of a tantrum than it would be after the child has been screaming and crying for 10 minutes. (42, p. 136–137)

> The earlier in the response sequence one can administer punishment, the greater will be the suppressive effect. In addition, instead of punishing a child after he has already completed a piece of misbehavior, it is probably better to wait and punish him just as he begins to repeat the behavior, at which point the punishment will be more effective. The above evidence casts doubt on practices in which children are sent to the office for punishment "when the principal gets around to it" or in which a teacher watches a child complete an act of misbehavior, carefully waits for him to finish, and then punishes. (35, p. 90)

Although considerable evidence for this position exists, especially in laboratory studies of animals and children (20, 29, 34, 51–53), others argue against placing too much faith in such evidence.

Behavioristically based sources of advice for teachers sometimes state that punishment will be more effective when it follows immediately after a transgression rather than when it is delayed, or that it will be more effective if it comes early in a sequence of undesired behavior rather than after completion of the sequence. Principles of this kind do seem to have some application for shaping animal behavior, but they are of doubtful relevance to the classroom, or to human learning generally. Here, punishment is a last resort method for curbing undesired behavior, not a basic method of shaping desired behavior. (9, p. 61)

The position taken by this book is that you should delay punishing students when:

1. You are not absolutely sure that students will complete acts of misbehavior that they have just started.

2. There may be extenuating circumstances that students might tell you about if given the chance to tell their side of the story.

3. Students are too upset emotionally to understand or accept the punishment.

4. You are too upset to deal with the situation in a calm, thoughtful manner.

5. Punishing the students may be too disruptive to the class.

6. It would be better to have the principal or someone else with more authority mete out the punishment.

*Self-Quiz: On Flexibility*

Review the arguments for and against being flexible about the severity, consistency, and timing of punishment. What are your opinions about these issues? What reasons do you have for your opinion?

## Acceptable Consequences

Considering the fact that negative consequences work because they are distasteful enough to cause students to change their behavior to avoid them, educators should select consequences that are no more unpleasant than is necessary to achieve that goal. To choose punishments more severe than necessary or to use excessively harsh punishments because milder forms prove to be ineffective is an abuse of the educator's authority and an infringement on the rights of the students. Thus, when you use negative consequences with your students, select the least noxious consequences necessary to do the job from among the acceptable alternatives available. If none of the acceptable alternatives work, don't abuse your power. Go on to use the more individualized, in-depth approaches described in Chapter 9 instead.

# Natural, Arbitrary, and Logical Consequences

There are three types of negative consequences—natural, arbitrary, and logical (11). Natural consequences occur automatically as the naturally occurring result of a particular behavior. Arbitrary consequences are arranged by an authority figure and aren't clearly related to the behavior being punished. Logical consequences are consequences that are arranged and are also related to the behavior in question.

| BEHAVIOR | NATURAL CONSEQUENCE | ARBITRARY CONSEQUENCE | LOGICAL CONSEQUENCE |
|---|---|---|---|
| 1. A student constantly complains about his peers. | The student isn't chosen when the class plays during recess. | He loses three points or tokens that he has been saving for a prize. | The student is required to sit and play by himself for part of the day. |
| 2. A student lies. | The student's peers don't believe her. | The student loses her snack. | The teacher tells her he doesn't believe her. |
| 3. A student draws graffiti on the bathroom wall. | | The student loses free time. | The student has to wash the drawing off the wall. |
| 4. A student calls out answers. | | The student misses recess. | The student loses her next turn. |
| 5. A student tries to push ahead in line. | The student is pushed back by another student. | The student is sent to the office. | The student is sent to the end of the line. |
| 6. A student abuses her laboratory equipment. | The equipment breaks, and she can't do the experiment. | She is sent to time-out. | The equipment is confiscated, and the student is not allowed to continue the experiment. |
| 7. A student hits another student during recess. | The student is hit back. | The student misses a class trip. | The student misses recess for the rest of the week. |
| 8. A student throws a noisy temper tantrum. | | The student is sent to the principal to be reprimanded. | The student is removed from class until he calms down. |

*(continued)*

*(continued)*

| BEHAVIOR | NATURAL CONSEQUENCE | ARBITRARY CONSEQUENCE | LOGICAL CONSEQUENCE |
|---|---|---|---|
| 9. A student teases her peers. | The student has few friends. | She loses her snack. | She is required to sit by herself. |
| 10. The student doesn't return a social studies book to the library. | | The student's grade in social studies is lowered. | The student has to pay for the book or work its cost off in the library. |
| 11. A student refuses to participate in the cleanup with her group before recess. | Her share is left undone when the other members of her group go to recess. | The student is reprimanded and loses ten tokens. | The student remains in the class during recess until she does her share. |
| 12. A student doesn't show up for three rehearsals in a row. | The other members of the cast treat her poorly. | She is kept in after school. | She loses her part in the play. |
| 13. A student plays the clown when he is called on. | The other students laugh at him. | He is sent to the office. | He isn't called on for an hour. |

Sometimes the natural consequences that result from misbehavior are enough to convince students to behave more appropriately. In examples 1, 5, 6, and 7, it's possible, but not necessarily probable, that the natural consequences of the misbehavior will be distasteful enough to motivate students to change the way they behave. In examples 2, 9, 11, and 12, it's unlikely that the natural consequences alone would motivate students to change. In examples 3, 4, 8, and 10, no natural consequences for the students' misbehavior occur. And in example 13, the natural consequence of playing the clown can actually reinforce the behavior.

When the natural consequences of misbehavior aren't negative enough to bring about a change, educators can use arbitrary or else logical consequences to supplement them. Dreikurs and others have suggested that, of the two options, logical consequences are preferable (11, 58, 71, 72). They feel that logical consequences are more acceptable to students because they fit the crime and are understandable; they are less likely to create resistance and power struggles because they appear to be the result of the students' behavior, not their teachers' authority; and they tend to be less harsh than many arbitrary punishments.

This line of reasoning appears to have merit though no research has been carried out to study it (73). In some cases, though, the logical consequences of misbehaving may not be severe enough to counterbalance the intrinsic rewards of students' actions. Examples 2, 3, 5, 9, 11, and 13 in the table may well fit that category. Telling students who lie that one doesn't believe them, making a student wash graffiti off the wall, sending a student to the end of the line for cutting when he would have been at the end of the line anyway, and requiring a student who teases others to remain isolated may not affect the students as particularly unpleasant. Taking a student's part in a play away from her might actually be rewarding if the student is purposefully attempting to be dropped from the cast. And not moving a student who doesn't do his homework to the next level may merely confirm the student in his belief that he is poor at math. In such cases, applying logical consequences could be insufficient, and you would have to resort to other kinds of consequences.

---

## THEORY FOCUS: DREIKURS RECOMMENDS RESPECT AND OPTIMISM

Rudolf Dreikurs has expressed his views on classroom management in four books: *Psychology in the Classroom: A Manual for Teachers, Discipline without Tears: What to do with Children Who Misbehave, Encouraging Children to Learn: The Encouragement Process*, and *Logical Consequences*. According to Dreikurs, teachers can encourage students to behave appropriately by treating them appropriately. Among other things, this includes relating to them respectfully and optimistically and stressing cooperation over competition and improvement over perfection.

He believes that four main reasons explain why students misbehave, and he advises educators to first determine which one is operating and to respond accordingly. For example, when students misbehave to gain attention, teachers should make sure they don't receive it. When students try to exert power over others, educators should avoid involving themselves in power struggles. If students seek revenge for real or imagined events, they should be treated in ways that reduce their need to be avenged. When they misbehave out of feelings of helplessness and impotency, then teachers should build up their self-confidence.

Dreikurs recognizes that at times these approaches will be ineffective, and then students will have to pay the consequences of their misbehavior in order to learn to behave appropriately. At such times he advises educators to act democratically, not autocratically, and to use logical, not arbitrary, consequences. He equates arbitrary consequences with punishment.

---

## Self-Quiz: Logical Consequences

Describe a logical consequence a teacher might apply in each of the following cases.

1. A student calls out answers.
2. A student lies about not getting her snack.
3. A student gets into a fight during recess.
4. A student refuses to clear his place during lunch.
5. A student draws graffiti on the school building.
6. A student pushes ahead in line.
7. A student refuses to do her part of the assignment for the group she has been working in.
8. A student abuses the bathroom pass.
9. A student forges his parent's name to a permission slip for a class trip.

*Disapproval*    There is a difference between signaling to students that you are aware of their actions or are issuing desist orders and expressing disapproval and reprimanding them for their behavior. Signaling awareness or giving desist orders provides students with factual information designed to give them the extra external control they require to manage their behavior. In contrast, expressing disapproval and reprimanding students are purposely designed to be noxious enough to motivate students to stop misbehaving in order to avoid them. To be effective, the resulting discomfort has to be significant enough to counter the positive reinforcement students can receive from misbehaving.

Research shows that expressing disapproval and reprimanding students in a soft voice and in private so no one else can hear can be effective so long as it isn't done too often (59, 61, 63, 68, 69). But reprimanding students in a loud voice, in front of their peers, or too often can actually lead to a worsening of their behavior. This response may make students angry and resentful, lower their self-esteem, cause them to rebel against the teacher's authority, or withdraw from class physically and/or psychologically to avoid feeling bad. It can also lead to a worsening in their attitude toward school, decrease their time on-task, and lower scores on achievement tests (54, 55, 57, 60, 64, 65). Research also indicates that students rank public reprimands among the least acceptable interventions that teachers use (67). Despite these facts, studies of classrooms reveal that teachers tend to criticize and reprimand students to an excessive degree much more often than they praise them (66, 70).

*Reprimanding effectively:* When you decide that it would benefit your students to express disapproval of their behavior or reprimand them, the following suggestions should help you carry this out more effectively.

1. *Speak to students privately in a calm, soft voice.* Avoid yelling at students from across the room. Speak to them privately at your desk, at their seat, or somewhere where no one else can hear what you say. Speaking to students privately, especially older ones, can protect them from being embarrassed in front of their peers. This also can serve to demonstrate your concern for their feelings, eliminate their need to "stand up to you" to maintain their peer standing, and avoid the negative result possible when students see one of their own being reprimanded publicly. Speaking to students softly in a calm voice instead of yelling makes it less likely that they will react defensively to being reprimanded or become nervous, jumpy, or tense.

2. *Choose your words carefully.* Although little research evidence either supports or refutes the idea, authors of classroom management texts typically suggest that when teachers reprimand students they should discuss the students' behavior, not the students themselves. In addition, they suggest that teachers describe the behavior, not judge or label it. These authors advise that comments that focus on the students, especially if they are judgmental, can make students feel angry, resentful, and defensive. They can also lower students' self-esteem if they accept their teachers' assertions that they are indeed rude, lazy, dumb, stubborn, and so on. These labels can become self-fulfilling prophecies (56, 58, 68). In addition, judgmental and labeling statements give students little information about what they did wrong compared to statements that describe the inappropriate behavior, which make it clear what needs correcting.

| Descriptive:<br>Focus on the Behavior | Judgmental, Labeling:<br>Focus on the Student |
|---|---|
| It was a mistake to start before I finished explaining how to do it. | That was a dumb thing to do. |
| It's dangerous to put things into the wall socket. You could be electrocuted. | You sure act stupid sometimes. Didn't you know it's dangerous to put things into wall sockets? |
| Don't interrupt. Wait your turn. | Don't be rude. |
| You have to finish the rest of the assignment first. | Don't be lazy. |
| Harold was waiting in line when you pushed ahead of him. | You weren't very nice to Harold. You weren't very fair. |
| Once the group votes, everyone has to abide by the decision of the majority. | Don't be stubborn. |

The advice to describe the students' behavior and to avoid judgmental terms applies to most students, but certain students may require another approach. In particular, when students need to learn to accept responsibility for their behavior, it may be more appropriate to focus in on what *they* did and how *their* behavior affected others. Likewise when students need to learn to control themselves because it's the right thing to do, it may be desirable to use such terms as *unfair* and *unjust* to describe their behavior. (This rationale, of course, would never justify the use of terms such as *stupid, dumb, lazy, stubborn, bad, jerky,* and the like.)

3. *Don't reprimand students when you are angry or frustrated with them.* The goal of reprimanding is to change students' motivation, not to discharge your feelings. If you are too angry or upset to choose your words wisely or to focus on the students' needs, wait until you have calmed down enough to do so. Otherwise, you may unintentionally reprimand them publicly or use harsh and judgmental terms that you wouldn't normally choose.

Expressing disapproval and reprimanding students tend to work best with students who value their teachers' opinions of them and seek their teachers' attention and affection. Merely signaling to such students' awareness of their behavior and/or telling them to stop is often sufficient so that reprimanding them is unnecessary. But, as reprimands may be too inconsequential for students who require negative consequences to be shown they can't get away with misbehaving and often unnecessary for students who respond to signals, the position of this book is that their usefulness as classroom management techniques is minimal at best.

*Overcorrection*   In examples 3, 10, and 11 in the table on natural, arbitrary, and logical consequences in which students drew graffiti on the wall, failed to return a library book, and refused to participate in cleanup activities, the logical consequences of their

## Self-Quiz: Reprimands

The following are examples of reprimands that can be improved on. In each case, identify the principle or principles that were overlooked, and improve the reprimand accordingly.

1. When the teacher saw Henry taking something from the closet, she called out, "Put that back. How many times do I have to tell you that I'm the only one allowed to remove things from the closet?"
2. When the teacher noticed Katherine looking covertly at her book during a test,

she walked up to her and quietly said, "Katherine, I'm surprised at you. I never thought you were a cheat."
3. When Steve refused to let Billy take a turn during recess, his teacher said, "Don't be bad. Let Billy have his turn."
4. The teacher was so angry when he heard Harold make an ethnic comment about Ira that he said, "Harold, you should be ashamed of yourself. You know that we don't say those things in class. Now say you're sorry."
5. When Jim started playing the clown for the class, his teacher reminded the other students that they were supposed to ignore him whenever he did stupid things.

misbehavior would be to require them to correct the situation they had caused by removing the graffiti, paying for the library book, and finishing the cleanup during recess. If merely making restitution for misbehavior isn't enough to change their behavior, the teacher could require the students to overcorrect the situation they had created. In the examples above, overcorrection might consist of having the student clean the complete wall, not just the section with graffiti; spend more time in the library than necessary to pay for the book; and do more than just her fair share of the cleanup. Other situations in which overcorrection might be appropriate include littering, carving school desks, breaking other students' property or projects, purposely excluding children from the group, throwing food in the cafeteria, and refusing to share.

Though overcorrection has been successful (75–78, 81), it has also been criticized for being too punitive and for only being effective in changing behavior so long as the threat of punishment is present (74, 79, 80).

*Time-Out*    Time-out is a term for a number of punitive classroom management procedures that involve removing students from regular classroom activities in ways designed to be unpleasant, distasteful, or boring. This should not be confused with the antiseptic bouncing (100), which is removing students from classroom situations that make them anxious, afraid, or guilty in order to prevent them from experiencing emotional problems.

When students want to take part in the classroom activities they are removed from, removing them can be unpleasant enough to make them modify their behavior. Students who enjoy classroom learning tasks and are motivated to complete their assignments in school instead of at home may want to avoid being sent to a time-out area, and very sociable students may control their talkative behavior if they are denied access to their friends. For such students, making them spend a short period in a time-out area at the back of the room, behind a screen, in the hall, or at their desks with their heads down on their arms may do the trick.

*A time-out situation that is lonely and boring may cause a student to think twice before misbehaving again.*

A time-out procedure, termed *contingent observation*, which is especially appropriate for preschoolers, has been described by Porterfield, Herbert-Jackson, and Risley (98). In their approach students who misbehave are first told why their behavior was unacceptable and how they should behave; then they are required to sit on the periphery of the group and watch while teachers call their attention to examples of the desired behavior among their classmates.

When time-out works, a short period of time-out is all that is necessary to create an effective deterrent to misbehavior. White, Nielson, and Johnson (107) report that time-out periods of 1 minute are as effective as lengthy time-out periods. Others have found that from 5 to a maximum of 15 minutes is adequate (87, 88, 93, 95, 103).

But students who aren't particularly interested in participating in classroom activities may not mind being removed from a situation they don't find reinforcing to begin with. For these students, some authors have suggested that educators should increase the unpleasant aspects associated with time-out. Suggestions for how to do this include requiring students to sit in a time-out chair facing the corner of the room (a technique some feel is not too different from requiring students to wear a "dunce cap" and sit in the corner or on the dunce's stool), sending students to an area designed to be a boring, unpleasant experience, or having them visit the dean of discipline or the principal's office.

Authors who reject the idea of making time-out worse by having the time-out area be unpleasant advise educators to make time-out unappealing by making "time-in" more appealing. The typical way to do this is to offer students the opportunity to earn points or tokens that can be turned in for a prize, special privileges, or the like by behaving appropriately and to deny this opportunity to students when they misbehave. In this approach teachers tell students who have misbehaved that they will be unable to earn points for a specified period of time. Then they place a ribbon on the students or some type of symbol on their desks, signaling that they can't earn points or tokens until it is removed, or else they move students to a time-out area of the room (89).

Considerable evidence shows that various forms of time-out work with some students (82, 84–86, 88, 91, 92, 96–98, 101–103, 105, 107). Weber, Roff, Crawford, and Robinson (106) list 21 texts that recommend time-out procedures to modify students' behavior. Still, the various forms of time-out have received their share of criticism for being overly punitive and unethical (38, 94, 99, 104).

*Using time-out effectively:* The following general guidelines are designed to help you use time-out techniques effectively.

1. Determine whether the use of negative consequences is the correct procedure. As noted previously, negative consequences are appropriate for some, but students, for example, who misbehave because they are angry at being teased by others may require another approach.

2. Decide which type of time-out would be most effective: preventing students from participating in the rewarding aspects of normal classroom activities, denying students the opportunity to earn points or tokens for acceptable behavior, or placing students in an unpleasant time-out area.

3. Establish a baseline of how often the undesirable behavior occurs that you can use to measure the effectiveness of your intervention. (Be as accurate as time allows.)

4. Make sure students know which behaviors they have to change and why these are unacceptable.

5. Establish the consequences that students will receive when they misbehave, and be sure students understand both the consequences and what they must do to avoid them.

6. Use the time-out procedure you have chosen, and evaluate its effectiveness in reducing or eliminating the target behavior.

7. If it is not effective, modify your procedure or select a different time-out technique.

8. If it is effective, eliminate the time-out procedure, and see whether students continue to behave appropriately. If the improvement isn't maintained, use other procedures to supplement those that you have been using. (See Chapter 9.)

Educators who support the use of time-out procedures offer the following specific suggestions for implementing them.

1. If not permitting students to participate in regular class activities is sufficient punishment to motivate them to modify their behavior, then select the least restrictive time-out area for the purpose. You can, for example, separate students who are too talkative from their friends by changing their seats. Place attention-seeking students behind a partition or screen, but banish disruptive students to the hall.

2. In order to use time-out from the opportunity to earn points or tokens, you have to establish a procedure whereby students can both earn points and lose the opportunity to earn them (see the next section on contingency contracting) as well as some signaling device to indicate that students are in time-out for a specified time period. You can use a private signal with students such as a tap on the shoulder or placing a hand on her desk in order to avoid calling attention to the "punishment." Or you can use a more public signal if you believe it's necessary to let other students know you are "with it" and are handling the problem.

3. If you choose to remove students to an unpleasant time-out area, be sure they experience this as unpleasant. Using such procedures with students who are trying to be kicked out of class or who want to impress other students with their delinquent stance is an ineffective way of handling their misbehavior.

4. When you remove students from class, make sure you aren't too angry or frustrated with them to make the right choice of consequences.

5. If necessary, send students to the hall, a detention center that is a regular classroom supervised by an adult, or the dean of discipline or principal's office.

6. Encourage students to do their work during their time-out periods. Make sure they don't have any other reading materials, games, or other objects they can entertain themselves with; advise secretaries and others not to talk to or commiserate with students in time-out.

7. Use the shortest period of time necessary to affect the students' behavior. Most authors consider 5 to 15 minutes reasonable. Don't increase the time students spend in time-out beyond a reasonable period if students resist leaving the classroom or if the procedure isn't effective. To do so would be abusive and a misuse of your authority.

*Contingency Contracting*   Contingency contracts are written out and typically signed by both students and teachers. They specify how students are expected to behave and the positive and negative consequences they will receive when they either comply or fail to comply with their contracts. Ideally, these contracts result from a period of negotiation between teacher and student during which the student participates in determining both the behavioral change expected of him and the consequences that will occur.

*Advantages and disadvantages*: Theorists claim several advantages for this approach to setting and enforcing expectations for appropriate behavior (9, 87, 93, 110). First, research indicates that contingency contracting is an effective method of achieving behavioral change in a variety of settings and with a variety of problems (108–110, 114, 116, 119, 120). A second factor is that students are more willing to abide by contracts they help formulate. They are also more likely to conform to formal agreements than informal ones. Next, writing down behavioral expectations and consequences makes it less likely that students will forget them. Another important point is that students who have agreed that their behavior needs changing are more likely to attribute any negative consequences they may incur to their behavior rather than to the teacher's whims. This is especially helpful with students who resent or resist their teachers' authority. Students participating in the development of contracts are taking a first step toward learning to manage their own behavior.

Finally, students themselves prefer contingency contracting over many other classroom management techniques.

But contingency contracting has also been criticized. Some feel that rewarding students for appropriate behavior can create overdependency, loss of creativity, and the kinds of problems discussed in Chapter 3. Also, when used in conjunction with negative consequences, contingency contracting doesn't produce long-term changes in behavior. This approach can provide the illusion of student participation, when in fact students often only pretend to agree with the contracts they have signed because of their teachers' power over them (9, 49, 112). Tanner states:

> Can teachers combine contracts with intrinsic motivation? This seems theoretically untenable since contingency management is based on the principle of operant conditioning with the use of extrinsic rewards . . . Contracts are manipulative. The learner is doing something unappealing for the privilege of doing something less unappealing and so on until the chain is completed. (49, p. 105–106)

*Using contingency contracting effectively*: Practitioners of contingency contracting have offered the following suggestions for implementing the technique (93, 111, 113, 115, 117, 118).

1. Develop contracts with students in ways that maximize their participation in order to gain their cooperation and enhance their growth toward self-management. (See section on self-management below.)

2. Specify the desirable and undesirable behaviors and what the consequences of each will be. For example,

   - Each day that I don't call out, I will be allowed to feed the rabbits.

   - I will earn 5 points for each half hour I don't call out. I will lose 5 points each time I speak to other students without permission. When I have 40 points, I will be allowed to feed the rabbits.

   - I will earn 10 points for each day I don't use foul language in class. I will lose 2 points each time I use foul language in class. I will earn 5 points each day I keep my hands to myself. I will lose recess if I hit or push other students.

3. Be realistic about the amount of change you can expect students to make, especially at the start of a contract. Reward small changes of behavior in the right direction so that students can be successful immediately.

4. Emphasize positive rather than negative consequences so that students are likely to profit from their contracts. Emphasize what students will get or earn by behaving appropriately, not what they will lose by misbehaving.

5. Make sure the terms of the agreement are clear.

6. Make sure students agree that the contract is fair.

7. Include a provision that entitles both parties to renegotiate the contract.

8. Include beginning and ending dates.

9. Have both parties to the contract express their agreement by their signature, a handshake, or the like.

10. Evaluate the results periodically. If the contract isn't working, renegotiate the terms; decrease your expectations for behavior change or increase the incentives you are offering students to modify their behavior. If the contract is a success, evaluate your students' behavior after the contract has terminated to determine whether the improvement is maintained without extrinsic consequences. If it isn't, develop new contracts with your students or use some of the techniques designed to motivate students to want to behave appropriately in the absence of consequences.

# Unacceptable and Controversial Consequences

The previous section described a number of punitive techniques that many educators feel are acceptable ways of dealing with misbehavior. This section discusses punitive techniques that many authors find unacceptable.

*Harsh Reprimands*   Numerous authors have reported that harsh reprimands—criticizing students publicly, frequently, angrily, or in a loud voice can be counterproductive. Instead of reducing disruptive behavior, harsh reprimands often increase undesirable behavior both on the part of students who are reprimanded and other class members as well. Research also indicates that harsh reprimands make students more aggressive and anxious and decrease their interest in learning (60, 62, 121, 124, 141, 160).

*Serious Consequences for Minor Infractions*   Although no research exists as yet on this subject, many educators disapprove of applying serious, time-consuming, or highly distasteful consequences for minor infractions; they feel that "the punishment should fit the crime." Examples of consequences that may not meet this requirement include taking away classroom responsibilities such as feeding the fish, taking messages to the office, being the line monitor, and so on for talking in class or in the halls; being kept in school after hours for not completing seatwork; and having to write, "I will not . . ." a hundred times for doing something only once or twice.

*Negative Practice*   Negative practice is a technique in which students are required to repeat an undesirable behavior until it loses its original reinforcing effects. For example, a teacher would require students who spit at other children or on the hallway floors to spit into a toilet or in a grassy area until they feel like they never want to spit again. Another example is making students who throw temper tantrums perform the same antics until they will think twice before doing so the next time they feel angry or frustrated. Though negative practice has its proponents and detractors, there is as yet no evidence of either the effectiveness or the side effects of this technique.

*Blame, Shame, Embarrassment, and Ridicule*   Purposely calling on inattentive or unprepared students to recite in class in order to embarrass them in front of their peers; using terms such as *stupid, lazy, idiotic, childish, foolish, dumb, egotistical, self-centered,* and the like to describe students or their behavior; and making comments like, "Would you like to sit with the kindergarteners?" may suppress students' undesirable behavior for the moment. But using this approach may also seriously damage their self-image and their relationships with their teachers (163).

*Peer Pressure*   A student's motivation to behave appropriately can be increased by the peer pressure that occurs when the consequences for the entire group depend on the behavior of one or a small group of individuals (142, 146). This approach can be both advantageous and disadvantageous as the following statement indicates.

> A well-executed dependent group contingency can have a distinct advantage: Problem students' peers tend to "root for" them and do what they can to encourage improvement because they have something to gain by doing so. A disadvantage is that it can easily be mismanaged, resulting in possible threats, criticism, or harassment from peers when the target student or subgroup does not perform adequately. (137, p. 7)

Telling the class that everyone except Harry and Lenny are ready to leave for recess can get these two to stop talking, but it can also encourage other students to harass them during recess for holding up the class. Due to the inherent possibility that students may exert negative pressure on their peers, peer pressure is not a safe way to motivate nonconforming students. Instead of making the class wait for Harry and Lenny, it would be more prudent to dismiss everyone except the two boys, who must stay behind until they are ready.

*Isolation/Seclusion*   Although many educators consider time-out an acceptable technique, putting students in seclusion or isolation during time-out is highly controversial. Clarizio (11) and Bereiter and Englemann (83), among others, favor the use of isolation as a technique to control extreme forms of misbehavior as the following quotes indicate.

> To use time-out procedures effectively, a teacher must be sure that removal from the class is a punishment . . . Ideally, the students should be placed in a dull, unstimulating room containing a chair and a light. The area should be well ventilated, lighted, and consistent with fire code regulations. (11, p. 142)

> The "isolation" room, if it is to be effective, should be an unpleasant place, providing an atmosphere that is far less enjoyable than that of the study room. A small, poorly lighted closet with a single chair will serve quite well. (83, p. 88)

Gast and Nelson (90) have published guidelines that they believe will enable educators to use seclusion ethically and effectively. These guidelines include the following suggestions.

1. Students should be advised about which behaviors will result in seclusion or time-out beforehand.

2. Teachers should document their attempts to control students' misbehavior by employing milder forms of time-out before using seclusion.

3. Teachers should have a written statement of the procedures to be followed.

4. The time-out room should be at least 6 by 6 feet, properly lighted and ventilated, and free of dangerous objects. It should contain a window for observing the student, and it should only be locked when necessary.

5. Teachers should keep records of all time-out events.

6. Seclusion in excess of 30 minutes should require consultation with supervisory school staff.

7. Teachers should reward students for behaving appropriately after they have completed a period of seclusion.

8. If seclusion appears to be ineffective in suppressing the behavior, an advisory committee should determine whether it should continue to be used.

Locking students in small rooms by themselves and not allowing them to leave until they have stopped crying or screaming should be unacceptable to all educators, and many do consider that kind of treatment as abusive, counterproductive, and wrong. The position of this author is that secluding students in isolation rooms is unjustified regardless of the way they behave in school. Much more humane and effective ways of dealing with behavior problems are readily available.

*Corporal Punishment*   Corporal punishment typically takes the form of a principal or some other school authority administering a paddling on the backside to a student. While most educators tend to agree that such forms of harsh punishment as ridicule, sarcasm, embarrassment, abusive reprimands, and excessive criticism are undesirable, much less agreement exists about corporal punishment.

Many educators favor using corporal punishment within clearly defined guidelines when, in the judgment of professionals, it is warranted (83, 129, 147, 151, 155). For example, Sabatino, Sabatino, and Mann state:

> This author does not advocate corporal punishment as the best alternative to solving behavioral problems in school. However, in lieu of the ineffectiveness of other tried alternatives, punishment may be necessary as a last resort, and in some cases, may be a better solution than others. (155, p. 12)

The following are two representative statements by superintendents of schools who favor the use of corporal punishment:

> The necessity for the use of corporal punishment as a means of managing behavior in schools arises from two particular sources. First, education is compulsory; children between the ages of 6 and 16 must attend school unless otherwise excused by local or state statute. Secondly, there is often no positive alternative institution to which a child can turn when he/she is suspended from school. If they are suspended from school, where are you going to suggest the parents of the child go for assistance in obtaining a public education for that child? All of us recognize that public education is desirable; it is desirable for children to learn the basic skills that they need to support themselves and to be contributing members of society. The basic knowledge must come from the public

school in this country, for there isn't any other source. Therefore, if we suspend a child from school as a possible alternative to corporal punishment, there is no place to send him/her except to the street. (151, p. 11)

I was not abused by my parents, and they used corporal punishment. I do not consider that I was abused by my teachers who used corporal punishment on me when I was coming up through the public schools. I perceive that I have a positive self-concept and that I have a pretty good attitude toward life. (147, p. 5)

*Advantages*: Supporters of the use of corporal punishment tend to point out the following facts to bolster their position: Corporal punishment has been approved as a disciplinary technique in schools by the Supreme Court; very few states have regulations disapproving its use in school (123); national surveys indicate that corporal punishment is widely used and approved of by school personnel and parents (138, 140, 148, 153, 162, 165).

Educators who favor corporal punishment also use a variety of arguments to justify its use (83, 129, 131, 147, 151, 155). They maintain that other techniques don't work with certain students who seem to need to experience pain before they are willing to conform. Even with students who do respond to other management techniques, the process can be so time-consuming that it may be more efficient to use corporal punishment. Also, corporal punishment is the most logical consequence to employ when students behave violently, defiantly, disrespectfully, destructively, or dangerously—when they directly challenge their teachers' authority, lie, refuse to admit their mistakes, and so on. Some suggest that the use of corporal punishment demonstrates that teachers care enough about their students to do what is necessary to help them learn self-control—to do what is best for themselves and the other members of the class. Others feel that corporal punishment builds character by teaching students to accept the consequences of their actions. It also enables school administrators to handle difficult students without suspending or expelling them. And, finally, corporal punishment is not abusive if used correctly:

- It is administered in a calm, rational atmosphere in private.
- Students are told what they did wrong and why they are being punished.
- Students are not paddled excessively.
- Students are forgiven and consoled immediately afterward in order to demonstrate to them that they were punished out of love and concern for them, not anger.

*Disadvantages*: A great many educators oppose the use of corporal punishment in school (40, 56, 104, 128, 130, 132, 134, 135, 136, 139, 145, 152, 153, 158, 159, 161, 164). The following statements are examples of this position.

If the technology of discipline management could be linked to an animal, then corporal punishment would surely be its ass end. Of all the discipline techniques in existence, corporal punishment distinguishes itself as having the fewest assets and the greatest number of liabilities. In terms of locking adult and child into a series of coercive cycles, it is the all-time champion. (136, p. 344)

Corporal punishment should never be used to motivate students. It not only is morally questionable, but, of critical importance to the school's mission, it just doesn't work. In fact, it is usually counterproductive. Students obviously do not wish to attend schools where corporal punishment is common, and so any later attempts to motivate them to learn are uphill battles. (104, p. 34)

Educators who are opposed to the use of corporal punishment have offered many reasons for their thinking. First, no evidence shows that corporal punishment decreases off-task behavior (126). They feel that corporal punishment is an unethical, overly punitive, and abusive technique. It is also significant that no legal guidelines have been established to determine when it would be reasonable to use corporal punishment or what type of corporal punishment is reasonable. Specifically, many cases of abusive use of corporal punishment have resulted in physical and psychological damage to students (127, 143). Critics note that corporal punishment tends to be used more with poor, minority, and handicapped students than with white, middle-class, nonhandicapped students (123, 133, 149, 156, 157).

Additional critiques by educators include the observation that teachers who use corporal punishment tend to be less experienced, less thoughtful, more close minded, and less educated (154). They posit that using corporal punishment can mask such real causes of students' misbehavior as poor instruction, overcrowded classrooms, cultural and linguistic differences, emotional problems, learning disabilities, and so forth. They also feel a danger exists that students may copy the physical aggression their teachers model (40, 122, 125, 155). And corporal punishment can cause students to be truant and drop out of school, to retaliate aggressively against teachers or school property, and to displace their anger onto other convenient victims (40, 125, 130, 135, 140, 150, 155). Finally, corporal punishment can make students too anxious or too angry to learn effectively (127, 144, 155). For all these reasons, the author is opposed to the use of corporal punishment in the schools.

# Mild Punishment—
# Pros and Cons

The previous section included a discussion of the pros and cons of using various controversial forms of punishment in the classroom. This section summarizes the arguments for and against using so-called acceptable forms of mild punishment.

*Pros*    Educators who favor using punishment provide several arguments in support of their position. First, they believe punishment plays a necessary, inevitable, and pervasive role in socializing children (34) and in the daily lives of both children and adults in the real world. No matter how much educators try not to use punishment, their students are bound to have aversive experiences in the classroom even if it's just the natural consequences of their own misbehavior. Thus, the question isn't whether to punish students but rather how to punish them (35).

Second, teachers can't rely on rules alone to manage classroom behavior. Just as sanctions are necessary to make sure adults obey traffic rules, parking and smoking regulations, and other public conventions, it has been demonstrated experimentally that teachers need sanctions to back up school rules (19, 179). Students, especially young ones, need to know that they will be noticed and punished if they misbehave. Once they realize this, most students will behave appropriately without actually having to be punished.

The next argument suggests that punishment also works for students who need the experience of actually being punished to control themselves. Punishment suppresses undesirable behavior quickly and for long periods of time (35, 38, 51, 82, 84–86, 88, 92, 96–98, 101–103, 105–107, 108–110, 114, 116, 119, 120, 170, 172, 174, 181–183, 187–190). As Walters and Grusec and MacMillan, Forness, and Trumball have put it,

> Although punishment does have its undesirable side effects, they are not as detrimental as some people have suggested. Used judiciously, punishment can be quite effective in suppressing unwanted behavior, without adversely affecting desirable behavior. This excludes extremely severe punishment that is administered randomly so that the contingencies are unclear to the recipient, and that which is administered by a hostile and rejecting caretaker. (50, p. 177)

> Punishment is particularly effective if at the same time the socializing agents (e.g. teachers) provide information concerning alternative prosocial behavior . . . For example, it is not enough that a teacher reprimand a child from grabbing a toy away from another child or scold him for fighting. One must also show the child how to share the toy or ask for it politely and must reinforce (i.e., praise) the child for doing so. Such behavior competes with, and hopefully supplants, the antisocial behavior. (35, p. 92)

Educators taking this position feel that punishment can have positive side effects on students. For example, behaving more appropriately can improve their relationships with their peers and teachers. As a result, students may experience more affection and acceptance from others, which can improve their self-esteem and self-confidence (166, 178). Also, when students observe their peers being punished, they are less likely to misbehave themselves.

The final argument is that, used appropriately, punishment seldom has the undesirable side effects mentioned in the literature (178).

*Cons*   Many authors see little, if any, role for punishment in the schools. The following quote is representative of this thinking.

> If punishment works, it does so only under very precise and complicated conditions, much too complicated for us to consistently use in classrooms. The controls that one must utilize to optimize the effectiveness of punishment are not possible in day-to-day operations either within families or schools. I (and, I suspect, you) will continue to respond in punitive ways to frustrating situations. However, I don't expect that the consequence of this punitive action will have the desired effect of helping others function more productively. I therefore will be searching for alternatives. Fortunately, there are other, less complicated, more promising alternatives. (167, p. 39–40)

These educators feel punishment doesn't work because, at best, it suppresses undesirable behavior; it doesn't teach students how to behave appropriately (9, 93). Also, the effects of punishment last only so long as the risk of it is present. Once the threat of punishment is removed, students tend to revert back to their previous behavior (9, 83, 170, 183). As Clarizio states:

> Punished behavior can come back . . . How many times have you scolded students, kept them from recess, retained them after school, put them out in the hall, threatened to lower their grades, or sent them to the principal's office only to find that they engage in the very same misbehavior after a short while? (87, p. 130)

Further, they contend that some forms of punishment work best on students who need it least (60). For example, reprimanding students for misbehaving works only for students who are concerned about their teachers' opinions of them. Students who don't care are the ones more likely to misbehave and less likely to be affected by such punishment. Educators opposed to punishment also suggest that punishment doesn't increase students' intrinsic motivation to want to behave appropriately in the absence of consequences. If it did, correctional facilities for adolescents and adults would have much higher success rates than they, in fact, do. If the goal of education is to prepare students to take their places as law-abiding, moral citizens in a democracy, schools need to increase students' intrinsic motivation (9, 168, 171, 173). Finally, the improved behavior punishment produces is often illusory, merely reflecting the fact that students are more careful not to get caught, are biding their time until better opportunities present themselves, or are using other equally unacceptable forms of behavior to attain their ends.

Educators who are against using punishment point out that punishment systems can be time-consuming and disruptive. Keeping records of students' points and tokens, arguing with students who resist relinquishing tokens they have already acquired, keeping track of students' on- and off-task behavior, and the like can use up class time and would better be spent in teaching students (9, 12, 167, 175, 186).

Those opposed to punishment argue that punishment can have a negative effect on students. For example, some students copy the punitive approaches their teachers model (169, 177, 185). They add that punishing students can cause them to become more aggressive, be less concerned about learning and other school values, be overly concerned about fitting in, have a less rational attitude toward misbehavior, and be less efficient learners (7, 74, 164, 207). Punishment can also increase students' anxiety and decrease their self-esteem (57, 141, 174, 184). In addition, some students avoid their teachers and other school-related activities after they have been punished (180). Punishment can also make students resentful, rebellious, and uncooperative as well as cause them to take pleasure in undermining their teachers' authority (136). And then, punishing students can have a negative ripple effect on their peers, upsetting them, making them anxious, and causing them to be less efficient learners (60, 176).

These educators also point out that punishment can mask the real causes of student problems. Specifically, it can suppress the behavior of students with learning disabilities and/or emotional problems temporarily, thereby eliminating the need to use more appropriate techniques for helping such students. It can also coerce students who are teased and victimized because they are handicapped, members of racial or ethnic minorities, or too small, passive, or frightened to defend themselves to act as if nothing is bothering them because they fear being punished if they react angrily, physically, or loudly. And it can mask the existence of an irrelevant curriculum, overcrowded classes, and underfinanced school systems.

Finally, punishing students is unpleasurable and distasteful. It is the least desirable form of classroom management and should only be used as a last resort, if at all.

*Conclusions*   Weighing the arguments for and against punishing students, the author has arrived at three conclusions based on his review of the literature and his personal experiences. First, punishment is a pervasive, inescapable, and necessary part of life. Both in school and out, teachers, parents, and other persons in charge can't rely on rules alone to ensure that people will behave appropriately. Punishment or the threat of it is necessary for young children who are still in the first stage of moral development. It also plays a minor deterrent role in keeping honest, law-abiding individuals from succumbing to the temptation to copy someone's work, park their cars illegally, exaggerate their deductions on their income tax returns, and so on. And it is an important technique to use with those few older youngsters, adolescents, and adults who are likely to break whatever rules they think they can get away with breaking.

In particular, students in the first stage of moral development may need several experiences of mild punishment both in school and elsewhere before learning to behave as expected. For well-behaved students, the mere existence of possible punishment and its occasional use should be enough to help them behave appropriately. Yet, while punishment may be a necessary technique to manage the behavior of students who will misbehave when they think they can get away with it, it does little if anything to increase their intrinsic motivation to want to behave in the absence of consequences. These students require the techniques described in Chapter 9 that are designed to change their intrinsic motivation.

The second conclusion is that even the so-called acceptable forms of punishment can be abused. If used inappropriately or with the wrong students, punishment can have the kinds of undesirable side effects that have been reported in the literature. It can also mask the genuine reason for students' behaviors, which deprives them of the help they require. And it can be used to sustain ineffective teaching, irrelevant curriculum, overcrowded classes, and underfinanced schools.

Finally, punishment should exist more as a possibility than an actuality in the classroom. That is, its primary role should be to deter students from misbehaving because they are aware of the consequences that will result if they do. When teachers have to punish students regularly, this indicates either that they have an unusually large number of students who want to get away with things or—and much more likely—that they are resorting to using punishment to temporarily suppress behavior that could and should be handled more effectively and more pleasantly by other, nonpunitive means.

---

## Self-Quiz: On Punishment

Decide what your opinion is about the following statement, and list the reasons for your opinion. This may help you clarify your thoughts about the use of punishment to modify students' behavior.

"Punishment is an acceptable classroom management technique if used appropriately."

State whether you think each of the following techniques is appropriate in some situations with some students or inappropriate in all situations and with all students; state the reasons for your opinion.

- Rewarding incompatible behavior
- Rewarding improvement
- Using peers as models
- Planned ignoring
- Expressing disapproval/reprimanding
- Applying logical consequences
- Overcorrection
- Time-out from earning rewards
- Time-out in a time-out area
- Contingency contracting
- Harsh reprimands
- Negative practice
- Blame, shame, embarrassment, and ridicule
- Peer pressure
- Isolation/seclusion
- Corporal punishment

# Self-Management

In recent years, educators have learned that students can manage their own reinforcement systems to a far greater degree than they had originally thought. This section describes some of the ways students can apply positive and negative reinforcements to their own behavior and describes what research indicates about the effectiveness of student-managed versus teacher-managed reinforcement systems.

As the term implies, students are in charge of the consequences when they use self-management techniques. But because students generally know little about the principles of behavior management, they have to be taught how to do it, helped to get started, and supervised periodically to make sure they are doing it correctly. Thus, in a very real sense, self-management requires a collaborative effort between teachers and students.

## Using Self-Management Effectively

Practitioners of the technique usually include the following steps in a self-management approach.

1. Motivate students to want to modify their behavior through active listening, reasoning with them, and other respectful, interactive behaviors so they will cooperate voluntarily.

2. Identify the inappropriate behavior to be modified.

3. Make sure students understand why their behavior is inappropriate.

4. Help students establish a baseline of how often, how long, and in which situations students behave inappropriately.

5. Assist students in identifying an appropriate behavior that they can substitute for inappropriate ones if possible.

6. Help students set *realistic* goals for behavioral change. Discourage students from setting goals that are so unrealistic that they won't be able to earn rewards or avoid punishments.

7. Help students establish consequences that are significant to them and positive if possible, negative if necessary.

8. Teach students how to develop a system for self-observation and record-keeping.

   - Teach them how to count the number of times they do behaviors that only last for a short time, such as calling out, bringing comic books to school, pushing other students, not raising their hands to ask for help.

*Teachers need to supervise the results of their students' self-management programs.*

- Teach them how to time how long they engage in behavior that is more continuous, such as on- or off-task behavior.

- Help students develop a schedule for periodic observation that will enable them to spend as much time as possible engaged in productive learning, not self-observation. For example, a timer can be set to go off every 15 or 20 minutes, and the students can record what they were doing at the moment or observe their behavior for the next few minutes.

- Teach students how to record their observations on charts or graphs so they can monitor their behavior.

9. Supervise students periodically to make sure their observations are accurate.

10. Teach students how to evaluate their behavior so they can determine the kinds and amounts of positive and/or negative reinforcements they have earned during each observation period. Rhode, Morgan, and Young (218) taught students to evaluate the improvement in their behavior accurately by having them compare their evaluations to those of their teacher. If the two were exactly the same, the students received a bonus. If they were close, the students kept the reward they had earned.

11. Make sure students reward themselves as soon as possible after each observation period.

12. Supervise students periodically to make sure they are reinforcing themselves properly and accurately.

13. Teach students to evaluate their progress periodically and to modify their program (goals, consequences, observation schedules, and so on) when necessary.

14. Help students generalize their improved behavior to other situations and in relationships with other people.

15. Eliminate the extrinsic reinforcements, and teach students to reinforce themselves by thinking about how much better they feel, how much better they get along with others, how they stay out of trouble now that they aren't misbehaving, and other internal satisfactions.

16. Help students determine whether their behavioral improvement is maintained in the absence of extrinsic consequences.

## *Advantages*

Educators who favor the application of self-managed rather than teacher-managed consequences offer several reasons to support their position. First, they point out that self-management works as well as, if not better than, teacher-managed consequences (192–195, 197, 200, 206, 207, 210, 212–214, 218–220, 222–224). Specifically, students who are in charge of their own reinforcements are more motivated to change; rebellious and resistant students are less likely to resent the application of consequences if they are in charge of applying them; students often know better than their teachers what is and isn't rewarding and punishing to them; in some cases, only students know when they are behaving inappropriately (i.e., daydreaming, thinking about going to the bathroom in order to miss class, and so on); and, finally, students who have managed their own behavior-modification programs are more likely to maintain their improved behavior in the absence of consequences. Second, they point out that self-management has positive side effects (198, 204). In particular, it teaches students how to manage their own behavior, which is a necessary skill in the real world; it gives students a sense of being in charge of their own destiny; and students who manage their own consequences are more likely to accept responsibility for their behavior than to blame others.

These educators note that student-managed programs require less teacher time (216, 225). They add that the effects of self-managing consequences are more likely to generalize to other situations and to be maintained when the program of reinforcement is terminated than teacher-managed consequences (192, 196, 197, 199, 201, 215, 224). Finally, they comment that self-managed consequences avoid the ethical and legal issues that are sometimes involved in teacher-managed, extrinsic reinforcement programs (12, 223).

To date, research regarding the effectiveness of self-managing reinforcement programs indicates that students can modify their behavior to a considerable degree by managing their own reward systems for behaving appropriately and for fulfilling contingency contracts (115, 194, 195, 197, 200, 201, 214, 218, 224). Students can also manage their time-out from the opportunity to earn rewards (205, 208) and the duration they spend in time-out areas to some degree (203, 209, 217). Finally, they can also punish themselves for misbehaving (202).

## *Disadvantages*

Other educators believe that having students manage their own extrinsic reinforcement systems isn't as effective as its proponents claim. They argue that it's no more effective than teacher-managed consequences (211, 213), and it involves a great deal of teacher time. For instance, teachers have to train students to manage their reinforcement systems and then supervise them periodically or else students will lie, cheat, and make mistakes (216). They suggest that self-management can produce the same negative side effects as systems of external consequences, and it encourages students who aren't really motivated to change their behavior to lie and cheat in order to gain rewards and avoid punishment (197, 221). In addition, it's more effective at improving academic performance than undesirable behavior (225), and it works best with students who have already been exposed to a teacher-managed reinforcement system (191, 213). They point out that self-management also works best with students who are motivated to behave appropriately, not students who need to be taught that it's necessary to change (216, 221, 224). Finally, it doesn't increase students' intrinsic motivation to behave correctly, and it often doesn't generalize. Even when it's effective in reducing certain target behaviors, it has little or no effect on the undesirable behaviors of students that aren't included in the reinforcement program. In addition, it doesn't generalize to other situations, and when the consequences are eliminated, the improvement often disappears (191, 224, 225).

*Conclusions*   The available evidence suggests that self-management suppresses undesirable behavior as well as teacher management does; however, the effects of both approaches don't generalize very well to other situations. Also, it is unclear how long changes are maintained over time in the absence of consequences. While self-management may require somewhat less teacher time in the long run, it does take considerable teacher time to train and supervise students at the outset. Very little evidence exists regarding the positive and negative side effects claimed for the technique or the types and ages of students it works best with, but the technique does seem to be more effective in keeping students on-task than in reducing their disruptive behavior. Despite these limitations, when it's advisable to use consequences to modify students' behavior, it may be worthwhile to employ a student-managed reinforcement system before resorting to a teacher-managed one.

## *Summary*

In the real world, people conform to rules and regulations not only because they want to but also because they have to. Positive and negative consequences are a necessary and inescapable part of life both in and out of school. Using consequences to obtain students' compliance may be appropriate for young students still in the first stage of moral development. The possibility of incurring negative consequences is sometimes necessary to keep students from yielding to the temptation to misbehave, but with such students, the primary role of consequences should be to deter. Students who aren't willing to behave appropriately if they can get away with it have to know that they will have to pay the consequences of their behavior. But punishment alone isn't sufficient because it doesn't deal with the cause of the students' behavior, and it doesn't increase their intrinsic motivation to want to behave appropriately in the absence of consequences. Even when punishment suppresses behavior, it is an abuse of teacher authority to punish students whose misbehavior is caused by other factors besides an unwillingness to conform to rules and regulations or an inability to resist temptations.

## *Activities*

A. For each of the following behavior problems, decide whether the use of consequences to modify the behavior:
   a. would definitely be appropriate
   b. might be appropriate
   c. might be inappropriate
   d. would definitely be inappropriate

B. Give the reasons for your opinions.

   1. A 13-year-old student becomes angry and defensive whenever he is criticized.

   2. A 17-year-old plays the clown.

   3. A 7-year-old student has such a short attention span that she begins to talk to her neighbors, look or wander around the room, and so on before the seatwork time is half over.

   4. A 9-year-old brings electronic games to class although this is against the rules.

   5. An 11-year-old rips up her artwork if she isn't satisfied with it.

   6. A 14-year-old refuses to do remedial work at his level, claiming it's too easy.

   7. A 6-year-old takes things from other students' cubbies.

   8. After failing the last three tests, a 15-year-old has been cutting class two to four times a week.

   9. An 8-year-old constantly talks to his neighbor despite being told not to.

   10. A 12-year-old regularly comes to class without her homework, claiming she left it at home, lost it, left her books in school, and so forth.

# *References*

REWARDING INCOMPATIBLE BEHAVIOR

1. Ayllon, T., & Roberts, M. D. (1974). Eliminating discipline problems by strengthening academic performance. *Journal of Applied Behavior Analysis, 7,* 71–76.

2. Campbell-Goymer, N., & Rickard, H. C. (1981). Academic contracting with emotionally disturbed children. *Psychological Reports, 48,* 605–606.

3. La Vigna, G. W., & Donnellan-Walsh, A. (1976). *Alternatives to Punishment in the Control of Undesirable Behavior.* Paper presented at the Annual Southern California Conference on Behavior Modification. California State University, Los Angeles.

4. Masden, C. H., Becker, U. C., & Thomas, D. R. (1968). Rules, praise and ignoring: Elements of elementary classroom control. *Journal of Applied Behavior Analysis, 1,* 139–150.

5. Twardosz, S., & Sajwaj, T. (1972). Multiple effects of a procedure to increase sitting in a hyperactive, retarded boy. *Journal of Applied Behavior Analysis, 5,* 73–78.


REWARDING IMPROVEMENT

6. Bolstad, O. D., & Johnson, S. M. (1972). Self-regulation in the modification of disruptive classroom behavior. *Journal of Applied Behavior Analysis, 5,* 443–454.

7. Deitz, S. M., & Repp, R. (1973). Decreasing classroom misbehavior through DRL schedules of reinforcement. *Journal of Applied Behavior Analysis, 6,* 457–463.


USING PEERS AS MODELS

8. Broden, H., Bruce, C., Mitchell, M. A., Carter, V., & Hall, R. V. (1970). Effects of teacher attention on attending behavior of two boys at adjacent desks. *Journal of Applied Behavior Analysis, 3,* 199–203.

9. Brophy, J. E., & Putnam, J. C. (1978). *Classroom Management in the Elementary Grades.* ERIC ED 167 537.

10. Charles, C. M. (1981). *Building Classroom Discipline: From Models to Practice.* White Plains, NY: Longman.

11. Clarizio, H. F. (1986). *Toward Positive Classroom Discipline* (3rd ed.). New York: Wiley & Sons.

12. Long, J. D., & Frye, H. V. (1981). *Making It Till Friday: A Guide to Successful Classroom Management.* Princeton: Princeton Book Company.

13. Sabatino, D. A. (1987). Preventive discipline as a practice in special education. *Teaching Exceptional Children, 19* (4), 8–11.

PLANNED IGNORING

14. Becker, W. C., Masden, C. H., Arnold, C. R., & Thomas, D. R. (1967). The contingent use of teacher attention and praising in reducing classroom behavior problems. *Journal of Special Education, 1,* 287–307.

15. Brown, P., & Elliot, R. (1965). Control of aggression in a nursery school class. *Journal of Experimental Child Psychology, 2,* 102–107.

16. Hall, R. V., Fox, R., Willard, D., Goldsmith, L., Emerson, M., Owen, M., Davis, F., & Porcia, E. (1971). The teacher as observer and experimentor in the modification of disputing and talking-out behaviors. *Journal of Applied Behavior Analysis, 4,* 141–149.

17. Jones, F., & Miller, W. H. (1971). *The Effective Use of Negative Attention for Reducing Group Disruption in Special Elementary Classrooms.* Department of Psychiatry, University of California at Los Angeles.

18. Kazdin, A. E. (1973). The effect of vicarious reinforcement on attentive behavior in the classroom. *Journal of Applied Behavior Analysis, 6,* 71–78.

19. Masden, C. H., Becker, W. C., & Thomas, D. R. (1968). Rules, praise and ignoring: Elements of elementary classroom control. *Journal of Applied Behavior Analysis, 1,* 139–150.

20. Masden, C. H., Becker, W. C., Thomas, D. R., Koser, L., & Plager, E. (1968). An analysis of the reinforcing function of 'sit down' commands. In R. K. Parker (Ed.), *Readings in Educational Psychology.* Boston: Allyn & Bacon.

21. O'Leary, K. D., Kaufman, K. F., Kass, R. E., & Drabman, R. S. (1970). The effects of loud and soft reprimands on the behavior of disruptive students. *Exceptional Children, 37,* 145–155.

22. Patterson, G. R. (1965). An application of conditioning techniques to the control of a hyperactive child. In L. P. Ullman & L. Krasner (Eds.), *Case Studies in Behavior Modification.* New York: Holt, Rinehart & Winston.

23. Warren, S. A. (1971). Behavior modification—Boon, bane or both? *Mental Retardation, 9,* 2.

24. Zimmerman, E. H., & Zimmerman, J. (1962). The alteration of behavior in a special class situation. *Journal of Experimental Analysis of Behavior, 5,* 59–60.


DEFINING PUNISHMENT

25. Azrin, N. H., & Holz, W. C. (1966). Punishment. In W. K. Honig (Ed.), *Operant Behavior: Area of Research and Application.* New York: Appleton-Century-Crofts.

26. Burchard, J. D., & Barrera, F. (1972). An analysis of time-out and response cost in a programmed environment. *Journal of Applied Behavior Analysis, 51,* 271–282.

27. Favell, J. E., McGimsey, J. S., & Jones, M. L. (1978). The use of physical restraint in the treatment of self-injury and positive reinforcement. *Journal of Applied Behavior Analysis, 11,* 225–241.

28. Lovaas, I. O., & Bucher, B. D. (1974). *Perspectives in Behavior Modification with Deviant Children.* Englewood Cliffs, NJ: Prentice-Hall.

PROVIDING A RATIONAL COGNITIVE STRUCTURE

29. Chayne, J. A., & Walters, R. H. (1969). Intensity of punishment, timing of punishment, and cognitive structure as determinants of response inhibition. *Journal of Experimental Child Psychology, 7,* 231–244.

30. MacMillan, D. L., Forness, S., & Trumbull, B. M. (1973). The role of punishment in the classroom. *Exceptional Children, 40,* 85–96.

31. Parke, R. D. (1969). Effectiveness of punishment as an interaction of intensity, timing, and cognitive structuring. *Child Development, 49,* 213–235.

32. Parke, R. D. (1977). Punishment in children: Effects, side effects, and alternative strategies. In H. L. Hom & P. A. Robins (Eds.), *Psychological Processes in Early Education.* New York: Academic Press.

ALTERNATIVE BEHAVIORS

33. Anderson, L. M., Evertson, C. M., & Emmer, E. T. (1979). *Dimensions in Classroom Management Derived from Recent Research.* ERIC ED 175 860.

34. Aronfreed, J. M. (1968). Aversive control of socialization. In W. J. Arnold (Ed.), *National Symposium on Motivation 1968.* Lincoln, NE: University of Nebraska Press.

35. MacMillan, D. L., Forness, S. R., & Trumbull, B. M. (1973). The role of punishment in the classroom. *Exceptional Children, 40,* 85–96.

36. Walters, R. H., & Parke, R. D. (1967). The influence of punishment and related disciplinary techniques on the social behavior of children: Theory and empirical findings. In B. Maher (Ed.), *Progress in Experimental Personality Research, Vol. 4.* New York: Academic Press.

INTENSITY

37. Aronfreed, J. M., & Leff, R. (1963). *Effects of Intensity of Punishment and Complexity of Discrimination upon the Learning of an Internalized Inhibition.* Unpublished manuscript. University of Pennsylvania, College Park, PA.

38. Arzin, N., & Holz, W. (1966). Punishment. In W. K. Honig (Ed.), *Operant Behavior: Areas of Research and Application.* New York: Appleton-Century-Crofts.

39. Burchard, J. D., & Barrera, F. (1972). An analysis of time-out and response cost in a programmed environment. *Journal of Applied Behavior Analysis, 5,* 271–282.

40. Gnagey, W. J. (1981). *Motivating Classroom Discipline.* New York: Macmillan.

41. Hobbs, S. A., Forehand, R., & Murray, R. G. (1978). Effects of various durations of time-out on the non-compliant behavior of children. *Behavior Therapy, 9,* 652–656.

42. Morgan, D. P., & Jenson, W. R. (1988). *Teaching Behaviorally Disordered Students: Preferred Practice.* Columbus, OH: Charles E. Merrill.

43. Solomon, R. L. (1964). Punishment. *American Psychologist, 19,* 239–253.

CONSISTENCY

44. Banks, R. K. (1966). Persistence to continuous punishment following intermittent training. *Journal of Experimental Psychology, 71,* 373–377.

45. Deur, J. L., & Parke, R. D. (1970). Effects of inconsistent punishment on aggression in children. *Developmental Psychology, 2* (5).

46. Ott, J. F. (1958). Teaching the emotionally disturbed. *National Association of Secondary School Principals Bulletin No. 238.*

47. Parke, R. D., & Sawin, D. B. (1975). *The Effects of Inter-agent Inconsistent Discipline and Aggressive Children.* Unpublished manuscript. Fels Research Institute, Wayne State University, Yellow Springs, OH.

48. Stouwie, R. J. (1972). An experimental study of adult dominance and warmth, conflicting verbal instruction and children's moral behavior. *Child Development, 43,* 959–972.

49. Tanner, L. N. (1978). *Classroom Discipline for Effective Teaching and Learning.* New York: Holt, Rinehart & Winston.

50. Walters, G. C., & Grusec, J. E. (1977). *Punishment.* San Francisco: W. H. Freeman.

51. Walters, R., Parke, R., & Cane, V. (1965). Timing of punishment and the observation of consequences to others as determinants of response inhibition. *Journal of Experimental Child Psychology, 2,* 10–30.

TIMING

52. Aronfreed, J., & Reber, A. (1965). Internalized behavioral suppression and the timing of social punishment. *Journal of Personality and Social Psychology, 1,* 3–16.

53. Parke, R. D. (1970). The role of punishment in the socialization process. In R. A. Hoppe, G. A. Milton, & E. Simmel (Eds.), *Early Experiences in the Process of Socialization.* New York: Academic Press.

ACCEPTABLE CONSEQUENCES

The listings below discuss expressing disapproval of students' actions or behavior.

54. Becker, W., Engelmann, S., & Thomas, D. (1975). *Teaching 1: Classroom Management.* Chicago: Research Press.

55. Berliner, D. (1978). *Changing Academic Learning Time: Clinical Intervention in Four Classrooms.* Paper presented at the annual meeting of the American Education Research Association, Toronto, Canada.

56. Cangelosi, J. S. (1988). *Classroom Management Strategies: Gaining and Maintaining Students' Cooperation.* White Plains, NY: Longman.

57. Fisher, C. W., Berliner, D. C., Filby, N. N., Marliave, R., Cahen, L. S., & Dishaw, M. M. (1980). Teaching behaviors, academic learning time, and student achievement: An overview. In C. Denham and A. Lieberman (Eds.), *Time to Learn.* Washington, DC: National Institute of Education.

58. Ginott, H. G. (1972). *Teacher and Child.* New York: Avon.

59. Hall, R. V., Axelrod, S., Foundopoulos, M., Campbell, R. A., & Cranston, S. S. (1971). The effective use of punishment to modify behavior in the classroom. *Educational Technology, 11,* 24–26.

60. Kounin, J. S. (1970). *Discipline and Group Management in Classrooms.* New York: Holt, Rinehart & Winston.

61. Masden, C. H., Jr., Becker, W. C., Thomas, D. R., Koser, L., & Plazer, E. (1968). An analysis of the reinforcing function of 'sit down' commands. In R. K. Parker (Ed.), *Readings in Educational Psychology.* Boston: Allyn & Bacon.

62. O'Leary, K. D., & Becker, W. C. (1968). The effects of the intensity of a teacher's reprimands on children's behavior. *Journal of School Psychology, 7,* 8–11.

63. O'Leary, K. D., Kaufman, K. F., Kass, R. E., & Drabman, R. S. (1970). The effects of loud and soft reprimands on the behavior of disruptive students. *Exceptional Children, 37,* 145–155.

64. Spear, P. S. (1970). Motivational effects of praise and criticism on children's learning. *Developmental Psychology, 3* (1), 124–132.

65. Thomas, D. R., Becker, W. C., & Armstrong, M. (1968). Production and elimination of disruptive classroom behavior by systematically varying teachers' behavior. *Journal of Applied Behavior Analysis, 1,* 35–45.

66. Thomas, J. D., Presland, I. E., Grant, M. D., & Glynn, T. L. (1978). Natural rates of teacher approval and disapproval in grade 7 classrooms. *Journal of Applied Behavior Analysis, 11* (1), 91–94.

67. Turco, T. L., & Elliott, S. N. (1986). Assessment of students' acceptability ratings of teacher-initiated interventions for classroom misbehavior. *Journal of School Psychology, 24,* 277–283.

68. Van Horn, K. L. (1982). *The Utah Pupil/Teacher Self-Concept Program: Teacher Strategies that Invite Improvement of Pupil and Teacher Self-Concept.* Paper presented at the annual meeting of the American Educational Research Association, New York.

69. Van Houten, R., Mau, P. A., MacKenzie-Keating, S. E., Sameoto, D., & Colavecchia, B. (1980). An analysis of some variables influencing the effectiveness of reprimands. *Journal of Applied Behavior Analysis, 15,* 65–83.

70. White, M. A. (1975). Natural rates of teacher approval and disapproval in the classroom. *Journal of Applied Behavior Analysis, 8* (4), 367–372.

The citations that follow discuss the topic of applying logical consequences.

71. Dreikurs, R., Grunwald, B., & Pepper, F. (1982). *Maintaining Sanity in the Classroom* (2nd ed.). New York: Harper & Row.

72. Glasser, W. (1969). *Schools Without Failure.* New York: Harper & Row.

73. Weber, W. A., Roff, L. A., Crawford, J., & Robinson, C. (1983). *Classroom Management: Reviews of the Teacher Education and Research Literature.* Princeton: Educational Testing Service.

OVERCORRECTION

74. Axelrod, S., Branter, J. P., & Meddock, T. D. (1978). Overcorrection: A review and critical analysis. *Journal of Special Education, 12,* 367–391.

75. Arzin, N. H., & Powers, M. A. (1975). Eliminating classroom disturbances of emotionally disturbed children by positive practice procedures. *Behavior Therapy, 6,* 525–534.

76. Barton, E. J., & Osborne, J. G. (1978). The development of classroom sharing by a teacher using positive practice. *Behavior Modification, 2,* 231–250.

77. Doleys, S. M., Wells, K. C., Hobbs, S. A., Roberts, M. W., & Cartelli, L. M. (1976). The effects of social punishment on non-compliance: A comparison of time-out and positive practice. *Journal of Applied Behavior Analysis, 9,* 471–482.

78. Foxx, R. M., & Arzin, N. H. (1972). Restitution: A method of eliminating aggressive-disruptive behavior of mentally retarded and brain damaged patients. *Behavior Research and Therapy, 10,* 15–27.

79. Hobbs, S. A. (1976). Modifying stereotyped behavior by overcorrection: A critical review. *Rehabilitation Psychology, 23,* 1–11.

80. Matson, J. L., Ollendick, T. H., & Martin, J. E. (1979). Overcorrection: A long-term follow-up. *Journal of Behavior Therapy and Experimental Psychiatry, 10,* 11–13.

81. Osborne, J. G. (1976). Overcorrection and behavior therapy: A reply to Hobbs. *Rehabilitation Psychology, 23,* 13–31.

TIME-OUT

82. Bean, A. W., & Roberts, M. W. (1981). The effects of time-out release contingencies on changes in child non-compliance. *Journal of Abnormal Child Psychology, 9,* 95–105.

83. Bereiter, C., & Engelmann, S. (1966). *Teaching Disadvantaged Children in the Preschool.* Englewood Cliffs, NJ: Prentice-Hall.

84. Bostow, D. E., & Bailey, J. B. (1969). Modification of severe disruptive and aggressive behavior using brief time-out and reinforcement procedures. *Journal of Applied Behavior Analysis, 2,* 31–37.

85. Broden, M., Hall, R. V., Dunlap, A., & Clark, R. (1970). Effects of teacher attention and a token reinforcement system in a junior high school special education class. *Exceptional Children, 36,* 341–349.

86. Burchard, J. D. (1967). Systematic socialization: A programmed environment for the habilitation of antisocial retardates. *Psychological Records, 17,* 461–476.

87. Clarizio, H. F. (1980). *Toward Positive Classroom Discipline* (3rd ed.). New York: John Wiley.

88. Clark, H. B., Rowburry, T., Baer, A. M., & Baer, D. M. (1973). Time-out as a punishing stimulus in continuous and intermittent schedules. *Journal of Applied Behavior Analysis, 6,* 443–455.

89. Foxx, R. M., & Shapiro, S. T. (1978). The time-out ribbon: A nonexclusionary time-out procedure. *Journal of Applied Behavior Analysis, 11,* 125–136.

90. Gast, D. L., & Nelson, C. M. (1977). Legal and ethical considerations for the use of time-out in special education settings. *Journal of Special Education, 11* (4), 457–467.

91. Lakey, B. B., McNess, M. P., & McNess, M. C. (1973). Control of an obscene 'verbal tic' through time-out in an elementary classroom. *Journal of Applied Behavior Analysis, 6,* 101–104.

92. LeBlanc, J. M., Busby, K. H., & Thomson, C. L. (1974). The function of time-out for changing the aggressive behaviors of a preschool child: A multiple base line analysis. In R. Ulrich, T. Stachnik, & J. Mabry (Eds.), *Control of Human Behavior, Vol. 3.* Glenview, IL: Scott, Foresman.

93. Long, J. D., & Frye, V. H. (1981). *Making It Till Friday: A Guide to Successful Classroom Management* (2nd ed.). Princeton: Princeton Book Company.

94. Mauer, R. E. (1985). *Elementary Discipline Handbook: Solutions for the K–8 Teacher.* West Nyack, NY: Center for Applied Research in Education.

95. Morgan, D. P., & Jenson, D. P. (1988). *Teaching Behaviorally Disordered Students: Preferred Practices.* Columbus, OH: Charles E. Merrill.

96. Pease, G. A., & Tyler, O. T., Jr. (1979). Self-regulation of time-out duration in the modification of disruptive classroom behavior. *Psychology in the Schools, 16* (27), 101–105.

97. Phillips, E. L. (1968). Achievement place: Token reinforcement procedures in a home-style rehabilitation setting for 'predelinquent' boys. *Journal of Applied Behavior Analysis, 3,* 213–223.

98. Porterfield, J. K., Herbert-Jackson, E., & Risley, T. R. (1976). Contingent observation: An effective and acceptable procedure for reducing disruptive behavior of young children in a group setting. *Journal of Applied Behavior Analysis, 9,* 55–64.

99. Powell, T. H., & Powell, I. Q. (1982). The use and abuse of using time-out procedures for disruptive pupils. *Pointer, 26,* 18–22.

100. Redl, F., & Wattenberg, W. (1959). *Mental Hygiene in Teaching* (2nd ed.). New York: Harcourt, Brace.

101. Roberts, M. W. (1982). The effects of warned versus unwarned time-out procedures on child noncompliance. *Child and Family Behavior Therapy, 4,* 37–53.

102. Sloane, H. N., Buckholdt, D. R., Jenson, W. R., & Crandal, J. A. (1979). *Structured Teaching: A Design for Classroom Management and Instruction.* Champaign, IL: Research Press.

103. Tyler, V. O., & Brown, G. D. (1967). The use of swift brief isolation as a group control device for institutionalized delinquents. *Behavior Research and Therapy, 5,* 1–9.

104. Wallen, C. J., & Wallen, L. L. (1978). *Effective Classroom Management.* Boston: Allyn & Bacon.

105. Wasik, B. H., Senn, K., Welch, R. H., & Cooper, B. R. (1969). Behavior modification with culturally deprived school children: Two case studies. *Journal of Applied Behavior Analysis, 2,* 181–194.

106. Weber, W. A., Roff, L. A., Crawford, J., & Robinson, C. (1983). *Classroom Management: Reviews of the Teacher Education and Research Literature.* Princeton: Educational Testing Service.

107. White, G. D., Nielson, G., & Johnson, S. M. (1972). Time-out duration and the suppression of deviant behavior in children. *Journal of Applied Behavior Analysis, 5,* 111–120.

CONTINGENCY CONTRACTING

108. Arwood, B., Williams, R. L., & Long, J. D. (1974). The effects of behavior contracts and behavior proclamations on social conduct and academic achievement in a ninth grade English class. *Adolescence, 9,* 425–436.

109. Cantrell, R. P., Cantrell, M. L., Huddleston, C. M., & Woolridge, R. L. (1969). Contingency contracting with school problems. *Journal of Applied Behavior Analysis, 2,* 215–220.

110. Clark, L. N. (1978). Let's make a deal: Contingency contracting with adolescents. *American Secondary Education, 8,* 12–23.

111. De Risi, W., & Butz, G. (1975). *Writing Behavioral Contracts.* Champaign, IL: Research Press.

112. Good, T. L., Biddle, B. J., & Brophy, J. E. (1975). *Teachers Make a Difference.* New York: Holt, Rinehart & Winston.

113. Hackney, H. (1974). Applying behavior contracts to chronic problems. *School Counselor, 22,* 23–30.

114. Homme, L. (1966). Human motivation and the environment. In N. Haring & R. Whelan (Eds.), *The Learning Environment: Relationship to Behavior Modification and Implications for Special Education.* Laurence, KS: University Press of Kansas.

115. Homme, L., Csanyi, A. P., Gonzales, M. A., & Rechs, J. R. (1970). *How to Use Contingency Contracting in the Classroom*. Champaign, IL: Research Press.

116. Sapp, G. L. (1971). *The Application of Contingency Management Systems to the Classroom Behavior of Negro Adolescents*. Paper presented at the annual meeting of the American Personnel and Guidance Association, Atlantic City, NJ.

117. Sulzer-Azaroff, B., & Mayer, G. (1977). *Applying Behavior Analysis Procedures with Children*. New York: Holt, Rinehart & Winston.

118. Tharp, R. G., & Wentzel, R. J. (1969). *Behavior Modification in the Natural Environment*. New York: Academic Press.

119. White-Blackburn, G., Semb, S., & Semb, G. (1977). The effects of a good-behavior contract on the classroom behavior of sixth grade students. *Journal of Applied Behavior Analysis, 10,* 312.

120. Williams, R. L., Long, J. D., & Yoakley, R. W. (1972). The utility of behavior contracts and behavior proclamations with advantaged senior high school students. *Journal of School Psychology, 10,* 329–338.

UNACCEPTABLE AND CONTROVERSIAL PUNISHMENTS

121. Anderson, H. H., & Brewer, J. E. (1946). Studies of teachers' classroom personalities II: Effects of teachers' dominative and integrative contacts on children's classroom behavior. *Applied Psychological Monographs, 8.*

122. Altman, R., & Talkington, L. W. (1971). Modeling: An alternative behavior modification approach for retardates. *Mental Retardation, 9* (3), 20–23.

123. Barba, L. (1979). *A Survey of the Literature on the Attitudes Toward the Administration of Corporal Punishment in Schools*. ERIC ED 186 538.

124. Becker, W. C., Engelmann, S., & Thomas, D. *Teaching I: Classroom Management*. Chicago: Science Research Associates.

125. Bongiovanni, A. F. (1977). A review of research on the effects of punishment: Implications for corporal punishment in the schools. In Wise, J. H. (Ed.), *Proceedings: Conference on Corporal Punishment in the Schools: A National Debate*. ERIC ED 144 185.

126. Bongiovanni, A. F. (1979). An analysis of research on punishment and its relation to the use of corporal punishment in schools. In I. A. Hyman & J. Wise (Eds.), *Corporal Punishment in American Education*. Philadelphia: Temple University Press.

127. Clarke, J., et al. (1984). *Analysis of Recent Corporal Punishment Cases Reported in National Newspapers*. Paper presented at the annual convention of the National Association of School Psychologists, Philadelphia.

128. Cryan, J. R. (1987). The banning of corporal punishment: In child care, school and other educative settings in the U.S. *Childhood Education, 53* (3), 145–153.

129. Dobson, J. (1970). *Dare to Discipline*. Wheaton, IL: Tyndale House Publishers.

130. Dubanoski, R. A., et al. (1983). Corporal punishment in schools: Myths, problems and alternatives. *Child Abuse and Neglect, 7* (3), 271–278.

131. Englemann, S. (1969). *Preventing Failure in the Primary Grades.* New York: Simon & Schuster.

132. Forness, S. R., & Sinclair, E. (1984). Avoiding corporal punishment in schools: Issues for school counselors. *Elementary School Guidance and Counseling, 18* (4), 268–275.

133. Guess, D., Helmsetter, E., Turnbull, R. H., & Knowlton, S. (1987). *Use of Aversive Procedures with Persons Who Are Disabled: A Historical Review and Critical Analysis.* Seattle: Association for Persons with Severe Handicaps.

134. Henson, K. T. (1985). Corporal punishment: Ten popular myths. *High School Journal, 69* (2), 107–109.

135. Hyman, I. A., & Wise, J. H. (Eds.). (1979). *Corporal Punishment in American Schools.* Philadelphia: Temple University Press.

136. Jones, F. H. (1987). *Positive Classroom Discipline.* New York: McGraw-Hill.

137. Kauffman, J. M., Pullen, P. L., & Akers, E. (1986). Classroom management: Teacher-child-peer relationships. *Focus on Exceptional Children, 19* (1), 1–10.

138. Kelly, P. C., Weir, M. R., & Fearnow, R. G. (1985). A survey of parental opinions of corporal punishment in schools. *Journal of Developmental and Behavioral Pediatrics, 6* (3), 143–145.

139. Kessler, G. (1985). Spanking in schools: Deterrent or barbarism? *Childhood Education, 61* (3), 175–176.

140. Kinnard, K. W., & Rust, J. O. (1981). Corporal punishment in Tennessee schools. *Tennessee Education, 7* (2), 11–17.

141. Kounin, J., & Gump, P. (1961). The comparative influence of punitive and non-punitive teachers on children's concept of school misconduct. *Journal of Educational Psychology, 52,* 44–49.

142. Litow, L., & Pumroy, D. (1975). A brief review of classroom oriented contingencies. *Journal of Applied Behavior Analysis, 8,* 341–347.

143. Mauer, A. (1977). All in the name of the 'last resort.' In J. H. Wise (Ed.), *Proceedings: Conference on Corporal Punishment in the Schools: A National Debate.* ERIC ED 144 185.

144. Mauer, A., & Wallerstein, J. S. (1984). *The Influence of Corporal Punishment on Learning: A Statistical Analysis.* Berkeley, CA: Generation Books.

145. Nash, R. (1963). Corporal punishment in an age of violence. *Educational Theory, 13,* 295–308.

146. Nevin, A., Johnson, D. W., & Johnson, R. (1982). Effects of group and individual contingencies on academic performance and social relation of special needs students. *Journal of Social Psychology, 116* (1), 41–59.

147. Newbold, K. R. (1976). Use of corporal punishment in North Carolina public schools. In R. S. Welsh, et al., *The Supreme Court Spanking Ruling: An Issue in Debate*. ERIC ED 151 644.

148. Patterson, J. (1974). How popular is the paddle? *Phi Delta Kappan, 55,* 707.

149. Ramella, R. (1974). Anatomy of discipline: Should punishment be corporal? *PTA Magazine, 67,* 24–27.

150. Redd, W. H., Morris, E. K., & Martin, J. A. (1975). Effects of positive and negative adult-child interaction on children's social preferences. *Journal of Experimental Child Psychology, 19,* 153–164.

151. Reinholz, L. (1976). A practical defense of corporal punishment. In R. S. Welsh, et al., *The Supreme Court Spanking Ruling: An Issue in Debate*. ERIC ED 151 644.

152. Rose, T. L. (1981). The corporal punishment cycle: A behavioral analysis of the maintenance of corporal punishment in schools. *Education and Treatment of Children, 4,* 157–169.

153. Rose, T. L. (1984). Current uses of corporal punishment in American public schools. *Journal of Educational Psychology, 76* (3), 427–444.

154. Rust, J. O., & Kinnard, K. Q. (1983). Personality characteristics of the users of corporal punishment in the schools. *Journal of School Psychology, 21,* 91–105.

155. Sabatino, D. A., Sabatino, A. C., & Mann, L. (1983). *Discipline and Behavioral Management: A Handbook of Tactics, Strategies, and Programs*. Rockville, MD: Aspen.

156. Smith, J. D., Polloway, E. A., & West, G. K. (1979). Corporal punishment and its implications for exceptional children. *Journal for Exceptional Children, 45* (4), 264–268.

157. Stevens, L. B. (1983). *Suspension and Corporal Punishment of Students in the Cleveland Public Schools, 1981–1982*. Cleveland, OH: Office of School Monitoring and Community Relations.

158. Strike, K., & Soltis, J. (1986). Who broke the fish tank? And other ethical dilemmas. *Instructor, 95,* 36–37.

159. Sulzer-Azaroff, B., & Mayer, G. R. (1977). *Applying Behavior Analysis Procedures with Children and Youth*. New York: Holt, Rinehart & Winston.

160. Thomas, D. R., Becker, W. C., & Armstrong, M. (1968). Production and elimination of disruptive behavior by systematically varying teachers' behavior. *Journal of Applied Behavior Analysis, 1,* 35–45.

161. Tuhus, M. (1987). It's time we stop paddling kids. *Instructor, 95* (7), 16–19.

162. Van Dyke, H. T. (1984). Corporal punishments in our schools. *Clearing House, 57,* 296–300.

163. Vrederoe, L. E. (1974). Embarrassment and ridicule. In *Discipline in the Classroom* (rev. ed.). Washington, DC: National Education Association.

164. Welsh, R. S. (1985). Spanking: A grand old American tradition. *Children Today, 17*, 25–29.

165. Wright, D., & Moles, O. (1985). *Legal Issues in Educational Order: Principals' Perceptions of School Discipline Policies and Practices.* Paper presented in the annual meeting of the American Educational Research Association, Chicago.

MILD PUNISHMENT: PROS AND CONS

166. Drabman, R., & Lakey, B. (1974). Feedback in classroom behavior modification: Effects on the target child and her classmates. *Journal of Applied Behavior Analysis, 7*, 591–598.

167. Englander, M. E. (1986). *Strategies for Classroom Discipline.* New York: Praeger.

168. Garner, H. S. (1976). A truce in the war for the child. *Exceptional Children, 42* (6), 315–320.

169. Gelfand, D. M., Hartmann, D. P., Lamb, A. K., Smith, C. L., Makan, M. A., & Paul, S. C. (1974). The effects of adult models and descriptive alternatives on children's choice of behavior management techniques. *Child Development, 45*, 585–593.

170. Iwata, B. A., & Bailey, J. S. (1974). Reward vs. cost token systems: An analysis of the effects on students and teachers. *Journal of Applied Behavior Analysis, 7*, 567–576.

171. Johnson, L. V., & Bany, M. A. (1976). *Classroom Management: Theory and Skill Training.* New York: Macmillan.

172. Kalish, H. I. (1981). *From Behavioral Science to Behavior Modification.* New York: McGraw-Hill.

173. Lawrence, E. A., & Winschel, J. F. (1975). Locus of control: Implications for special education. *Exceptional Children, 41*, 483–489.

174. Mayer, G. R., Sulzer, B., & Cody, J. (1968). The use of punishment in modifying student behavior. *Journal of Special Education, 2*, 323–328.

175. McLaughlin, F. T., & Malaby, J. (1972). Reducing and measuring inappropriate verbalizations in a token classroom. *Journal of Applied Behavior Analysis, 5*, 329–333.

176. McManis, D. L. (1967). Marble sorting persistence in mixed verbal incentive and performance level pairings. *American Journal of Mental Deficiency, 71*, 811–817.

177. Mischel, W., & Grusec, J. E. (1966). Determinants of the rehearsal and transmission of neutral and aversive behaviors. *Journal of Personality and Social Psychology, 3*, 197–205.

178. Newsom, C., Favell, J. E., & Rincover, A. (1983). Side effects of punishment. In S. Axelrod & J. Apsche (Eds.), *The Effects of Punishment on Human Behavior.* New York: Academic Press.

179. O'Leary, D., Becker, W., Evans, M., & Saudergas, R. (1969). A token reinforcement program in a public school: A replication and systematic analysis. *Journal of Applied Behavior Analysis, 2,* 3–13.

180. Oliver, S. D., West, R. C., & Sloane, N. H. (1974). Some effects on human behavior of aversive events. *Behavior Therapy, 5,* 481–493.

181. Pace, D. M., & Foreman, S. G. (1982). Variables related to the effectiveness of response cost. *Psychology in the Schools, 19* (3), 365–370.

182. Pazulinec, R., Meyerrose, M., & Sajwaj, T. (1983). Punishment via response cost. In S. Axelrod and J. Apsche (Eds.), *The Effects of Punishment on Human Behavior.* New York: Academic Press.

183. Phillips, E. L., Phillips, E. A., Fixsen, D. L., & Wolf, M. M. (1971). Achievement place: Token reinforcement procedures in a home-styled rehabilitation setting for predelinquent boys. *Journal of Applied Behavior Analysis, 4,* 45–59.

184. Ryan, B. A. (1979). A case against behavior modification in the 'ordinary' classroom. *Journal of School Psychology, 17* (2), 131–136.

185. Steuer, F. B., Applefield, J. M., & Smith, R. (1971). Televised aggression and the interpersonal aggression of preschool children. *Journal of Experimental Child Psychology, 11,* 442–447.

186. Sulzer, B., & Mayer, G. B. (1972). *Behavior Modification Procedures for School Personnel.* Hinsdale, IL: Dryden Press.

187. Swanson, L. (1979). Removal of positive reinforcement to alter LD adolescents' preacademic problems. *Psychology in the Schools, 16* (2), 286–292.

188. Walker, H. M. (1983). Application of response costs in school setting: Outcomes, issues and recommendations. *Exceptional Education Quarterly, 3,* 47–55.

189. Warren, S. A. (1971). Behavior modification—Boon, bane, or both? *Mental Retardation, 9,* 2.

190. Witt, J. C., Elliot, S. N. (1982). The response cost lottery: A time efficient and effective classroom intervention. *Journal of School Psychology, 20,* 155–161.

SELF-MANAGEMENT

191. Baer, D. M., Fowler, S. A., & Carden-Smith, L. (1984). Using reinforcement and independent grading to promote and maintain task accuracy in a mainstreamed class. *Analysis and Intervention in Developmental Disabilities, 4,* 157–169.

192. Bolstad, O. D., & Johnson, S. M. (1972). Self-regulation in the modification of disruptive classroom behavior. *Journal of Applied Behavior Analysis, 5,* 443–454.

193. Broden, H., Hall, R. V., & Mitts, B. (1971). The effect of self-recording on the classroom behavior of two eighth grade students. *Journal of Applied Behavior Analysis, 4,* 191–199.

194. Clement, P. W. (1973). Training children to be their own behavior therapists. *Journal of School Health, 43,* 615–620.

195. Drabman, R. S., Spitalnik, R., & O'Leary, K. D. (1973). Teaching self-control to disruptive children. *Journal of Abnormal Psychology, 82,* 10–16.

196. Epstein, R., & Goss, C. M. (1978). A self-control procedure for the maintenance of nondisruptive behavior in an elementary school child. *Behavior Therapy, 9,* 109–117.

197. Felixbrod, J., & O'Leary, K. D. (1973). Effects of reinforcement on children's academic behavior as a function of self-determined and externally imposed contingencies. *Journal of Applied Behavior Analysis, 6,* 241–250.

198. Frith, G. H., & Armstrong, S. W. (1986). Self-monitoring for behavior disordered students. *Teaching Exceptional Children, 18,* 144–148.

199. Glynn, E. L. (1970). Classroom applications of self-determined reinforcement. *Journal of Applied Behavior Analysis, 3,* 123–132.

200. Glynn, E. L., & Thomas, J. D. (1974). Effects of cueing on self-control of classroom behavior. *Journal of Applied Behavior Analysis, 7,* 299–306.

201. Glynn, E. L., Thomas, J. D., & Shee, S. M. (1973). Behavioral self-control of on-task behavior in an elementary classroom. *Journal of Applied Behavior Analysis, 6,* 105–114.

202. Grusec, J. E., & Kuczynski, L. (1977). Teaching children to punish themselves and effects on subsequent compliance. *Child Development, 48,* 1296–1300.

203. Hall, N. E. (1966). The youth development project: A school based delinquency prevention program. *Journal of School Health, 36,* 97–103.

204. Henker, B., Whalen, C. K., & Henshaw, S. P. (1980). The attributional contexts of cognitive intervention strategies. *Exceptional Education Quarterly, 1,* 17–30.

205. Humphrey, L. L., Karoly, P., & Kirschenbaum, D. S. (1978). Self-management in the classroom: Self-imposed response cost versus self-reward. *Behavior Therapy, 9,* 592–601.

206. Johnson, S. M. (1970). Self-reinforcement versus external reinforcement in behavior modification with children. *Developmental Psychology, 3,* 147–148.

207. Kanfer, F. H., & Duerfeldt, P. H. (1967). Effects on retention of externally to self-reinforced rehearsal trials following acquisition. *Psychological Reports, 21,* 194–196.

208. Kaufman, K. F., & O'Leary, K. D. (1972). Reward, cost, and self-evaluation procedures for disruptive adolescents in a psychiatric hospital school. *Journal of Applied Behavior Analysis, 5,* 293–309.

209. Keirsey, D. W. (1965). *Transactional Case Work.* Paper presented at the annual convention of the California Association of School Psychologists and Psychometrists, San Francisco.

210. Kneedler, R. D., & Hallahan, D. P. (1981). Self-monitoring of on-task behavior with learning disabled children: Current studies and directions. *Exceptional Education Quarterly, 2* (3), 73–82.

211. Ledwidge, B. (1978). Cognitive behavior modification: A step in the wrong direction? *Psychological Bulletin, 85,* 353–375.

212. McKenzie, T., & Rushall, B. (1974). Effects of self-recording on attendance and performance in a competitive swimming training program. *Journal of Applied Behavior Analysis, 7,* 199–206.

213. McLaughlin, T. F. (1976). Self-control in the classroom. *Review of Educational Research, 46,* 631–663.

214. McLaughlin, T. F., & Malaby, J. E. (1974). Increasing and maintaining assignment completion with teacher and pupil controlled individual contingency programs: Three case studies. *Psychology, 11* (3), 45–51.

215. Molitzky, B. (1974). Behavior recording as treatment: A brief note. *Behavior Therapy, 5,* 107–111.

216. O'Leary, S. G., & Dubey, D. R. (1979). Applications of self-control procedures by children: A review. *Journal of Applied Behavior Analysis, 12,* 449–465.

217. Pease, G. A., & Tyler, O. T., Jr. (1979). Self-regulation of time-out duration in the modification of disruptive behavior. *Psychology in the Schools, 16,* 101–105.

218. Rhode, G., Morgan, D. P., & Young, K. R. (1983). Generalization and maintenance of treatment gains of behaviorally handicapped students from resource rooms to regular classrooms using self-evaluation procedures. *Journal of Applied Behavior Analysis, 16,* 171–188.

219. Rosenbaum, M. S., & Drabman, R. S. (1979). Self-control training in the classroom: A review and critique. *Journal of Applied Behavior Analysis, 12,* 467–485.

220. Sagotsky, G., Patterson, C. J., & Lepper, M. R. (1978). Training children's self-control: A field experiment in self-monitoring and goal setting in the classroom. *Journal of Experimental Child Psychology, 25,* 242–253.

221. Santogrossi, D. A., O'Leary, K. D., Romanczyk, R. G., & Kaufman, K. F. (1973). Self-evaluation by adolescents in a psychiatric hospital school token program. *Journal of Applied Behavior Analysis, 6,* 277–287.

222. Sugai, G., & Rowe, P. (1984). The effect of self-recording on out-of-seat behavior of an EMR student. *Education and Training of the Mentally Retarded, 19,* 23–28.

223. Thomas, J. W. (1980). Agency and achievement: Self-management and self-regard. *Review of Educational Research, 50,* 213–240.

224. Turkewitz, H., O'Leary, K. D., & Ironsmith, M. (1975). Generalization and maintenance of appropriate behavior through self-control. *Journal of Consulting and Clinical Psychology, 43,* 577–583.

225. Workman, E. A., & Hector, M. A. (1978). Behavioral self-control in classroom settings: A review of the literature. *Journal of School Psychology, 16,* 227–236.

# PART THREE

# SOLUTIONS TO INDIVIDUAL BEHAVIOR PROBLEMS

## *Introduction*

This part is designed to help you deal with the behavior problems of the few students in your class who don't respond to the techniques described in the previous two chapters because they need a more individualized, in-depth approach. The chapters in this part will help you determine what specifically causes your students' problems so you can then provide the appropriate individualized approach. Chapter 8 discusses educational factors that can cause behavior problems. Chapter 9 discusses how you can handle the problems of students who aren't able to conform to the demands of school because they aren't prepared to share, wait their turn, work cooperatively, or follow rules and procedures. Chapter 10 describes techniques for students who are too insecure to function independently, to accept and profit from an objective evaluation of their work, and the like. Chapter 11 explains how you can use managing and accommodating techniques to help students who are experiencing problems adjusting to the unusual demands of school because they are immature or temperamentally different or else have problems sustaining attention or controlling their high activity levels. The difficulties culturally different students experience in school are discussed in Chapter 12. Chapter 13 explains how you can handle school problems that are the result of current sex-role differences.

Although many educators believe it's important to individualize classroom management techniques with some students (1–6), others do not agree. They advocate a set response for each of the behavior problems they confront. For example, when they catch students cheating during an exam, they invariably punish them. Or when students answer without waiting to be called on, they reprimand them. If students turn in their assignments late, they routinely lower their grades.

But different students can behave the same way for entirely different reasons. Students cheat during exams for a whole range of reasons. For some, cheating, lying, getting away with things, and taking the easy way out are how they do things. Others cheat because their parents put tremendous pressure on them to earn high grades, or they set unrealistically high goals for themselves, or they don't have the background or skills necessary to learn what is being taught in class without additional help.

While students should not be allowed to cheat on exams, punishing them for doing so may not deal with the cause of the problem. Punishment may be a reasonable approach with students who lie, cheat, and steal as a way of life to help them learn that "crime doesn't pay." But with the other students, appropriate solutions might involve convincing their parents to put less pressure on them, helping them develop realistic standards, or making sure they get the extra help they need so they can do well on exams without cheating.

## *Some Typical Concerns*

While you are reading this part, one or more of the following questions about the feasibility of handling students' behavior problems on an individual basis will probably cross your mind.

1. *Is it really necessary to know the cause of students' inappropriate behavior in order to deal effectively with it?* Research clearly supports the approach that it's possible for educators to choose the correct solution to students' behavior problems without knowing what causes them. But it is much more likely that educators will choose the appropriate techniques and avoid those that are ineffective or that make the problems worse if they consider the causes of their students' problems when choosing how to respond. For example, using consequences to teach students not to steal, cheat, lie, or take advantage of younger children may work if their misconduct is caused by a lack of exposure to appropriate consequences. But it won't work to change the attitudes of students who act this way because they haven't received enough love, attention, and caring to want to behave ethically. Likewise, providing added assistance may help anxious students with poor self-concepts who believe they can't succeed on their own get started or continue to work and so teach them that they can succeed. But giving such assistance will only aggravate the problems of students who aren't used to working on frustrating, difficult, or tedious things on their own because they have been able to manipulate adults into doing such things for them. Finally, requiring students to behave themselves "or else" may work with students who know what appropriate behavior is. But culturally different students may need to be taught how to behave in new ways and told why behavior that is acceptable in their homes and neighborhoods isn't acceptable in school.

2. *Is it really possible to know why students behave as they do?* Teachers with access to information about their students' developmental histories, home lives, previous school records, and the ways they behave outside of school are in a good position to understand why their students behave as they do. Teachers with some of this information can make educated guesses about what causes their students' behavior problems. Even teachers who know very little about their students except what they learn from their own observations have at least that much information on which to base their judgments.

   Special education teachers who work with 8 to 20 students and elementary schoolteachers who may have 25 to 30 some-odd students in their classes are in excellent positions to get the information they need to draw reasonably accurate conclusions about the causes of their students' behavior problems. In contrast, secondary schoolteachers, who deal with six or seven different classes of 25 or more students each, may have more difficulty finding the time it takes to gather adequate information about their students, especially if they have large numbers of students with behavior problems. If they only have a few students with behavior problems in each of their classes, though, the individualized approach described in this part is quite feasible.

   While it's best if educators have all the necessary information at their disposal, they are still better off making an educated guess based on the information they have and adapting their strategies and techniques to what they think causes the problems than they would be using the same techniques with all students. Even educated guesses increase the odds that the strategies and techniques they choose will be effective.

3. *Can one person relate to students in so many different ways?* It's absolutely true that educators are all individuals with their own unique personalities that in turn determine which techniques they can and can't be comfortable using with their students. But it's also true that what usually limits the range of techniques educators use isn't teachers' personalities but rather a lack of understanding about the causes of their students' behavior problems, too little information about alternative strategies and techniques, and an absence of self-awareness about how they habitually respond to their students' behavior. As educators grow more knowledgeable about what causes different behavior problems, which techniques work best with each of them, and what approaches they typically use from force of habit, they will be better able to select techniques that suit both their personalities and the causes of their students' behavior problems.

4. *Can students accept different rules, expectations, and consequences for other students without becoming jealous, resentful, or rebellious?* If different rules and expectations and different consequences for various students are used in an arbitrary manner, without rhyme or reason, then they probably will make students jealous, resentful, angry, or rebellious. But if teachers tailor their expectations and so on to the needs of each of their students, and students can see that they are all being treated fairly, then they will be more accepting of this approach because they will all be getting what they need.

# *References*

1. Brophy, J., & Evertson, S. M. (1976). *Learning from Teaching: A Developmental Perspective.* Boston: Allyn & Bacon.

2. Morse, W. C., & Smith, J. M. (1980). *Understanding Child Variance.* Reston, VA: Council for Exceptional Children.

3. Rhodes, W. C., & Tracy, M. (1975). A *Study of Child Variance.* Ann Arbor, MI: University of Michigan Press.

4. Rich, H. L. (1978). A matching model for educating the emotionally disturbed and behavior disordered. *Focus on Exceptional Children, 10* (3), 1–11.

5. Shea, T. M., & Bauer, A. M. (1987). *Teaching Children and Youth with Behavior Disorders* (2nd ed.). Englewood Cliffs, NJ: Prentice-Hall.

6. Quay, H. C. (1969). Dimensions of problem behavior in educational programming. In P. S. Graubard (Ed.), *Children Against Schools.* Chicago: Follett.

# *EDUCATIONAL DIFFICULTIES*

## *The School's Impact*

Providing an educational program that suits the individual needs of thousands of different students in the same building is a challenging task, but no more challenging than selecting instructional strategies, curriculum, and classroom management techniques that will work for a class of diverse students. No wonder so many students experience school-related problems.

## *Inherent Difficulties*

The demands placed on youngsters in school are different from those placed on them in the "real world" (1, 2). These school-related demands can cause youngsters who are fine elsewhere to have problems even in the best-run schools and classrooms.

*Interpersonal Relationships*   At home most youngsters have to learn to live with only a few people—their parents and siblings. These relationships are usually stable and develop over a long period of time. In school, though, students have to contend with new teachers and the teachers' own ways of managing and relating to students each year. At home children are gradually prepared by their parents to fulfill the roles their parents assign them. In school new teachers expect students to adjust quickly to their ways even if these conflict with what the students are used to at home. Youngsters are also very special to their parents at home. In school they are one of many students. Whereas at home youngsters receive personal attention and usually a lot of it, at school they receive much less and what they do get tends to be much more impersonal. If, like many children, they are used to receiving their parents' praise and encouragement for almost everything they do at home,

*Expectations at school and at home are often different.*

they may react poorly to their teachers' more realistic appraisals of their accomplishments and to the inevitable comparisons children make between themselves and their peers.

*Structure*    The structure in and out of school is also very different. Although definite limits exist at home, children and teenagers have more opportunity to choose what to do, how to do it, when to do it, and when to stop doing it there. Even when it comes to such things as cleaning up their rooms or doing chores, youngsters have some say about when they will do them and how fast they will work, even though their parents may not like it. In school the same youngsters have precious little choice. Their teachers decide what they will do, how they will do it, when they will do it, and how long they will spend doing it. Instead of being able to pace themselves, students are usually obliged to keep up with the group— to start when the group starts, whether they are ready or not, and to stop when the group stops, whether they have finished or not.

In the world outside of school, children and teenagers can gradually choose to engage in activities they like and do well in and avoid those that are hard for them. In school students must participate in all classroom activities and study all subjects, whether they like them and do well in them or not. Outside school walls, they are generally allowed to question the authority of their parents, scout leaders, camp counselors, and so on to some extent; in school, questioning teachers' authority is commonly taboo. At home when they are doing their homework, they can move around as they wish, take breaks, and listen to music or talk and laugh. The structure of school may often be necessary, but it is certainly unnatural and extremely constricted and restrictive.

*Tasks*    The tasks required of youngsters in school are also very different from what they are asked to do at home. While they certainly learn a great deal from their play, for example, playing outside of school and learning in school are highly dissimilar. At school learning is likely to involve learning by listening or by reading. In addition, the tasks youngsters confront in school are both more complex and abstract. It's much easier for most children to learn how to make their beds, fold their clothes, take care of their younger brothers and sisters, figure out the rules of their new board games, and hit and catch a baseball than it is to learn to spell, print or write, speak and read a foreign language, or solve algebra problems. To do a good job of learning in school, youngsters need even more chances to set their own paces and more individualized help than they need outside of school. Unfortunately, they rarely receive this extra amount of choice and help.

*Private Versus Public Time*    Outside of school, children and teenagers can have private time. By closing a door, they can shut out others if they want to be alone when they are upset, need time to themselves, or want to do or try things they aren't ready for other people to witness. In school, everything students do is scrutinized by their teachers and peers. Even when they have private thoughts, they may be disciplined for being off-task.

*Atypical Students*    Most students gradually adjust to the special demands school makes on them within a reasonable period of time. Others continue to have difficulty adjusting to school long after their peers have made the adjustment and have accepted schooling on its own terms. It is these students, who have problems for a variety of reasons discussed in this and the following chapters, that will require some kind of individualized response from you.

## *Avoidable Difficulties*

Unfortunately, in the imperfect world we live in, few schools or school systems are run as well as they could be. Many suffer from one or more of the following failings, which naturally impact on students.

*Underfinancing, Overcrowding, Undertraining, and Overworking*    Due to substantially reduced financial support to education, too many school systems are unable to provide the educational services students require. Lower school budgets have also led to overcrowded classrooms and inadequate teacher salaries. These factors, in turn, have made it difficult for school systems to attract and retain high-caliber educators and to provide the in-service training teachers need to improve their skills. While many students excel in school despite the effects of these cutbacks, others fall victim to them.

*Inadequate Physical Environments*    As Gordon states:

> Most classrooms unfortunately are designed, constructed, and furnished in ways that make it difficult for students to stay motivated and involved in the learning process; and when students are distracted and bothered by the classroom environment, many of their coping mechanisms turn into behavior unacceptable to teachers and interfere with efforts to teach. (6, p. 156)

*Poor Instruction and Management Techniques*    Students' behavior is influenced by how well their teachers instruct them, how interesting and relevant the courses are, how effectively teachers manage their classrooms, how often teachers resort to punishment, how available and approachable teachers are, how well teachers match the difficulty level

## THEORY FOCUS: JONES ON POSITIVE CLASSROOM DISCIPLINE

Fredric Jones derived many of his ideas about classroom management from working as a clinical psychologist with youngsters who had emotional problems, but his two volumes entitled *Positive Classroom Discipline* and *Positive Classroom Instruction* were written specifically for educators. Jones's main emphasis is on managing group behavior in order to reduce disruptions and increase cooperative behavior. The four major elements in his approach are classroom structure, limit-setting, responsibility training, and backup systems.

According to Jones, educators can avoid many behavior problems by establishing good classroom structure. This includes not only rules, routines, and standards of appropriate behavior but also good teacher-student relations that are positive, gentle, and cooperative. When students misbehave despite good classroom structure, Jones advises setting limits, expecting and teaching them to assume responsibility for their behavior, and finally using backup systems (positive consequences) to motivate them. Because Jones believes educators can motivate students enough by providing them with the opportunity to gain or lose positive consequences, he feels it's unnecessary to punish them.

Jones describes the four major aspects of his approach to classroom discipline as follows.

1. *Preliminary structure:* "Natural" teachers make "proactive" into an art form. They know exactly what they want done, and they have routines for getting things done that are simple and effective. Preliminary structure includes such things as a specific choreography to the first hour, day, and week of the school year, room arrangement, the organization of chores, the clarification of rules and values, and the communication of those rules and values to parents. Common to all, however, is an investment in getting to know the students and an ongoing effort to make the learning environment personal, safe, and comfortable.

2. *Limit-setting:* Limit-setting or "meaning business" is the teacher's physical demeanor that communicates to the students at all times that the teacher is "in charge." Limit-setting . . . is body language—the sum total of the teacher's body language that is visible at all times and can be read like a book by any two-year-old.

Body language is the language of emotions and intentions both conscious and unconscious. It is part of our biological equipment—neither invented nor changeable. We either understand it and use it to our advantage or experience exhaustion and exasperation as "creative" students use it to their advantage.

There are two keys to understanding limit-setting:

   a. Effective discipline management begins at the *emotional* level.
   b. *Calm is strength whereas upset is weakness.* When you consider

of individual students' work to their level of functioning, and how fair teachers are. Research clearly demonstrates that "better" teachers have fewer discipline problems than poorer teachers (4, 7, 8, 11).

In reviewing the instructional errors teachers make, Jones suggests that one mistake is especially damaging:

Almost all the chronic motivation problems and overt helplessness in any classroom are a by-product of one simple thing—the way a teacher helps a student who is stuck . . . It

---

**THEORY FOCUS: JONES ON POSITIVE CLASSROOM DISCIPLINE** *(continued)*

that your body is designed to get upset when provoked (a "fight-flight" reflex that becomes nagging and threatening as soon as we add dialogue), it is clear that our "natural equipment" is a considerable liability when social power rather than physical power is the issue.

3. *Building patterns of cooperation:* To be positive, discipline management must ultimately be voluntary on the part of students. We ask for cooperation thousands of times a day as we ask the entire class to be at the right place at the right time with the right materials doing the right thing. If we want all of this cooperation, we must answer one eternal question over and over again . . . "Why should I?" We will need very good answers to reach all the students in the class.

Those answers are called incentives. Yet incentives as they typically exist in classrooms are inadequate. They expect the students to behave appropriately in order to get some type of reinforcer. Any kid who will "prime the pump" by giving cooperation before they get anything doesn't need much management to start with. How do you get noncooperative students to repeatedly do what you want them to do the first time you ask by using learning as the reinforcer? This will require the more sophisticated incentives we refer to as Responsibility Training.

4. *Back-up systems:* What do you do when push comes to shove in discipline management . . . ? The answer to this question is the stuff of which school discipline codes are made. Warnings, detentions, trips to the office, suspensions—it hasn't changed in 75 years, and 5 percent of the student body still produce 90 percent of office referrals. So what's new?

It would be new if our within-classroom back-up system prevented the need for continual reliance upon the school site back-up system. It would be new if teachers had a specific and effective plan for responding to common provocations so that they got smaller rather than larger.

But first think of limit-setting and remember that at its foundation discipline management is emotional, and calm is strength. If you "lose it" and demean the student in front of their peers due to your "upset," you will pay and pay fast. There is no such thing as win/lose in discipline. Either you and the students win together, or the students will guarantee that you pay more dearly than they do.

But exactly how do you respond in the heat of the moment to diffuse a rough situation—to protect the student in order to protect yourself? Don't expect your "biological equipment" to be of any help. It will take a lot of training and practice to overcome the fight/flight reflex. (F. Jones, personal communication, June 8, 1989)

---

is universally assumed that when students are stuck, you explain to them what they do not understand and then help them to do it right. Unfortunately, this unexamined and ordinary piece of teacher behavior is an unmitigated educational disaster. (7, p. 23)

Jones explains that rushing in to help students reinforces their helplessness by giving them teacher time and attention; it keeps them from learning how to solve problems for themselves and uses time that should be spent on group instruction and supervision.

*Unnecessary Anxiety and Stress*    Anxiety and stress can cause students to misbehave (5, 9, 10, 12). Although we probably can't make schools totally stress free, many students are subjected to unnecessary levels of anxiety and stress. Phillips (12) has identified a number of stress-causing situations in school. Among them are the students' inability to understand and learn what they are taught when teachers proceed too rapidly, academic competition between students, not fulfilling teachers' academic expectations, being laughed at for giving the wrong answer, taking tests, and having teachers report to parents.

## Self-Quiz: On Personal Characteristics

Kauffman, Pullen, and Akers identify eight teacher characteristics that contribute to student misbehavior:

a. Inconsistency in management techniques
b. Reinforcement of the wrong behavior
c. Formation of inappropriate expectations for children
d. Nonfunctional or irrelevant instruction
e. Insensitivity to children's legitimate individuality
f. Demonstration or encouragement of undesirable models
g. Irritability and overreliance on punishment
h. Unwillingness to try new strategies or to seek suggestions from other professionals. (75, p. 2)

If you have had teaching experience, answer the following eight questions about yourself. These authors suggest your answers will give you insight into the way you function in class.

1. Am I consistent in responding to children's behavior?
2. Am I rewarding the right behavior?
3. Are my expectations and demands appropriate for children's abilities?
4. Am I tolerant enough of children's individuality?
5. Am I providing instruction that is useful to children?
6. Are children seeking desirable models?
7. Am I generally irritable and overreliant on punishment as a control technique?
8. Am I willing to try a different tack on the problem or to seek the help of colleagues or consultants?

*Behavior Problems*    Numerous authors have provided anecdotal descriptions of the ways in which such things as underfinancing, overcrowding, inadequate physical environments, poor instruction and classroom management techniques, and so on cause students to misbehave (13–21). Research has confirmed many of these anecdotal descriptions. For example, studies indicate that as students progress through the grades, they often perceive themselves as doing schoolwork because they are required to do so in order to receive good grades, not because they are interested in the material (4, 9, 13, 14). They also become less proud of their work, less likely to believe they are doing as well as they should, less likely to say they are trying their best, less likely to feel positive about school, and more likely to say they are discouraged about their school careers (22–24, 28, 31–33). Naturally students who feel and think these ways about themselves are unlikely to give their all in school.

Failing students have an especially difficult time in school. Lack of success or outright failure are experiences that all students react to poorly. While most youngsters can handle an occasional setback, constant repetitive failure, even if it occurs only in one area or subject, is something with which few children or adolescents can cope without some problems. The experience of failure can be even more devastating when teachers show preference for students who do well.

Sometimes students react to failure by doubling their efforts to succeed. All too often, they become anxious and insecure. They may, if possible, avoid challenging situations. Or they may blame themselves for their failure and feel guilty or depressed. They may also defend themselves against such feelings by blaming the situation, their teachers, or their peers for the difficulty they experience and then feel angry and resentful (3, 5).

By the time they are teenagers, some students are so far behind they see little if any point to school. Some are willing to put the time in until they can drop out legally. But many others are unwilling to continue to play the part of the well-motivated, well-behaved student.

No wonder research indicates that students who score high on tests and who get high grades behave better than those who do poorly (3, 5, 8). Research also indicates that students' misbehavior both in school (26, 27, 30) and out (25, 29) is related to their school experiences to a considerable degree. For example, Rutter et al. (30) found that students who were well matched with each other when they entered school differed dramatically in terms of both the frequency and seriousness of their misbehavior after a few years depending on the school they attended and their experiences in school.

Suggestions for improving your classroom management techniques and decreasing student anxiety and stress are included throughout this book, though Chapters 2 and 3 are especially relevant.

# Solving School-Caused Behavior Problems

As a single individual, you cannot solve all school difficulties that cause students to misbehave. You have very little control over things like school finances, inadequate physical environments, and so on. But you can do your best within your own working conditions. The important thing is to recognize when students' behavior problems are caused by school-related factors.

## Three-Step Process

When, despite your best efforts, students experience educational difficulties that lead them to misbehave, you can use the following three-step approach to identify and solve the problem.

1. *Determine if the cause of your student's behavior problem is educational and identify, if possible, the particular educational cause.* A student's behavior problems are more likely to be related to difficulties in school if he or she only misbehaves in

school. If, on the other hand, the student misbehaves both in and out of school, chances are the cause of the problem lies elsewhere. Or if a student is doing fine, then suddenly begins to behave inappropriately and you think the cause is educational, ask yourself if the change could have been precipitated by a particular event or situation in school. Has the student recently failed an exam, had a run-in with a teacher, or had a falling out with some peers?

If a student only behaves inappropriately some of the time, determine when and under what circumstances he or she misbehaves. Students with educationally related behavior problems who are generally well-behaved may act up when it's time to go to a particular class or study a particular subject, time for recess, or time to go home by bus. Relating misbehavior to a certain time or stimulus may give you some clues about the possible cause.

2. *Correct any classroom problems that could be causing the misbehavior.* For example, change the seat of a student who is inattentive or disruptive because she can't read the blackboard or hear you lecture. Use more hands-on teaching techniques with kindergarteners who are still highly kinesthetic learners and so learn by doing. Be less critical of students who "push your buttons." Don't assign work that is too easy or too difficult for students who aren't working on the same level as the majority of their peers. Make sure students understand assignments before you allow them to begin.

3. *Change the situation if necessary so that it no longer evokes the reaction you are trying to eliminate.* Accommodate your curriculum as much as possible to a student who lacks the readiness skills other students have acquired by beginning with the student at his level. For example, when feasible, teach to the strengths of a learning-disabled student, or allow a student who does poorly in an activity, despite his best efforts, to engage in a different activity. You might also allow a student from a culture where showing others you know the answer is frowned on to put off volunteering answers until she is ready to do so.

## Applying the Process

This section describes how you can use the three-step process to identify and solve behavior problems caused by educational difficulties. Because this text deals with classroom management and not instruction, space doesn't permit a detailed discussion of the many instructional techniques you can use to solve these problems as part of the three-step process. Thus, rather than focusing on instructional strategy, this section shows how the three-step process is applied to the behavior problems of two types of students especially susceptible to experiencing educational difficulties.

*Students Lacking Readiness Skills*   Some children enter school without the social and academic skills their teachers and the school system expect them to have. Certain preschoolers and kindergarteners may not, for example, have experienced and accepted many of the rules and routines such as waiting in line or taking turns that educators rely on to manage large groups of students. Others may not be used to the pace at which the group functions. Some young students may find it hard to adjust to teachers who treat them differently from the ways their parents do. Often this happens when teachers don't give a student as much individual attention, assistance, praise, or freedom as he is used to. In other cases, the teacher may not hold the same opinion as a student's parents do about the relative value of cooperation versus competition, the rights of the individual versus the rights of the group, or the best methods to manage a group or to discipline youngsters.

Some preschoolers and kindergarteners, especially from working-class and minority families, may not have the academic skills necessary to succeed in school at the same level as their better prepared peers. Unless educators are willing and able to individualize their social and academic expectations for students and work with each one at their entering level, many students will not have the skills they need to succeed. This in turn may cause them to become tense, anxious, angry, rebellious, or withdrawn (35).

Teachers in the upper grades face similar problems with students who function below grade level. Secondary school teachers often have to deal with the problems that result when students are allowed to enroll in their courses without the necessary prerequisites. Accommodating one's teaching techniques and instructional materials to students' levels of functioning can solve many behavior problems; however, this is often difficult to accomplish especially at the secondary level without the cooperation of one's colleagues and administrators.

If a kindergartener or first grader is having difficulty learning, seems anxious and tense, and daydreams or talks instead of staying on-task, she may not be able to function at the level of the other students in the class. To determine whether you are giving a student work that she isn't ready for, you can do an informal assessment of what the student knows and doesn't know and can and can't do. Then compare the results with the skills needed to succeed at the level of your expectations. Or you could use one of the many formal assessment procedures that research indicates are valid for evaluating students' readiness skills (36, 38, 39, 40, 43, 44).

If your assessment of the student indicates that she lacks certain readiness skills, accommodate your expectations, materials, and teaching techniques to the student's actual level of functioning. Research indicates that accommodating to students' readiness levels can help avoid the kinds of educational difficulties that often cause young students to misbehave (34, 37, 41, 42).

*Mismatched Learning and Teaching*   In recent years research has clearly demonstrated that students learn more efficiently when they are taught in ways that conform to their learning styles—conditions in which they learn most efficiently (45, 46, 48, 51, 55, 60, 61, 64, 67, 68, 71–73). Many differences among students' learning styles have been substantiated by research, including the finding that some students prefer to work independently, while others want more feedback and supervision from their teachers (66). Also, although many students seem to respond well to competition, many others function better in cooperative situations, especially if they come from a culture that encourages cooperation (66). Research has shown that not all students are motivated by the same types of rewards. Such material rewards as candy, toys, trips, and the like are effective with some students, but others are more responsive to interpersonal rewards such as praise and teacher attention (66). In terms of learning modality, although kindergarten students are kinesthetic learners and learn best by doing, touching, feeling, and manipulating (46), by the time they reach the upper elementary grades some students learn better when material is presented to them orally. Others, however, learn more when material is presented visually

(48, 59, 65, 70, 73). Another area in which students differ is in terms of whether they require silence or sound to do their best work. Some are distracted by the sounds around them; others concentrate best when the radio, tape deck, or television is on (64).

Other findings show that some students concentrate best in bright light, while others do better when the light is dim (60). Like adults, students tend to be day or night people. Night owls do better late in the day, and early birds function best in the morning (47, 65). Students who prefer a formal atmosphere like to work at their desks or at a table in the library, but students who enjoy informality do better lying or sitting on the floor, lounging in a chair, or reading in bed (65, 68).

In addition, students work at different paces. Some are comfortable working fast; others learn more when they are allowed to proceed at a pace that is slower than most students (57, 69). A related characteristic is that while some students can sit still for long periods of time, others function better when they can move about fairly often (52). In general, students become less impulsive and more reflective as they mature, but students tend to be either reflective or impulsive throughout their educational careers (74). Students who are reflective need to think for a while before answering questions and beginning activities, whereas impulsive students "get off the mark" almost immediately (56, 58, 62). Certain students

*Kindergartners tend to be kinesthetic learners, but older students have a variety of learning styles.*

can concentrate for long periods of time on one activity, while others require periodic breaks in order to maintain their concentration (52). Analytic students use a step-by-step approach to solve problems and understand things. In contrast, global students need to see the big picture before they can deal with the details involved (51, 53, 57, 72).

Because students learn more effectively when the teaching style matches their learning style, some behavior problems occur when students have to consistently function in ways that hinder rather than enhance their learning. In such cases, teachers can improve their students' behavior by individualizing their teaching styles as much as possible. When you feel your students may be misbehaving because your teaching style doesn't match their learning styles, you can assess them informally according to the descriptions given above or use published instruments. Two helpful instruments are the Learning Style Inventory— Regular and Primary Versions (54, 63, 67) and the Ramirez and Castañeda Behavior Rating Scale (66).

The Learning Style Inventory involves students in the assessment process by having them state whether or not various statements apply to them. Below are sample items from the instrument:

I remember things best when I study them early in the morning.

Noise usually keeps me from concentrating.

The things I remember best are the things I hear.

I like to be given choices of how I can do things.

I like to be told exactly what to do.

The Ramirez and Castañeda Behavior Rating Scale assesses both students' preferred learning styles and teachers' teaching styles. This joint assessment enables educators to determine whether their teaching styles match a particular student's learning style. The following are some representative items from the students' and teachers' versions of the Behavior Rating Scale.

| Field-Sensitive Students | Field-Independent Students |
|---|---|
| —likes to work with others to achieve a common goal | —prefers to work independently |
| —Seeks guidance and demonstration from teacher | —likes to try new tasks without teacher's help |
| —is sensitive to feelings and opinions of others | —task oriented: is inattentive to social environments when working |

| Field-Sensitive Teachers | Field-Independent Teachers |
|---|---|
| —encourages cooperation and development of group feeling | —encourages competition between students |
| —humanizes curriculum | —relies on graphs, charts, and formulas |

---

## THEORY FOCUS: RAMIREZ AND CASTAÑEDA ON BICOGNITIVE EDUCATION

Manuel Ramirez and Alfredo Castañeda believe that minority students have the legal and moral right to maintain their own ethnic group values and learning styles in school while at the same time they are exposed to and acquire mainstream values and learning styles. In their book *Cultural Democracy, Bicognitive Development and Education*, they describe the learning styles of nonacculturated Mexican-American field-sensitive students and the field-independent teaching styles of the majority of educators. And they attribute many of the problems these students

have in school to this mismatch between their learning styles and their teachers' teaching styles. Ramirez and Castañeda have developed instruments that an educator can use to evaluate to what degree students are acculturated to the mainstream society. The instrument also compares the students' learning styles to their teachers' teaching styles. These authors also suggest ways to both adapt teaching styles to students' learning styles and help students learn to function biculturally and bicognitively.

---

Once you have identified your students' learning styles and compared them to your usual teaching style, you can accommodate your teaching techniques to their needs as much as possible so they can learn more effectively (46, 49, 54, 60, 64, 66, 68, 71, 72). For example, if you use competition and material rewards a lot, you can make an effort to include more cooperative learning and interpersonal rewards in your classroom activities. If you basically lecture students as your primary instructional strategy, you can supplement your usual presentation with visual materials—pictures, films, reading materials—for the visual learners among your students. Such changes should lead to improvements in their behavior.

## Case Studies

The following case studies illustrate how you can determine when students' behavior problems are caused by educational difficulties, identify the specific causes of their misbehavior, and then correct them so students will stop misbehaving.

## Carlos

Carlos, a third-grade student, immigrated to the United States from El Salvador when he was three. He was transferred from a bilingual class to a regular class after second grade because he passed an English proficiency test. But his third-grade teacher, Ms. Allen, described Carlos as "requiring excessive teacher direction, feedback, and praise" in order to complete learning tasks. Typically, he raised his hand or went up to the teacher's desk three or four times during a 30-minute period to ask if he was doing his assignment correctly. If he wasn't able to get such feedback, he stopped what he was doing and waited. His teacher felt he was overly dependent on her and couldn't work independently enough to succeed in a class of 33 students.

Initially, Ms. Allen attributed Carlos's dependency to "insecurity and anxiety caused by a low self-concept." But after having Carlos in class for two months, she realized Carlos had much more self-confidence than she had given him credit for: he made friends easily, volunteered for a part in the class play, was always eager to read books that were difficult for him because of his earlier lack of English proficiency, and seemed to expect that she would tell him he was on the right track whenever he asked her for feedback about how he was doing.

Carlos's former bilingual education teacher agreed that he had a good self-concept and thought that he probably wasn't unusually anxious about being in an all-English class. Rather, she assumed that Carlos's behavior was a reflection of his field-sensitive learning style, a characteristic of many Hispanic students, and suggested that Ms. Allen use the Ramirez and Castañeda Behavior Rating Scale to determine and compare his learning style to her teaching style.

When she did, Ms. Allen discovered that Carlos was indeed a field-sensitive learner, while she was using a field-independent teaching style. He scored high on "likes to work with others to achieve a common goal," "seeks guidance and demonstration from teachers," and "seeks rewards which strengthen relationship with teacher and is highly motivated when working with teacher." In contrast, she scored high on "encourages independent student achievement" and "maintains formal relationships with students" but low on "uses personalized rewards which strengthen the relationship with students" and "encourages cooperation and development of group feeling."

Armed with the knowledge she gained from the rating scale, Ms. Allen concluded that she wasn't encouraging cooperative-learning enough or expressing enough physical and verbal approval for many of the students in her class. So she decided to change her approach with both the entire class and Carlos. First, she stopped her unnecessary attempts to build up Carlos's self-confidence, and she accommodated to his requests for her feedback. At the same time, she also told him that in the United States students are expected to work more on their own, which would prepare him for success in other classrooms. And she made a point of praising him whenever he completed assignments without asking her opinion. By the end of the school year, Carlos was working much more independently, although he continued to show her his finished work more often than most other students.

## Jo Ann

Jo Ann was doing worse in the sixth grade than she had done before in school. Instead of getting mostly B's with an occasional A or C, she was earning all C's except for D's in math and science. Mr. Davidson, a second-year teacher, noticed that she rushed through her assignments, made many careless errors, almost never volunteered answers, daydreamed a lot, and seemed extremely anxious during tests.

Thinking that she might have been experiencing problems outside of school that were affecting her functioning in class, he contacted her parents. They said that as far as they knew Jo Ann had no serious problems, but they also reported she had been complaining about school for the first time since third grade. When pressed by Mr. Davidson, they said that Jo Ann felt that her teacher was going too fast, gave students tests before they were ready, and didn't like them to ask questions about things they didn't understand.

After thinking about what he had heard, Mr. Davidson decided to slow the pace down. He told the class he wanted them to ask questions if they didn't understand something and made a point of commenting, "That's a good question" or "I guess I didn't explain that too well," when they did. He also conducted a review before each test. Although he never spoke individually to Jo Ann about the problem, he noticed a dramatic improvement in her behavior and test scores within just a few weeks.

## Frank

Ms. Russo, Frank's 11th-grade social studies teacher, found him to be a "fresh," "impudent," "rebellious" student. Yet when she spoke to his other teachers, none reported any problems with him. Concerned about whether it was the subject matter, the time of day, or just the chemistry between them, Ms. Russo did some self-evaluation. This led her to admit that she was intensely uncomfortable with the way Frank related to the girls in the class. She especially disliked the way he strutted in as if were "God's gift to women," smiling at each pretty girl as he passed. She was also revolted by the bits and pieces of his conversations with girls that she overheard.

In giving this more thought, Ms. Russo decided she didn't have the right to allow her feelings about Frank's relationships with the girls to affect the way she dealt with him, especially since he was earning an A in her course. She met with him after class, expressed her opinion about his behavior, and stated that she was wrong to have let it influence the way she dealt with him. Then she suggested that they start all over. Although her opinion of him remained the same, their relationship improved somewhat so that it was at least bearable. At times, though, Ms. Russo had the feeling that Frank purposely did things to annoy her.

## Summary

Students may react to the difficulties they experience in school by misbehaving. Because the interpersonal relationships between students and teachers and the classroom structure and tasks required of students are so different than those of the outside world, many students experience adjustment problems in school.

Underfinancing, overcrowding, understaffing, inadequate facilities, poor teaching, and the unnecessary stress students are often placed under can create additional school-related behavior problems. Teachers can use a three-step process to both identify and correct the educational causes of students' behavior problems.

## *Activities*

I. Evaluate the physical environment of your classroom and your instructional techniques in terms of the criteria described in Chapter 3 in the section about transitions.

II. Use the description of learning-style differences above to evaluate the learning styles of several students. Then determine how well your usual teaching style suits their learning styles.

## *References*

THE SCHOOL'S IMPACT

1. Brophy, J. E., & Putnam, J. G. (1978). *Classroom Management in the Elementary Grades*. ERIC ED 167 537.

2. Jackson, P. (1968). *Life in Classrooms*. New York: Holt, Rinehart & Winston.

AVOIDABLE DIFFICULTIES

3. Duke, D. I. (1976). Who misbehaves? A high school studies its discipline problems. *Educational Administration Quarterly, 12*, 65–85.

4. Dweck, C. (1975). The role of expectations and attributions in the alleviation of learned helplessness. *Journal of Personality and Social Psychology, 31*, 674–685.

5. Gnagey, W. J. (1978). *Attitudes, Motives and Values of Facilitators and Inhibitors*. Paper presented at the annual conference of the American Educational Research Association, Toronto, Canada.

6. Gordon, T. (1974). *Teacher Effectiveness Training*. New York: Wyden.

7. Jones, F. H. (1987). *Positive Classroom Instruction*. New York: McGraw-Hill.

8. Jorgenson, G. W. (1977). Relationship of classroom behavior to the accurate match between material difficulty and student ability. *Journal of Educational Psychology, 69* (1), 24–32.

9. Kirschenbaum, H., Napier, R. W., & Simon, S. B. (1971). *Wad-ja-Get? The Grading Game in American Education*. New York: Hart.

10. Leffingwell, R. J. (1977). Misbehavior in the classroom: Anxiety a possible cause. *Education, 97* (4), 360–363.

11. Moore, T. (1966). Difficulties of the ordinary child in adjusting to primary school. *Journal of Child Psychology and Psychiatry, 7,* 17–38.

12. Phillips, B. (1978). *School Stress and Anxiety: Theory, Research and Intervention.* New York: Human Science Press.

The citations below deal with the subject of the negative effects of poor schooling based on anecdotal descriptions.

13. Cormany, R. (1975). Guidance and Counseling in Pennsylvania: Status and Needs. Lemoyne, PA: ESEA Title III Project, West Shore School District.

14. Glasser, W. (1969). *Schools Without Failure.* New York: Harper & Row.

15. Hargreaves, D. H., Hester, S. K., & Mellor, F. J. (1975). *Deviance in Classrooms.* Boston: Kegan & Paul.

16. Hentoff, N. (1966). *Our Children Are Dying.* New York: Viking Press.

17. Holt, J. (1979). *The Underachieving School.* New York: Pitman.

18. Kozol, J. (1967). *Death at an Early Age.* New York: Bantam.

19. Laurence, J., Steed, D., & Young, P. (1984). *Disruptive Children, Disruptive Schools.* New York: Nichols.

20. Melton, D. (1975). *Burn the Schools—Save the Children.* New York: Thomas Crowell.

21. Purkey, W., & Novak, J. (1984). *Inviting School Success: A Self-Concept Approach to Teaching and Learning* (2nd ed.). Belmont, CA: Wadsworth.

The following references are research studies that document the negative impact poor schooling can have.

22. Blumenfeld, P., Pintrich, P., Meece, J., & Wessels, K. (1982). The formation and role of self-perceptions of ability in elementary classrooms. *Elementary School Journal, 82,* 400–420.

23. Currence, C. (1984). School performance tops list of adolescent worries. *Education Week, 3,* 8.

24. Flanders, N., Morrison, B., & Brode, E. (1968). Changes in pupil attitudes during the school year. *Journal of Educational Psychology, 59,* 334–338.

25. Heal, J. (1978). Misbehavior among school children: The role of the school in strategies for prevention. *Policy and Politics, 6,* 321–332.

26. Johnson, K. D., & Krovetz, M. L. (1976). Levels of aggression in a traditional and a pluralistic school. *Educational Research, 18* (2), 146–151.

27. Laurence, J., Steed, D., & Young, P. (1977). *Disruptive Behavior in a Secondary School.* London: University of London Goldsmiths College.

28. Morse, W. (1964). Self-concept in the school setting. *Childhood Education, 41,* 195–198.

29. Reynolds, D. (1976). The delinquent school. In M. Hammersley & P. Woods (Eds.), *The Process of Schooling: A Sociological Reader.* London: Routledge & Kegan Paul.

30. Rutter, M., Maughan, B., Montimore, P., Ouston, J., & Smith, A. (1979). *Fifteen Thousand Hours: Secondary Schools and Their Effects on Children.* Cambridge, MA: Harvard University Press.

31. Stake, R., & Easley, J. (1978). *Case Studies in Science Education* (Vols. 1 & 2). Urbana, IL: Center for Instructional Research and Curriculum Evaluation.

32. Stanwyck, D., & Felker, D. (1974). *Self-Concept and Anxiety in Middle Elementary School Children: A Developmental Survey.* Paper presented at the Annual American Education Research Association Convention, Chicago.

33. Yamamoto, K., Thomas, E., & Karnes, E. (1969). School-related attitudes in middle school age students. *American Educational Research Journal, 6,* 191–206.

The references cited below deal with the readiness skills of high-risk students.

34. Au, K. H. (1974). *A Preliminary Report on Teaching Academics Readiness.* ERIC ED 158 852.

35. Caspari, I. (1976). *Troublesome Children in Class.* London: Routledge & Kegan Paul.

36. Colligan, R. C. (1976). Prediction of kindergarten reading success from preschool reports of parents. *Psychology in the Schools, 13* (3), 304–308.

37. Goolsby, T. M., Jr., & Frary, R. B. (1969). *Enhancement of Educational Effect Through Extensive and Intensive Intervention—The Gulfport Project.* ERIC ED 047 012.

38. Hayes, M., Mason, E., & Covert, R. (1975). Validity and reliability of a simple device for readiness screening. *Educational and Psychological Measurement, 35,* 495–498.

39. Ireton, H., Kampen, M., & Shing-Lun, K. (1981). Minnesota Preschool Inventory Identification of children at risk for kindergarten failure. *Psychology in the Schools, 18* (4), 394–401.

40. Nagle, R. J. (1979). The predictive validity of the Metropolitan Readiness Tests, 1976 Edition. *Educational and Psychological Measurements, 39* (4), 1043–1045.

41. Pheasant, M. (1985). *Aumsville School District's Readiness Program: Helping First Graders Succeed.* ERIC ED 252 967.

42. Terens, S. (1984). *Second Year Full Day Kindergarten Program Evaluation, Laurence Public Schools, Number Four School.* ERIC ED 251 177.

43. University City School District, Missouri. (1970). *Primary Mental Abilities and Metropolitan Readiness Tests as Predictors of Achievement in the First Primary Grade.* ERIC ED 043 683.

44. Wood, C. M. (1979). *Cognitive Style, School Readiness and Behavior as Predictors of First Grade Achievement.* ERIC ED 182 014.

The citations that follow discuss the learning styles of high-risk students.

45. Cofferty, E. (1980). *An Analysis of Student Performance Based on the Degree of Match Between the Educational Cognitive Style of the Students.* Unpublished doctoral dissertation, University of Nebraska, Lincoln, NE.

46. Carbo, M. (1980). *An Analysis of the Relationship Between the Modality Preferences of Kindergarteners and Selected Reading Treatments as They Affect the Learning of a Basic Sight-Word Vocabulary.* Unpublished doctoral dissertation, St. John's University, Jamaica, NY.

47. Carruthers, S., & Young, A. (1980). Preference of condition concerning time in learning environments of rural versus city eighth-grade students. *Learning Styles Network Newsletter, 1* (2), 1.

48. de Hirsch, K., Jansky, J., & Langford, W. (1966). *Predicting Reading Failure.* New York: Harper & Row.

49. Dixon, C. N. (1977). *Matching Reading Instruction to Cognitive Style for Mexican-American Children.* ERIC ED 158 269.

50. Domino, G. (1970). Interactive effects of achievement orientation and teaching styles on academic achievement. *ACT Research Report, 39,* 1–9.

51. Douglass, C. B. (1979). Making biology easier to understand. *The American Biology Teacher, 41* (5), 277–299.

52. Dunn, R. (1983). Learning style and its relation to exceptionality at both ends of the spectrum. *Exceptional Children, 49,* 496–506.

53. Dunn, R., Cavanough, D., Eberle, B., & Zenhausern, R. (1982). Hemispheric preference: The newest element of learning style. *American Biology Teacher, 44* (5), 291–294.

54. Dunn, R., & Dunn, K. (1978). *Teaching Students Through Their Individual Learning Styles: A Practical Approach.* Reston, VA: Reston Publishing Company.

55. Gregorc, A. (1982). *An Adult's Guide to Style.* Maynard, MA: Gabriel Systems.

56. Kagan, J. (1966). Reflection-impulsivity. *Journal of Abnormal Psychology, 71,* 17–24.

57. Kagan, J., Moss, H., & Siegel, I. (1963). Psychological significance of styles of conceptualization. In J. C. Wright & J. Kagan (Eds.), Basic Cognitive Processes in Children. *Monographs of the Society for Research in Child Development, 28,* 260.

58. Kagan, J., Rosman, B. L., Day, D., Albert, J., & Phillips, W. (1964). Information processing in the child: Significance of analytic and reflective attitudes. *Psychological Monographs, 78* (1), 578.

59. Keefe, J. W. (1979). Learning style: An overview. In *Student Learning Styles: Diagnosing and Prescribing Programs*. Reston, VA: National Association of Secondary School Principals.

60. Krimsky, J. S. (1982). *A Comparative Analysis of the Effects of Matching and Mismatching Fourth Grade Students with Their Learning Styles Preferences for the Environmental Element of Light and Their Subsequent Reading Speech and Accuracy Scores*. Unpublished doctoral dissertation, St. John's University, Jamaica, NY.

61. McCarthy, B. (1980). *The 4Mat System: Teaching to Learning Styles with Right/Left Mode Techniques*. Oak Brook, IL: Excel.

62. Messick, S. (1970). The criterion problem in the evaluation of instruction. In M. C. Wittrock & D. E. Wiley (Eds.), *The Evaluation of Instruction: Issues and Problems*. New York: Holt, Rinehart & Winston.

63. Perrin, J. (1982). *Learning Style Inventory: Primary Version*. Jamaica, NY: St. John's University.

64. Pizzo, J. (1981). *An Investigation of the Relationships Between Selected Acoustic Environments and Sound, an Element of Learning Style, as They Affect Sixth Grade Students' Reading Achievement and Attitudes*. Unpublished doctoral dissertation, St. John's University, Jamaica, NY.

65. Price, G. (1980). Which learning style elements are stable and which tend to change? *Learning Styles Network Newsletter, 1* (3), 1.

66. Ramirez, M., & Castañeda, A. (1974). *Cultural Democracy, Bicognitive Development and Education*. New York: Academic Press.

67. Renzulli, J., & Smith, L. (1978). *The Learning Style Inventory: A Measure of Student Preference for Instructional Techniques*. Mansfield Center, CT: Creative Learning Press.

68. Shea, T. C. (1983). *An Investigation of the Relationship among Preferences for the Learning Style Element of Design, Selected Instructional Environments, and Reading Achievement of Ninth Grade Students to Improve Administrative Determinations Concerning Effective Educational Facilities*. Unpublished doctoral dissertation, St. John's University, Jamaica, NY.

69. Shumsky, A. (1968). *In Search of Teaching Style*. New York: Appleton-Century-Crofts.

70. Smith, I. (1964). *Spatial Ability*. San Diego, CA: Knapp.

71. Tannenbaum, R. (1982). *An Investigation of the Relationships Between Selected Instructional Techniques and Identified Field Dependent and Field Independent Cognitive Styles as Evidenced among High School Students Enrolled in Studies of Nutrition*. Unpublished doctoral dissertation, St. John's University, Jamaica, NY.

72. Trautman, P. (1979). *An Investigation of the Relationship Between Selected Instructional Techniques and Identified Cognitive Style.* Unpublished doctoral dissertation, St. John's University, Jamaica, NY.

73. Urbschat, K. S. (1977). *A Study of Preferred Learning Models and Their Relationship to the Amount of Recall of CVC Trigrams.* Unpublished doctoral dissertation, Wayne State University, Yellow Springs, OH.

74. Witkins, H. A., Goodenough, D. R., & Kays, S. A. (1967). Stability of cognitive style from childhood to young adulthood. *Journal of Personality and Social Psychology, 1,* 291–300.

SELF QUIZ: ON PERSONAL CHARACTERISTICS

75. Kauffman, J. M., Pullen, P. L., & Akers, E. (1986). Classroom management: Teacher-child-peer relationships. *Focus on Exceptional Children, 19* (1), 1–10.

# CHAPTER 9

# *CONDUCT PROBLEMS*

This chapter begins by defining conduct problems from a developmental point of view. It then goes on to explain why some students have conduct problems and offers guidelines for identifying such students. A major portion of the chapter describes techniques you can use to deal with conduct problems in your classroom. The final section includes suggestions for working with parents.

Humans are social beings, born completely dependent on others to care for them. Even when fully grown, they almost always continue to live with or near other people. While different groups (societies and cultures) expect different things from their members, they all require that, at certain times, their members submit to authority, adhere to norms of acceptable behavior, and sacrifice personal desires for the benefit of the entire group. Individuals in any society who have not accepted these obligations and who thus don't exercise the necessary self-control over their behavior to meet these obligations have conduct problems. Put another way, individuals with conduct problems are unwilling to control their behavior when it interferes with the rights of others.

People generally fulfill these three obligations for several reasons. First, they anticipate positive consequences if they do so and negative consequences if they don't. Second, they are emulating others whose behavior is acceptable to society. Also, most understand that groups can't function properly if each individual does as she or he pleases. Finally, they internalize the values and morals that the society instills in them, which in turn make them want to behave in ways approved by society even when it's clear that no negative consequences will occur if they don't.

## Defining Conduct Problems

Individuals with conduct problems are unwilling to control their behavior for three reasons. First, they haven't learned that they will suffer undesirable consequences if they don't. Second, they don't understand or care that society can't function unless people exercise self-control. And third, they haven't internalized the morals and values necessary to help them control their behavior in the absence of consequences.

Modern society cannot rely on consequences in most situations because most people aren't under constant surveillance. No one watches to see whether people give money to charity or add a tip for the waiter when they pay restaurant bills with credit cards. No one makes people return the extra change the clerk in the department store hands them by mistake. And no one forces parents to give their children the best care possible even to the point of making considerable financial sacrifices to put them through college. People do these things not because they have to by law but because they see the necessity of doing so and accept the morals and values that make them believe it's right and good to do these things.

No society can rely on rewards and punishments alone to control its members' behavior for very long. It would take more enforcement agents to do the job well than would be practical. Hopefully no society ever will. But society can't rely on values and morals alone either. Societies must use a combination of both forms of influence to make sure that its members fulfill their obligations to each other.

## The School's Role

Some educators would argue that moral development is the sole responsibility of parents and religious leaders and not the schools. But American schools have always been active in the moral development of their students merely by establishing rules, procedures, and expectations for students to live up to, for example. Today's educators, like their predecessors, have an important—though not primary—role to play in ensuring that students develop morality. This is especially true of students with conduct problems. As you will see below, although it's unlikely that you will be able to eliminate your students' conduct problems on your own, you can make an important contribution if their problems aren't serious enough to require the services of other professions.

## Developmental Approach

The approach to helping students with conduct problems recommended in this book is developmental. It assumes that students with conduct problems misbehave because they haven't attained the stage of moral development that is appropriate for their age (see Chapter 3), so the solution to their problem is to help them in reaching their age-appropriate stage of moral development. You can assist students to achieve this goal by using classroom management techniques that will enhance their moral growth; using managing, tolerating, and preventing techniques while you are assisting your students to reach their appropriate stages of moral development; and counseling the students' parents, as needed.

For purposes of this discussion, the moral development of students is divided into three stages that are similar to, but not exactly the same as, three of the six stages described by Kohlberg and Piaget (1, 2).

# First Stage—Extrinsic Consequences

When children are very young, the adults caring for them are more concerned about satisfying their physical and emotional needs than teaching them to control themselves and do things independently. As children get older, though, caretaking adults become less willing to permit them to behave in an uncontrolled way or to do everything for them. To teach young children self-control, adults use several approaches: they model the behavior they expect youngsters to emulate, communicate their expectations that youngsters will control themselves, reward them when they do, and punish them when they don't. As a result, little by little, youngsters adjust to the fact that they have to control their behavior and become more independent. Primary grade students who have not learned this, and who therefore resist conforming to adult expectations, have conduct problems.

## Identification

Few real children are angels—they all misbehave occasionally. Students who haven't yet reached the first stage of moral development and haven't learned that it's necessary to behave appropriately are less likely than older students to do what they are told to do without first ignoring the teacher in charge, resorting to some delaying tactic, or resisting in some way. For example, they may balk at putting their things away, stopping an activity they enjoy, or starting an activity they dislike. They may play with things they have been told not to touch or else break things they are told to be careful with unless you keep them from doing so. They would rather be "done for" than to "do" for themselves. For instance, they may insist that their teachers help them dress, tie their shoes, or straighten up after them. The idea that whoever messes up should straighten up is totally unacceptable to them. They also tend to take things from others, resist sharing or cooperating with others and taking turns. In fact, they often act as if they expect to have their desires satisfied immediately and become upset if they don't get what they want, *when* they want it. They call out answers or push ahead of others instead of waiting to be called on or attended to. For them, waiting is a deprivation they are unwilling to accept unless absolutely necessary.

They haven't yet been taught that they have to "control their behavior or else." So when they are told to do something they don't want to do, they often don't believe they really have to comply. Instead they pretend that they haven't heard their teachers in the

*Students who have not reached the first stage of moral development become upset if they don't get what they want when they want it.*

hope that the adults will do it for them, or they play up to teachers or else try to intimidate them to get them to change their minds. They will sometimes also disregard what they are told until it becomes obvious to them that they had better listen.

Students who have learned that they have to control their behavior usually acquiesce to authority without experiencing a lot of anger or resentment. In contrast, children who have not yet learned that it's necessary to do so may whine, cry, and throw temper tantrums as an expression of their anger at being controlled. Adolescents who have not adjusted to these obligations may sulk, start arguments, or throw temper tantrums as well for the same reason.

Research indicates that teachers can, with a high degree of accuracy, informally identify students in regular classes who have conduct problems (3). Educators can also supplement their own observations with the results of formal assessment instruments such as the Behavior Problems Checklist (4) and the Devereux Child Behavior Rating Scale (5).

Behaviors that may indicate students have conduct problems include the following. They frequently:

Ignore the teacher's directions

Use delaying tactics

Resist following directions

Try to get others to do their chores for them

Take things from others

Refuse to share or cooperate with others

Demand immediate gratification

Call out answers

Push ahead in line

Try to manipulate teachers

Whine, cry, or throw temper tantrums when required to acquiesce

*Chris: A Case Example*    Chris was a six-year-old who had conduct problems because he had not reached the first stage of moral development. He was not readmitted by the two preschools he attended because of his behavior problems and was instead enrolled in a public school kindergarten because he wasn't accepted by any of the private schools in the area. In kindergarten he was described as "unruly," "stubborn," and "lacking in social skills." His first-grade teacher reported that he had difficulty sharing and taking turns. He hit other children when they didn't give him his way and often rebelled or had temper tantrums when his teacher reprimanded him or enforced the consequences that resulted from his misbehavior.

Interviews with Chris's parents indicated that they were both career-oriented individuals with little time to devote to Chris, their only child, who was basically being brought up by two child-care workers. During the time they did spend with Chris, they indulged him without setting limits rather than discipline him because they believed that whatever time they spent with him should be quality time, which they interpreted as always being fun or feeling good.

## *Fostering Moral Development*

Educators can help students, like Chris, who have conduct problems to attain the moral development appropriate for their chronological age. They can do this by relating to them in ways that counteract the effects of the experiences that delayed their moral development in the first place.

*Causes of Moral Development Delays*    The following are some of the typical reasons why certain students' moral development is delayed. Consider how these relate to Chris's situation.

*Models:* Youngsters often learn as much or more from what adults do as from what they say. For example, if adults tell young children not to lie, not to interrupt, and not to be selfish with their things, but then they themselves lie to children, interrupt them, and avoid sharing with them, children will probably learn from what they see and experience, not from what they are told is right.

*Expectations:* Children and teenagers learn to control themselves when adults require them to do so. But some parents don't require that their youngsters control themselves. And youngsters who don't learn to control their behavior for the benefit of others at home aren't prepared to do so in school.

Also, some adults are inconsistent in their expectations and rules. This means they allow youngsters to get away with things either when they are in a good mood or a bad mood. As a result, their children don't learn that it is actually necessary to follow rules or obey adults. In addition, parents may disagree about what youngsters should and shouldn't be allowed to do and countermand each other's orders. When this happens, youngsters learn who to ask for what, or they play one adult against another instead of complying when they are told to do something.

*Consequences:* Some parents don't use consequences effectively. Specifically, once parents have told youngsters to do or not to do something, they have to follow through. And the consequences of the children's noncompliance have to be strong enough to make a difference. A mild reprimand or another slight consequence may have very little effect on youngsters who have just gotten great satisfaction from some forbidden pleasure.

Negative consequences may also be ineffective if they don't have the intended effect. Parents who really "lay the law down" to youngsters by shouting and screaming threats about what will happen to them if they ever dare to do the same thing again may believe their youngsters will certainly think twice about repeating the behavior. In reality, though, their children could be so accustomed to such angry outbursts and empty threats that they hardly listen to them. Youngsters who have not been exposed to effective consequences at home may have conduct problems at school and elsewhere because they don't expect to have to pay any serious consequences for misbehaving.

*Individual differences:* Physiological factors can also impede a child's moral development. For example, youngsters born with stubborn or persistent temperaments may find it especially difficult to do what others tell them to do. Immature children may be unable to exercise the kind of self-control typical of their more mature peers. (See Chapter 11.) In addition, extenuating circumstances such as illness, poverty, or pressure on the job can prevent adults from bringing up youngsters as they would like to. Thus, although adults are responsible for the moral development of their children, they are not necessarily to blame when their youngsters have conduct problems.

*Enhancing Moral Growth*    As we noted above, children can develop conduct problems if the adults who care for them don't model the behavior society expects of its members, expect youngsters to behave appropriately, or use consequences properly. Teachers can help students with conduct problems change their attitudes and behavior by relating to them in ways that make up for what they have missed.

*Appropriate models and expectations:* Your students may change their attitudes and behavior if you truly expect them to wait their turn, share, speak respectfully, take "no" for an answer, and so on, and if you yourself behave that way. For this reason, when working with a student who has conduct problems, begin by exposing him to expectations for correct behavior. Point out that both you and the other students in the class behave the way you expect him to behave.

The following are some general principles to consider when exposing students to appropriate expectations in order to change their attitudes toward good behavior.

1. Base your expectations on how much and what kinds of self-control are appropriate for children or adolescents of their age.

2. Make your expectations clear—avoid any vagueness.

3. Maintain consistent expectations. While it may be necessary to occasionally be flexible, for the most part your expectations should be consistent.

4. Maintain a good balance between justifying your expectations and insisting that your students do what they are told because you are the teacher in charge.

5. Don't weaken if they cry, throw a temper tantrum, say nasty things, or promise to do better next time.

6. Don't expect your students to always comply the first time they are told to do something or to comply without occasionally testing you to see how serious you are. And don't expect your students to be able to change overnight, to control all of their inappropriate behaviors at once, or to show continual progress without occasionally slipping back into old patterns.

7. It is unrealistic to expect your students to change their behaviors without feeling resentful or angry and occasionally showing these strong feelings by pouting, carrying on a temper tantrum, claiming you are mean or unfair, and the like. Anger is a natural reaction to being forced to do what one doesn't want to do. All children go through this phase until they finally accept the fact that they have to submit, conform, and sacrifice some of their personal desires. In certain cases, students are just passing through this phase at an older age.

*Effective consequences*: Providing good role models and appropriate expectations is sometimes all you need to change a student's behavior. But if your students weren't exposed to appropriate consequences at home, it will be necessary to teach them the positive consequences of desirable behavior as well as the negative consequences of any misbehavior.

The techniques for using positive and negative consequences discussed in Chapter 7 are particularly suitable for convincing students that it not only pays to behave appropriately but is also necessary to do so. The process described below outlines how to use a number of these techniques in an organized way. In most cases, after using the techniques in Chapter 7 or following the process for a few weeks, you should see a real improvement in your students' behavior.

1. *Select just a few behaviors to change at first.* To require students to stop doing all the things they shouldn't be doing and start doing all the things they should at once is to invite failure. A much better approach is for you and your students to select a few behaviors (target behaviors) to change *together*. If your student is an active participant in the process, if she agrees that the behavior should be changed, it's more likely that your efforts will be successful. Then you can manage, tolerate, or prevent the other behaviors until they can be changed. When you select behaviors, pick those that your student is most likely to have success with. Like adults, students find some bad habits easier to break than others, so start with something easy for them. Save the behaviors that annoy you the most for later.

2. *Make sure your student knows which specific behavior he will have to change.* "Play nice with other children" is too vague. "Don't take other children's toys and don't hit other children" is more specific, and it's important to be specific.

3. *Determine how often the targeted behavior occurs to give you a baseline for evaluating the results of your efforts.* Some educators like to chart the frequency of the undesirable behavior so they can have a visual picture of how this changes as the student learns to behave more appropriately.

4. *Make sure, if possible, that your student no longer gains any rewards or positive consequences from the undesirable behavior.* If you can eliminate the positive consequences of your student's unacceptable behavior, he may stop doing it because there's no longer any payoff. Unfortunately, this isn't always possible. For example, you can't always prevent students from getting an inherent payoff when they take others' toys or steal things from other students' lockers. In these instances, you may have to resort to extrinsic consequences to control your students' behavior. (See step six.)

5. *If possible, substitute an acceptable behavior for an unacceptable one.* It's easier for anyone to give up unacceptable ways of achieving satisfaction when they are given other acceptable ways of doing so. Stealing, pushing ahead of others, and lying are unacceptable behaviors that have no acceptable substitutes. So this step does not apply to such behaviors. But students who grab things from others can be taught how to ask in a way that makes it more likely they will hear a "yes," and students who call out answers can learn to raise their hands and be called on.

6. *If necessary, use consequences to get your student to change her behavior.* Reward your student for behaving appropriately. If that doesn't work, which is unfortunately common with students who have conduct problems, punish the student when she behaves inappropriately. The specific consequences you choose should depend on which ones will have the desired effect on your student and which ones you are comfortable using. Smiles, pats on the back, praise, and approval can be effective positive rewards. Expressing your disapproval or just ignoring students is sometimes enough to discourage some young students from inappropriate behavior. Often, though, it's necessary to resort to other forms of rewards such as gold stars, points, prizes, and/or the loss of such rewards or a time-out to motivate such students. Whether you use positive or negative consequences, they may work better if your student has a hand in selecting them.

   When using consequences to change a student's behavior, keep the following principles in mind. (See Chapter 7 for a more detailed discussion of these principles.)

   - With older students, self-managed reward systems are generally preferable to those teachers manage. If possible, teach your student to reward himself for behaving appropriately. For example, students can reward themselves by reminding themselves that they are in control of their behavior, by focusing on what they are achieving, and by thinking about the positive natural consequences of their changed behavior such as getting along better with their peers, learning to read better, or getting better grades. If these kinds of intrinsic, mental rewards aren't enough, students can give themselves checks or points that can be converted to extrinsic rewards of their choice. But since many students with conduct problems may not be trustworthy enough to reward themselves only when they behave appropriately, you will have to determine whether this technique is feasible with a particular student.

- A successful beginning is essential. Reward students at the start of the program for behavior even if it only approximates the eventual goal in order to give them a feeling of success and to avoid feelings of discouragement and disappointment.

  Remember, some behaviors, especially new ones students haven't practiced, take time to learn correctly. Students may try to do what is expected of them but only accomplish something that resembles the desired behavior. In such cases, you will have to shape your student's behavior by making sure she is rewarded for closer and closer approximations to the desirable behavior. For example, at first young students who haven't learned to share their things may only allow others to examine something for a moment. If they haven't been willing to do even that before, reward them. Next, reward them for allowing others a short turn and later only when they give other students a fair turn.
- Substitute natural/intrinsic reinforcers for extrinsic reinforcers as soon as possible.
- Positive consequences are preferable to negative consequences.
- When you have to resort to negative consequences, logical, fair, and reasonable ones are more likely to be acceptable to youngsters.
- Apply negative consequences consistently but with flexibility.
- Following through convinces youngsters that you mean business.
- Proper timing enhances the effectiveness of consequences. In general—with some exceptions—reward students immediately for behaving appropriately, and punish them as soon as practical for misbehaving.

7. *Evaluate the results of your efforts.* After a trial period of giving the student time to learn the consequences of his behavior, determine whether it has improved. If your student's behavior has changed both in your classroom and outside of it, not only with you but also with others who aren't using consequences, your efforts have succeeded.

   But if the student's behavior has only changed when you are there to administer consequences, he hasn't changed his attitude about exercising self-control but only behaves appropriately when it's necessary due to external circumstances—namely, you. In such cases, he will still have to change his basic attitude.

   If your student hasn't changed her behavior even with consequences to pay, your efforts haven't worked at all. There are at least three possible explanations.

   - The student may be getting some positive reward from her negative behavior that you have overlooked. If so, eliminate this positive consequence.
   - You may have selected the wrong consequences. They may be too strong or too unfair and so spark rebellion. Or else they may not be significant enough to motivate the student to behave differently.
   - It may be more difficult than you realized for the student to change the particular behaviors you targeted. If you think this might be the case, continue your efforts a while longer. But if there's still no change, choose some other behavior that will be easier for the student to change.

8. *Eliminate any extrinsic reinforcements that may be maintaining the desired behavior and see if the behavior continues even with these gone.* This is an important step because the ultimate goal is to help the student behave appropriately even without external extrinsic consequences.

9. *Work toward attitudinal change.* When your student has changed the few behaviors you have been working on, use the occasion of these successes to try to get your student to change his basic attitude. Point out how he is better off than before by saying things like: "Now that you are sharing things with other students, you have more friends. How does that make you feel? Don't you think you should wait your turn on the equipment during recess?" "Now that you're doing your own homework instead of copying, you're doing so much better in the course." "Remember all the arguments we used to have because you used to keep asking me for permission when I told you that you couldn't do something? Isn't it much better now that you take 'no' for an answer?"

This final step is extremely important because the goal of this process is more than getting your student to change a few behaviors; rather, you are trying to change his attitude about the necessity of behaving appropriately.

# *Second Stage—*
# *Natural Consequences*

By the time students leave the primary grades to enter upper elementary, they can understand why rules are necessary. Now instead of behaving appropriately primarily because of what will happen as a result, they also follow rules and procedures because they can appreciate their reasonableness. For example, primary grade students raise their hands and wait to be called on, keep silent while others are reciting, keep working at boring tasks, share with others, and put things away where they belong when they don't really want to in order to gain their teachers' approval and avoid disapproval. Upper elementary students do these things because they understand that only one student can recite at a time, that students can't hear the speaker when others are talking, that it's necessary to stay on-task even when assignments are boring in order to learn or complete the work during the allotted time, that if they want others to share with them they have to share with others, and that they have to put things where they belong so they and others can find them again. Unlike students in the first stage of moral development, who exercise self-control due to the extrinsic consequences of their actions, students in the second stage exercise self-control not ony because of extrinsic consequences but also because they appreciate the natural consequences of their behavior.

## *Identification*

Students who are in upper elementary but have not reached the second stage of moral development still need consequences to motivate them to behave appropriately. They seem to base their decisions about how to behave on a "what's-in-it-for-me" standard. Sometimes they may actually ask their teachers what will happen if they don't comply. They often complain about having to conform to rules and question their necessity. When they are caught misbehaving, they resist paying the consequences, claiming they are unfair. They may feign regret or guilt, but they rarely experience these emotions to the same degree as their classmates. They also commonly maintain a double standard in their relationships. They expect others to listen to them, share with them, and treat them nicely even though they don't behave in these ways themselves. They do this because they don't yet understand that others will treat them the way they treat others.

*Audrey: A Case Example*    Audrey, a ten-year-old, has been a problem since she entered school. She came late, attended irregularly, was disobedient toward her teachers, and complained that they were too strict and unfair when they insisted that she abide by the same rules and do the same assignments as her classmates.

Audrey's parents were described as suspicious of school authorities and uncooperative. During the few parent-teacher conferences they had attended, they said they didn't believe in the rigidity of school because it stunted children's creativity and development. One of the teachers described them as artists who didn't believe in rules either at home or at school. They claimed to be bringing up Audrey to question authority and to think for herself so that she could discover who she was and become self-directing and self-actualizing. Knowing Audrey's background, it is understandable that she resisted her teachers' authority, truly believed that they treated her unfairly, and exhibited conduct problems in school.

## Fostering Moral Development

Unfortunately, no studies presently explain why some youngsters don't progress to this second stage of moral development. The following criteria have been mentioned as possible causes by educators and psychologists.

*Causes of Moral Development Delay*    *Poor modeling*: As noted, children may learn more from what adults do than what they say. Children who see adults cheating at games, breaking traffic rules, and lying to others may learn to mock rules and procedures in the same way.

*Lack of explanations*: Youngsters need to be taught why rules and procedures are necessary so they can learn to appreciate why everyone can't do as she pleases. If adults merely tell youngsters, "Do it because I say so," or "Do it or else," they may learn to obey but not to reason. It is important to teach youngsters the practical reasons to behave appropriately.

*Lack of group identification*: If youngsters don't identify with the group—their friends and classmates—they may not care how their actions impede or infringe on the rights and goals of others. This means they may understand quite well that others can't hear the speaker when they are talking and that others may not get their share or turn if they take too much or too long, but they may simply not care enough about "others" to control their own desires.

*Immaturity*: Youngsters who develop at slower rates than their peers may be too immature socially and emotionally to understand or appreciate the practical reasons why they should abide by rules and procedures in the absence of extrinsic consequences.

*Enhancing Moral Growth*    Educators can help students with conduct problems acquire the kind of moral self-control characteristic of second-stage development by modeling appropriate behavior, explaining the practical necessity for rules and procedures, helping students understand the effects of their behavior on others through role playing, providing students with cooperative-learning experiences, and fostering group identification.

As the following quotation aptly explains, students may learn to behave morally by following their teachers' examples.

> Students do not learn moral values solely through reasoned debate. They may learn by example and from behavioral reinforcement. For example, if teachers praise students for helping one another understand their assignments, the children may come to value cooperative learning. Or students who consistently see the teacher listening respectfully to everybody's point of view adopt this practice too. Teachers need to show young children how to be fair in concrete ways, for children seem to learn situation-specific rules of behavior before they are able to grasp universal principles of justice. (8, p. 45–46)

To encourage the second stage of moral development, deemphasize your role as the authority and your use of extrinsic consequences as management techniques. Instead of telling students about the extrinsic consequences of various behaviors, explain the practical reasons why it's necessary to share, take turns, raise one's hands, and so forth. When students ask what will happen to them if they do or don't follow rules, explain that the issue isn't what will happen to them but rather how their actions will affect others. Make sure students know and understand why the rules and procedures established for the class are necessary, not arbitrary, and why acceptable alternative ways of behavior are more appropriate than undesirable ones.

You can help your students develop to the second stage by asking them to think about the implications of their actions for the group. Direct them to imagine what would happen if:

Everyone called out whenever they wanted to.

No one cleaned up or put things back where others could find them.

No one listened to the umpires when they were told they were out.

Help students understand the principle of reciprocity in human relationships. You can do this by explaining the kinds of reactions their behavior evokes in others. Another approach is to ask students to imagine how they would feel, what they would think, and how they might react if someone did to them what they do to others if:

You had been waiting ten minutes and someone cut in line ahead of you.

The school library had no books for you to do your report because someone had taken more than they needed.

Someone called out the correct answer to a difficult question when it was your turn, and you knew the answer.

Someone took your book because he had lost his.

No one chose you for the team during recess.

Deemphasize competition and individual assignments. Instead, involve students in cooperative-learning experiences so they learn how they can benefit from helping each other and working together. Remind students often that others are more likely to help them if they help others.

Research indicates that using role playing and having students who behave inappropriately assume the role of the victim or injured party can improve the way some of them relate to their peers (6, 7, 9, 10). But these studies are not clear about which students are most likely to benefit from role playing and exactly why they benefit from the technique. It may be that role playing works best with students who are unaware of or try not to think about how their actions affect others because they get a firsthand experience of what it feels like to be treated as they usually treat others.

You can also help students identify with their classmates so they care about the effects their misbehavior has on the group. Use the techniques described in Chapter 2 to foster group cohesiveness and group identity.

# Third Stage— Intrinsic Consequences

Adolescents who have reached the third stage of moral development behave appropriately because it's the right thing to do. They do this even when they would have no extrinsic consequences to pay because of the intrinsic consequences they feel. In particular, when they do the right thing, they feel good about themselves; when they misbehave, they feel bad, guilty, or ashamed of themselves. Since many adolescents and adults only exhibit this type of morality some of the time, even honest, law-abiding citizens require the watchful eye of parking meter attendants, IRS agents, and the Highway Patrol from time to time.

## Identification

Older students who have internalized or accepted the values and moral behavior they need to control themselves in the absence of consequences feel good about doing so and bad when they don't. Students who haven't yet internalized these values and morals don't experience these feelings as intrinsic consequences of their behavior. They often cheat on exams, in sports, and in competitive games and are apparently not bothered by this. It also doesn't upset them to allow others to do their share of the work. They don't seem to care about other people's feelings and feel little remorse or guilt about taking advantage of others who are younger or weaker. If caught lying, cheating, or stealing, they only regret being caught, not what they did. They may feign remorse and guilt, but unless they are good actors, it's usually obvious that they really don't experience these feelings.

*Ernie: A Case Example*   When Ernie, a 15-year-old, was caught breaking into his school, he and two others had removed audiovisual, musical, and office equipment worth several thousand dollars. Ernie had a history of stealing from other students when he was in elementary school, but that appeared to have stopped once he entered junior high, though one of his teachers suspected, but couldn't prove, that he continued to steal. In junior and senior high, he was suspected of copying homework, and he was observed cheating on tests a number of times, but he denied doing so when confronted by his teachers. His teachers considered him to be devious, dishonest, and manipulative but also bright enough to avoid being caught with the "smoking gun." When asked why he had broken into the school, Ernie claimed he stole the equipment to get money to buy the clothes and other things he needed for school and a guitar to take guitar lessons because there were no jobs for someone his age, and his mother wouldn't help him out.

Ernie lived with his mother and two sisters in a rundown neighborhood. His father was serving a second sentence for robbery. His mother advised the authorities to lock up Ernie with his father since he had turned out to be "just like him."

## Fostering Moral Development

Adolescents are motivated to behave appropriately for moral reasons. This happens as a result of adults teaching them the moral principles that guide behavior, modeling the kind of behavior they want them to copy, and giving them the love and attention they need in order to learn to care about others. Clearly, this did not happen in Ernie's case.

*Causes of Delayed Moral Development*   Adults who just either reward or punish youngsters like Ernie for respecting or not respecting others' rights without explaining the ethical reasons behind their actions may succeed in convincing young people that they should behave appropriately when there are consequences to pay. This approach does not, however, help youngsters learn to control themselves in the absence of consequences. In addition, adults who model immoral behavior because they themselves have conduct problems tend to raise adolescents with conduct problems. And, finally, youngsters who aren't treated lovingly with caring attention often have less love to give. It's as if we need to have our own batteries charged before we are able to give to or care about others.

*Enhancing Moral Growth*   Hersh, Miller, and Fielding (8) believe that the type of self-control characterizing the third level of moral development has three aspects: judging, caring, and behaving. According to their theory, to function at the stage of moral development where one acts appropriately for intrinsic reasons, individuals must have certain abilities. Specifically, they have to be able to reason or judge moral issues by weighing conflicting interests and principles and choosing in favor of the higher morality. They must care enough about others on a basic, emotional level to want to help, support, and protect them regardless of whether a payoff is in it for them. They must also be able to act on their moral feelings and judgments in situations where internal and external pressures push them not to act.

Take, for example, a student offered a great deal of money by a drug dealer to help him sell drugs to his classmates. The student might refuse if he is afraid of being caught (a nonmoral decision), but he might also refuse if he *judged* that it was wrong to sell illegal drugs or if he *cared* enough about his fellow students not to want to profit from their misery. If he was poor and needed the money or if the drug dealer threatened to harm him if he didn't cooperate, he would then also have to face internal and external pressures on him not to *act* on his feelings or moral judgments.

Another example is a teenager who, having lost the textbook for an upcoming exam, sees someone else's on an empty table in the lunchroom. She would either have to *judge* that it was wrong to take someone else's book or *care* enough about the unknown individual in order to decide not to take it for moral reasons. If the exam was really important to her or she desperately needed a good grade, she would also have to cope with internal pressures on her not to *act* on her judgment and feeling that it is wrong to steal.

You can help teenagers who haven't yet reached the third stage of moral development by working with them to improve their moral judgment or reasoning, which means working at the cognitive level. You can encourage their caring for others, the affective level of experience. Finally, you can help them act on their judgments and feelings, to fulfill themselves as moral people on the behavioral level.

*Cognitive level—judging:* Explain to students why they should behave morally. For example, give them reasons why they should treat others as they would like to be treated, why they shouldn't take things that belong to others, why they shouldn't copy on tests, and so on. Point out to them when other students or newsworthy adults behave morally. Model the behavior you want them to copy, and tell them how and why you live by the principles you do. Tell them you would like the same principles to guide their behavior. Or if you are uncomfortable discussing your personal beliefs and lifestyle with students, use other people they can identify with as examples for them to emulate.

When students argue that other people behave immorally, explain that life isn't perfect and that each person has to live his or her life in the best way possible. Help students think about how they could handle situations in which moral behavior doesn't seem to "pay" because others aren't acting ethically. Examples might include students copying from each other during an exam while the teacher is out of the room or students grabbing what they need when there aren't enough materials to go around.

Numerous moral education programs for use in the schools have been published in recent years (1, 17–19, 30, 33, 34, 38, 39, 41). Most of these programs are based on two assumptions: (1) if students don't know moral principles, then they can't apply them to moral issues, such as competing unfairly, lying, respecting the rights of the majority, and so on; and (2) students who do know such principles will apply them to moral issues. Although these programs are designed to be used with groups of students, you can use many of these materials with individual students.

These programs typically present students with situations involving moral dilemmas that they are then asked to solve. To use this technique, you can make up your own situations as well. For example, you can ask your students what they think would be the best thing to do if:

Paul's friend makes a wisecrack to a third student in front of Paul about his excessive weight and expects Paul to laugh at his remark.

Teresa's best friend asks to copy her homework because even though she wanted to do her report she had to go somewhere with her parents, and she can't afford to get a zero. Teresa believes that allowing someone to copy one's homework is wrong.

Someone hits Armando first, and he knows the boy will continue to hit him if he doesn't defend himself, but Armando has been taught that fighting isn't a good way to solve problems between people.

Harvey wants to help his parents who are abusing drugs to the point that they are hurting both themselves, his brother, and him. To do this he wants to turn them in for their own benefit, but they have ordered him not to do this.

Lupe, a little girl that Helen takes care of after school, gets into the medicine cabinet and swallows something a few minutes before her parents return. Helen thinks she ought to tell them in case Lupe swallowed something dangerous, but she is afraid she will lose her job if she does. Besides, she tells herself, she doesn't really know if it was dangerous.

Some of these programs also teach values that are necessary in a democratic society. You can adopt this approach with students by giving them reasons why all students should have the right to state their opinions and be *listened* to, why it's necessary for individuals to generally accept the decisions of the majority even when they don't agree with them, and why all students should do their fair share of the work the group is assigned. Using role playing as well can give students the experiences necessary to understand the explanations you have given them.

Research (14) indicates that these cognitive approaches (moral education) increase students' scores on such tests of moral reasoning as Kohlberg's Standard Moral Judgment Interview (26) and the Defining Issues Test (35). Yet no clear relationship shows up between students' scores on tests of moral reasoning and their behavior either in or out of the classroom (12). The finding relating directly to behavior is that only some delinquents and students with conduct problems score low on tests of moral reasoning. But many students who score low on such tests don't exhibit conduct problems in school or delinquent behavior outside of school (13, 15, 16, 20, 22, 24, 25). As Junell explains, while moral education produces increased moral awareness and the ability to reason morally:

> The fact remains that the link between moral reasoning and behaving morally is very weak if not virtually nonexistent. (23, p. 79)

The current state of affairs is summarized succinctly by Rest:

> To date, no studies have demonstrated directly that changes wrought by these moral education programs have brought about changes in behavior. (35, p. 87)

Perhaps the cognitive approach is only appropriate for teenagers who misbehave because they haven't been taught that they should behave morally. It may be that most students with conduct problems need to be able to care about others and withstand the internal and external pressures that inhibit them from acting morally. It's now clear that cognitive development alone won't bring about behavioral change (11–13, 21, 27, 29, 31, 40). Adults must also motivate students to want to behave morally (28, 32, 36, 37).

*Affective level—caring:* The moral development literature includes a variety of techniques, mostly not yet researched, that educators can use to help students learn to care enough about others so that they want to treat them morally (42, 43). One involves students in activities where they learn firsthand about the feelings and experiences of others. For example, students with conduct problems can visit programs that serve abused children or poverty families. Or they can talk to students who have been beaten up, had their money stolen, been exposed to racial abuse, and so on so they can learn what it feels like to be the victim of someone else's misbehavior. Or the students they have victimized can confront them directly. These techniques seem to have the potential of affecting students more powerfully than role playing the victim, but their actual effectiveness has not been researched. One possible shortcoming of providing students with direct experiences or involving them in role playing is that if they don't care enough about their victims to feel for them, learning about their suffering isn't going to change their behavior.

Another technique for helping students care more about others is to give them chances to help others so they learn from experience how helping people can make them feel good about themselves. Newman and others (44, 45) have described techniques for involving students in worthwhile projects designed to achieve this goal. No current research exists to show that students with conduct problems would behave differently after having been involved in such a program though.

A third approach is to involve students in cooperative-learning projects. In theory, working together in small groups will give students enough satisfaction so that they will want to relate better to their peers as a result. Again, the effectiveness of such an approach with students who have conduct problems is as yet unresearched.

Many educators believe that teachers can increase the caring behavior of students by acting in a caring manner toward them. During class, teachers can demonstrate their interest and concern for certain students by providing them with a little extra attention, writing extra or more detailed comments on their work, and actively listening when the students voice their personal concerns. Teachers can also spend time with students doing things that the students choose whether it's shooting baskets, having a soda, or lending a sympathetic ear to what they have to say.

The idea that caring for students can indeed "charge up their batteries" is very appealing. It certainly appears that youngsters who are well cared for and who receive love and affection are more likely to love and care for others than youngsters who have been abused, neglected, or rejected. But there are real limits involved. Secondary schoolteachers with thirty or more students per period for six periods can model caring behavior, but they can only provide so much actual care, love, and attention to individual students. Since anecdotal reports of successful programs for students with serious conduct problems indicate that they need lots of individual attention, it doesn't appear feasible for regular education teachers to provide adolescents who have serious conduct problems with such individual attention. Often they require abundant extra care if they have experienced serious neglect or deprivation. On the other hand, teenagers with mild conduct problems may decide to behave better if they are exposed to caring and concerned educators. For these reasons, it is likely that you can sometimes help teenagers with mild conduct problems. Adolescents with serious problems, though, will probably require additional services from other professionals.

*Behavioral level—acting:* As noted at the beginning of this chapter, people don't always act on their moral convictions. Certain situations bring out the best in people; others the worst. Some adolescents may misbehave even though their moral reasoning is sound and they care for others because they can't resist the pressures to behave inappropriately. They may be unable to resist a request from a good friend to copy their answers during a test even though they believe it's wrong to do this. Or they may be unable to do anything but defend their honor physically when someone makes a derogatory remark about their mothers even though they agree that students shouldn't fight in school. Students who have difficulty acting on their beliefs need to have their resolve strengthened. They also need to practice how to resolve situations in more acceptable ways so they don't keep giving in to pressures to behave inappropriately.

A number of educators have suggested that teachers can help students decide to behave morally in conflict situations by helping them clarify their values (46, 47, 49, 50). The assumption underlying this "values clarification" approach is that students will be able to use their values to make decisions about how to behave better when they are clear about them. One way to use this approach with students who don't yet act on their values is to teach them to apply the process below to conflict situations.

- *List the alternative ways of behaving.* In the first example above, a student could either allow a friend to copy her test answers or not.

- *Consider the consequences of each alternative way of behaving both to oneself and others.* If the student cooperated with her friend, she might feel bad about cheating and anxious that she would be caught. She might also actually be caught and get herself into trouble, but her friend would be appreciative. Possible consequences for her friend might be that she would get a better grade on the exam, but she might be tempted to continue to rely on her instead of doing her own work, which would be bad for her friend in the long run.

- *Identify one's personal values that are involved.* The personal values the student identifies might include not cheating, helping a friend, being liked by a friend, doing what one thinks is right.

- *Identify the values that are most important or significant, and select the alternative that fits these values.* If the student identified not cheating as her highest value, she would probably agree that not cooperating with her friend would be the best alternative. If she identified being liked by a friend as first, she would probably believe cooperating would be the alternative to choose. If she identified helping a friend as paramount, she might choose either alternative depending on which she thought was more helpful—assisting her friend to get a higher grade or encouraging her to do her own work.

You can also use this process with students after they have misbehaved to help them evaluate what they did and to understand why they should or could have behaved differently. For example, you could guide Alex, who hit another student who had said something about Alex's mother, to examine and evaluate alternative ways he could have reacted to the situation.

- *In what alternative ways could Alex have reacted to the situation?* He could have fought in school, fought after school, or not fought.

- *What would have been the consequences to Alex and the other student of each alternative?* By fighting in school, Alex defended his honor, but he also got into trouble. The other student received a bloody nose, got into trouble for fighting, and may have learned not to provoke Alex and others. If they had fought after school, the consequences may have been roughly the same except that they wouldn't have gotten into trouble. If Alex hadn't fought the other student, he would have felt shame for not defending his honor physically, and the other student might have lost respect for him and might continue to provoke him.

- *What personal values were involved in the situation?* To defend one's honor and to do well in school.

- *Which values were most important to Alex, and which alternative would have fit these values?* Fighting after school would have satisfied both values and led to the greatest number of desirable consequences.

Helping students clarify their values is no guarantee, however, that they will either choose values that parallel the school's or act on their values when pressure exists not to do so. In fact, current research doesn't indicate that helping students in groups clarify their values results in improved behavior (48). The process described above, however, is a modification of the group process. While there is as yet no research evidence regarding the effectiveness of using this individualized approach with students who have conduct problems, many teachers believe it has been useful with such students.

---

*Self-Quiz:*
*On Techniques*
*for Handling*
*Conduct Problems*

How would you feel about employing each of the following techniques with teenage students who have conduct problems?

    Discussing moral dilemmas in class

Teaching the values that are assumed to be necessary in a democratic society

Involving students in activities in which they learn firsthand about the feelings and experiences of individuals who are the victims of injustice

Providing students opportunities to help others

Involving students in cooperative-learning projects

Providing students with extra attention after school

Utilizing values clarification techniques

---

## *Managing, Tolerating, and Preventing*

While you are attempting to change them, you can work with students who have conduct problems using three approaches. You may use more than one at a time, depending on the circumstances.

# *Managing*

While fostering your student's moral development—and waiting for the results—you may have to manage her inappropriate behavior. The following examples of managing techniques might work for you during this transition time.

1. When you see a student on the verge of doing something wrong, distract her attention to something else. Ask her to do something for you or engage her in a conversation about something that will hold her interest.

2. Remind the student about the acceptable alternative ways she could accomplish the same goal.

3. Stay near at hand when a student appears to be about to get into trouble. The knowledge that you are watching may be all that is needed to help a student control her impulse.

4. If that doesn't deter the student, signal your disapproval by a look or a gesture that conveys your attitude. Remind the student that what she is about to do is wrong.

5. If the student is about to commit a target behavior you are trying to modify through using consequences, remind the student of that consequence.

6. Help the student manage her own behavior. Explain the importance of avoiding situations that are so tempting or where much pressure is on her to misbehave. Help the student draw up a list of situations that she should try to avoid.

# *Tolerating*

You won't be able to manage all of your students' inappropriate behaviors, so you will have to tolerate or prevent some. Certainly you'll want to prevent behaviors that are dangerous or that seriously interfere with the rights of others. Whether you should tolerate or try to prevent behaviors that aren's so serious is a matter for you to decide based on your own preferences.

The following are some general principles to keep in mind when you tolerate your students' behaviors.

1. *Try not to feel resentful or disappointed that you have to tolerate their behavior.* It may help you to remember the reason you are doing this—because the students can't control all of their behavior immediately. If you get angry or disappointed, you will give your students conflicting messages. You may try to communicate temporary acceptance of their behavior, but this won't work if you really feel resentful and they can sense this.

2. *Tolerate behavior only temporarily.* Sometimes it's easier to tolerate students' behavior problems than to continue to try to change them. However, since conduct problems can be changed, don't tolerate behavior as a substitute for trying to change it.

3. *Make sure your students know which behavior you are tolerating and which you aren't.* Both you and your students should be clear about this distinction.

# *Preventing*

Behaviors that are unfair to other youngsters or that seriously interfere with their rights and behaviors should be prevented if possible. "If possible" is included because educators can't be in more than one place at a time; they don't—regardless of what their students sometimes think—have eyes in the back of their heads, and they can't anticipate each and every thing students will do. All they can do is their best.

The following are some examples of techniques you can use to prevent students from behaving inappropriately while you are fostering their moral development.

1. Schedule activities that usually generate misbehavior for times when you or someone else can provide the needed supervision.

2. Supervise students closely in situations likely to cause problems. Keep a ready eye out for trouble and intervene before anything happens. For example, if a student is a poor loser and will cheat or lie to win, try to be watchful when he is playing competitive games.

3. Protect students from situations they can't handle without supervision when you aren't in a position to provide close supervision. For example, don't allow students to borrow things from other students or books from the class library if they don't yet take care of other things well or return them. Don't place students who take advantage of others in charge of groups. Don't allow students to use valuable or irreplaceable equipment when you know they won't be careful. Don't allow students who won't share or give up things to others to have the first turn.

4. When your intervention isn't effective and the problem is threatening to get out of hand, remove students from the situation before they seriously interfere with the rights of others.

5. Use physical control if necessary to make sure students don't harm anyone. In case of an emergency, don't hesitate to call on the authorities for help when students are on the verge of doing something dangerous. Many educators are wary of using physical force with their students due to the possibility of litigation. But when all else fails or it's obvious nothing else will work and you need an immediate response, consider physically preventing your students from doing harm. If you do, use the minimum amount of force necessary but make sure you use enough. Then get help from others as soon as possible.

Whether these or other techniques will work depends on such factors as your students' ages, the kinds of behaviors you want to prevent, and your personality. Thus, you may be able to physically prevent a young student from taking something that belongs to another student; but if your student is a teenager, this technique may be totally inappropriate. If a student is about to do something that isn't so serious, you might be okay trying a technique that has only a reasonable chance of succeeding. But if your student might hurt someone or get himself into serious trouble, choose a technique that is guaranteed to be effective even if it is a drastic solution to the problem. Finally, your particular personality will influence your choice of the preventive techniques you use. When a student is on the verge of getting into trouble, you may feel comfortable allowing her to remain in the situation while you maintain a watchful eye and prepare to intervene if necessary. Or you may prefer to remove the student from situations that require close supervision.

# *Counseling Students' Parents*

Students are more likely to change their attitudes and behavior if their parents (or the adults in charge of bringing them up) *and* their teachers all expect and model the same behavior, use consequences appropriately, teach them to behave morally, and treat them with the attention and affection they need. When parents don't relate to students with conduct problems in these ways, it may be necessary to encourage them to change how they handle their youngsters so they won't be at cross purposes with you.

Some teachers believe that helping parents change for the better is the job of the school social worker or the guidance counselor. They feel they have neither the training nor time to counsel parents. But other educators disagree. They believe teachers can be instrumental in helping many adults improve the way they handle youngsters with conduct problems. For example, Morgan and Jenson suggest that:

> Including parents takes extra time and planning, but if it is effective, it can facilitate the teaching process and may actually reduce the demands on the teacher. (51, p. 402)

This section describes a general approach you can use to counsel parents. This approach is based on the assumption that you can meet with the parents of a few of your students from three to five times during the school year. The section also identifies three reasons adults typically don't use appropriate parenting skills with youngsters who have conduct problems: lack of information, situational difficulties, and psychological problems. It goes on to offer suggestions for how you can help these adults improve their child care skills within your limited training and the short amount of time you can spend counseling them.

During your first meeting with the parents of your student, discuss the problems in class that made you want to meet with them. Then explain how they can assist you in doing a better job with the student by helping you understand her better. The meeting can also help you obtain the additional information you require and give you a chance to deal with any questions or concerns they may have. If, during the meeting, you arrive at conclusions concerning the parents' role in maintaining the student's behavior and how you might help them improve the way they handle their youngster, you might suggest ways that you can all work together to improve the student's behavior if time permits. But more than likely, you will need time to think over what you have learned during this initial meeting and to plan your approach to them for your next meeting.

You can devote the second meeting to the joint formulation of a plan of action that specifies in detail what you and they will do. During your subsequent conferences with the

*Teachers can often help parents improve the way they handle their children, which can make everyone's job more positive.*

parents, evaluate the effectiveness of your plan together: Are they carrying out their part of the contract? Have they noticed any problems? Are they still in agreement with the plan of action? How has the youngster reacted to the new approach at home and in school? Is it necessary to modify the plan? Is it still feasible to work with the parents, or would it be better to refer them to the school social worker, guidance counselor, or psychologist?

Your final meeting with the parents should be a wrap-up session. Discuss what you have all learned about the student and about effective ways of dealing with his problems. Review the progress he has made, and discuss how each of you plan to continue working with the student.

## *Lack of Information*

Some adults don't have the information they need to bring up youngsters free of conduct problems. Perhaps they have unrealistic expectations because they don't know enough about normal child and adolescent development, or they may not know how to communicate their expectations. Some adults don't use consequences effectively. Others are unaware of the importance of explaining to youngsters why they should behave appropriately. Providing the information parents lack can sometimes be all the assistance they need to improve how they handle their youngsters.

*Expectations*    Do the adults in charge of raising the student expect him or her to exercise a realistic amount of self-control, or do they expect too much self-control too soon or too little too late? Children and teenagers learn to control themselves when adults require them to do so. Some parents don't demand that their youngsters exercise enough self-control because they don't realize they are able to do so. They may not know, for example, what to expect from a typical three-year-old, five-year-old, or eight-year-old, or they may think "too much" self-control will frustrate youngsters and stunt their personal growth.

In contrast, parents can also require too much self-control from their youngsters, insisting that their children not touch tempting but breakable objects, not mess up their rooms when they play, or not talk into the night when a friend is sleeping over long before the children are able to control these behaviors. They may also expect their youngsters to control their behavior 100 percent of the time without allowing the occasional slip we all make from time to time. When adults expect too much self-control from youngsters, children may learn they are unable to do what is expected of them. Attributing their inability to a lack in themselves rather than to the adults' inappropriate expectations, they may give up trying or rebel against the parents' unrealistic demands.

Ask the following types of questions: "What is Harry allowed and not allowed to do?" "What things do you expect Marie to do on her own, and when do you have to supervise her closely?" "In what ways does Vincent live up to your expectations, and in what ways does he not?" These can give you clues about the parents' expectations. If the adults who care for your students have inappropriate expectations, explain how they are inappropriate. Describe how the students' peers behave in class, and help the parents arrive at more realistic expectations for their child at home.

*Do the adults in charge of your student communicate their expectations clearly in a way that indicates they mean them?* Youngsters can fulfill adults' expectations only when they know what they are. Some things adults habitually say are too vague: "You can close the door to your room, but don't do anything you are not supposed to do," "You two can talk for a while, but then you have to stop and try to fall asleep," "Be good, listen to the baby sitter, and don't go to sleep late." Youngsters may not mind when their parents say such things because they really don't know what they aren't supposed to do in their rooms, how long they can talk, and when exactly to go to bed. Some adults also phrase things ambiguously: "It would be nice if you ———," "Don't you think it's a good idea to ———?" "You would really make me happy if you ———." In cases like this, children may not get a clear message that they are supposed to do something, yet their parents think they are making demands. They may also not learn that they have to submit to their parents' authority if the parents do not exercise that authority.

Ask parents to give you some examples of how they communicate their expectations to their youngsters. You can suggest that, if it's easier, they can do this by role playing an interchange between them and their youngster. If you find that their expectations are unclear or they aren't communicated in a businesslike, serious manner, explain how that can mislead youngsters. You can also suggest alternative ways to communicate expectations and give them examples of how you speak to the student in class.

*Are the expectations consistent?* Youngsters are more likely to fulfill adult expectations that are consistent. As noted, if parents prohibit their youngsters from behaving in certain ways sometimes, but not at other times, or if they disagree with each other about what youngsters should and shouldn't be allowed to do and countermand each other, their youngsters may not learn that it's actually necessary to follow the rules or listen to their parents.

Ask the parents of youngsters how flexible and how consistent their expectations are. If they are inconsistent, explain the importance of holding the line. Find out whether both parents have similar expectations for their youngster. If they don't, guide them through a discussion of one or two expectations until they reach an agreement. Suggest that they continue the process on their own.

*Consequences*   Ask the parents to describe how, when, and why they reward and punish their child. Try to determine the ratio of positive to negative consequences and the specific kinds of positive and negative consequences they use. Also ascertain whether they follow through on the consequences they say will result for different types of behavior and if they apply consequences in a timely fashion.

*Do parents employ a good balance between positive and negative reinforcements to motivate youngsters?* It is understandable that adults would rather discipline children by rewarding them for good behavior than by punishing them for bad behavior; however, some parents of youngsters with conduct problems rely too much on rewards. As a result, their children don't learn that it's necessary to behave or else. If you find that parents overrely on positive reinforcement, explain why it's necessary to "lay down the law" with children and to teach them that they can't misbehave with impunity. If they resist using negative consequences because they believe that would make them be terrible parents, stunt their children's growth, or destroy their relationship with their child, explain that such repercussions are unlikely so long as the punishments they use aren't abusive. Ask them what they would consider abusive and nonabusive negative consequences, and help them select consequences that they will feel comfortable with.

Don't be surprised if you and the parents disagree somewhat. Some adults, for example, believe it's okay to take away a youngster's privileges, such as sweets, desserts, treats, and the like, but not rights like supper; others think it's fine to send a youngster to bed without supper. Some adults feel that an occasional spanking or strapping with a belt followed up with a sincere statement of caring about the youngster is okay; many others can't abide any sort of physical punishment. Some adults feel that parents shouldn't punish children when they are angry or upset at their youngsters, while others feel that an appropriate punishment fairly administered can teach youngsters they can't do things that anger other people without paying the consequences of their behavior.

Adults can also err in the opposite direction by overrelying on negative consequences to try to motivate their children. When working with such parents, explain that even the best result of this approach is that their youngsters will fear them enough to obey them. But their children might also be angry enough to disobey them even though they also fear them. Either way, their children won't learn to love them enough to obey them voluntarily, which is the real goal. Help such parents identify positive rewards and replace some of the negative consequences they have been employing. If necessary, teach them how to reward their youngsters. (See Chapter 7.) Help parents who use excessively harsh punishment to make their "punishments fit the crime." Explain that the consequences of a youngster's transgressions should be natural if possible, in proportion to what the youngster has done, and no more severe than a youngster that age can tolerate. Also help them understand why they shouldn't choose punishments that reflect their anger and frustration. Instead they should base their choice on punishment that will get their points across fairly and clearly. Suggest that they say nothing until the heat of the moment passes and they can once more deal calmly with the problem. Some parents may not take kindly to being advised about how to discipline their child, especially by a young teacher who may not yet even have any children. If this appears to be the case, you might want to consider referring them to some books or classes on parenting that you believe are relevant to their problem.

*Ethical Principles*   *Do parents teach youngsters ethical principles?* It would certainly be presumptuous of you to tell parents which ethical principles to teach children. But if you find that parents are overrelying on consequences to discipline their teenagers, it would be appropriate to explain why it's important for them to communicate the values and ethical principles they believe in to their youngster as a way of motivating him or her to behave in a more acceptable manner. Older children and adolescents can understand the ethical concepts in such questions as "How would you feel if someone treated you that way?" or "How can you expect them to treat you one way and everyone else another way?" And suggesting such questions may help parents.

## Situational Difficulties

Some parents are caught up in situations that make it extremely difficult for them to bring up their youngsters as they would like. For example, one spouse may disagree with the other about how to teach their child self-discipline but acquiesce to keep the peace. A parent may know what to do about his son but be unable to do it because legally he is only permitted to see the youngster once or twice a week. Parents may be so busy trying to earn enough to pay the bills, they can't devote the time they know they should to their families. They may also be experiencing tremendous pressure at work to stay late or bring work home if they want to be promoted or just keep their jobs. Or they may be so worn out by their own problems that they just can't cope with those of their youngsters.

Educators can do little if anything to help parents solve the kinds of situational difficulties that limit their ability to bring up their children free of conduct problems. But they can help parents appreciate the effects they are having on their youngsters if they are unaware of them. They can also help strengthen and support the parents' resolve to do everything in their power to solve their situational difficulties. When appropriate, educators can refer parents to appropriate sources of needed assistance.

## Psychological Problems

Some parents are highly motivated to change how they relate to their youngsters and are willing and able to act on the suggestions educators offer them. But many others need more help than you can provide despite their motivation to change. Still other parents resist help with their problems and may even be difficult clients for mental health professionals (52). The following are some examples of how parents' psychological problems interfere with their ability to teach youngsters self-control. The first two are problems that educators may be able to help parents with. The others would most likely require that you refer the parents to a school social worker, guidance counselor, or psychologist who might in turn refer them to a mental health professional.

The first example involves parents who find it hard to accept their anger at other people no matter how justified it is. They may be uncomfortable about punishing children when they do things that make them angry. Thus, they may tolerate behavior they should try to change, give in to their children rather than stand up to them in order to avoid conflicts, and threaten to punish them without following through. With such parents, you might try reminding them that their youngsters shouldn't be allowed to do things that make their parents and other people angry. You could also explain why it's no help to children to permit them to develop behavior patterns at home that can get them into trouble in school or elsewhere.

The second kind of psychological problem that educators may have success with are parents who have difficulty disciplining their youngsters because of guilt. They may believe they haven't given them enough time and attention because of their careers, or they feel they are to blame for depriving their children of a parent because they wanted a divorce. They may also feel guilty because they are too tired and overwhelmed by their own problems to care for their youngsters properly or are too resentful about having to care for their youngsters by themselves as a single parent to provide them with the love and attention they need. If they are also afraid of losing their youngsters' love, they may be even less able to discipline them.

Parents of handicapped children are particularly susceptible to this problem because they often mistakenly feel somehow responsible for their youngster's handicaps. They also often feel so sorry for their youngsters that they can't bring themselves to add to their burdens by insisting that they behave themselves and disciplining them when they don't.

If parents seem to be suffering from inappropriate guilt, you can listen to their feelings and even validate them ("Yes, I can see why you might feel that way"), but then offer some support for the choices they've made. Explain that everyone has a right to his or her own life, divorce can be the best solution for everyone concerned if the situation is bad enough, or that parents don't knowingly cause their children to be handicapped.

Youngsters whose parents have difficulty disciplining them for psychological reasons often develop ways of keeping their parents from carrying through on discipline. "I'm sorry, I'm sorry. I didn't mean to do it;" they apologize, and their parents give in. "I didn't know, I forgot, I promise, I'll never do it again;" they promise, and their parents yield. "Give me one more chance, just one more chance, please;" they beseech their parents, putting on a look of fright or helplessness, and their parents melt. "I hate you, you don't love me, you're so mean;" they proclaim angrily, and their parents cave in. "It's your fault, you didn't remind me to . . . ;" they complain defensively, and their parents agree. If the parents of your student are being manipulated by their youngsters, help them identify when their youngsters are manipulating them so they can stand firm for their youngster's benefit.

The third example involves psychological factors that cause parents to demand too much from their youngsters rather than being too permissive. Instances include parents who are resentful because they are single and have to care for their youngsters by themselves, parents who are themselves too immature and needy to take care of the needs of their children, and parents who had unplanned youngsters late in life. In each case, they may take their resentment out on their children. They may pressure their youngsters to do things for themselves such as dress themselves, straighten their rooms, and do things on their own like homework before they can do so. The lack of tender loving care that these premature demands reflect can make youngsters unwilling to behave appropriately, sacrifice their desires for the benefit of others, and respect the rights of others.

The fourth example occurs when power is an issue in parents' lives, which can influence their relationships with their youngsters. Such parents may experience the task of disciplining children as a battle of wills and evaluate success in terms of who is controlling whom rather than in terms of how much self-control their youngsters have acquired. Many youngsters are not too adversely affected by this kind of power struggle so long as they also receive plenty of tender loving care from their parents. But if parents fail to balance power plays with enough caring or they become so angry and full of rage when their youngsters misbehave that they constantly resort to harsh punishments to win their power struggles, then instead of acquiescing, their youngsters may rebel. In addition, by teaching their youngsters that power is the "name of the game," they provide poor models and even less motivation for them to control their behavior in the absence of consequences.

In another example, parents who are nervous, unhappy, or depressed may be unable to cope with the daily tasks of bringing up children and teenagers. Nervous parents may avoid getting into conflicts with their youngsters about things they should and shouldn't do. Depressed parents may not have the energy to discipline their youngsters or to give them the care they need no matter how much they would like to do or how badly they feel about not doing so.

Finally, parents who have conduct problems themselves often pass these on to their children. By not modeling appropriate behavior and not teaching youngsters to behave morally, they make it difficult for youngsters to control themselves in situations where there are no consequences.

## Self-Quiz: On Counseling Parents

Do you think counseling parents of students who have conduct problems should be part of your role as a classroom teacher? Do you think classroom teachers should counsel parents who need help with their youngsters because of lack of information, situational difficulties, and psychological problems?

## Case Studies

The following case studies illustrate how you can use techniques described in this chapter to help students with conduct problems.

# *Randi*

Randi, an eight-year-old, was considered "disruptive and unmanageable" by Ms. Finney, her third-grade teacher. At the start of the second month of the school year, Ms. Finney asked for consultation with a district behavior therapist. The specific behaviors she listed on the referral forms included "calling out, not waiting her turn, difficulty sharing, taking things from other students' cubbies, aggressive behavior toward peers, resisting cleaning up and putting things away." After meeting with Ms. Finney, Randi's first-grade teacher, and her parents, as well as observing Randi in class and reviewing her cumulative folder, the behavior specialist, Mr. Singfield, thought they should deal with Randi's behavior problems as conduct problems, and he devised the following program.

Before saying anything to Randi, Ms. Finney determined how often each of the behaviors occurred during two mornings and two afternoons over a four-day period. Following this she met with Randi, listed five of her undesirable behaviors, and clearly explained why they were unacceptable. Together they selected two behaviors from the list that Randi agreed to modify—calling out and refusing to put her things away. They also identified two alternative acceptable behaviors—raising her hand and waiting to be called on and putting her things away. In addition, they selected the rewards Randi would receive for behaving in an acceptable way and the negative consequences that would result when she behaved inappropriately. For raising her hand instead of calling out and for putting her things away, she was awarded points that she could later use for playing jacks with Ms. Finney. She received one point each time she raised her hand and five points each time she put her things away. But she lost one point each time she called out and five points each time she refused to put her things away. She could purchase a minute of jacks-playing time with five points. In addition, Ms. Finney told Randi that she would ignore her whenever she called out. (Mr. Singfield had observed that Ms. Finney often acknowledged Randi's contributions when she called out, thereby reinforcing her behavior.) Randi was also told that the other three unacceptable behaviors on the list weren't a part of the deal for the time being. She wouldn't receive any positive or negative consequences regarding them except that if she hit or pushed other students she would be sent to the principal's office (a technique that Ms. Finney had been using without any observable success).

During the first three days of the program, Randi called out only four times and put her things away each time she was required to. During the morning of the fourth day, she was sent to the office for hitting, and when she returned she reverted to her previous level of calling out. Her behavior improved again during the fifth day. By the end of the second week, Randi raised her hand and put her things away consistently. But the program had little effect on her other undesirable classroom behaviors.

After the third week during which Randi had five almost perfect days, Ms. Finney and Mr. Singfield decided to eliminate the extrinsic consequences. This resulted in a rapid deterioration of Randi's behavior, and they reinstated the point system. The two target behaviors improved immediately, and waiting her turn and participating in group cleanup improved somewhat. But Randi continued to take things from other students' cubbies and to resist sharing materials and equipment.

At this point, Mr. Singfield decided it would be necessary to include Randi's parents in the program. During his interview with them, he had noted that Randi's parents presented a "divided front" in that her father permitted her to get away with a great deal, and he often "undercut" her mother's efforts to discipline her. As a result of a meeting with him, Randi's parents adapted a consistent approach with her. In addition, Ms. Finney began to place more emphasis on consistently praising Randi for behaving appropriately and pointing out how much better it would be for her if she also modified the three other undesirable behaviors on her list. After two additional weeks, all of Randi's undesirable behaviors in school improved considerably. Her parents also reported that her behavior at home had improved a little.

Six weeks later, the program was discontinued in school but maintained at home with very little deterioration in Randi's behavior in class. She seldom called out, consistently put her things away, and participated in group cleanup. No instances of taking things from other students' cubbies were observed. She still resisted sharing with others on occasion, however, and infrequently hit or pushed other students when they wouldn't acquiesce to her wishes.

## Barry

Barry, a 16-year-old, was a bright student who was just barely passing in school. He was two years behind in math and three in reading. Although he had been a disruptive student until the eighth grade, his behavior changed drastically when he entered high school. He stopped "defying" his teachers and fighting with other students. His teachers felt that he had gone "underground." They suspected him of copying his homework, stealing equipment from science labs, forging his mother's signature on absence reports, and selling drugs, but they were unable to prove anything.

When some inexpensive equipment from the science laboratory was discovered in his locker, two letters requesting a meeting were sent to his home without an answer. In response to a telephone call, his mother told the school authorities that they could do as they pleased with Barry. She couldn't afford to take a day off from work, and her husband was in prison for the third time.

Mr. Johnson, Barry's science teacher who had grown up in the same neighborhood as Barry, volunteered to be his mentor if he wasn't suspended or referred to the police. Given the option of working with Mr. Johnson or having his case referred to the police, Barry chose Mr. Johnson.

During the first few meetings, Barry said nothing about the science equipment. They talked mostly about Barry's poor grades and irregular attendance. Mr. Johnson offered to obtain a tutor for Barry, but he declined, saying he didn't need one because he just wanted to finish high school and get a job. But it turned out that the jobs Barry was interested in required more than a high school diploma. In response to Mr. Johnson's question about what he liked to do, Barry answered sports and art, both of which he was good at.

Mr. Johnson located a commercial artist who hired Barry part-time after school, and he took him to two basketball games before Barry brought up the stolen science equipment. When Barry justified his behavior on the grounds that kids like him had to survive in any way they could since they couldn't make it in the system, Mr. Johnson let him know that he had also grown up in Barry's neighborhood—without, however, communicating an attitude of "Look at me, I made it, why can't you?"

Two months later Barry asked Mr. Johnson if he could still find him a tutor since he had decided that he wanted to study commercial art in college.

# *Summary*

Youngsters must learn to accept the fact that there are times when they must submit to authority, conform to norms of acceptable behavior, and sacrifice their personal desires for the benefit of others. To teach them to accept these obligations when they are young, adults provide good models for youngsters to follow, motivate them to copy appropriate adult behaviors, and teach them that desirable consequences follow when they submit, conform, or sacrifice, and negative consequences follow when they don't. When children are older, adults motivate them to accept these three obligations even when they don't have to suffer the consequences of their actions by explaining the reasons why they should do so, teaching them ethical principles, and providing them with the affection and concerned caring needed to motivate them to want to behave morally. Young children who don't fulfill these three obligations, and older children and adolescents who do so only when there are consequences to pay, have conduct problems.

To help students who have conduct problems, you should use techniques that will assist them in attaining the stage of moral development that is appropriate for their age. While you are doing this, you can also use managing, tolerating, and preventing techniques and counsel their parents if necessary.

# *Activities*

Read each of the following descriptions and decide whether the behavior described is more likely to be caused by conduct problems or some other kinds of problems.

John was a nine-year-old who had been behaving poorly since kindergarten. He was slow to do what he was told and did so only under pressure. He argued and fought with the other students in his classes and seldom shared, waited his turn, or allowed others to speak if he wanted to say something. His parents reported that he refused to listen to them, demanded their complete and immediate attention, and didn't get along with his younger brother and sister. Some of the specific behaviors they described were nagging them and making a general nuisance of himself until he either got what he wanted or was punished, interrupting them whenever he felt like it, and taking his siblings' toys without permission.

Ophelia was a five-year-old preschool student who was well behaved at school. However, her teachers were concerned about the fact that she seldom interacted with other children and almost never spoke to anyone about anything. On a few occasions she even wet herself rather than ask to go to the bathroom. What struck them was the difference between her behavior when she was with her mother at the beginning of the school day and then after her mother left. In her mother's presence, she was lively, energetic, full of smiles, spontaneous, and talkative. As soon as her mother left, she became quiet and never smiled. Ophelia's parents were also worried about her behavior. Their three main concerns were that she was still unable to fall asleep unless one of them kept her company, she cried and threw temper tantrums when they left her with her baby sitter, and she showed little interest in playing with other children her age. On the other hand, she got along well with her younger sister and older brother and was well behaved except when she was put to bed or left with baby-sitters.

Tyrone, a 13-year-old, got along well with his teachers but not with the other students. He was often in trouble for getting into fights that he invariably started because of some slight insult he imagined he had suffered at the hands of his peers. His parents reported that he always listened to them except when it came to his two younger sisters. Although his parents had warned and punished him repeatedly, he still made life miserable for his sisters. He hit them, teased them, took things away from them, called them names, and did anything he could to upset them. The more they cried and complained to their parents, the more he annoyed them. When he was younger, the neighbors complained that he shot their pets with his pellet gun, tied things to their tails, and set fires in the street. However, except for one neighbor who suspected that Tyrone had broken some windows of his cottage, it had been over two years since any of the neighbors had complained about him.

# *References*

DEVELOPMENTAL APPROACH

1. Kohlberg, L. (1984). Moral stages and moralization. In A. Garrod, R. Bartell, W. Rampaul, & K. Siefert (Eds.), *Perspective on Teaching, Learning and Development*. Dubuque, IA: Kendall/Hunt.

2. Piaget, J. (1965). *The Moral Judgment of Children*. New York: Free Press.

ENHANCING MORAL GROWTH—FIRST STAGE

3. Nelson, C. M. (1971). Techniques for screening conduct disturbed children. *Exceptional Children, 37*, 501–507.

4. Quay, H. C., & Peterson, D. R. (1979). *Manual for the Behavior Problems Checklist*. Miami: Quay & Peterson.

5. Spivack, G., & Spotts, J. (1966). *Devereux Child Behavior Rating Scale*. Devon, PA: Devereux Foundation.

ENHANCING MORAL GROWTH—SECOND STAGE

6. Chandler, M. (1973). Egocentrism and antisocial behavior: The assessment and training of social perspective-taking skills. *Developmental Psychology, 9*, 326–332.

7. Feshbach, N. (1978). Studies in developing empathy. In B. Maker (Ed.), *Progress in Experimental Personality Research*. New York: Academic Press.

8. Hersh, R. H., Miller, J. P., & Fielding, G. D. (1980). *Models of Moral Education*. White Plains, NY: Longman.

9. Schmuck, R., & Schmuck, P. (1984). *Group Process in the Classroom* (4th ed.). Dubuque, IA: Brown.

10. Selman, R. L. (1976). Social cognitive understanding: A guide to educational and clinical practice. In T. Lickona (Ed.), *Moral Development: Theory Research and Social Issues*. New York: Holt, Rinehart & Winston.

ENHANCING MORAL GROWTH—THIRD STAGE—COGNITIVE LEVEL

11. Arndt, A. W., Jr. (1976). Maturity of moral reasoning about hypothetical dilemmas and behavior in an actual setting. *Dissertation Abstracts International, 37*, 435B. (University Microfilms No. 75-15, 009)

12. Bear, G. G. (1980). The relationship of moral reasoning to conduct problems and intelligence. *Dissertation Abstracts International, 40*, 4961A. (University Microfilms No. 80-04, 677)

13. Bear, G. G., & Richards, H. C. (1981). Moral reasoning and conduct problems in the classroom. *Journal of Educational Psychology, 73* (5), 644–670.

14. Blatt, M., & Kohlberg, L. (1975). The effects of classroom moral discussion upon children's level of moral judgment. In L. Kohlberg & E. Toriel (Eds.), *Recent Research in Moral Development*. New York: Holt, Rinehart & Winston.

15. Campagna, A. F., & Hartner, S. (1975). Moral judgment in socio-pathic and normal children. *Journal of Personality and Social Psychology, 31*, 199–205.

16. Fodor, E. M. (1972). Delinquency and susceptibility to social influence among adolescents as a function of level of moral development. *Journal of Social Psychology, 86*, 257–260.

17. Fraenkel, J. R. (1977). *How to Teach About Values: An Analytic Approach*. Englewood Cliffs, NJ: Prentice-Hall.

18. Gardner, E. M. (1983). *Moral Education for Emotionally Disturbed Adolescents: An Application of Kohlbergian Techniques and Spiritual Principles*. Lexington, MA: Lexington Books.

19. Hersh, R. H., Miller, J. P., & Fielding, G. D. (1980). *Models of Moral Education: An Appraisal*. White Plains, NY: Longman.

20. Hickey, J. E. (1972). The effects of guided moral discussion upon youthful offender's level of moral judgment. *Dissertation Abstracts International, 33*, 1551A. (University Microfilms No. 72-25, 438)

21. Hogan, R. (1975). The structure of moral character and the explanation of moral action. *Journal of Youth and Adolescence, 4*, 1–15.

22. Hudgins, W., & Prentice, N. M. (1973). Moral judgment in delinquent and non-delinquent adolescents and their mothers. *Journal of Abnormal Psychology, 82*, 145–152.

23. Junell, J. S. (1979). *Matters of Feeling: Values Education Reconsidered*. Bloomington, IN: Phi Delta Kappa Educational Foundation.

24. Jurkovic, G., & Prentice, N. M. (1974). Dimensions of moral interaction and moral judgment in delinquent and nondelinquent families. *Journal of Consulting and Clinical Psychology, 42,* 256–262.

25. Kohlberg, L. (1958). *The Development of Modes of Moral Thinking and Choice in the Years 10 to 16.* Unpublished doctoral dissertation, University of Chicago, Chicago.

26. Kohlberg, L., Colby, A., Gibbs, J., & Speicher-Dubin, B. (1978). *Standard Form Scoring Manual.* Cambridge, MA: Harvard University, Center for Moral Education.

27. Kohlberg, L., & Hersch, R. H. (1977). Moral development: A review of the theory. *Theory into Practice, 16,* 53–58.

28. Kohlberg, L., Kauffman, K., Scharf, P., & Hickey, J. (1974). *The Just Community Approach to Corrections: A Manual* (Part I). Unpublished manuscript, Harvard University, Cambridge, MA.

29. Leming, J. S. (1978). Intrapersonal variations in stage of moral reasoning among adolescents as a function of situational context. *Journal of Youth and Adolescence, 4,* 405–416.

30. McPhail, P., Ungoed-Thomas, J. R., & Chapman, H. (1975). *Lifeline.* Niles, IL: Argus Communications.

31. Muson, H. (1979, February). Moral thinking: Can it be taught? *Psychology Today,* pp. 48–68.

32. Power, C., & Reimer, J. (1978). Moral atmosphere: An educational bridge between moral judgment and action. In W. Damon (Ed.), *New Directions in Child Development: Moral Development.* San Francisco: Jossey-Bass.

33. Presno, V., & Presno, C. (1980). *The Values Realm: Activities for Helping Students Develop Values.* New York: Teachers College Press.

34. Reimer, J., Paolitto, D. P., & Hersch, R. H. (1983). *Promoting Moral Growth: From Piaget to Kohlberg* (2nd ed.). White Plains, NY: Longman.

35. Rest, J. R. (1986). *Moral Development: Advances in Research and Theory.* New York: Praeger.

36. Scharf, P. (1978). *Moral Education.* Davis, CA: Responsible Action.

37. Scharf, P., Hickey, J. E., & Moriarty, T. (1973). Moral conflict and change in correctional settings. *Personnel and Guidance Journal, 51,* 660–663.

38. Shaver, J., & Strong, W. (1976). *Facing Value Decisions: Rationale Building for Teachers.* Belmont, CA: Wadsworth.

39. Silver, M. (1976). *Values Education.* Washington, DC: National Education Association.

40. Stein, J. L. (1973). *Adolescent Reasoning About Moral and Sex Dilemmas: A Longitudinal Study.* Unpublished doctoral dissertation, Harvard University, Cambridge, MA.

41. Sullivan, E. V. (1975). *Moral Learning: Finding Issues and Questions*. New York: Paulist Press.

The entries below deal with enhancing moral growth on the affective level.

42. Lickona, T. (1977). Creating the just community with children. *Theory into Practice, 16* (2), 103.

43. McPhail, P. (1975). *Learning to Care*. Niles, IL: Argus Communications.

44. Newman, F. (1975). *Education for Citizen Action: Challenge for Secondary Curriculum*. Berkeley, CA: McCutchan.

45. Newman, F., Bertocci, T. A., & Landsness, R. M. (1977). *Skills in Citizen Action*. Skokie, IL: National Textbook.

These references discuss working with moral growth on the behavioral level.

46. Kirschenbaum, H. (1977). *Advanced Value Clarification*. La Jolla, CA: University Associates.

47. Kirschenbaum, H., & Simon, S. (1973). *Readings in Values Clarification*. Minneapolis, MN: Winston Press.

48. Lockwood, A. L. (1978). The effects of values clarification and moral development curricula on school age subjects. *Review of Educational Research, 48*, 325–364.

49. Raths, L., Harmin, M., & Simon, S. (1966). *Values and Teaching: Working with Values in the Classroom*. Columbus, OH: Charles E. Merrill.

50. Simon, S., Howe, L., & Kirschenbaum, H. (1972). *Values Clarification: A Handbook of Practical Strategies for Teachers and Students*. New York: Hart.

COUNSELING PARENTS

51. Morgan, D. P., & Jenson, W. R. (1988). *Teaching Behaviorally Disordered Students: Preferred Practices*. Columbus, OH: Charles E. Merrill.

52. Patterson, G. R. (1982). *Coercive Family Process*. Eugene, OR: Castalia.

# CHAPTER 10

# *EMOTIONAL PROBLEMS*

This chapter is concerned with students who misbehave in the classroom because they come to school with emotional problems that originate elsewhere. It discusses what emotional problems are, how they cause students to misbehave, and what educators can do to help such students in school.

## *Role of Emotions*

Emotions both stimulate us to react to events and help us select appropriate responses to these events. Let's look at an example of how the process works.

The bell signaling the end of the period will ring in two minutes, and the teacher in charge hasn't quite finished returning the class test papers. Mary, Jaime, and Latanya are about to receive their papers. Mary looks apprehensively at the top of the page—C. She is relieved. "I finally passed," she announces to her friend sitting alongside her. Jaime looks at his paper, sees a C, and moans. Latanya examines her paper—C. "Oh no!" she thinks. "I can't show this to my dad. He'll kill me."

The bell rings. Mary walks out of the room happy. Jaime stops at the door, anxiously waiting for his friend, Carlos. Carlos sees the worried look on his face. "Hey man," Jaime says to him, "you gotta help me with this sucker." Latanya is still sitting in her seat, stunned. She is in no hurry to go home where she will have to fulfill the family ritual of showing her parents her test papers because she is petrified of the consequences.

With each of these three students and their test grades, the process is the same. First, something happens that is given meaning by the student's intellect. In this example, they see their grades. For Mary, the C is good; for Jaime and Latanya, the C is a disaster.

Next, each student has an emotional experience including a bodily response that prepares them to react to the situation. Mary feels happy, Jaime becomes anxious, and Latanya is afraid.

Then, their intellect determines how they will react, based on their previous experiences, training, expectations, and the like. Mary bounds out of the room humming; Jaime seeks assistance; and Latanya sits motionless, trying to summon up the courage to face her parents.

# Emotional Problems

This process of an event, a feeling, and a behavior is the way things should happen and the way they usually do happen. But some students' emotional responses don't guide their behavior appropriately. As a result we say that they have emotional problems.

## Overly Intense Emotions

Certain students have emotional responses that are too strong. For example, you may have or know students with whom you really have to be careful about what you say because they are devastated by the slightest criticism. Or you may have students who feel intensely anxious when they have to talk in front of a group. Some students build up the little positive things in their lives out of proportion so that other students can't understand what they are so excited about. Students who experience their emotions too intensely and so behave inappropriately usually have emotional problems.

Most of the time, you will have to make on-the-spot decisions about your students' emotional responses. You can make fairly accurate informal assessments by using their behaviors to indicate whether their responses are appropriate or not.

Emotional responses that are too intense are characterized by extreme reactions to small or relatively inconsequential events or events that, at the student's current age, should no longer evoke such strong responses. Below are examples of behaviors from students whose emotional responses are too intense.

They are petrified by a little blood from a scrape on the knee or a small cut on the finger.

They become extremely anxious when they have to answer questions, take tests, make a report, or the like.

They are easily upset by even a minor criticism or correction of their work or behavior.

They become very angry about small things and seem to have a chip on their shoulders.

*Sad, worried, and depressed students have difficulty concentrating on school work.*

They are frustrated over very minor delays, small obstacles, and other irritants.

They get depressed over the little disappointments that other students seem able to take in stride.

If, for example, Jaime's emotional response had been too intense, he might have felt so anxious that he would have had to avoid talking about the exam or learning the right answers because it would make him much more anxious. If Latanya's emotional response had been too strong, she might have stayed out all night or thrown away her test and told her parents she received an "A" but lost the paper. In both cases, Jaime and Latanya would have overreacted to their grades and behaved inappropriately.

## *Weak Emotions*

Certain students have just the opposite problem. Instead of being too strong, their emotional responses are too weak. For example, most students mistreated or abused by their peers will eventually rise up and protest such treatment. But students with weak emotional responses just feel a little resentful but not resentful enough to do something about it. Most students have their ups and downs, but some seem incapable of feeling really happy. Though nice things happen to them, these things don't excite or energize them as they would other people. Educators with a student that fits this description sometimes feel like shaking her and saying, "Wake up, you're alive, you've got feelings, stand up for yourself, enjoy yourself, live a little."

The following are examples of students' emotional responses that are too weak.

They don't experience enough anger to defend or protect themselves when others take advantage of them.

They aren't upset enough by their mistakes and failures to try to correct them or do better.

They aren't particularly pleased by the pleasant things they experience.

If Mary's emotional responsiveness had been weak, she wouldn't have felt good, despite the fact that she had passed her first test in the course thanks to tutoring sessions. If Jaime's response had been too weak, he wouldn't have cared enough that he was earning a "C" average in the course instead of the "B" he needed to earn a college scholarship. As a result of their weak responses, neither Mary nor Jaime would have been motivated or energized to respond positively to their grades.

## *Incorrect Emotions*

Many students experience unwarranted emotional responses. Some are insecure about their abilities to do well even though no objective reason exists for them to think this way. Other students seem to love to be unhappy and virtually wallow in their misery. They never seem "happier" than when relating some misfortune or complaint. Some students enjoy hurting others. Instead of empathizing with their peers' pain and hurt, they take pleasure in it. They seem to delight in putting others down, ridiculing them for their mistakes, and teasing and abusing weaker students.

The following are examples of unwarranted emotional responses.

Students worry about things they know are extremely unlikely to happen. For instance, they may worry about failing a test they have studied for in a course that they are doing well in.

They torment other children, pets, or animals and laugh at the pain they inflict on them.

They do dangerous things and appear exhilarated by the possibility of being hurt.

They seem uncomfortable and anxious when others show that they like or respect them.

Latanya could have experienced an unwarranted emotion. Instead of being afraid of her parents' reaction to her "C" grade, she could have convinced herself that she had been marked unfairly and complained angrily about her teacher to her parents. It is obvious that such emotional responses can cause problems for the student who has a mistaken view of reality. And they can also generate problems for the teacher who has to deal with these students on a day-to-day basis.

## Conflicting Emotions

Students sometimes experience conflicting emotions. They get angry at someone, but then they feel too guilty to act on their anger. Or they think they know the answer and want to participate, but then they are too afraid they will be wrong to raise their hands. They may be afraid to do something dangerous, but they are also too ashamed to tell their friends they don't want to do it. To experience conflicting emotions is natural. It only becomes a problem for students when they can't sort out their emotions enough to act one way or the other.

Students with conflicting emotions often appear to be immobilized by their problems.

Instead of showing resentment or anger when taken advantage of, they may act as if nothing bothers them because they are too guilty to admit to themselves that they are resentful.

Instead of trying to learn to play an instrument, build a project, or make a team, they act as if they didn't care one way or the other because down deep they are afraid of failure.

Rather than ask for help when they need it, they persist even though they know what they are doing is inadequate or wrong.

If Jaime, for example, had experienced conflicting emotions, he might have felt both anxious about his average and also too ashamed to ask anyone for help.

At times, intense, weak, and conflicting emotions can be appropriate. Intense emotional responses fit intense situations. When students are having serious problems in school, when something wonderful and unexpected happens to them, or when they have done something terrible that they regret, it is appropriate that they experience strong emotional responses. Weak emotional responses are also natural in the rhythm of life. If every event produced the same level of response, little delays, obstacles, or disappointments would upset students as much as major frustrations, and they would be overwhelmed by the little problems that confront everyone from time to time. Conflicting emotions are a part of life, too. Students should feel too guilty or too ashamed to act on some of their feelings if these actions would hurt or be unfair to others. Emotional responses only cause students problems when they are *too* strong, *too* weak, or *incorrect* for the situations at hand or when, instead of dealing with their conflicting emotions, students can't act on them.

## Inappropriate Emotions and Inappropriate Behavior

When students experience emotional responses that are too strong, too weak, the wrong ones, or in conflict, their behavior is appropriate for their emotional response but inappropriate for the situation. Due to this mismatch between emotion and situation, these students usually adopt one of three ineffective strategies instead of applying appropriate solutions to the problems and opportunities of daily living. Either they *avoid* facing up to situations, *defend* against them, or merely *suffer* through them without being able to even try dealing with them.

*Avoiding*    Students may avoid situations if they can't cope with the emotions these situations arouse. For example, they may feign illness to avoid a test, a teacher, or a bully on the bus who is too threatening to handle. Avoiding these situations may temporarily alleviate their fears and anxieties, but it doesn't solve the problem they are too anxious or too afraid to handle.

The following examples of avoidance behavior characterize many students with emotional problems.

They cut classes or are truant.

They don't try to accomplish things that they anticipate will be difficult, or they stop attempting things as soon as they reach a difficult stage or obstacle in the process.

Instead of discussing the things that bother them, they retreat into themselves and give others the silent treatment.

They tend to break up relationships rather than try to work on them when they run into difficulties with other people.

When their peers do annoying things or interfere with what they are doing, they let them have their way in order to avoid confrontations.

*Defending*    While the word *defend* has many meanings, here it means to fool oneself, to pretend to oneself that one doesn't feel or think the way one in fact does. By being defensive, a person keeps himself from experiencing feelings and thoughts that are too threatening or unacceptable. Students act defensively when they convince themselves that their teachers can't teach when in fact they actually haven't made an effort to learn. Another example is when students persuade themselves that a test they failed due to lack of preparation was unfair and picayune.

Students are especially likely to act defensively when they experience conflicting emotions. For example, if a student is afraid of failing an audition for the school play, she can skip the audition. If she also feels ashamed about being insecure, the student may overcome her fear enough to show up. But if the student cannot admit to herself that she is insecure because she can't deal with the shame such an admission would produce, she may "forget" to show up for the audition. Then the student can blame a poor memory for the fact that she didn't show up, thereby missing the audition and avoiding the shame she might feel if she had missed it intentionally.

Defending oneself to oneself and lying to others are different behaviors. When students act defensively, they delude themselves. At least on one level, they really believe their self-deceptions. But when students lie to others, they know the truth yet prefer not to admit it to others.

Like all of us, students have a variety of ways they can act defensively.

They blame their teachers and peers for their own mistakes and shortcomings, fail to see how they play a role in their own rejection and failure, or believe the constructive criticism and necessary punishment they receive is unjustified and uncalled for.

They justify inappropriate behavior to themselves with a variety of excuses that are obviously false to others.

When things don't turn out as they expect them to or when they don't succeed in doing what they attempted to do, they adopt a sour grapes attitude, saying things like "It didn't really matter" and "Who needed it anyway?"

They feel too sick or too tired to try doing something they really don't want to do or are afraid to try to do in order not to have to face up to the fact that they don't want to or are afraid to do it.

*Suffering*    Suffering an emotion means experiencing it so intensely that one can't do anything about it except suffer. Students who suffer with emotions or emotional problems may experience emotional blocks when they are extremely anxious about taking a test, speaking in front of a group, or reading answers aloud. Other students may be immobilized by depression or guilt.

The unproductive, unhelpful suffering some students experience can take many forms.

They bite their nails, twitch, develop a variety of facial grimaces, or simply cry when they are anxious or afraid.

More extreme suffering can cause them to have blocks when they have to talk, read, or perform before a group.

They fall apart on examinations and are unable to do what would be easy for them to do if they weren't so anxious.

When their work is difficult, they rip up their papers, throw their books across the room, or take their frustration and tension out on inanimate objects in other ways.

They sit silently, stare out the window, draw at their desk, and so on when they are too depressed to mobilize themselves to do anything.

Only excessive avoiding, defending, or suffering cause problems. The examples of avoidance, defensiveness, and suffering above illustrate some of the nonconstructive ways students react to the daily problems and challenges in their lives. That doesn't mean, however, that avoiding, defending, and suffering are always inappropriate. For example, avoidance may sometimes be necessary. Students can't always face up to every challenge as soon as it presents itself—they don't operate that way. Students need to take breaks from the difficulties they encounter in school so they can return to them refreshed and ready to do battle again. In these cases, avoidance is natural and necessary.

Defensive behavior can also be appropriate at times. For instance, when students are learning a new skill or sport, it sometimes helps them to believe they are doing better than they are. If beginners knew how poorly they wrote, how clumsy they looked on the basketball court, or how their violin playing really sounded, they might be too discouraged to continue to strive to achieve their goals.

Suffering is a normal part of life, too. Students may have to suffer for a time before they can act. Sometimes they have to fail badly at something before they are moved enough to change their behavior. A little suffering may not stir them to action. Instead they need to suffer a lot first.

Students' emotional problems are caused by emotional responses that lead them to consistently avoid, defend, and suffer with their problems instead of trying to solve them. Everyone experiences inappropriate emotional responses from time to time. And at times or when necessary, everyone avoids, defends, and suffers instead of trying to solve their problems. But when students do these things to excess, too often, and in situations that are nonconstructive so that they have few successes and fail to develop competency or confidence, they have emotional problems.

Students avoid, defend, and suffer inappropriately when doing so impedes rather than fosters their progress. Experienced teachers usually know when a student who is avoiding a challenge should be allowed to take a break from it and when he should be encouraged or required to tackle it head on. They can also tell when to go along with a student's behavior because she isn't prepared to accept the truth or when she needs a dose of reality, and when allowing a student to suffer the results of her mistakes and inappropriate behavior would be good for her and when it would be better to provide her with support, understanding, and forgiveness.

---

## Self-Quiz: Behavior Adjustment Mechanisms

Categorize each of the following behaviors in terms of the four adjustment mechanisms (avoiding, suffering, defending, solving).

1. She leaves the room to go to the bathroom when the work is difficult.
2. He convinces himself that what one does not know is not important.
3. He asks the teacher for help when he does not understand the problem.
4. He believes that his teacher is too strict when it is obvious to others that he is not.
5. She scribbles on the page instead of working.
6. She studies before the examination.
7. He has a stomach pain or a headache when he has to go to school.
8. She pretends to feel sick when she has to go to school.
9. He believes that school isn't important because he is going to be a professional football player so it doesn't matter that he is flunking three subjects.
10. She becomes so nervous when she has to give a report in front of the class that she can't speak.

---

# Identification

If a student's behavior problem is caused by an inappropriate emotional response, you need to be able to identify the emotion and decide whether it is too strong, too weak, incorrect, or in conflict with another feeling. For example, you might realize that a student is hitting someone else because she is extremely jealous (too intense). Or you may discover that a student is being teased by other youngsters because he doesn't become angry enough to defend himself (too weak). You might conclude that a third student won't answer in class because he is afraid for no good reason that you and the other students are going to make fun of him (incorrect). And you may learn that a fourth student hasn't been doing any homework for the last month because she is worried that she might be pregnant, but at the same time she is afraid to confide in anyone or take a pregnancy test because she feels ashamed (conflicting emotions). In each example, it's possible to both identify the emotion that is causing the behavior and to know whether it is too strong, too weak, incorrect, or in conflict.

## Informal Assessment

If a student's behavior is caused by an emotional problem, you should also be able to determine whether she or he is avoiding, defending, or suffering. It may be clear to you, for example, that a teenager spends less time with her girlfriends because she is *avoiding* situations where she has to relate to boys. Or you may discover that a student's anger and vindictiveness when you point out what he has done wrong is his way of *defending* himself because he can't admit that he has made a mistake. Or you may realize that even though a student has written a good composition, if you try to make her read it to the class, she may *suffer* a panic attack and do a terrible job of reading it aloud.

---

## Self-Quiz: Causes of Problem Behaviors

Below are seven descriptions of problem behaviors. Imagine at least one emotional cause and one nonemotional cause for each behavior.

1. When the teacher asks her a question, she continues to look out the window.

2. He never plays soccer with the other students during recess.
3. When the teacher doesn't do what he wants, he makes angry noises, shouts, and on occasion threatens the teacher.
4. When it's her turn to be called on, she lowers her head and looks down at her desk.
5. When she has seatwork, she often asks her neighbors to do it for her.

---

## Formal Assessment

You can also use formal assessment instruments to identify students with emotional problems. Such instruments as the Behavior Checklist (3), the Behavior Problems Checklist (1, 2, 6), the Devereux Elementary School and Adolescent Behavior Rating Scales (4, 5), and the Walker Problem Identification Checklist (7, 8) can help you determine when the causes of students' behavior problems are emotional.

# *Emotional Versus Conduct Problems*

Students have emotional problems because their emotional responses to situations are too intense, too weak, incorrect, or in conflict, and they commonly avoid, defend, and suffer rather than trying to solve the problems and challenges of their daily lives. In contrast, students with conduct problems are unwilling to control their behavior. They know how adults expect them to behave, but they don't believe they need to or should behave that way. Conduct problems and emotional problems differ in two important respects.

First, students with conduct problems are able to behave differently, but they neither want to do so nor do they think it's necessary to do so. Students with emotional problems, however, cannot behave differently. Thus, if students have conduct problems, they need a change in their attitudes to change their conduct. If students have emotional problems, however, they need to have chances to experience more appropriate emotional responses and to be able to avoid, defend, and suffer less and resolve their problems more.

The second way in which conduct and emotional problems differ is that students with conduct problems do things to benefit themselves even at the expense of others. But students with emotional problems may do things even though they benefit no one, not even themselves. Thus, for change to take place, students with conduct problems have to learn they can't and shouldn't always place their own benefit before the welfare of others. Students with emotional problems, however, need help so they don't continue to do things that aren't beneficial to themselves.

Now let's look at some examples of these differences. Two students may both act as if they don't hear their teacher ask them to move a cage with a harmless garden snake inside, but each may have a different reason. A student with conduct problems may not want to do his share of the classroom chores. But a student with emotional problems may want to do his share yet be too afraid of snakes to be able to follow through. In another example, a student with conduct problems may copy test answers because she thinks it's okay to do so. A student with emotional problems may be so anxious about doing poorly on the test that she copies someone else's answers even though she knows it's wrong to do so. In a third example, a student with conduct problems pushes in front of another student to avoid waiting his turn. A student with emotional problems may do the same because he enjoys dominating weaker students.

# *Two Kinds of Emotional Problems*

Some students' emotional problems are part of their personalities, and they bring their problems with them wherever they go. They are anxious and insecure in situations that most students can take in stride. They are angry, sullen, and resentful in situations that don't upset most other children and teenagers. Or they fear all authority figures, not just those that are punitive. Other students without such personality problems who are doing well in general may have problems dealing with particular situations. The necessity of adjusting to a divorce, a new stepparent and perhaps stepbrothers and sisters, a death in the family, a serious illness, a move to a new neighborhood, and other life crises cause them to react in ways that can create additional difficulties for themselves and others. They may suddenly become anxious, angry, rebellious, or depressed, but they aren't basically anxious, angry, rebellious, or depressed young people. Because difficult situations rather than their personalities cause their emotional problems, mental health professionals often label their difficulties adjustment problems or reactive problems.

Students with adjustment or reactive problems that affect their functioning in school need individualized attention from their teachers. Students with personality problems require a somewhat different approach than students who have situational problems because the cause of their problems is different. Thus, educators need to distinguish between these two types of emotional problems because this distinction is critical to coming up with a sensitive and effective response.

## Comparing Personality and Situational Problems

Your answers to the following questions will help you determine whether a student's behavior problems are situational or part of the student's personality.

1. *Did the student's behavior problem appear suddenly or is it long-standing?* Did she suddenly change from well-adjusted to anxious or from easy to get along with to angry and disobedient? One indication that a student's behavior problems are situational is that they tend to be recent. Commonly what happens is that the student does quite well until a particular situation or event causes a sudden behavior change.

2. *Can you identify a particular event or circumstance that triggered the change in the student's behavior?* When a student has problems that arise outside of school, a teacher can often get the student to talk about the problem if the teacher approaches the student in the right way. Sometimes when a student is obviously troubled but is reluctant to discuss the problem, a call home often confirms a teacher's suspicion that something outside of school is interfering with a student's classroom functioning.

## Situational Problems

Since not all students are alike, some can handle situations that cause others to have problems. Certain situations, though, are so challenging, threatening, or emotionally charged that they are likely to cause most students to have some situational problems. For

## Self-Quiz: Is It a Situational or Personality Problem?

The following examples illustrate the difference between situational and personality problems. Read each one and decide whether the behavior problem is more likely to be situational or a personality problem.

1. Rocco, a 7-year-old who is afraid of his older brother and sister, the children in his neighborhood, and the other children his age or older in school, only plays with younger children during recess.
2. After having heard for the last five years that she can't and shouldn't try to do what normal children do because of her heart condition, Cindy, a 9-year-old, is afraid to run, play ball, walk up hilly streets, or do anything that requires a lot of physical exertion. But she isn't at all hesitant about engaging in challenging activities that don't involve physical exertion.
3. Michael, an 11-year-old student, lies both at home and at school whenever he is confronted with his inappropriate behavior.
4. Harry, a 12-year-old, lies to a teacher who punishes the students in her class rather severely for the infractions they commit, but he is as honest as most students his age with his other teachers.
5. Vincente, a 13-year-old student in the honors program of his intermediate school, has been inattentive in class for the last few days. He doesn't volunteer answers and, when called on, says he doesn't know the answer, gives his teachers a blank look, or glares at them. In one of his classes, he either reads comic books surreptitiously or lays his head down on his desk and tunes out the world.

example, the death of a parent usually has a profound effect on people regardless of their age. Students of any age may suffer extreme forms of anxiety, panic, sadness, depression, or a combination of all these feelings if one of their parents dies. Adolescents—being less dependent upon and attached to their parents—may have these reactions to a lesser degree, but they may suffer from bouts of guilt and remorse for the way they behaved toward the parent before.

Divorce has a similar effect on students, especially young ones, though it's usually less severe than an actual death. Concerns about such things as who will take care of them, who will support them, whether they will lose the parent they aren't living with, is it their fault that their parents separated, and so on cause most youngsters to feel frightened, anxious, guilty, resentful, angry, sad, or depressed. If their parents put them in the middle of their own conflicts and require them to take sides, they may experience even more problems. Students experiencing the emotional side effects of a death or divorce in the family typically have difficulty functioning well in school.

Many other home-based problems can influence school behavior, too. A new sibling can be a problem for young "only children" who are suddenly no longer the center of attention. Especially vulnerable youngsters may become jealous of their peers in school or try to make up for what they are missing at home by seeking extra attention from their teachers. Or deteriorations in students' relationships with their parents can affect the way they function in school. In particular, students whose parents start to abuse alcohol or drugs or who become the victims of physical or sexual abuse at home may demonstrate the psychological effects of such situations in school.

*Some students welcome the opportunity to discuss their problems with an understanding teacher.*

In addition, experiences unrelated to the home can create situational emotional problems that can interfere with students' classroom functioning. For example, a serious illness or prolonged hospitalization, preoccupation with an unwanted pregnancy, racial or ethnic conflicts on the school bus or in the streets near the school can each take their toll on students' performance in school.

If a well-behaved student suddenly comes to class looking tired, depressed, or sullen, withdraws from his or her peers, stops participating in class and turning in homework, cuts class or acts rebellious for no apparent reason, and you suspect his behavior may be due to situational problems outside of school, a good first step is to try finding out what the student is reacting to. A very young child may respond to a question such as, "What's the matter, Betty, you seem so sad?" An older child might be approached with a question like, "Everything seems to upset you lately, Billy. Is something wrong?" An inquiry to a teenager might be phrased, "You have really had a short fuse (chip on your shoulder) the last couple of weeks. Is something bothering (upsetting) you that you want to talk about?" or "You really seem down. Has something happened to upset you?"

If a student seems hesitant to discuss the cause of the problem with you, let your student know that your goal is to be helpful, not critical. Assure the student that you want to help him decide how *he* wants to handle the problem, not tell the student what to do. If your intuition tells you the problem may be serious or confidential, inform the student that if he wants to talk with you, you won't interfere by going to talk to anyone involved without his consent unless it is absolutely necessary to do so. You might have to explain what these circumstances are.

If the student still won't confide in you, the problem may be the kind that students typically prefer to talk over with someone besides their teachers. Sexual problems, discord at home, drug-related problems, unwanted pregnancies, and abuse at home are topics that many students feel uncomfortable discussing with teachers, even when they and their teachers have had excellent relationships. If you think your student is unable to confide in you, you might suggest someone else she or he could talk to or an agency or organization that might be able to help.

If your student does confide in you, you may learn that the student is reacting to a situation that can't be changed, such as a death or divorce. If that is the case, you may be able to help the student deal with his or her feelings and also adapt your expectations to the student's current emotional state. (See below.) Also treat your student with understanding, patience, and compassion. You can readily adjust your expectations and demands until the passage of time heals the wounds.

If, in contrast, your student is confronted by a situation that can be remedied, you will have to decide whether you can help or whether she should be referred to another individual, agency, or organization. In dealing with a minor problem, you may be able to provide your student with the advice she needs. But if your student is confronting a serious problem that requires the attention of other professionals and is not yet receiving such assistance, the most helpful thing you could probably do would be to help her contact the appropriate agency or professional. In particular, if your student's difficulty in school is caused by conflicts at home, you would need to determine whether you have the training and time to counsel the student's parents about the problem or whether you should refer the family to an agency that provides such services. Also, if your student's problems in school stem from some kind of abuse, you may be required by law to inform the proper authorities of what you have learned.

## Self-Quiz: Choosing Responses to Situational Problems

Which of the following techniques would you feel comfortable using if you thought one of your students was experiencing situational problems?

Asking students if something is bothering them and what it might be.

Temporarily adjusting your expectations to the student's emotional state.

Counseling the student about how to deal with the problem.

Suggesting specific agencies that provide help to an older student.

Contacting a younger student's parents for additional information.

Contacting an older student's parents for additional information.

Counseling the student's parents.

Referring the student's parents to specific agencies that provide the assistance they require.

Informing the appropriate school personnel about the student's problem.

Informing the appropriate authorities if you suspect child abuse.

# *Personality Problems*

Students whose emotional problems are part of their personalities present teachers with two related, but different, challenges. The first is to overcome the learning and behavior problems caused by their students' emotional problems. The second is to contribute toward eliminating—or at least reducing—emotional problems themselves. Many educators doubt that classroom teachers can handle the learning and behavior problems of students with mild emotional problems, let alone make a contribution toward eliminating the problems. However, the view in this book is well expressed by Brophy and Putnam, who have stated:

> Teachers with the willingness and skills to do so can play important roles in helping their disturbed students to improve their general personal adjustments, in addition to helping them cope with the demands of the student role. (9, p. 13)

This section describes techniques you can use to play a role in helping your students with emotional problems make a change for the better. Subsequent sections describe techniques you can use to improve their behavior despite their problems (managing, tolerating, and preventing).

## *Helping Students Change*

Because you will see and interact with your students daily, you are a key figure in their lives. You have an opportunity to influence not only how they behave but also how they feel about themselves.

*Enhancing Self-Concepts*   People's self-concepts, the characteristics they attribute to themselves, have a highly significant effect on the way they behave. Virtually no limits restrict the types of characteristics individual students can attribute to themselves—how tall they are, who they take after, whether or not they are good eaters, how intelligent they are, and so on. Despite this, four groups of attributes appear particularly relevant for understanding students' behavior (22, 40, 54).

Ability or competency: the extent to which students believe they can attain, achieve, and succeed.

Power or locus of control: the extent to which they believe they, not others, are in control of their lives.

Virtuousness: the extent to which they think they have lived up to the moral and ethical standards they have acquired.

Acceptance: the degree to which they experience others as liking, respecting, and wanting them.

Self-esteem, which is related to self-defining characteristics but is actually a different concept, refers to students' appraisal of the qualities they attribute to themselves. Specifically, if their self-concept matches what they think they should be like (ideal self), then they are likely to esteem themselves highly. If, however, a great discrepancy occurs between their self-concept and their ideal self, they may disparage themselves (46).

Research indicates that students with poor self-concepts or low self-esteem often develop emotional problems that in turn create learning and behavior problems (10, 11, 14–20, 23, 26, 29–32, 36, 39, 43–45, 47, 48, 51, 52, 54, 56, 57). For example, students who believe they are unable to do things or are incompetent, who think they can't learn or solve problems because they are stupid, can't play sports because they are clumsy and uncoordinated, and the like can become anxious or fearful when confronted with the very things they mistakenly believe they won't be able to succeed at. Their anxiety or fear may be so strong that they avoid the task or challenges altogether. Or they may try to rise to the challenge but experience an emotional block. They might also give up at the first sign of difficulty because they are convinced they will fail if they persist. If they do this, they may give up quietly and feel sad or depressed, fly into a rage and rip up or destroy whatever they were working on, or take their anger and frustration out on others who only want to help them succeed.

Feeling incapable and inept, some students develop "learned helplessness" and come to believe that the locus of control over their lives is external. That is, they assume that they aren't the masters of their own destiny. Instead of taking charge, they give up setting goals for themselves and become passive.

In the same circumstances, other students become defensive. They fool around in class, forget to do their homework, cut school, and are generally negligent so they can blame their failure on lack of effort rather than lack of ability. They tend to have difficulty accepting criticism no matter how constructive, well meaning, or well put it may be. Instead of accepting the truth, they defend themselves against the hurt they experience by blaming others and feeling angry. Their avoiding, blocking, giving up easily, and acting defensively cause them to fail. And this only fulfills or confirms their original fear that they are unable to succeed and makes it likely that they will experience even more anxiety and fear the next time.

Students who believe they aren't virtuous have their own type of emotional problems. They may think that they are spoiled, selfish, mean, uncooperative, stubborn, or willful when in reality they aren't. But thinking that they are bad and prone to blame themselves when things go wrong, they often feel guilty, ashamed, and depressed. Students with these burdensome feelings have difficulty keeping their minds on their work in school or mobilizing the energy they need to function adequately. Some try extra hard to be good in order to combat their notion that they are bad. This can prevent them from defending themselves when their peers take advantage of them because they think it's bad to do so.

Students who believe they aren't worthy of attention, respect, love, or acceptance tend either to avoid relationships with their peers and teachers or try currying favor with them. They feel they have to work hard or do something special to be accepted. Such students often feel sorry for themselves and can become sad and even depressed. Whatever specific form students' poor self-concepts take, so long as they think poorly of themselves, they experience emotional problems that can affect how well they function in school.

The good news is that research indicates that dedicated teachers can improve their students' self-concepts and self-esteem when they make the effort to do so (21, 24, 26, 29, 34, 38, 49, 50). As Knoblock states:

> Students can be assisted to feel better about themselves as a specific aspect of the school day. Self-awareness and understanding can be put into the context of skill development and can be taught systematically over time. (37, p. 158)

The process of change, however, takes time. Canfield and Wells offer this caution:

> It is possible to change self-concepts, and it is possible for teachers to effect the changes . . . It isn't easy. Changes take place slowly over a long period of time. (21, p. 4)

Although in theory it's possible for students to attribute only negative characteristics to themselves, more typically they attribute both positive and negative qualities to themselves. Thus, one student may think of himself as competent and powerful but not as accepted or virtuous, while another believes just the opposite of herself. So in order to target your efforts at improving students' self-concepts accurately, it's essential to first know what they think of themselves in various areas.

You can gather this kind of information informally by observing students at work, at play, and during their interactions with others. You can also talk with them about what they think of themselves. In addition, several validated formal assessment instruments are available for this purpose. The Piers-Harris Children's Self-Concept Scale (42) and the Self-Observation Scales (35) provide information about students' overall perceptions of themselves. Other instruments have a more narrow focus: the Perceived Competency Scale for Children (33), the Nowicki Strickland Locus of Control Scale for Children (41), and the Coopersmith Self-Esteem Inventory (22).

Your daily interactions with your students give you lots of opportunities to make a significant contribution toward helping them improve their self-concept. This is actually important for all students, but it's crucial for students with poor self-concepts and low self-esteem. The recommended way to best help such students is to provide them with information and experiences that contradict the negative ways they currently perceive themselves. If they think they are inadequate or stupid, help them learn that they are capable and smart. If they believe they are powerless, help them see that they have some control of their own destinies. If they believe they are bad, help them realize that they aren't. And if they feel they aren't accepted by others, treat them with acceptance and respect.

Negative self-concepts that have built up over many years will not be changed overnight by a few well-chosen words. It takes consistent and determined effort for a considerable period of time to help students think better of themselves. The following suggestions are designed to assist you in achieving this goal.

*Lack of ability:* You can employ the following techniques with students who believe they don't have the capacity to attain their goals.

1. If your students think they are incapable or stupid, good instructional techniques individualized to their strengths and weaknesses are probably the most effective way to work with these students. Selecting work at their ability levels, organizing their as-

signments to ensure success, and providing support and information when they need it can help many students with poor self-concepts succeed despite their beliefs that they can't.

2. You may be able to counteract students' pessimistic self-perceptions by helping them see the strengths and skills they bring to each task, by expressing your personal belief that they can succeed, and by explaining how their past experiences can be poor predictors of the present if they practice, study, and concentrate more and learn from their mistakes.

3. Research shows that students with emotional problems can learn vicariously by reading books and seeing films about others who have had experiences like theirs (bibliotherapy) (48). Exposing students who don't believe that they can overcome their past to stories of real life people who have actually done so can be inspirational. A number of literature lists that you can use to inspire troubled students are readily available (12, 25, 27, 48).

4. If students see their accomplishments as inadequate because they judge themselves by perfectionistic standards, help them be more realistic about what to expect of themselves. Explain that no one can do well in everything.

5. According to research, providing students with opportunities to succeed in areas where they feel adequate improves their general perceptions of their ability in other areas (55). An example of how you might put this to use with students who are anxious about reading or social studies is to encourage them to decorate their reports with artwork or maps or prepare dioramas if that is an area in which they have talent or skill.

6. Merely encouraging students to make positive rather than negative statements about themselves and reinforcing them when they do so can improve their self-concepts (34, 38). While this approach alone may not be enough to solve the problem, it does help.

*Lack of power:* You can help students who think the control over their lives is external to believe they can influence their own destinies in a variety of ways.

1. Demonstrate your trust and faith that they can be self-managing and self-motivating enough to attain the goals they determine themselves with a minimum of external guidance.

2. In keeping with their maturity level, allow students to choose among alternative learning activities, centers, manipulatives, and instructional materials and permit them to generate or develop some of the alternatives themselves within limits you set. This will enhance their perceptions that they, and not others, are responsible for what they do in class. This also gives them another opportunity to experience your faith in them.

3. Allow students to work at their own pace within limits set by the needs of the group as a whole.

4. Provide dependent students with assistance only when they request it, and gradually wean them from needing your assistance.

5. Ask students what they think about their own work rather than expressing your opinion. This demonstrates your faith in them that they can evaluate themselves.

6. Teach students who seek extrinsic rewards to reward themselves.

*Lack of virtue:* The first thing you can do to help students who feel guilty and depressed because they think they are bad is to avoid saying or doing things that will feed their guilt. Accentuate the positive in your relationships with them. If you have to say something negative, try to mention something positive first by saying such things as, "You were doing really well putting your art work away until you began to . . . " Or "Sometimes you do wait patiently until you're called on and other times, like now, you don't." When talking about unacceptable behavior, instead of saying that a young student is naughty or a teenager is irresponsible, say that his *behavior* or the way she acted was wrong or unacceptable. This condemns the action, not the person (see section on reprimands in Chapter 7).

*Lack of acceptance:* Students who believe that they aren't respected, cared for, or loved by others will grow to feel better about themselves as they experience acceptance from others. Coopersmith and Feldman describe acceptance in the following terms.

> Acceptance implies liking and showing concern for the child as he is, with his capacities, limitations, strengths, and weaknesses. This acceptance is expressed by interest in the child, concern for his welfare, involvement in his activities and development, support for him in his times of stress and appreciation of what he is, and can do. Acceptance is also expressed by recognition of the child's frailties and difficulties and by the awareness that the child can only do so much and be his particular kind of person at this time of his life. . . . It is the quality of expression rather than the sheer quantity that is critical. Children can sense concern, interest, and appreciation and are not easily fooled by mere words of praise and affection or by insincere demonstrations of physical affection. (23, p. 206)

Your daily interaction gives you many chances to demonstrate your interest, concern, and acceptance of students. While you should do this with all students, students who feel they aren't accepted and loved by others especially need such caring, compassionate treatment.

*Self-concept enhancement programs:* A number of structured programs exist that have proven to be effective in helping enhance many students' self-concepts (13, 21, 24, 28, 50, 53). But their effectiveness with students who have emotional problems hasn't yet been researched. Some authorities (37) believe, though, that they will work effectively with such students. Others disagree. For example, Morse suggests:

> There are programs to improve self-concept, but self-concept is so much a part of a person's totality that it is hard to imagine a specific curricular method that could accomplish this. (40, p. 255)

*Correcting Overgeneralizations*   Some students have emotional problems in school because they overgeneralize their emotional reactions. For example, students abused at home may fear and avoid adults in general including their teachers. Or students who have

## THEORY FOCUS: MORSE ON UNDERSTANDING CHILD VARIANCE

William Morse began training educators to work with students who had emotional problems in the 1950s. The training program he directed was especially noted for preparing educators to use the "life-space interview" and many other techniques first described by Redl to help students deal with emotional crises in the classroom. *Public School Classes for the Emotionally Handicapped: A Research Analysis*, which Morse coauthored, was the first detailed study of how students with emotional problems were handled and mis-

handled in the public schools. His book *Understanding Child Variance* suggests that behavior problems can be the result of a variety of causes, each of which is more amenable to some solutions than others. Two of the many other books he has written that contain a wealth of suggestions for how to help students with emotional and conduct problems are *The Education and Treatment of Socio-Emotionally Impaired Children and Youth* and *Affective Education for Special Children and Youth*.

learned to say as little as possible at home to avoid being criticized or ridiculed may be too anxious to volunteer opinions or answers in school if they anticipate a similar response. It's not that they think they are bad or ridiculous, but rather they expect to be treated badly or ridiculed. They transfer their experience at home to similar situations and assume the outcome will be the same.

It's not necessary to find out the past histories of students who flinch at a sudden move in their vicinity, act startled at a sudden noise, seem devastated by the slightest criticism, or tremble when called on to recite. Their reactions in class are enough to make you realize that their past experiences—whatever they were—caused them to respond inappropriately. Nor is it necessary to know the details in order to develop a plan to help them change their emotional responses, though such knowledge could certainly assist the process. Two approaches in particular can make a contribution toward changing the emotional reactions of such students—a helping relationship and gradual desensitization.

*Helping relationships:* Just telling students they have nothing to worry about, be angry about, or feel jealous about and explaining why is rarely enough to change their expectations. The saying "Actions speak louder than words" is operative here. You can show these students that all adults or all authority figures aren't alike by relating to them in ways that disprove their expectations. The suggestions in Chapter 2 for relating to students in non-authoritarian ways, being fair, listening actively, being friendly, communicating acceptance and empathy, and avoiding negative and destructive consequences are particularly relevant for students with emotional problems.

*Gradual desensitization:* You can begin to help a student who won't volunteer in class because she is afraid others will laugh at her by convincing her that she has nothing to be afraid of. You could also help her feel relaxed enough so that despite her idea that she may be laughed at, she still volunteers an answer. If she does well on one try, and no one laughs or ridicules her, the experience will change her original apprehension. Then the next time she knows the answer, she will be more likely to raise her hand.

The difficulty with this approach is helping to relax a student who is highly upset because he anticipates dire consequences even though you can't change his expectations.

Gradual desensitization, which is one way to accomplish this, is based on the fact that people are less likely to feel upset about something that usually bothers them if they take tranquilizers or sedatives, eat a very satisfying meal, or have a good massage. The physical effects these activities have on them counteract the effects of the anxiety and anger-producing ideas and experiences that are upsetting them. They may still remember what it was that made them anxious or angry—they may still be aware that they aren't ready for a test or that someone treated them unfairly—but they just aren't bothered as much.

Gradual desensitization is a technique in which students are first relaxed and then gradually desensitized to the experience they can't deal with. Proceeding gradually is extremely important because although at times some people can jump right into upsetting situations, more often they have to first test out the waters, then accustom themselves to the temperature, and finally jump into the challenging experience.

To use gradual desensitization effectively with your students, follow these six steps:

1. Identify the situation that arouses the wrong emotional response, such as taking a test, reading aloud, trying out for a play, and so on.

2. Determine how you can best help your students to feel calm, relaxed, and comfortable. Techniques you can use to relax students include
    Deep rhythmic breathing, stretching, or vigorous exercise
    Thinking about something pleasant that happened or that the student would like to happen (emotive imagery)
    A favorite snack
    Calm, soothing music
    A favorite toy, stuffed animal, and the like (for younger children)
    The physical presence of a friend, parent, or teacher

3. Identify a series of small, gradual steps your students can take on the way toward confronting the actual stimulus they can't cope with. You have several options here—you can graduate steps in terms of how close students are to actually doing the threatening challenge, how close they are in time to the threat, or whether they are going through the steps in the threatening situation in their imagination or in reality. (You may choose to have them do the steps in their imagination first as a safe way to start.)

4. Help your students attain each step while they are feeling relaxed and calm. Be sure not to pressure them to proceed more rapidly than they are ready to.

5. Call your students' attention to the fact that they accomplished the goal without experiencing any negative results.

6. Encourage them to try to do the same thing again.

Let's look at two examples of this approach. Clara, an anxious third-grade student, is unwilling to participate in the class play because she is afraid she will forget her poem and everyone will laugh at her. The last time she participated, she was so anxious that she forgot her lines. How can her teacher use gradual desensitization to help Clara overcome her problem? First, he could help relax Clara by having her think about something pleasant, giving her a favorite snack, or waiting until she was feeling very good about something and

*Gradual desensitization can help students overcome their fears of speaking in front of others.*

then asking her to recite her poem for him when none of the other students were present. If she did this, and it was a positive experience for her, the teacher might wait to catch her in a good mood next time or do something to put her in a good mood and then ask her to recite the poem in front of one or two students. Finally, he would work up to having Clara do it in front of the whole class. Then if that worked out well, he could ask her to think about participating when the class performs for the whole school in the auditorium. He would have to do everything possible to make her feel calm and relaxed before she goes on stage, however.

The second example involves a sixth-grade student named Steve who, after repeatedly suffering "test anxiety" and blocking on examinations, announces he won't take any more tests because he always fails. How can a teacher gradually desensitize Steve to taking tests? First, the teacher can identify a series of steps leading up to taking tests that Steve can proceed through gradually and use an appropriate way of helping Steve during each step. For example, after making sure Steve is relaxed, the teacher can ask him to imagine the following situations one by one: You have just been told that there will be a test in three days. You are studying for the test at home two days before the test. You are studying for the test the night before you are to take it. It's the morning of the test. You have completed your studies, and you feel confident that you will do well. You are in class waiting for the tests to be distributed. You receive your copy and begin. You complete the test and pass it in. Now, it's the day after the test, and you are waiting for the test papers to be returned. You look at your grade—it's an A.

After completing these imaginary steps, which may take a few days, the teacher can help Steve get used to real tests in stages. The teacher can ask Steve to read the test over without taking it. Then the next few times Steve takes a test, he can first take it without handing it in, take the test with the understanding that he can have a makeup if he isn't satisfied with how he did, and finally take the test under the same conditions as the other students.

Some educators feel that gradual desensitization is outside the scope and role of classroom teachers, but research indicates that teachers can use it effectively with students who have emotional problems (58–63). Moreover, once students learn ways to relax themselves and how to develop their own series of graduated steps, they can use these techniques independently for any subsequent challenges they encounter.

*Resolving Conflicting Emotions*    Students can have emotional problems because their values and standards of behavior prevent them from acting out their emotions in appropriate ways. For example, students may learn at home that nice boys and girls discuss their differences instead of fighting, and when someone teases, pesters, annoys, or pushes them, they should try to find out why, ignore the provocation, or walk away, but never tease or push back. The idea that it's wrong to act out their anger or even feel angry can put them in a bind because feeling angry also makes them feel guilty. Then if the guilt is strong enough to keep them from asserting or defending themselves when they feel angry or resentful, other students may take advantage of, pick on, or scapegoat them. Similarly, students who have been taught that they should always want to share their things with others, always be considerate of others, and always allow others to go first may feel too guilty to stick up for their own rights or speak out for their own interests when it's appropriate to do so.

You can help such inhibited students by giving them more realistic expectations and standards of behavior that allow for flexibility when the situation calls for it. Consider telling students who believe good boys *never* fight that they try not to fight or don't fight unless they have to. Help students who think that good children *always* share their things with others by telling them good children share *most* things *most* of the time with others who also share their things with them. Explain to your students that it's natural to feel angry when they are treated unfairly or punished unjustly, and help them express these feelings appropriately. One way to do this is to model the appropriate behavior yourself. When the opportunity presents itself, you can also point out when other students behave in ways that you and most people find acceptable even if your student doesn't. This helps them see and accept a broader range of behavior.

*Correcting Defensive Behavior*    As we noted earlier, students can defend themselves against experiencing uncomfortable emotions by distorting the way they see and experience the world. Specifically, students can defend themselves against taking responsibility for their low grades in school by believing that their teachers are inadequate, their exams are unfair, or their assignments are tricky. They can also defend themselves against thinking they are bad when they lash out at others in anger or pick on other students for the fun of it by believing that "the other student started the problem," "they had it coming to them," "it was an accident," "everyone else does it anyway," or with similar rationalizations.

Defensive students can be highly exasperating. Teachers often want to confront them with the truth to clear away their excuses and self-deceptions. But such direct attacks on students' defenses often backfire. Instead of helping students face reality, such attacks often cause students who are highly motivated to defend themselves to become even more defensive. To escape such painful confrontations with their teachers, students may cause incidents that result in their being excluded from class, or they may cut class or drop out of school.

*Life-space interview:* A nonconfrontational approach, life-space interviewing was developed to assist teachers to deal with their students' defenses (67–69). Somewhat like Gordon's (65) concept of active listening (Chapter 2), the life-space interview is designed to engage defensive students in a communications process with teachers that will lead them to correct their misperceptions and modify their behavior. To do this, the technique is designed to help students gradually face the truth they have been hiding from themselves without forcing them to give up their defenses before they are ready to do so. This approach is based on the assumption that students will be more open to modifying their inappropriate behavior once they have admitted to themselves what they really have been doing and the real reasons they have been doing it. By helping students perceive themselves and their experiences more accurately and by aiding them in developing alternative ways of coping with their feelings, the life-space interview enhances feelings of being in control of one's life (71).

Below is a description of the major aspects of life-space interviewing and an example of how it is used with defensive students. Although the concepts are presented in a logical order, they aren't thought of as fixed steps but rather as aspects to be considered and included at some point in the process.

Harold is a 15-year-old who breaks other students' things "by accident," says nasty things to them "without realizing it," interrupts them when they are talking, and constantly gets himself rejected. But he never admits either that he starts things or that he brings about his own rejection. As far as he is concerned, he is always the victim, never the instigator.

Harold's parents always found him to be much more difficult to deal with than his older brother. By the time Harold was three, his parents were already engaged in fruitless battles with him. By now, they and his older brother rely almost exclusively on threats and punishments to manage his behavior. When he was younger, Harold showed his anger toward them because of how he was treated. But as he got older, he began to defend himself against experiencing his anger by doing the things he did to bother his family and others "accidentally."

*Establish a relationship of confidence and acceptance with your students.* Students are much more likely to admit the truth to you if they believe that you won't laugh, feel disgusted, or react punitively but instead will say that what they tell you isn't nearly as bad, wrong, disgusting, or difficult as the students think. If you establish a trusting, accepting relationship before you broach a subject that may make a student defensive, it's less likely they will feel it necessary to maintain their defenses during the discussion.

In Harold's case, you might establish a relationship of confidence and acceptance by telling him the good things about himself and, most importantly, by trying not to respond negatively and punitively when he "accidentally" does obnoxious and provocative things in class.

*Choose problems or incidents that your students can deal with realistically and cooperatively.* After you have established a relationship of trust, select a situation that isn't too threatening for your student to deal with. Helping a student face the truth about something that is less threatening is usually more effective than tackling something that would make a student feel really terrible to admit. With Harold, you might pick an incident when he caused a student to yell at him by "accidentally" sticking his feet out just as the student walked by and then complained because the student yelled at him.

*Interview students under circumstances that encourage their participation.* Students are more likely to discuss their thoughts and feelings in private. Long and Frye (66) advise allowing 10 to 20 minutes to provide enough time for such a conversation.

*Find out your students' perceptions.* After you have selected an incident or situation to discuss with your student, find out how he sees it. Listen as long as necessary and ask whatever questions you need to in order to be sure you understand the students' point of view. Do this in a nonjudgmental way, without any sign of disagreement or disapproval. Remember that your students are distorting the situation not because they want to but because they have to defend against the truth for the moment. This step is critical because you have to understand the students' point of view if you want to correct it. It's also important because you communicate your interest and respect by listening to what they have to say. As Morse points out:

> We want to know how the youngster sees and thinks about an event . . . Once we are clear how the child perceives the problem (even if the pupil's view cannot be accepted as satisfactory), we are in a position to work out, hopefully with concurrence, a possible resolution. (68, p. 214)

Tanner (71) also recommends that the teacher try to determine the meaning of the incident to the student. Is it really a central issue? Is it related to a particular vulnerability or concern, such as jealousy, pride, ethnic or racial sensitivity, issues over power, and so on? If a student explodes in anger when a group of students laugh at him, is it because he was laughed at by his peers or because his teacher failed to protect him from their ridicule?

In Harold's case, you would listen while Harold complained that the student yelled at him, that no one likes him, and that he feels left out. Then you would ask what he thought caused the student to yell at him. When Harold answered that the student just liked to yell at him, you wouldn't try to correct him.

*Communicate your understanding and acceptance of both the students' perception of the incident and their feelings about it (without expressing agreement).* Few things are more satisfying in our relationships with others than knowing that we are understood and accepted—except perhaps when others also agree with us. Communicating your understanding and acceptance of your students' perceptions can motivate them to want to discuss their feelings with you. Keep in mind that acceptance is not agreement, however. Acceptance means you can appreciate that they think and feel the way they do because of the way they experienced the incident. Acceptance also means listening in a noncritical and nonjudgmental manner. It doesn't necessarily mean that you see things the same way as the student does.

In working with Harold, you could express your acceptance of his feelings by saying you understand that he was angry about being yelled at for no reason. You could add that he would be justified to feel that way *if* the incident happened as he described it. You aren't saying here that you agree with his perception, only that you can understand and appreciate the way he feels given how he sees the situation.

*Explore other possible perceptions of the incident or situation.* After you have indicated that you understand your students' point of view and accept how they feel or think about what happened, ask your students if they can think of any other ways to look at or understand the event. Do this without suggesting that the students' points of view are incorrect. If they don't come up with an alternative, you can suggest one or two. For example, you might say, "I can understand why you think that you had a right to hit Molly for laughing at what you said when I called on you, but how do you know she was laughing at what you said? Is it possible that someone else had just said something funny to her or had told her a joke?" If the students are adamant that there is no other possible explanation, don't make an issue of it. This indicates that they aren't ready to face the truth. But if your students can admit that other possibilities might make sense, then together you can look at which alternative is the most likely or plausible one. Again, do this in a nonjudgmental way.

After communicating your understanding and acceptance of Harold's feelings, you would ask him whether it was possible that the student had some other reason for yelling at him. If he says "no," you would ask him if he remembers the student saying, "You almost tripped me with your stupid, fat feet." If Harold doesn't want to discuss it, let it drop. But if he seems receptive, you would ask Harold to think about why he decided to stretch his feet out in the aisle at the very moment the student walked by. If he is willing to admit that he might have been at fault after all, you would proceed to the next step.

*Maximize your students' motivation to perceive things realistically rather than defensively.* Students are more likely to admit that they made a mistake, that they were wrong, or that they were responsible for what happened if they will benefit by facing the truth or at least if nothing too terrible will result if they do look at what really happened. Therefore, to encourage students to give up their defenses, help them see the benefit in doing so. For example, you can explain that by not admitting their mistakes, students are forced to repeat them over and over again. You can also say that by not giving their peers the benefit of the doubt they are making it difficult for themselves to make and keep friends. Being clear that you are willing and eager to help them avoid making the same mistakes over again might also help them be less defensive.

At this step in the process, you could help Harold understand that if he actually started the problem by almost tripping the other student—and he can admit it and stop doing this kind of thing—he will be taking the first step toward having the student as a friend. On the other hand, if he can't admit it, keeps on doing it, and complains that the student is picking on him, he will continue to have the student as an enemy. Be positive as you explain this. Mention all the positive benefits Harold might derive from seeing things more clearly. Avoid pressuring him by suggesting any type of negative repercussions if he doesn't change his ways.

*Provide the help, support, and rewards your students need to face the truth they have been denying.* If students admit they are worried and anxious about not being able to succeed at things, give them extra help, sign them up for an after-school program, or arrange for peer tutoring. If students feel guilty or ashamed about the "bad" things they have been doing to you, forgive them and give them extra attention in class. Regardless of what they admit to, don't scold them for what they did. Instead, reward them for confronting things that they couldn't face before.

In Harold's case, you could praise him for being willing to admit his role in his problems. Remind him that this takes real courage, and help him see how his relationship with other students improves over time as his behavior toward them changes.

*Assist students in identifying more appropriate ways of behaving that are in tune with their nondefensive perceptions of themselves and their experiences.* Tanner advises:

> Elicit from the pupil how the pupil thinks he or she might be helped and what the teacher might be able to do to help the pupil control the behavior impulse in question. Develop a follow-through plan with the pupil. What will we have to do if this happens again? . . . any plan must be conceived within the limitations of school resources. (71, p. 168)

Student-identified and -managed solutions are preferable to those that teachers select and enforce because the students are more motivated to follow through on plans they determine or help determine. But as Morse (40) suggests, the teacher should also approve any plan.

With Harold, you could ask him what he thinks he should do if he believes it was his responsibility that his feet tripped the student. If he decides he should apologize to the student for tripping him, congratulate him for deciding on such a mature response and praise him when he actually does apologize.

*Evaluate the effectiveness of your efforts.* You should evaluate your attempts to change your students' behavior using the same types of criteria you would use to evaluate any technique: Does the unacceptable behavior occur less often? Is it less severe or less serious? Has it been replaced by more appropriate behavior? Include any other questions that help you objectively assess possible improvement.

You can evaluate Harold's progress by observing any change in how often he inflicts accidental mishaps on others and by comparing the number of times he is willing to admit that he was at fault with the number of times he blames others for things he does to them.

To summarize, the steps in the life-space interview process are:

1. Establish a relationship of confidence and acceptance with your students.

2. Choose situations or incidents that your students can deal with realistically and cooperatively.

3. Interview students under circumstances that encourage their participation.

4. Find out your students' perceptions.

5. Communicate your understanding and acceptance of both the students' perception of the incident and their feelings about it (without expressing agreement).

6. Explore other possible perceptions of the incident or situation.

7. Maximize your students' motivation to perceive things realistically rather than defensively.

8. Provide the help, support, and rewards your students need to face the truth they have been denying.

9. Assist students in identifying more appropriate ways of behaving that are in tune with their nondefensive perceptions of themselves and their experiences.

10. Evaluate the effectiveness of your efforts.

Several authors have recommended life-space interviews to classroom teachers (8, 66, 68, 71). Others criticize it, claiming that it is time-consuming and requires more individual attention than teachers can provide students. The little research available on this technique indicates that it can be effective, especially with older students who are able to think about and evaluate their own behavior (64, 70).

*Confronting students' defenses:* When educators need to get results faster than they can with the indirect life-space interview, they can be more direct. For example, they can present students with a true picture of reality without pressuring them to accept it. This approach is more confronting than life-space interviewing because students are presented with the educator's perception without any real preparation. It's not, however, as confronting as it could be because the teacher doesn't pressure the students to accept their perception.

One way to use this technique is to behave in ways that contradict what your student believes or actually say that you disagree with the student without getting into an argument about it. For example, if you think a student might be worried that she can't do something but can't admit it and so can't ask for help, you can just say to her, "Don't forget, I'm here to help you" or "It's all right to ask for help if you get stuck." If necessary, you can be even more direct and say, "I really don't think you can do that by yourself." If a student causes his own problems with other students and then runs to you to complain, hoping to receive sympathy, you can say, "I can't give you sympathy because it's your own fault. You are making them act mean by the way you are treating them." Another option is to say, "You don't have to agree with me, but I think they act mean to you because you try to boss them around. If you stop acting the way you do, maybe they will stop acting the way they do." The important thing in this approach is to give the student a clearer picture of reality *without* insisting or even trying to convince the student to accept your point of view unless he continues the conversation voluntarily.

Some educators are even more confrontational. They not only tell students how they perceive situations, but they also present their evidence and arguments until the students either see the truth or escape from the situation by refusing to continue the discussion, starting an argument, pretending to agree, calling them liars, or some other diversion. While this head-on approach can work, it also has the potential for making the situation worse. Even when teachers succeed in making students see things more objectively, the students may be so overwhelmed by the guilt, shame, fear, or anxiety they were defending against that they do something drastic. For this reason, it is best to avoid pressured, direct confrontation.

## Managing Emotional Problems

This section describes techniques you can use to make it less likely that students will act out their emotions in class in nonconstructive ways. Unlike the techniques described above, they are designed to manage students' misbehavior, not solve it.

As noted in Part Two, educators can use three kinds of techniques to manage students' behavior: managing without consequences, managing with consequences, and self-managing. The application of these three types of techniques to students with emotional problems is discussed below.

*Managing Without Consequences*   Although it is often possible to manage many students' behavior by the use of consequences, the following are some of the reasons why it's preferable for educators to manage their students' *emotional* problems without using positive or negative consequences whenever possible.

First, trying to pressure or coerce students with emotional problems to change their behavior when they are too upset to do so is like pushing them into the deep end of a pool without letting them get used to the cold water in the shallow end first. Educators can certainly make the consequences of not participating in the school play, not reading a composition to the rest of the class, or not answering when called on so distasteful that students who would otherwise be too embarrassed, ashamed, or anxious to participate feel compelled to do so. Sometimes this works, and students participate and learn that they were concerned about nothing. But many times this approach fails because working only on the behavioral level without changing the students' physical responses doesn't counteract the effects of their incorrect emotions. As a result, their intense embarrassment, shame, or anxiety causes them to block, stammer, clutch up, and so fail.

A second reason to avoid using consequences with these students is that students who experience incorrect emotions often misperceive things. This means that they may not be able to understand why their teachers are trying to pressure or coerce them to do things that these youngsters mistakenly—but firmly—believe they can't do or will harm them in some way.

Students whose emotions are too strong may also be too afraid to face something, too anxious to try something, too angry to make peace with someone, or too upset to sit down and talk calmly about something regardless of the rewards they are offered or the negative consequences educators may impose on them. Promising such students positive consequences if they change behavior that is often beyond their control or negative consequences if they don't may create unbearable conflicts in these students, drive them to tears, cause them to develop such "nervous" symptoms as twitches and sniffles, and push them to become truant or drop out of school.

Even if using techniques with consequences does get students to change their behavior for the moment, the price may not be worth it. When educators can get students to control their behavior without correcting their misperceptions or calming their emotional over-reactions, they may actually be putting even more pressure on the students to act out their feelings until they explode.

The use of consequences is also likely to prove ineffective or even counterproductive with students who are angry and resentful about being under the control of others or who are suspicious about others' motives. Even attempts to change these students' behavior by using only positive consequences can make them angrier, more resentful and suspicious, and cause them to rebel against one more dose of the very type of external control they can't accept.

Finally, the use of consequences can increase learned helplessness and foster an external locus of control. Many students with emotional problems already experience these and they don't need any reinforcement.

Below in the numbered lists are examples of managing techniques without consequences (73–75). They are divided into three groups. The first group involves ways you can adapt how *you* react to the students. The second group focuses on suggestions for calming *students* down or draining off part of their emotions so they are less likely to cause an inappropriate reaction. The third group are ways of adapting the *situation* to accomplish this end. The choice of which techniques would be the most appropriate for you to use depends both on the kinds of problems your students exhibit and the kinds of techniques you are comfortable using.

*Adapting to students*: These are things you can do to manage your students with emotional problems.

1. *Impersonalize your commands*: Older, rebellious, angry, or resentful students often react better when orders and directions are given in an impersonal way. You may get a more positive response from students if you say, "You are supposed to raise your hand" or "You are supposed to put away the equipment you use" instead of "*I want you to raise your hand*" or "Didn't I tell you to straighten up?" Likewise, they may react better to statements such as, "That's nothing to be proud of" than to statements like, "I'm not very proud of you."

2. *Avoid challenging statements*: Students, especially teenagers, with emotional problems may rebel when they are told what they can and can't do. When they hear the word *can't*, it's as if they experience a challenge to their independence. Sometimes it helps to phrase statements differently. "You aren't supposed to" can sound more acceptable than either "You can't" or "I won't allow you to."

3. *Suggest rather than order*: Students may also react better if you make suggestions rather than give orders.

The three techniques above are only temporary measures to manage behavior problems. In the long run, your students should be able to accept statements that reflect *your* authority or state clearly what they are or aren't allowed to do. But while you are helping these students grow and change so that they don't become resentful, angry, or rebellious when you "tell it like it is," you can make life easier for everyone concerned by rephrasing statements that could cause problems.

4. *Avoid moralizing*: Students who have problems with excessive guilt and shame may have difficulty coping with criticism that is expressed in moral terms. When they are told they are bad, unfair, and so on, they may feel so devastated that they become too defensive to accept the truth. It may be much easier for them to hear when they are told that their actions aren't helpful, appropriate, or acceptable. These words are less moralistic and focus on and describe the behavior rather than the person.

5. *Ignore provocative or argumentative behavior*: Some students create incidents so they have a chance to express their angry feelings. It's as if they are looking for an excuse or a reason to be angry and are trying to pick a fight. When students do this, you may be able to avoid these predictable outbursts by ignoring their behavior. Certain students purposely provoke teachers into punishing or rejecting them so they can then feel sorry for themselves. Others who can't cope with schoolwork may use provocative and argumentative behavior in order to get sent to the office or study hall. You may be able to manage these behaviors easily simply by ignoring them. This may not deal with the cause of the problem, but ignoring attempts to provoke a reaction from you may enable you to manage the situation until you can use some of the techniques described in the previous section to help these students change.

6. *Relieve tension using humor.* Sometimes, when they're very upset, students with emotional problems say things they don't mean and don't believe. They can also unwittingly take positions they know are wrong or blow things out of proportion. Then, later, they can't admit their mistakes gracefully. When educators take these situations seriously and respond by trying to maintain their own positions and points of view, this aggravates things. The results would be ludicrous if they weren't so unfortunate—two individuals unable to extricate themselves from a situation that both realize is ridiculous. At such times, making light of the situation, pointing out the humor in it, laughing *at* oneself but *with* one's student can turn a potential confrontation into a moment of shared humor.

The approaches described below are aimed at calming students. You can use these three techniques to help diminish the strength of your students' emotional overreactions so they are less likely to cause inappropriate behavior.

1. *Use relaxation techniques to counteract strong emotions.* You can try the relaxation methods described in the section on gradual desensitization when students are so afraid, angry, anxious, or upset that they are on the verge of misbehaving. You can also use relaxation techniques before students engage in activities that are potentially upsetting.

2. *Assure students that they will receive the support they need.* If students are anxious about not being able to do something alone, offer to help them whenever it becomes necessary.

3. *Prepare students for upsetting events ahead of time.* If you give students advance notice about something that may upset them and help them work through their anxieties and fears, they may be able to handle the event by the time it actually occurs.

Adapting to the situation is a third way to work with students who have emotional problems. These techniques include examples of ways you can modify the situations confronting your students to make it more likely that their emotional reactions will be manageable.

1. *Use the space to your students' advantage.* If certain students tease others or get into arguments with them over small things, separate them from their peers as much as possible. If they are anxious about being in school without the support of their parents, seat them close to you.

2. *Arrange the timing of activities to your students' advantage.* Schedule confrontations with students so they don't occur at difficult times such as the end of the day or right before tests. If students are so anxious they can only do certain activities when they can count on your help, then schedule such activities for times you can give them the attention they need.

3. *Distract students before their emotions get too strong to control.* When students are about to have a frustration fit over something they are trying to do or are starting to have an argument with another student, distract them from the problem situation to another activity. This technique is especially effective with younger students.

*Managing With Consequences*    Unfortunately, like many things in life, techniques for managing without consequences only work some of the time. If you believe your students will be able to accept and profit from consequences, you may decide to try using management techniques with consequences. If so, look at some of the management techniques described in Chapters 7 and 9, which you can also use with students who have emotional problems. If you do so, be mindful of the potential problems discussed above, and also avoid the use of negative or harsh consequences (72, 76). The rationale for avoiding such consequences with students in general and especially students who have emotional problems is expressed very well by Hewett:

> Teaching children to behave in certain ways and to acquire complex skills such as reading because they are afraid not to represents an educational "dead end" since our major goal is to make appropriate behavior and acquisition of reading eventually rewarding in and of itself. (72, p. 71)

*Self-Management*    Research indicates that educators can teach some students who have emotional problems to self-correct and self-moderate their emotional reactions by using techniques that are labeled self-control, self-mediation, self-instruction, self-management, cognitive behavior therapy, and cognitive behavior modification by various practitioners of this approach. The literature on self-control approaches for students with emotional problems includes a wide variety of techniques (78, 80, 82, 84, 85, 88, 90, 91, 93–95, 97, 99). Typically these involve teaching students to do some, but not necessarily all, of the following:

Delay acting out their feelings and impulses

Relax

Examine the reasons for their feelings and correct their misperceptions

Identify alternative ways of reacting to their feelings

Consider the consequences that are likely to result from each alternative

Select the most appropriate alternative

Instruct themselves about appropriate ways of reacting to their feelings

Evaluate their behavior and reinforce themselves for appropriate behavior

This section describes some of the ways students can implement procedures to manage their emotional reactions. It also discusses approaches educators have used to teach students how to follow these procedures. Finally, it reviews the research on the effectiveness of self-management techniques.

*Delay:* Students can try to delay acting out their emotions until they can think about their behavior by counting to ten, reminding themselves not to say or do anything while they are upset, instructing themselves to walk away when they are tempted to "lay hands on" someone else, telling themselves rule number 1 is always to "cool off" before you say or do anything. Any other helpful self-reminders that create a time gap between the emotional response and follow-up behavior can help the student cope.

*Relaxation:* Once students have inhibited their initial impulsive reactions to their feelings, they can relax themselves in any of the ways already described such as deep breathing or muscle relaxing exercises, allowing the body to go limp, emotive imagery, vigorous physical exercise, and so on.

*Reasoning:* Once they are relaxed rather than upset, students will be able to think reasonably about their reactions. One way to do this is for them to label their feelings and/or question their appropriateness. This is particularly important for students who aren't "in touch with" their feelings, such as students who act out their anger or frustration without even realizing that they are angry or frustrated. A student who gets easily frustrated whenever he runs into trouble in his schoolwork and rips up his papers without realizing why he does so can be taught to monitor himself. You can teach him to tell himself, "Oh, oh! I am getting frustrated. I feel like throwing my paper away again. Why should I feel frustrated? There's always a hard part to learning something new." Another student, disappointed that she wasn't called on when she knew the answer to a tough question and about to complain, can remind herself that students can't expect to be called on whenever they raise their hands. A student who gets angry whenever he receives a poor grade on a test and blames the teacher or the test in a loud, disruptive manner can remind himself that he should check the answers marked wrong with another student before deciding that his answers are absolutely right. A student who gets jealous when students she tends to play with are playing with someone else can remind herself that students, including herself, don't play with the same friend all the time. And a student who tends to believe that others pick on him unfairly can ask himself if he did anything to cause another student to reject him.

A second approach is for students to develop a set of alternative behaviors, explore the possible results of each, and select the most beneficial or effective one. For example, a student who gets so angry when she drops the ball playing poison ball that she wants to throw the ball over the fence can ask herself how the other students will react if she does this. Or a student who experiences the urge to hit another student for something he said can remind himself that if he does, he will get into trouble. But if he only says something nasty back to the student, there won't be any repercussions.

*Self-instruction:* Just as in creating a delay, students can instruct themselves to react more appropriately. Self-instructions can remind students how to react to their emotions in more constructive ways. Examples of self-instructions give an idea of how many situations they cover: "Tell people how you feel," "Don't act your feelings out," "Tell people you're angry with them," "Don't hit others," "Don't rip up your paper—ask the teacher for help," and "Take a short break when you feel tense."

*Self-evaluation and reinforcement:* Each time students follow self-management procedures, they should evaluate the results in terms of how they feel about their behavior and their increased self-control. They also need to look at the favorable consequences that resulted from their behavior as well as the unfavorable consequences they avoided by controlling themselves. Noting the positive results of following self-management procedures should be intrinsically rewarding. But students can also reward themselves for modifying their behavior with a positive reinforcement of their choice. (See Chapter 2 for examples of positive rewards.)

*Turtle Technique:* The Turtle Technique, a structured program for helping students manage their emotions, has been successful with some elementary school students (97). In this technique, the teacher tells the students a story about a little turtle who gets into trouble in school for becoming angry and fighting with other students until a tortoise tells him to withdraw into his shell whenever he gets angry and just rest until he feels better. The teacher then shows the students how to pull their arms and legs in close to their bodies, lay their heads on their desks, put their arms over their heads, and relax. They also learn to use problem-solving approaches for selecting appropriate ways to react to their feelings before coming out of their "shells."

*Teaching self-management:* It is possible to teach students to correct and moderate their behavior when they experience strong emotions that they would otherwise act out nonconstructively. Meichenbaum and Goodman (93–95) suggest using the following approach to train students to control their own behavior.

1. The teacher models the behavior students should copy while saying aloud the things students should eventually think.

2. Students perform the same behavior under the teacher's supervision.

3. Students perform the behavior while instructing themselves aloud.

4. Students perform the behavior while whispering the instructions to themselves.

5. Students perform the behavior and instruct themselves mentally.

## THEORY FOCUS: MEICHENBAUM ON SELF-MANAGEMENT

Donald Meichenbaum is one of the founders of cognitive behavior modification, a self-management strategy that emphasizes helping students think before acting. His published works have helped educators appreciate the fact that students are more capable of managing their own behavior than was originally thought. In a number of articles and books, including *Cognitive Behavior Modification: An Integrative Approach*, Meichenbaum describes self-management techniques students can use to gain control over their actions as well as effective procedures for teaching students to employ these techniques correctly and consistently in school.

Recently Meichenbaum stated, "Consider the child in the classroom who 'knows what to do and does it,' who has a series of adaptive routines and procedural scripts to perform both academic and social tasks. If teachers had their wish they would 'clone' such children. My present research efforts are designed to understand such children and the learning conditions under which self-directed behavior can be nurtured.

"In contrast, children who evidence attentional problems, such as hyperactive children, tend to have difficulty in following rules, especially when those rules are designed to sustain their behavior over a period of time and when there is not continual feedback. Similarly, conduct disorder children have difficulty complying with teacher requests. Our work on teaching children self-control strategies, under the headings of cognitive behavior modification and meta-cognitive training (cognitive strategy instruction), is designed to help make both teaching and learning trouble free." (Donald Meichenbaum, personal communication, April 15, 1989)

Educators have used bibliotherapy—stories of how others have managed similar emotions and overcome similar problems—to provide models for students to learn from. Educators have also had students observe how others in class handle similar problems or watch videotapes with helpful models. Having students role play the parts of others affected by their inappropriate emotional reactions also helps enhance students' understanding of the consequences their inappropriate behavior has had.

*Effectiveness:* Self-managing techniques have been effective for some, but not all, of the students they have been used with. Specifically, they have helped some students control behavior that is angry and aggressive (80, 87, 92, 97), anxious (93, 98), and fearful (89, 96). Research reviews of the efficacy of self-management techniques with students who have emotional problems indicate that their effectiveness is limited (77, 79, 81, 86, 100). It also isn't clear which techniques will work with which students and why. As Bornstein has said:

> Self-instructional training will probably be of great benefit to some, moderate benefit to others, and minimal or no benefit to yet a final grouping of individuals. Our job is to identify those variables that substantially affect the success of our treatment. (79, p. 71)

Ephanchin and Paul arrived at virtually the same conclusion about self-managing techniques:

> Given the paucity of information, it is not yet possible to say how and for whom this approach works best, although it appears to be promising. (83, p. 187)

Although many conceivable reasons might explain why self-management techniques aren't equally effective with all students, four explanations appear particularly plausible.

First, older students appear to profit more than younger ones from self-managing techniques (108, 109). This may be because children's abilities to control themselves mature as they do. They are also better able to remember and follow a number of instructions, develop their own plans of action, and generate their own visual images.

While a number of studies indicate that preschoolers can be taught to control their motor behavior, resist temptations, and influence their emotional states (101, 104–107, 110), they require more training than older children on identifying the cues that indicate they should begin to self-instruct themselves. They require a specific, uncomplicated, short set of instructions from adults that they can tell themselves to follow (they are relatively unable to formulate instructional commands on their own). They also respond better to self-instruction if they receive extrinsic rewards for doing it (103, 109).

Self-management techniques may also not help some students because they aren't mature enough to follow the procedures this approach requires. In particular, since many students with emotional problems are immature, they may not be able to use self-managing techniques that are appropriate for their ages but not their developmental levels. As Pressley has stated:

> Cognitive rationales can increase children's self-control, but only if the content of the rationale is consistent with what the child can comprehend (as a function of developmental level). (109, p. 347)

A second possible explanation for why self-management is effective with some students and not others is that these techniques appear to work better with students whose locus of control is internal (102). Students with an internal locus believe they are in control of their own lives, but students with emotional problems who have poor self-concepts may not believe in their self-power and efficacy enough to put self-managing techniques to use effectively. A third explanation is that some students become too upset to delay their reactions long enough to think before acting. Others may be unable to control themselves in the intensity of feeling even though they know full well the possible negative consequences that could follow. The same happens with adults who are so angry they lose control and say things they are sorry for or do things they know will cause them grief. The satisfaction they get from expressing their anger at the moment simply outweighs the more distant, undesirable results they anticipate later. Finally, defensive students who misperceive both themselves and their experiences may not be able to objectively perceive and evaluate alternative ways of behaving even though they delay acting out their feelings. This can happen if they are too defensive to correct their perceptions on their own.

*Developmental Level*    It is best to decide on the types of self-managing techniques you teach students to use, how you teach them to use these techniques, and the extent to which you rely on self-managing rather than teacher-initiated techniques partly based on your students' developmental levels.

*Self-control:* Preschool and primary grade students may be able to exercise some self-control, but it's generally more effective to emphasize teacher-initiated managing techniques at this level. Secondary students may be able to manage much more of their emotional reactions providing they aren't immature or defensive and they believe they can control their own lives.

*Number of instructions:* Younger students may only be able to give themselves simple directives that involve a single idea such as: work slow, ask for help, think of fun things. Older students should be able to remember increasingly longer series of instructions. For example: count to ten before saying or doing anything, then breathe deeply and let your body go limp; next, ask yourself if the other person could somehow be right and you wrong; then think of all the different ways you might react, and choose the best one.

*Specificity of instructions:* Young students require teachers to formulate the directives they will use to self-instruct themselves. Teachers need to say, "When you want to hit somebody, say 'count to ten.'" Or "When you want to stop working because the work is too hard, say to yourself 'Ask the teacher for help.'" A final example: "When you're afraid about going to recess, say to yourself 'think of fun things you like to do during recess.'" In contrast, teachers can give older students general directives to follow. Instead of telling older students exactly what to say in order to delay their reactions, they might tell students that they can choose from a number of things to do such as counting to ten, thinking about something else, turning and walking away from the person, and so on. Then the teacher can encourage students to find out which approach works best for them.

*Cues:* Preschool and primary grade students usually can't generalize self-instructional techniques they have learned to use in one situation (to one cue) to other situations (with other cues). Thus, they need practice using the technique in each different situation where it applies. You also have to teach older students to generalize the self-managing techniques they have learned with one set of cues to other possible situations, but their training may not have to be so concrete and repetitious.

*Monitoring and evaluating:* Young students may not be able to evaluate how well their self-managing efforts are working and can require close supervision. But you can teach older students how to monitor and evaluate the results of their efforts to manage their own behavior.

*Reinforcement:* As noted, preschool and primary grade students may implement their self-managing systems more consistently if teachers give them extrinsic rewards. Older students, however, may be able to reward themselves by observing the improvement in their behavior and thinking about how much better off they are as a result.

## Tolerating Emotional Problems

Students who can't yet manage their own behavior and who don't respond to their teachers' management techniques all the time will occasionally act out inappropriately. At such times, teachers can either tolerate this behavior or try to prevent it from occurring. Sometimes it is especially appropriate to tolerate students' misbehavior.

To begin with, it's unrealistic to expect that you and your students will be able to manage all of their inappropriate behaviors. You and your students may be able to manage many such potential instances, but you may have to tolerate others.

Tolerating may also be appropriate if the behavior won't harm your students, hurt others, or seriously interfere with their rights. For example, you might decide to tolerate a student's occasional show of temper or complaint that you are unfair. But you would certainly try to prevent a student from hitting another student in anger or else destroying something in a fit of jealousy that another student has made.

Even when your students' behavior improves due to your efforts, you may have to occasionally tolerate their misbehavior when they slip back into old patterns temporarily because the going gets too rough or a situation is particularly upsetting. Likewise, as students attempt to cope with more and more of what would once have been too threatening to face or as they move closer to a goal that is very frightening, they may find it necessary to take a step back.

Another time tolerance is called for is when students, who have been inhibited from doing things due to excessive fear, guilt, or shame begin to do things that others their age have been doing for a long time. Often these students don't know how to behave appropriately. Under such circumstances, it's a good idea to tolerate their incorrect behavior until they learn to behave more appropriately. For example, when students who have been timid about standing up to their peers finally begin to do so, they often overreact or use highly aggressive ways of defending themselves due to their lack of experience. Tolerate this behavior (if it's not dangerous) while you teach your students more acceptable ways of standing up to others.

Finally, if you use consequences to manage your students' behavior, you may have more success with this approach if you tolerate their expression of anger or resentment. They are likely to be upset with you for requiring them to behave more appropriately, even though you are doing it for their benefit. Let them express these negative feelings as a byproduct of the goal you are striving toward.

When you choose to tolerate behavior, the principles for tolerating conduct problems discussed in Chapter 9 apply to tolerating emotional problems as well. They are:

1. Try not to feel resentful or discouraged that you have to tolerate behavior since you have no other possibility for the moment.

2. Tolerate behavior only temporarily.

3. Make sure the student understands which behaviors you are tolerating and which you aren't.

4. Never tolerate behavior that you can manage.

## Preventing Emotional Problems

Preventing emotional problems from occurring is the best strategy for behavior that would be harmful or significantly interfere with the rights of others. You have a great many ways to prevent students from acting out their emotional problems. The number is limited only by the creativeness and ingenuity you apply to the task. This section includes examples of certain techniques you can use with your students, but your personality and the situation will suggest others that can be just as effective with your particular students.

1. *Remove upsetting stimuli from your students' environment.* Remove things that are too upsetting or threatening for students to cope with. These might include pictures of war, disease, famine, and death.

2. *Protect students from situations they can't handle.* Extricate students from situations that are disintegrating before they become too anxious, too angry, or too afraid to maintain their self-control. Don't allow students to try things when you know they can't succeed.

3. *Provide the assistance your students need in order not to experience frustration or anxiety.* Helping your students succeed when they are verging on misbehavior due to frustration or anxiety about something they are trying to accomplish is a good prevention technique. If you know your students will need your help, provide it even before they begin to feel frustrated or anxious. This may mean giving students a calculator to do math problems or providing a peer tutor in algebra even though students need them for emotional rather than academic reasons.

4. *Adapt your demands and expectations to fit your students' emotional states.* When students are anxious, angry, or resentful, accept what they are capable of doing at the moment, not what they can do when they aren't upset.

5. *Excuse students from situations they will be unable to handle.* Allow students to decline from participating in class plays, reading their work aloud, and similar situations. Provide alternative activities for students who can't handle discussions or films about disease, war, crime, or kidnapping. Use cubicles and earphones to protect students from activities they can't deal with. If necessary, permit students to leave the room, run an errand, or otherwise get some distance to avoid a stressful situation.

6. *Depersonalize your teaching techniques when students can't handle attention from others.* Use such impersonal teaching materials as computers and programmed instruction texts for students who grow uncomfortable with personal help.

7. *Use physical control if necessary to make sure students don't harm anyone.* Don't hesitate to call authorities for help when students appear on the verge of doing

## Self-Quiz: Handling Emotional Problems

To determine the range of techniques you would use with students who have emotional problems, answer the following questions about the techniques listed below.

1. How comfortable would you feel about using each of the techniques?
2. How often have you used each of the techniques?
3. Which techniques do you overemphasize?
4. Which techniques would you like to use more often?

Improving students' self-concepts by:

Ensuring their success through selecting work at their levels, providing extra help, and so on

Expressing your belief that they can succeed

Having students read stories about others who have overcome similar obstacles and problems

Correcting students' perfectionistic standards

Providing opportunities for students to succeed in alternative activities

Encouraging students to make positive rather than negative statements about themselves

Helping students believe they have power over their own lives by:

Allowing them to select the activities they engage in, the materials they use, the pace at which they work, and other self-determining decisions.

Providing as little assistance as possible to dependent students

Encouraging students to evaluate their own work and efforts

Correcting students' overgeneralizations by:

Gradually desensitizing them to threatening stimuli

Encouraging inhibited students to act out their emotions without feeling guilty or embarrassed

*(continued)*

something dangerous. Many educators are wary of using physical force with their students due to the possibility of litigation. But if all else fails or nothing else will work, and the situation calls for an immediate response, you might consider physically preventing your students from doing harm. In doing so, always use the least amount of force necessary, but make sure you use enough. Then get help from others as soon as possible.

Prevention shouldn't be punitive. Students with emotional problems misbehave because their emotions are inappropriate. They don't mean to be willful, disobedient, mean, or nasty. When they have to be sent out of the room, physically restrained, and so on, it's because they *can't* control themselves, not because they *don't want to*. They neither deserve to be punished nor will punishing them help them solve their emotional problems. Thus, if you have to prevent students from misbehaving, treat them with kindness and

Correcting students' defensive behavior by:

Life-space interview techniques

Confronting students' defenses directly

Managing students' behavior by:

Impersonalizing your directives

Suggesting rather than ordering

Avoiding moralizing

Ignoring provocative and argumentative behavior

Releasing tension through humor

Using relaxation techniques

Preparing students for impending upsetting events

Using space advantageously

Distracting students before they become upset

Using consequences to encourage students to control themselves despite their emotional reactions

Teaching students to manage their own behavior by:

Delaying their responses

Relaxing themselves

Reasoning through problems

Reinforcing themselves for behaving appropriately

Tolerating behavior problems that can't be managed.

Preventing students from harming themselves or others or from infringing on others' rights by:

Removing upsetting stimuli from the environment

Protecting students from situations they can't handle

Adapting demands and expectations to students' emotional states

Allowing students to escape from upsetting situations

Depersonalizing teaching techniques

Using physical restraint when necessary

Employing nonpunitive preventive techniques

understanding as you do so. And, if at all possible, have your words, tone of voice, and actions all convey this attitude while you do what you have to. This may be an unrealistically idealistic goal, but it is a goal worth striving for.

## *Matching Techniques and Problems*

Educators can help improve the behavior of students with emotional problems by correcting the ideas that cause their inappropriate emotions, by calming and relaxing them so their upsetting emotions don't affect them as much, by using consequences to convince them to behave in acceptable ways despite their emotional problems, or by using a combination of these approaches. When educators give students more information, try to talk sense with them, or tell them to try being less defensive, they are working on the students' incorrect ideas. When they allow students to listen to calm music or eat a snack when they are anxious or have them do relaxation exercises to reduce the tension they have built up during the day, they are working on modifying the students' physical state. These physical interventions don't do anything about the ideas and situations that made the students tense or caused their worrisome thoughts, but they counteract the effects the students' ideas have on their bodies. This enables the students to relax and to function temporarily as if these troubling thoughts or situations didn't exist. Finally, when educators pressure students to attempt to do something even though the students believe they have almost no chance of succeeding, or when they force students to move onward despite their fears, they are working on the students' behavior itself.

Educators who tend to habitually emphasize one or another of these alternatives sometimes make the mistake of using their usual approach even when it isn't effective. For example, educators who rely almost exclusively on words to explain to students why they shouldn't be so upset, afraid, anxious, or angry may have a difficult time helping students when they are just too upset to respond to ideas and logic. This is clearly the case when students are too angry to discuss something no matter how much their teachers try to get them to think about the problem rationally. The students need first to relax before they can relate to ideas no matter how clearly the teacher presents them.

Educators who overuse relaxing their students when they are upset or afraid may do a good job of calming them down. But if they don't also deal with the ideas that cause their students' inappropriate behaviors, they won't be able to do anything to help these students avoid repeating the same behaviors again and again.

Finally, educators who push anxious, fearful students to do things can sometimes help them overcome their hesitancy. It's just as likely, though, that this may upset students even more, causing them to fail at things they aren't ready for or to mistrust their teachers whom they see as insensitive to their feelings.

To be genuinely effective with students who have emotional problems, you need to be knowledgeable about a variety of techniques. From these, you should choose the ones that you believe are most likely to work well with an individual student.

# Summary

When students' emotions function properly, they help guide their actions so they can adequately handle the many different situations they face daily. When their emotions don't perform this function or perform it inadequately, then students have emotional problems. A student's behavioral problems have an emotional basis if her emotional responses are *often* inappropriate for the situation and she *often* avoids, defends, or suffers instead of attempting to solve the problems of daily living.

If a student's behavior problems are caused by emotional factors, you should be able to identify his inappropriate emotions; state whether they are too strong, too weak, incorrect, or in conflict; and determine that he avoids, defends, or suffers *too much* and *too often*. Though some educators doubt that classroom teachers can handle the behavior problems of students with emotional problems, much less make a contribution toward eliminating these emotional problems, research and classroom experience indicate otherwise.

## *Activities*

I. Reread the three case studies in the activities section of Chapter 9 and decide which, if any, of the students described had emotional problems.

II. Decide whether each of the following behavior patterns is more likely to be a conduct problem or an emotional problem, and state the reasons for your opinion.

1. Harry pushes ahead of smaller children in line when the teacher isn't supervising the group.

2. Carlotta seldom participates in group cleanup activities unless her teacher uses consequences to motivate her.

3. Matilda teases weaker children and laughs when they act upset.

4. Although he has never been caught at it, Rudy has been selling drugs in school, according to reports from three students.

5. Although Placido is a bright student and can do the work on his own without any difficulty, he often copies other students' homework.

6. Antonia thinks so little of her math abilities that she often gives up whenever she encounters a difficult problem.

III. Decide whether each of the six problems described below is more likely to be a personality problem or a situational problem. Give reasons for your choices.

1. Because of the neglect and abuse she received since her early childhood, Barbara is very suspicious of children and adults and doesn't trust anyone.

2. Because he was not selected for the varsity football team, Peter feels very bad and no longer associates with any of his friends who made the team.

3. Mark is afraid of his brothers and sisters and the other children in the school. He always sits in the back row and doesn't play with anyone his own age or older.

4. Since she was hit by a car a few months ago, Barbara shakes whenever she has to cross the street.

5. The other children in the class laughed at Jason because he did so poorly on an exam. Now he doesn't want to go to school.

6. Because Susan is so anxious and dependent, she always tries to get attention from adults.

IV. Imagine a behavior problem that can result when students experience each of the following emotions in class: anger, fear, anxiety, jealousy, depression, guilt, shame. Suggest two management techniques educators can use to make it less likely that these potential behavior problems will occur.

# *References*

IDENTIFICATION

1. Quay, H. C. (1977). Measuring dimensions of deviant behavior: The Behavior Problem Checklist. *Journal of Abnormal Child Psychology, 5*, 277–289.

2. Quay, H. C., & Peterson, D. R. (1983). *Revised Behavior Problem Checklist.* Coral Gables, FL: University of Miami.

3. Rubin, E., Simpson, C., & Betwee, M. (1966). *Emotionally Handicapped Children and the Elementary School.* Detroit: Wayne State University Press.

4. Spivack, G., Spotts, J., & Haines, P. E. (1967). *The Devereux Adolescent Behavior Rating Scale.* Devon, PA: Devereux Foundation.

5. Spivack, G., & Swift, M. (1967). *Devereux Elementary School Behavior Rating Scale Manual.* Devon, PA: Devereux Foundation.

6. Von Isser, A., Quay, H. C., & Love, C. T. (1980). Interrelationships among three measures of deviant behavior. *Exceptional Children, 46*, 272–276.

7. Walker, H. (1969). Empirical assessment of deviant behavior in children. *Psychology in the Schools, 6*, 93–97.

8. Walker, H. (1976). *Walker Problem Behavior Identification Manual.* Los Angeles: Western Psychological Services.

PERSONALITY PROBLEMS

9. Brophy, J. E., & Putnam, J. G. (1978). *Classroom Management in the Elementary Grades.* ERIC ED 167 537.

ENHANCING SELF-CONCEPT

10. Backman, C. W., & Secord, P. V. (1968). *A Social Psychological View of Education.* New York: Harcourt, Brace, Jovanovich.

11. Bandina, A. (1982). Self-efficacy mechanism in human agency. *American Psychologist*, 37, 122–148.

12. Baskin, B. H., & Harris, K. S. (1977). *Notes from a Different Drummer: A Guide to Juvenile Fiction Portraying the Handicapped*. New York: Bowker.

13. Bessel, H., & Palomares, V. H. (1970). *Methods in Human Development*. El Cajon, CA: Human Development Training Institute.

14. Bledsoe, J. C. (1964). Self-concepts of children and their intelligence, achievement, interests and anxiety. *Journal of Individual Psychology*, 20, 55–58.

15. Bowdin, F. B. (1957). *The Relationship Between Immature Self-Concept and Educational Disability*. Unpublished doctoral dissertation, Michigan State University, East Lansing, MI.

16. Brookover, W. B., Erickson, E. L., & Joiner, L. M. (1967). *Self-Concept of Ability and School Achievement. III: Relationship of Self-Concept to Achievement in High School*. East Lansing, MI: Office of Research and Publications, Michigan State University.

17. Brookover, W. P., Patterson, A., & Thomas, S. (1962). *Self-Concept of Ability and School Achievement*. East Lansing, MI: Office of Research and Publications, Michigan State University.

18. Brookover, W. P., Patterson, A., & Thomas, S. (1964). Self-concept of ability and school achievement. *Sociology of Education*, 37, 271–278.

19. Burdett, K., & Jensen, L. C. (1983). The self-concept and aggressive behavior among elementary school children from two socioeconomic areas and two grade levels. *Psychology in the Schools*, 20, 370–375.

20. Campbell, P. (1967). School and self-concept. *Educational Leadership*, 24, 510–515.

21. Canfield, J., & Wells, H. C. (1976). *100 Ways to Enhance Self-Concept in the Classroom*. Englewood Cliffs, NJ: Prentice-Hall.

22. Coopersmith, S. (1981). *The Antecedents of Self-Esteem* (2nd ed.). Palo Alto, CA: Consulting Psychologists.

23. Coopersmith, S., & Feldman, R. (1974). Fostering a positive self-concept and high self-esteem in the classroom. In R. H. Coop & K. White (Eds.), *Psychological Concepts in the Classroom*. New York: Harper & Row.

24. De Charms, R. (1976). *Enhancing Motivation*. New York: Irvington.

25. Dreyer, S. S. (1977). *The Bookfinder: A Guide to Children's Literature about the Needs and Problems of Youth Aged Two Through Fifteen*. Circle Pines, MN: American Guidance Service.

26. Engle, K. B., Davis, D. A., & Meyer, G. (1968). Interpersonal effects on underachievers. *Journal of Educational Psychology*, 61, 208–210.

27. Fassler, J. (1978). *Helping Children Cope*. New York: Free Press.

28. Felker, D. W. (1974). *Building Positive Self-Concepts*. Minneapolis: Burgess.

29. Gillham, I. (1967). Self-concept and reading. *The Reading Teacher, 21,* 270–273.

30. Gose, A., Wooden, S., & Muller, D. (1980). The relative potential of self-concept and intelligence as predictors of achievement. *Journal of Psychology, 104,* 279–287.

31. Gowan, J. (1960). Factors of achievement in high school and college. *Journal of Counseling Psychology, 7,* 91–95.

32. Hansford, B. C., & Hattie, J. E. (1982). The relationship between self and achievement/performance measures. *Review of Educational Research, 52,* 123–142.

33. Harter, S. (1982). The perceived competency scale for children. *Child Development, 53,* 87–97.

34. Hauserman, N., Mitler, J. S., & Bond, F. T. (1976). A behavioral approach to changing self-concept in elementary school children. *Psychological Record, 26,* 111–116.

35. Katzenmer, W. G., & Stenner, A. J. (1970). *Self-Observation Scales*. Durham, NC: NTS Research Corporation.

36. Kinard, E. M. (1980). Emotional development in physically abused children. *American Journal of Orthopsychiatry, 50,* 686–696.

37. Knoblock, P. (1983). *Teaching Emotionally Disturbed Children*. Boston: Houghton Mifflin.

38. Lane, J., & Muller, D. (1977). The effect of altering self-descriptive behavior on self-concept and classroom behavior. *Journal of Psychology, 97,* 115–125.

39. Lefcourt, H. J. (1966). Internal versus external control of reinforcement. *Psychological Bulletin, 65,* 206–220.

40. Morse, W. C. (1985). *The Education and Treatment of Socioemotionally Impaired Children and Youth*. Syracuse, NY: Syracuse University Press.

41. Nowicki, S., & Strickland, B. (1973). A locus of control scale for children. *Journal of Consulting and Clinical Psychology, 40,* 148–154.

42. Piers, E. V., & Harris, D. B. (1969). *Children's Self-Concept Scale (The Way I Feel About Myself)*. Nashville, TN: Counselor Recordings and Tests.

43. Quimby, V. (1967). Differences in the self-ideal relationship of an achieved group and an underachieved group. *California Journal of Educational Research, 18,* 23–31.

44. Reynolds, W. M. (1980). Self-esteem and classroom behavior in elementary school children. *Psychology in the Schools, 17,* 273–277.

45. Rosenberg, F. R., & Rosenberg, M. (1978). Self-esteem and delinquency. *Journal of Youth and Adolescence, 7,* 279–291.

46. Rosenberg, M. (1979). *Conceiving the Self*. New York: Basic Books.

47. Rotter, J. B. (1966). Generalized expectancies for internal versus external rein-forcement. *Psychological Monographs, 80* (Whole No. 609).

48. Russell, A., & Russell, W. A. (1979). Using bibliotherapy with emotionally dis-turbed children. *Teaching Exceptional Children, 11,* 168–171.

49. Scheier, M. A., & Kraut, R. E. (1979). Increasing educational achievement via self-concept change. *Review of Educational Research, 49,* 131–149.

50. Schulman, J. L., Ford, R. C., & Busk, P. (1973). A classroom program to im-prove self-concept. *Psychology in the Schools, 10,* 481–487.

51. Shaw, M., & Alves, G. (1963). The self-concept of bright academic under-achievers: II. *Personnel and Guidance Journal, 42,* 401–403.

52. Wattenberg, W. W., & Clifford, C. (1964). Relation of self-concept to beginning achievement in reading. *Child Development, 35,* 461–467.

53. Weinstein, G., & Fantini, M. (1970). *Toward Humanistic Education.* New York: Praeger.

54. Wells, L., & Maxwell, G. (1976). *Self-Esteem: Its Conceptualization and Mea-surement.* Beverly Hills, CA: Sage.

55. White, K., & Allen, R. (1971). Art counseling in an educational setting: Self-concept change among preadolescent boys. *Journal of School Psychology, 9* (2), 218–225.

56. Williams, R., & Cole, S. (1968). Self-concept and adjustment. *Personnel and Guidance Journal, 46,* 478–481.

57. Yauman, B. E. (1980). Special education placements and the self-concepts of ele-mentary school-age children. *Learning Disabilities Quarterly, 3,* 30–35.

CORRECTING OVERGENERALIZATIONS

58. Deffenbacher, J., & Kemper, C. (1974). Systematic desensitization of test anxiety in junior high school students. *The School Counselor, 21,* 216–222.

59. Hosford, C. (1969). Overcoming of fear of speaking in a group. In J. Krumboltz & C. Thoresen (Eds.), *Behavioral Counseling.* New York: Holt, Rinehart & Winston.

60. Johnson, S. (1979). Children's fears in the classroom setting. *School Psychologist Digest, 8,* 382–396.

61. Lazarus, A. A., Davidson, G. C., & Polefka, D. A. (1965). Classical and operant factors in the treatment of a school phobia. *Journal of Abnormal Psychology, 70,* 225–229.

62. Mann, J. (1972). Vicarious desensitization of test anxiety through observation of videotaped treatment. *Journal of Counseling Psychology, 19,* 1–7.

63. Montenegro, H. (1968). Severe separation anxiety in two preschool children: Successfully treated by reciprocal inhibition. *Journal of Child Psychology and Psy-chiatry, 9,* 93–103.

CORRECTING DEFENSIVE BEHAVIOR

64. De Magistris, R. J., & Imber, S. C. (1980). The effects of life-space interviewing on academic and social performance of behaviorally disordered children. *Behavior Disorders, 6,* 12–25.

65. Gordon, R. (1974). *Teacher Effectiveness Training.* New York: Wyden.

66. Long, J. D., & Frye, V. H. (1981). *Making It Till Friday: A Guide to Successful Classroom Management* (2nd ed.). Princeton: Princeton Book Company.

67. Long, N. J., Morse, W. C., & Newman, R. G. (Eds.). (1980). *Conflict in the Classroom: The Education of Emotionally Disturbed Children* (4th ed.). Belmont, CA: Wadsworth.

68. Morse, W. C. (1963). Working paper: Training teachers in life-space interviewing. *American Journal of Orthopsychiatry, 33,* 727–730.

69. Redl, F. (1959). The concept of the life-space interview. *American Journal of Orthopsychiatry, 29,* 1–18.

70. Reilly, M. J., Imber, S. C., & Cremins, J. (1978). *The Effects of Life-Space Interviews on Social Behaviors of Junior High School Special Needs Students.* Paper presented at the 56th International Conference of the Council for Exceptional Children, Kansas City.

71. Tanner, L. N. (1978). *Classroom Discipline for Effective Teaching and Learning.* New York: Holt, Rinehart & Winston.


MANAGING EMOTIONAL PROBLEMS WITHOUT CONSEQUENCES

72. Hewett, F. M. (1968). *The Emotionally Disturbed Child in the Classroom.* Boston: Allyn & Bacon.

73. Jacobson, S., & Falgre, C. (1953). Neutralization: A tool for the teacher of disturbed children. *American Journal of Orthopsychiatry, 23,* 684–690.

74. Long, N. J., & Newman, R. G. (1965). Managing surface behavior of children in school. In N. J. Long, W. C. Morse, & R. G. Newman (Eds.), *Conflict in the Classroom.* Belmont, CA: Wadsworth.

75. Redl, F., & Wineman, D. (1957). *The Aggressive Child.* New York: Free Press.

76. Wood, F. H. (1978). Punishment and special education: Some concluding remarks. In F. H. Wood & K. C. Lakin (Eds.), *Punishment and Aversive Stimulation in Special Education: Legal, Theoretical, and Practical Issues in Their Use with Emotionally Disturbed Children and Youth.* Minneapolis, MN: Advanced Training Institute for Trainers of Teachers for Seriously Emotionally Disturbed Children and Youth.


SELF-MANAGEMENT

77. Albion, F. M. (1983). A methodological analysis of self-control in applied settings. *Behavior Disorders, 8,* 87–102.

78. Beck, A. T. (1976). *Cognitive Therapy and Emotional Disorders*. New York: International University Press.

79. Bornstein, P. H. (1985). Self-instructional training: A commentary and state of the art. *Journal of Applied Behavior Analysis, 18*, 69–72.

80. Camp, B., Blom, G., Herbert, F., & Van Doornenck, W. (1977). "Think Aloud": A program for developing self-control in young aggressive boys. *Journal of Abnormal Child Psychology, 5*, 192–199.

81. Carpenter, R. L., & Apter, S. J. (1987). Research in integration of cognitive-emotional interventions for behaviorally disordered children and youth. In M. C. Wang, H. J. Walberg, & M. C. Reynolds (Eds.), *Handbook of Special Education: Research and Practice*. Oxford, England: Pergamon Press.

82. Emery, G., Hollon, D. S., & Bedrosian, R. D. (1981). *New Directions in Cognitive Therapy*. New York: Guilford Press.

83. Epanchin, B. C., & Paul, J. L. (1987). *Emotional Problems of Childhood and Adolescence: A Multidisciplinary Prospective*. Columbus, OH: Charles E. Merrill.

84. Fagan, S. (1979). Psychoeducational management and self-control. In D. Cullinan & M. Epstein (Eds.), *Special Education for Adolescents: Issues and Perspectives*. Columbus, OH: Charles E. Merrill.

85. Fagan, S. A., Long, N. J., & Stevens, D. J. (1975). *Teaching Children Self-Control in the Classroom: A Psychoeducational Curriculum*. Columbus, OH: Charles E. Merrill.

86. Fick, L. (1979). Self-control strategies for emotionally disabled students. *Iowa Perspective*, May.

87. Goodwin, S., & Mahoney, M. (1975). Modification of aggression through modeling: An experimental probe. *Journal of Behavior Therapy and Experimental Psychiatry, 6*, 200–202.

88. Hallahan, D. P. (Ed.). (1980). Teaching exceptional children to use cognitive strategies. *Exceptional Education Quarterly, 1*.

89. Kanfer, F. H., Karoly, P., & Newman, A. (1975). Reduction of children's fear of the dark by competence-related and situation threat-related verbal cues. *Journal of Consulting and Clinical Psychology, 43*, 251–258.

90. Knaus, W. (1974). *Rational-Emotive Education: A Manual for Elementary School Teachers*. New York: Institute for Rational Living.

91. Kurtz, P. D., & Neisworth, J. T. (1976). Self-control possibilities for exceptional children. *Exceptional Children, 42*, 213–217.

92. McCullough, J. P., Huntsinger, G. N., & Nay, W. R. (1977). Self-controlled treatment of aggression in a 16-year-old male: Case study. *Journal of Consulting and Clinical Psychology, 45*, 322–331.

93. Meichenbaum, D. (1973). Cognitive factors in behavior modification: Modifying what clients say about themselves. In R. Rubin, J. Brady, & J. Henderson (Eds.), *Advances in Behavior Therapy, Vol. 4*. New York: Academic Press.

94. Meichenbaum, D. (1977). *Cognitive-Behavior Modification: An Integrative Approach*. New York: Plenum.

95. Meichenbaum, D., & Goodman, J. (1971). Training impulsive children to talk to themselves: A means of developing self-control. *Journal of Abnormal Psychology, 77*, 115–126.

96. Prout, H. T., & Harvey, J. R. (1976). Applications of desensitization procedures for school related problems. A review. *Psychology in the Schools, 13*, 533–540.

97. Robin, A., Schneider, M., & Dolnick, M. (1976). The Turtle Technique: An extended case study of self-control in the classroom. *Psychology in the Schools, 13*, 449–453.

98. Warren, R., Deffenbacher, J., & Brading, P. (1976). Rational emotive therapy and the reduction of test anxiety in elementary school children. *Rational Living, 11*, 26–29.

99. Workman, E. (1982). *Teaching Behavior Self-Control to Students*. Austin, TX: Pro-Ed.

100. Workman, E. A., & Hector, M. A. (1982). Behavior self-control in classroom settings: A review of the literature. *Journal of School Psychology, 16*, 227–236.

DEVELOPMENTAL LEVEL

101. Bornstein, P. H., & Quevillon, R. P. (1976). The effects of a self-instructional package on overactive preschool boys. *Journal of Applied Behavior Analysis, 9*, 179–188.

102. Bugenthal, D. B., Whalen, C. K., & Hencker, B. (1977). Casual attributions of hyperactive children and motivational assumptions of two behavior-change assumptions: Evidence for an interactionist position. *Child Development, 48*, 874–884.

103. Hartig, M., & Kanfer, F. (1973). The role of verbal self-instructions on children's resistance to temptation. *Journal of Personality and Social Psychology, 25*, 259–267.

104. Meacham, J. A. (1978). A verbal guidance through remembering the goals of actions. *Child Development, 49*, 188–193.

105. Mischel, W., Ebbensen, E. B., & Zeiss, A. (1972). Cognitive and attentional mechanisms in delay of gratification. *Journal of Personality and Social Psychology, 21*, 204–218.

106. Mischel, W., & Patterson, C. J. (1976). Substantive and structural elements of effective plans for self-control. *Journal of Personality and Social Psychology, 34*, 942–950.

107. Mischel, W., & Patterson, C. J. (1978). Effect plans for self-control in children. In W. A. Collins (Ed.), *Minnesota Symposium on Child Psychology, Vol. II*. Hillsdale, NJ: Earlbaum.

108. O'Leary, S. G., & Dubey, D. R. (1979). Application of self-control procedures by children: A review. *Journal of Applied Behavior Analysis, 12* (3), 449–465.

109. Pressley, M. (1979). Increasing children's self-control through cognitive interventions. *Review of Educational Research, 49* (2), 319–370.

110. Yates, B. T., & Mischel, W. C. (1979). Young children's preferred attentional strategies for delaying gratification. *Journal of Personality and Social Psychology, 37,* 286–300.

# *PHYSIOLOGICAL FACTORS*

Some students don't comply with the rules and procedures that are appropriate for most students because they are physiologically unable to do so. This chapter discusses three of the major physiological factors that make it difficult for certain students to fulfill their teachers' expectations—developmental lag, temperamental differences, and attention deficit disorder. The chapter explains how these factors can affect students' behavior, describes how you can help identify students whose behavior problems are caused by these factors, and offers suggestions for dealing with such problems in your classroom.

## *Developmental Lag*

Infants, children, and teenagers all develop at their own unique biologically determined rates. Children not only learn to crawl, walk, talk, and control their bowel and bladder movements at different ages, they also develop the skills necessary for success in kindergarten and elementary school at different ages. Unfortunately—with few exceptions—students all begin kindergarten in September when they are approximately five and first grade the following fall when they are close to six despite their different levels of maturity. As a result, significant numbers of children with developmental delays start school almost predestined to experience difficulty, frustration, and failure in the lower grades. Thus, by the time they catch up to their peers developmentally, they may lag far behind academically and be in trouble behaviorally.

# *Identification*

Because the consequences of developmental lag can influence a student's entire education, it is both valuable and important to discover these students as early as possible.

*Informal Assessment*   You can identify developmentally delayed, immature students informally by whether or not their behavior is age-inappropriate. The examples in the paragraphs below describe the immature behavior of students with developmental lag.

*Preschoolers:* Behaviors that characterize preschool children with developmental lag include speaking very little compared with their peers or speaking in "baby talk"; playing alone or engaging in parallel play rather than playing with children and showing a preference to play outdoors or with toys and games rather than to engage in activities that require more concentration and self-control; difficulty in waiting their turn and controlling their impulses to hit others or take what others have; tending not to follow directions; trouble settling into an activity; once they settle in, they don't sit still or pay attention for as long as other children their age. In addition, they may also cry more often and more easily than their peers and be unwilling to attend school without bringing along their "security blanket" or favorite stuffed animal.

Steve is an example of an immature preschool student. Although he had turned four in May, he was kept back with the three-year-olds in September by the faculty of the preschool he attended due to immaturity. Specifically, he was unable to sit still during circle time and demonstrated no interest in table work that involved art projects, puzzles, or any structured activities. He would play instead in the playhouse or on the rug with blocks. He had "great difficulty with delay of gratification" when it came to waiting for other students to have their turns at things.

*Elementary school students:* Some of the behaviors that can characterize immature elementary school students include: they have short attention spans and can't sit still for very long; they are easily frustrated and prefer playing, drawing, talking, and so on to academic activities. They also lack the social skills necessary to get along with their peers such as sharing with others, waiting their turns, and keeping their hands to themselves, and they demand a great deal of teacher attention.

Melany is an example of a youngster whose development was delayed. She didn't sit up until she was 6 months old, didn't start to crawl until she was 13 months, didn't walk until her 19th month, and didn't talk until she was almost three. At six years of age, her physical development still lagged behind her peers except for her fine-motor coordination.

Her attention span was extremely short both at home and at school. At home she would shift from one toy or game to another or one activity to another. In school she was observed looking at eight different books within a five-minute period.

Her social behavior was more like a four-year-old's than a six-year-old's. She never expressed any interest in inviting children to her house. When her schoolmates invited her to play, she only accepted after being coaxed and cajoled by her parents. In school she was often in difficulty with other students because she took things they were playing with, pushed them out of the way to get where she wanted to go, and interrupted them during sharing time to talk about herself.

*Secondary school students:* Secondary school students can also be developmentally immature, although their immaturity is sometimes less obvious to their teachers and

*Parallel play is characteristic of young and immature students.*

parents. Teenagers with developmental lags may prefer to spend time with younger children and have few friends among their classmates. They are often less motivated to do well in school out of a mature concern that what they learn and the grades they receive can affect their future. They tend to avoid activities that involve the opposite sex, and aren't as independent as many teenagers. Thus, while many adolescents are already acting as if they know it all and can go it alone, suggesting that parental guidance is an unnecessary interference, immature adolescents are unable to venture forth without a great deal of parental support.

Sonia is an example of an immature teenager. At almost 16, she still decorated her bedroom like a child's room and wore clothing styled for preteens. She lived very much in the present, never thinking of her future either at home or in school. She never demonstrated any interest in boys, whom she shunned like a contagious disease. She had been adamant about not having any kind of sweet 16 celebration until her parents suggested that she could invite a few close girlfriends for a weekend outing. In school she usually kept to herself, almost never attending school functions such as dances, athletic events, and after-school trips.

If your student's actions fit one of these descriptions, her or his behavior problem may be caused by a development lag. But you should ask yourself three additional questions before arriving at this conclusion.

1. *Does your student behave immaturely in all situations?* The truly immature child or teenager will seem immature in any situation that calls for mature behavior. Other teachers and the student's parents can either confirm the fact that your student behaves immaturely or let you know that he behaves one way with you and another with them.

2. *Has your student always behaved immaturely, or did she behave more maturely for a while and then regress to an earlier, more immature form of behavior?* A child or teenager who is developmentally immature doesn't waver, first behaving maturely, then reverting back to immature behavior. A student who regresses certainly requires his teacher's attention, but the cause is unlikely to be developmental delay.

3. *Is your student's immaturity caused by environmental rather than physiological factors?* Immaturelike behavior can also be caused by environmental factors. For example, students who have unpleasant or traumatic experiences with other children may lose interest in playing with them. Or students who have never been urged to keep trying when things get difficult or to accept the disappointments and frustrations of life without excessive complaining may have low or no tolerance for frustration. Also, traumatic experiences with the opposite sex can cause teenagers to avoid any male-female relationships, and insecurity can cause an adolescent to prefer the company of younger students who aren't threatening because they aren't seen as competitors with more academic or social skills, more strength, knowledge, beauty, and the like.

*Formal Assessment*   A number of valid developmental tests are available to help you identify preschool and primary grade students who are developmentally delayed. No instruments are currently available, however, for testing upper elementary and secondary school students.

Developmental Tests for Younger Students

Batelle Developmental Inventory, birth—eight years. DLM Teaching Resources, Allen, Texas.

Denver Developmental Screening Test, two weeks—six years. LADOCO Publishing Foundation, Denver, Colorado.

Developmental Profile II, birth—nine years. Psychological Development Publications, Aspen, Colorado.

Minnesota Child Development Inventory, birth—six years. Behavior Science Systems, Inc., Minneapolis, Minnesota.

VISCO Child Development Screening Test, three years—seven years. Educational Activities, Inc., Freeport, New York.

## *Helping Developmentally Delayed Students*

Research indicates that educators can help developmentally delayed students succeed in school despite their immaturity by adapting instructional and classroom management techniques to their students' developmental levels (1, 2). The discussion that follows describes some techniques you can use to accomplish this with students at different school levels.

*Preschool and Elementary School Students*    The speech problems and poor motor coordination that interfere with young developmentally delayed students' abilities to communicate with others and run, climb, ride tricycles, cut, paste, draw, print, and so on aren't behavior problems in themselves. But given the low frustration tolerance of children in general and especially those with developmental lags, these obstacles can certainly lead young students to behave inappropriately. By providing such students with the assistance they need to achieve what the other students do, educators can help keep them from becoming frustrated and venting their feelings in school.

You can provide poorly coordinated youngsters with equipment that is especially suitable for their motor problems and the help they need to succeed in such activities as climbing, cutting, pasting, and printing. This may improve their behavior. If they can't succeed even with your help, directing them to alternative activities is another option. Teaching other students not to make negative comments about the way developmentally delayed students do things can help protect such students from having their self-concept damaged by their peers.

Educators can also help developmentally delayed students avoid behavior problems by accommodating the length of seatwork assignments to their shorter attention spans, assigning them to a quiet nonstimulating area where they can be free of distractions, and providing them with alternative activities when they can't sit still. Placing these students on the periphery of the group during circle time or when telling or reading stories may make it easier for their attention to wander, but this also allows them to leave the group mentally or physically when they can no longer concentrate without distracting others.

You can manage students who haven't developed the social skills necessary to get along with others by keeping them under close supervision. Remind such students in advance not to hit, take things, or push ahead of others. It's unlikely, though, that these kinds of techniques will completely eliminate their behavior problems. Thus, be prepared to accept some immature, infantile, and even antisocial behavior so long as it doesn't seriously interfere with the rights of others. Certainly praise students when they conform to rules and procedures and make them aware when they don't, but don't use consequences to try to speed up the maturational process or scold students for behaving immaturely.

*Secondary School Students*    Secondary school students who are too immature to care about their future and lack the maturity to function independently in school shouldn't be allowed to fall by the wayside. Teachers should do whatever is possible to ensure that such students make enough progress in school so they will be able to move ahead when they mature. To do this, provide students with the extra support, structure, and guidance they need to participate and succeed despite their immaturity. But it's important to do this without pressuring them to "act their age." Immature teenagers cannot be more responsible in school than they really are. Requiring them to function independently may cause them to fall flat on their faces. Nor can they be motivated to want to participate in social activities that are only attractive to their more mature peers. Manipulating them into positions where they must participate in such activities can result in unnecessary embarrassment and shame for them.

---

| *Self-Quiz:* *Developmental Delays* | What kinds of developmental delays are you most and least able to accept? Review the problems that tend to characterize students with developmental delays, and state whether you react positively or negatively to each one. |

---

## *Temperamental Differences*

Ask a group of mothers and fathers what kinds of differences they observed among their sons and daughters when they were infants. One mother might tell you her firstborn was so full of energy she hardly slept, couldn't be kept in her crib and playpen, was totally unpredictable, and got into everything in the house, but then the second child slept through the night when he was two months old, was almost never cranky, and spent hours playing by himself in his crib. A father might focus on the fact that one child was finicky about foods, frightened of strangers, and just downright difficult to please, while the other was just the opposite. Ask the parents if these differences continued as their children grew, and they will tell you how little they were able to change them over the years.

Such informal observations of basic ways of being have been supported by formal research. Studies have demonstrated that infants have consistent, individual patterns of sleeping, eating, body movements, and physiological functioning. They differ in terms of whether they typically approach or withdraw from new things in their environment such as foods and strangers, in how active they are, and in how often they smile or cry. Studies that have followed groups of infants through childhood and adolescence have also found that some, but not all, individuals maintain these earliest behavior patterns. Studies of identical twins reared apart from birth also show evidence of inborn behavioral styles. These persistent, apparently inborn differences among infants have been called "temperamental traits" by theorists who believe that they help account for many of the personality differences among people.

## *Temperamental Traits*

Although authors have tended to agree on definitions of temperament, they vary considerably in the lists of temperamental traits and temperamental types they provide (3–7). Presently, research evidence does not clearly support any particular list of temperamental traits.

One of the most ambitious attempts to document temperamental differences among infants and to examine their effects on the development of personality is the New York Longitudinal Study initiated by Thomas, Chess, and Birch (18). These researchers followed a group of infants through to their young adulthood. They used nine "temperamental traits" to characterize the difference among the individuals they followed.

As they studied the life spans of these individuals, they discovered that youngsters with temperamental characteristics that didn't match the behavior styles commonly expected of students in school were more likely than others to have problems adjusting to school rules and procedures. The following are descriptions of the nine temperamental characteristics they included in their studies and the kinds of classroom behavior problems some are associated with (8–21).

*Activity*—the amount and tempo of motor activity. Highly active infants were described by their parents as so active that they couldn't be left alone on the bed. They crawled or ran around so much that they exhausted their parents. Nonactive babies lay quietly in bed, in the bath, and when they were being dressed, and they remained in the same position all night.

In school, highly active students wriggle around in their seats, start conversations with students sitting alongside them, and move around the classroom. They listen to only the first part of directions before starting an assignment. They don't hear what their teachers say when they are actively involved in doing something they shouldn't be doing because they are too energetic to sit still and listen.

Students with low activity levels usually work at a slow pace. They may not finish classroom assignments, timed tests, or lengthy homework assignments during the time allotted. When other students are ready for the next class or activity, they may still be putting their materials away. Sometimes they are misperceived as sluggish, apathetic, or even retarded because of their inability to accomplish the expected amount of work in the standard time.

*Rhythmicity*—the regularity of functions such as sleeping, eating, and bowel and bladder movement. Regular children fell asleep and woke up at approximately the same time each day or moved their bowels on a regularly predictable schedule. Irregular infants were unpredictable. Rhythmicity has not been found to cause behavior problems in school.

*Approach or withdrawal*—the initial response to newness. Children who approached new aspects in the environment were described as smiling at strangers or loving new toys. Those who withdrew were slow to accept new toys, people, places, or foods.

Withdrawers tend to react negatively to new teachers, new subjects, and new activities. If they are also slow to adapt, it may take them an inordinately long time to get involved in new tasks and activities, which could negatively impact their performance in school.

*Adaptability*—the extent to which an infant changes her initial responses in the ways desired by parents and other adults. Highly adaptable babies changed their initial avoidance responses to bathing, new foods, toys, and the like after a short time. Low-adaptable babies continued to reject new things even after they were no longer strange or new.

Low adaptability has been found to be related to behavior problems only when students also have certain other temperamental traits (see difficult children and those slow to warm up).

*Intensity of reaction*—the energy of response. Highly intense children screamed and spit out food they didn't like. Low-intensity children whimpered and let the food drool out.

Students who react intensely seem as if they love some teachers or some subjects and hate others. These students' intense ways of reacting don't actually reflect their true feelings nor do they predict how they will actually deal with a teacher, subject, or task because it is just their style of responding. Nevertheless, educators and sometimes the students themselves are fooled into believing these reactions express how they really feel about things.

Students who characteristically react with low intensity don't show others how they really feel because their words, facial expressions, and gestures are misleading. This means that educators may not realize when these students are upset, frustrated, or frightened. They also may not recognize the subtle clues that indicate these seemingly disinterested students are actually quite motivated to learn.

*Threshold of responsiveness*—the amount of stimulation required to cause a reaction. Babies with a high threshold of responsiveness were difficult to startle and inattentive to new foods mixed in with their meals. Babies with low thresholds seemed to notice anything new, any change, or any noise.

Students with high thresholds of responsiveness are slow to pick up both the subtle and not-so-subtle clues in their environments. Relatively insensitive to body language and other social clues, they often misread the feelings of peers and teachers. They may also have difficulty distinguishing the important from the unimportant and the central from the trivial in their teachers' lectures. In a general sense, they may not know what their teachers want or are driving at unless it's spelled out for them.

*Mood*—positive, pleasant, joyful, friendly, in contrast to negative, unpleasant, crying, unfriendly. Infants who had positive moods cooed, laughed, and smiled much more than average. Children with negative moods whined, cried, and fussed a lot.

Students with negative moods can allow their moods to affect how they function in school. If their moodiness puts their teachers off, they may be called on less often, praised less often, and given less attention by teachers who are unlikely to extend themselves for "ill-humored," "unfriendly" students.

*Distractibility*—the ease with which irrelevant events change ongoing actions. Distractible children stopped crying when they were picked up even though they were

*A long attention span is an asset and may indicate a student's maturity.*

still hungry or stopped playing with one toy when they spied another one. Non-distractible children continued to cry in their mothers' arms or continued to play with the same toy despite possible distractions.

Highly distractible students have difficulty attending to lectures and completing seatwork. The end result is often poor grades and arguments with teachers about paying attention and staying on task.

*Attention span and persistence*—attention span is the length of time a child continues in self-initiated activities. Persistence is the extent to which a child continues an activity despite obstacles. Children with long attention spans maintained interest in their activities much longer than children with short attention spans who quickly switched from one activity to another.

Persistent toddlers continued to try to walk though they repeatedly fell, and continued to do something even though their parents said "no." Nonpersistent children gave up easily and stopped when their parents told them to.

Students with short attention spans have problems staying on task. Persistent students are usually well received by their teachers when they persist in trying to solve problems and complete assignments despite difficulties and frustrations. But when they persist in doing what the teacher tells them to stop doing or when they nag their teachers after they have been told "no" repeatedly, the same temperamental characteristic can cause problems.

## THEORY FOCUS: CHESS AND THOMAS ON TEMPERAMENTAL CHARACTERISTICS

Stella Chess and Alexander Thomas have collaborated on a wide variety of research projects including the New York Longitudinal Study that investigates the role of temperament during the life span. This ongoing study of individuals from their early years through young adulthood has contributed immensely to our understanding of what types of behavior can be influenced by temperament. The study has also helped us learn more about the stability of temperamental characteristics over time and the relationship between extreme temperamental characteristics and the development of behavior problems. Through such books as *Temperament in Clinical Practice, Temperament and Development, Temperamental and Behavior Disorders*, and *Your Child Is A Person* as well as a large number of articles, these researchers have helped both professionals and parents realize the role physiological factors can play in determining people's personalities.

Chess describes the role of temperament and the purpose of her research as follows:

The many individual styles children bring to their everyday responses to the people and ac-

tions of their environment are to be seen in the classroom, too. Temperamental features will characterize their varied approaches both to social demands and expectations and also to the educational tasks of the educational institutions. This is a complicated set of ongoing interactions with mutual influences: the youngster's temperamental style, together with intellectual abilities and other features of personality, will influence the educators and the decisions they make—in ever continuing cycles. And, along with this, one must be aware that both expectations and abilities will depend also on the child, adolescent, or adult's developmental status. Only by following the same individuals through life can we distinguish their changing adaptations, see "winners" who coped well from infancy on as well as those with poor beginnings who discovered strengths and became "winners" as adults! Unfortunately the opposite also occurred.

Temperament, we found, plays a powerful part in filtering meaning and hopes, and even lighting educational fires well after none were expected any longer. (Stella Chess, personal communication, April 12, 1989)

The results of the New York Longitudinal Study also indicated that youngsters who had certain combinations of temperamental characteristics were especially likely to have problems adapting to school. Thomas, Chess, and Birch (18) labeled two of these groups of youngsters "difficult children" and "slow-to-warm-up children."

*Difficult children:* Students who are characteristically irregular in their biological functioning, put off by new aspects of their environment, slow to adapt to changing expectations, negative in mood, and intense in their reactions were the most likely to develop problems during childhood and adolescence. Seventy percent of the infants in this group had adjustment problems by age ten.

Since they had irregular functioning, they didn't develop patterns of eating, sleeping, and so on that their parents could plan their day around. Instead of adjusting to the schedules their parents attempted to set for them, they required their parents to adjust to their irregularity. Likely to withdraw from new situations and slow to adapt, they required many gently familiarizing exposures to new experiences before they could adjust to each new situation. Without this gentle lead-in, they tended to react with screams, temper tantrums, and threats. Since they often overreacted to even minor frustrations, parents were unable to judge how they really felt about things.

In school they reacted negatively to the beginning of the new school year, a new teacher, or a new social or academic demand. Teachers tended to misperceive their temperamentally determined, intensely negative responses as willful defiance or else emotional overreaction.

*Slow-to-warm-up children:* Children who were characterized by low activity levels, initial withdrawal responses, slow adaptability, low-intensity reactions, and negative moods initially responded to newness and strangers with mild fussing or turning away. When they started nursery school, they often wanted to have one of their parents remain for a while. Even with their parents present, they tended to remain on the sidelines watching the other children until they felt comfortable enough to join in.

In grade school they often met new situations and new tasks with an "I don't like it" announcement or, more typically, a silent refusal to participate. Because these students are quietly passive in their negativism, their reluctance often goes unnoticed. When it is noticed and teachers push them to participate by cajoling or coaxing them or by engaging in a battle of wills with them, the students tend either to retreat further into themselves or become less quiet and more intensely negative. On the other hand, when adults are able to wait while these youngsters adapt at their own slower pace, they often overcome their initial negativism to participate.

## Identification

Temperamentally different children need to be identified so that you can work with them in the classroom appropriately. Without such identification, you may respond to them with techniques that will not help the students or you.

*Informal Assessment*   Once you realize that your students' behavior is caused by temperamental factors, you can help them succeed in situations even when their temperament is a disadvantage, and you can help eliminate adjustment problems they may already have. But first you need to find out if a temperamental factor is involved. To informally determine whether a student's problems are caused by temperamental differences, you should ask yourself four questions:

1. *Does the problem fit descriptions that research suggests can be the result of temperamental differences?* Below is a list of fifteen traits substantiated by research as being possible aspects of temperament (3–7, 18). If your student's behavior doesn't appear on the list, it's unlikely that it is caused by temperamental factors. But if her behavior does appear on the list, it may be a reflection of her temperament. For example, it's unlikely that students who are jealous of their peers or poor sharers behave that way for temperamental reasons since no evidence shows that such behaviors have a temperamental base.

    *Daringness*—fearful versus courageous responses to challenging or risky situations.

    *Sociability*—an individual's desire to be with or avoid contact with others.

    *Reflectiveness*—the tendency to respond impulsively (spontaneously) or thoughtfully.

*Flexibility*—stubbornness or pliability in relationships with others.

*Diurnal-nocturnal*—whether an individual functions better early or late in the day.

*Activity level*—the amount and tempo of motor activity.

*Rhythmicity*—the regularity of functions.

*Approach-withdrawal*—an individual's initial response to newness.

*Adaptability*—ability to modify an initial response in light of additional information.

*Intensity of reaction*—the energy of an individual's response.

*Threshold of responsiveness*—the amount of stimulation required to evoke a reaction.

*Mood*—usual or customary emotional state.

*Distractibility*—the ease with which irrelevant events change ongoing activities.

*Persistence*—the tendency to continue an activity despite obstacles or difficulties.

*Attention span*—the length of time an individual engages in self-directed activities.

2. *Is the behavior present in all aspects of the student's life?* Consult with your student's other teachers to determine whether she consistently behaves the way she does in your class. Ask your student's parents how she behaves at home, or request the school social worker to obtain that information from them for you. Parents can be asked to informally describe their youngster's behavior or to complete a formal questionnaire designed to elicit the information from them (23).

3. *Has the student behaved that way since he was young?* Although research indicates that parents' recollections of their youngsters' behavior as infants and toddlers is sometimes distorted, in most instances your students' parents should be able to provide you with the information you require to determine whether his behavior has been consistent over time. The Dimensions of Temperament Survey (23) may also prove helpful. Again, consider working with the school social worker to obtain this information. Keep in mind that some parents have difficulty remembering how their youngsters behaved when they were infants and toddlers, while others may not remember their youngsters' behavior accurately. Most parents, however, recall their youngsters' behavior fairly accurately (27–31).

4. *Using appropriate techniques, have adults and teachers been unable to change the student's behavior?* To determine this, you would want to know what techniques were tried, when, where, under what conditions, and with what degree of success. Your student's parents and other teachers can give you the information you need to answer this question.

The following case examples illustrate an informal procedure to determine whether a student's behavior problems have a temperamental basis. You can use similar procedures with your own students.

*Larry* was a seven-year-old whose first- and second-grade teachers used words such as *shy, withdrawn, timid, insecure,* and *frightened* to describe him. They reported that he avoided new tasks and had trouble making friends. Three months into the school year, his second-grade teacher was trying unsuccessfully to get him to overcome his "insecurity." His first-grade teacher said, however, that if left alone Larry got over his initial fears and learned that he was able to succeed. Then he did as well, if not better, both academically and socially than many of his peers.

Larry's parents also saw him as "shy" and "timid." They reported that he had difficulty making friends and often stayed in his room with the door closed when guests were in the house unless he knew them very well. He balked at accompanying the family on visits to other people's houses and exasperated his parents on vacation trips abroad during which he seemed especially ill at ease. He often refused to try new foods when they went out to restaurants or to other people's homes. When he visited amusement parks, he would adamantly refuse to go on most rides designed for children his age. On the other hand, he had excellent relationships with his younger brother and two school friends and behaved perfectly normally with people he knew well and in situations where he was comfortable.

Larry's parents recalled that he had always been uncomfortable with strangers. Even as an infant, he would cry when handed over to or picked up by anyone except his parents. Each change of housekeeper or babysitter and the two times they had relocated had been traumatic for him. He had great difficulty adjusting to nursery school and preschool, and his mother had to remain with him in both programs for quite some time before he felt comfortable being left by himself. Until then, her attempts to coax him or pressure him to allow her to just drop him off were unsuccessful. Yet he eventually adjusted to the new program, housekeeper, or babysitter and could be left without any problem. Larry's parents also recalled that he was a finicky eater who tended to reject any new food out of hand. He also didn't seem to be interested in new toys, pets, or anything else at first sight, either. An evaluation of the technique his parents had been using to try to get him to accept new neighborhoods, children, housekeepers, babysitters, schools, food, and so on indicated that they were totally appropriate and would probably have worked quite well with an average child.

Larry's behavior fits the description of a youngster whose temperamental makeup included initial negative reactions to new things and a slowness to adapt. Background information about him revealed that the way he behaved at school was similar to the way he behaved at home and consistent with how he had been behaving his whole life. This information also indicated that neither Larry's parents nor his teachers had been able to change his behavior. These facts make it clear that the behavior problems his teachers and parents noted were indeed the result of his temperament.

*Mary* was a nine-year-old who was having difficulty in fourth grade. Her teacher stated that she refused to do as she was told. Instead, she would continue working on activities she liked long after the other students had moved on, and she wouldn't do things she didn't want to do until she was pressured or threatened. She interrupted when others were speaking and called out answers without raising her hand. Her teacher's major complaint was that she would do almost anything in her power to get her way. Interviews with her other teachers indicated that she had been particularly willful and stubborn with her second-grade teacher who was rather inexperienced, easygoing, and not a strict disciplinarian. But she had not been a problem with her first- and third-grade teachers who "knew how to control" their students.

Her parents reported that at home she interrupted them no matter what they were doing whenever she wished and pestered them until she either got her way or was punished. If she wanted to watch television when they thought she should be doing something else, or if she wanted a new dress or toy that they thought she didn't need, she would whine, throw temper tantrums, slam doors, and generally make their lives miserable until they either hit her or gave in to her in order to have some peace in the house. Her parents described themselves as alternating between feeling extreme rage at their inability to control her and feeling extremely badly about how punitive they had become toward her. At times they blamed her for not being able to "take 'no' for an answer." At other times they blamed themselves for not making sure that she did so.

Mary's parents remembered having had the same difficulty with her since she was able to get into things. She always tried to have things her own way. They didn't think, though, that she was particularly motivated to overcome obstacles nor did she have an unusual amount of persistence about difficult tasks. Like other children, when things got difficult she became bored or frustrated and gave up.

During an extended conversation, Mary's parents admitted that when she was little, they had both been so busy with their careers that they often gave in to her or did things for her that she should have done for herself because it was easier and less trouble. Her mother agreed that she still handled Mary the same way at times because, although she was no longer working, she was suffering from "battle fatigue" and preferred to avoid confrontations if possible.

The information available from both Mary's parents and teachers indicates that her behavior was not consistent in all situations. In addition, the techniques her parents used to change her behavior were inappropriate. Thus, it's likely that the cause of Mary's persistent behavior wasn't temperamental. Judging from how Mary's parents tried to discipline her, her behavior would probably improve if her parents and her teachers used techniques such as the ones suggested in Chapter 9 to teach her to take "no" for an answer.

*Formal Assessment*    A number of instruments have been specifically designed to help educators assess their students' temperaments (22–26). Research indicates that educators can use these assessments to arrive at valid conclusions about their students' temperaments (22–27).

| INSTRUMENT | RATER | AGE RANGE |
|---|---|---|
| Behavior Style Questionnaire | parents | 3–7 years |
| Dimensions of Temperamental Survey | parents | 3–adult |
| Preschool Temperament Inventory | teachers | 3–6 years |
| Teacher Temperament Questionnaire | teachers | 3–7 years |

## Helping Temperamentally Different Students

When teachers adjust their expectations to the unmodifiable aspects of youngsters' personalities, the youngsters do well. But many teachers don't recognize when youngsters' behavior problems are in fact caused by their temperaments. It's often much easier for

teachers to accept the fact that youngsters have been born with certain physiological apti-
tudes (or "gifts") that will help determine whether or not they do well in sports, music, art,
or academics than it is for them to accept that youngsters' responses to new situations, their
persistence, activity levels, and the pace at which they do things can also be influenced by
physiological factors.

*Two Problems*    The belief that youngsters can change their behavior if they try when
they really can't, and the perception that they are willful, disobedient, rebellious, lazy,
spoiled, selfish, and so on when they aren't can easily lead teachers to engage in fruitless
battles with their students. This can, in turn, create additional problems for youngsters who
are already experiencing difficulty in adjusting to the demands of family, school, and society. This was clearly seen in the studies Chess, Thomas, Birch, and their associates did (8,
11, 18) and has been confirmed by others (36–47). As they followed the development of the
youngsters in their study, Thomas, Chess, and Birch found that those who had extremes of
certain temperamental traits were more likely than others to have adjustment problems at
home and school. The authors concluded that these extreme temperamental characteristics tended to interfere with the youngsters' normal development because they were temperamentally unable to behave the way adults expected them to.

When adults tried to require these youngsters to behave according to their expectations, the youngsters were likely to respond by becoming negative, aggressive, or withdrawn. But when adults adapted their methods and expectations to the youngsters'
temperaments, then they didn't develop these additional problems. Instead they adjusted
well but still behaved somewhat differently than most youngsters because of their temperamental makeup (15, 18, 32–35).

This research shows that extreme temperamental differences can add two types of
behavior problems. First, students may have difficulty "adjusting" to school unless their
teachers individualize both instructional and classroom management techniques, to some
degree, to the unique temperaments of these students. Second, students may develop additional problems if their teachers misperceive the cause of their behavior and so use inappropriate techniques to try to change it. Educators who mistakenly believe such students
are willful, disobedient, stubborn, lazy, or rebellious may resort to punitive approaches to
force them to change what in reality are relatively fixed aspects of their personalities. Such
futile attempts to get students to change can lead to unnecessary conflicts and can also
cause students to believe they actually are bad, selfish, stubborn, uncooperative, lazy, and
the like.

But avoiding unnecessary conflicts with temperamentally different students doesn't
mean that teachers should merely accept their students' temperamentally determined behavior styles. If left totally to their own devices, students whose temperaments are characterized by withdrawal tendencies, slow adaptability, negative moods, or extreme
distractibility, and the like may experience problems at school. Thus, it is especially important that their teachers help them succeed in school despite their temperamental differences. Such help may prevent them from developing additional problems due to
mismatches between the demands of school and their temperaments.

*Self-Managing Techniques*    Presently virtually no research has studied the ability of
temperamentally different students to use self-managing techniques to modify their behavior. Thus, the discussion that follows on helping students manage their behavior is based
on several reasonable, but unproven, assumptions. The most basic assumption is that

students who are aware of their temperamental makeups are better able to manage their behavior. A corollary is that educators can increase students' self-awareness about their temperamental traits. To do this most effectively, educators should use techniques for enhancing students' self-awareness that are suitable for the students' developmental levels. For example, preschool and primary grade students cannot yet understand that individuals have different behavioral styles. Students in the upper elementary grades can begin to understand that people are all different, and secondary school students can comprehend the concept of temperamental traits in more or less the form it's presented in this chapter. Given this as background, temperamentally different students can use the techniques for self-reinforcement described in Chapter 7 and the techniques for self-instruction described in Chapter 10 to gain some degree of self-control over their temperamentally determined behavior styles. In addition, secondary school students can select school activities, courses, hobbies, and ultimately occupations that suit their temperaments.

Based on these concepts, to assist temperamentally different students to manage their behavior, you should help them become aware of their temperamental makeups and teach them self-managing skills. The following techniques for accomplishing these goals have proved successful with some students who have other kinds of problems. They may also be effective with temperamentally different students.

*Self-awareness*: Help students become aware of their temperamental characteristics. Adapt your techniques for enhancing students' awareness of their temperamental traits to the cognitive levels of elementary grade students by talking to them on a concrete rather than abstract level. High-activity-level students might be told, "Wow, you have a lot of energy." "You don't like to sit still for a long time like the other students, do you?" Or, "Where do you get all your energy from? Are you always like that?" If students are slow to warm up, you might say, "At first you didn't want to try the new game, but after a while you changed your mind, and you liked it, didn't you?" Or, "You did the same thing the first few times the music specialist came to the class. Now you're practically the first one to choose an instrument from the box. I guess it takes you a little longer than other students to get to like something new." Students with negative moods can be told, "Seems like you woke up in a bad mood today. I guess some days are better than others for you."

Have students read stories with characters who have temperaments similar to theirs; then ask, "Did Mitzy remind you of anyone?" Or, "Do you think Danny is like you?" Teach students to monitor their behavior, and discuss what they have learned about themselves with them. High-activity students can record how many times they get out of their seats. Low-activity students can record how many times they fail to complete seatwork during the time allotted. Moody students can assign themselves frowning and happy faces each day. Persistent students can monitor the number of times they were told to stop doing something or change activities more than once before they complied.

You can talk to secondary school students more directly about individual differences among people and engage them in discussions of their behavior styles in class. Such discussions, however, will probably be more acceptable and successful if you give the strengths and advantages of their temperamental characteristics at least as much if not more emphasis than the behavior problems their temperaments create. It is also important to explain to students as soon as possible how they can manage their temperaments and turn their own behavior styles to their advantage.

*Self-managing specific temperamental traits*: You can use the self-managing techniques described in Chapters 7 and 10 with students who have the kinds of temperaments that research indicates are likely to cause difficulties for students in school.

*High activity level:* Teach students to identify when they are becoming restless or tense. Show them how to relax, take a quiet break at their seats, stretch, or ask permission to leave the room if necessary.

*Low activity level:* Guide students to understand the advantage of using part of their recess or lunch times to catch up and to set aside more time than others need to complete their homework assignments.

*Initial withdrawal and/or slow adapting:* Teach students to remind themselves that they react negatively at first to new experiences, to question the validity of their initial responses, and to instruct themselves to join in new experiences despite initial negative reactions to them.

*High intensity of reaction:* Help students learn to instruct themselves to:

Identify when they are about to respond intensely

Delay their responses

Question whether their intense feelings actually reflect their true reactions

Express their feelings in less intense words such as "I feel angry," "This doesn't hold my interest," and "I don't want to be with you right now" instead of "I hate you," "This is the most boring class I have ever had," and "I can't stand you."

*Low intensity of reaction:* Help students practice expressing their opinions and feelings more directly and clearly. Teach students to monitor the reactions of others when they express their feelings and opinions in order to determine whether they have gotten their messages across. Have students practice asking themselves, "Does the person act like he or she really understands how I feel or think, or do I have to make myself clearer?"

*Negative mood:* Teach students to question their negative feelings and opinions about people, events, tasks, and so on when they are in a negative mood. Prepare them to use guided imagery to think about happy, optimistic, or pleasant experiences when they feel moody or pessimistic. Teach them to instruct themselves to avoid making negative comments and to tell others that they are in a bad mood.

*High persistence:* Help students instruct themselves to think that others aren't necessarily bossy or unfair when they issue desist orders or deny students' requests. Explain that requiring others to give them the same directives repeatedly is disruptive and that others may have good reasons for saying no.

*Teacher-Initiated Techniques*    Since we have no reason to believe that students can completely modify their behavior styles by using self-managing techniques, teachers can help temperamentally different students by using teacher-initiated techniques to manage some of their behavior problems. They can also help by accommodating their expectations and routines to aspects of their students' behavior styles that can't be managed. Finally, they can prevent students' extreme temperamental differences from causing serious problems in school. In the absence of research on the effectiveness of specific classroom management techniques with such students, the techniques described below are reasonable suggestions rather than proven solutions.

*Students with highly active temperaments need to let off a little steam occasionally.*

*High activity level:*

1. If possible, schedule sedentary activities such as reading and math after activities like physical education, lunch, and recess so students can discharge some of their energy before having to sit for long periods of time. If you use this technique, be sure to provide a relaxing, cooling-off transition period between the two activities to prepare students to be less active.

2. Provide students with plenty of desk room so they can stretch out and fidget without bothering other students.

3. Permit students to discharge some of their energy by taking breaks from sedentary activities. Allow them to stand, stretch, sharpen pencils, run errands—whatever

doesn't cause a problem or disrupt other students. Encourage responsible students to take breaks as needed. With less responsible students, though, you might have to schedule breaks at regular intervals. While most students should be able to take breaks without having to be supervised, some may abuse the privilege. If they do, you may have to convince them to control any inclinations to take advantage of their temperament by reasoning with them or by taking away the privilege (logical consequence).

4. Locating students in the back of the room may make it less likely that their high activity level will distract other students, but seating them close to you may decrease their overactive behavior.

5. If possible, use teaching techniques that require students to learn by doing, manipulating, moving around, or using other hands-on approaches.

6. Don't require students to sit still for long stretches of time during class trips. If students must eat together on trips or in school, allow your active students to leave the table as soon as they become restless.

7. Don't assume students hear and understand you when you say something while they are busily engaged in high-energy activities. Ask them to respond to a question or to follow directions to determine whether they understand. Better yet, have them stop what they are doing and attend before you say anything important.

8. Guide students into high-energy extracurricular activities, hobbies, sports, and so on.

9. If the students' parents or other teachers are not aware of their temperament, advise them that the students are not willful or disobedient but rather highly energetic.

*Low activity level:*

1. Give students extra time to complete things that other students can finish in less time when you aren't on a strict schedule. If you do have a schedule to keep, have these students start earlier than the others. If students are required to keep up with a group, remind them to try to stay with the group but do so without nagging or complaining.

2. Don't schedule activities that have to be finished in school for the final period of the day when there is no chance of extra time for the activity.

3. Except under extenuating circumstances, don't pitch in and help students complete things because they take too long—even when you or the class are late or in a rush. If you are too helpful too often, students may learn to expect you to do things for them.

4. Don't take it personally when students make you or the class wait—even when you give them a head start and remind them about the time. It's perfectly natural to feel angry and frustrated at such times, but don't treat the students as if they are unfair, inconsiderate, or selfish.

5. Use untimed power tests, not timed tests. If students do poorly on standardized tests, find out whether they didn't know the work or didn't have enough time to demonstrate what they knew.

6. Advise other adults who may not be aware of the students' temperaments that they are slow moving, not slow learners, slow thinkers, or perfectionists.

*Initial withdrawal:*

1. Keep in mind that these students' initial reaction is to withdraw, but they will eventually get involved if they are allowed to do so at their own pace, especially if the activity is intrinsically interesting or rewarding.

2. Allow students to withdraw from you and/or their peers if that is what they need to do. Keep your distance until they signal their readiness to be engaged, but be sure they understand that you are available if and when they need you.

3. If these students are just starting school and having difficulty adjusting to new situations, don't view their behavior as an indication that they are too dependent on their parents, suffering from separation anxiety, or afraid of school. If necessary, tell the appropriate school officials that their difficulty is only a temperamentally determined inability to jump right into a new situation and that these students need patience, understanding, and encouragement, not therapy.

4. Give students advance notice about impending changes. If possible, familiarize them with new activities before they are introduced by showing them pictures, telling them anecdotes, and so forth. Put new or novel situations in their best light by highlighting the positive, attractive, and advantageous. But don't hide any negatives because unpleasant surprises can be devastating.

5. If possible, introduce students to new things in a pleasant, familiar setting or in the company of a trusted friend.

6. If possible, allow students—especially young ones—to watch an activity a few times before getting involved in it. Although the students may seem only to be watching disinterestedly, more than likely they are actually learning and preparing to join in.

7. Praise students when they react positively to new situations even if it takes a while for them to do so, but don't scold or pressure them when they don't.

8. If students are also slow to adapt and take even longer to get over their initial negative reactions, keep at it. Muster up even more patience and understanding.

9. Guide students toward activities, hobbies, subjects, and careers that don't involve constant change and novelty.

10. Give students insight into their temperaments. Remind them of the many times they didn't like something at first but then changed their opinions.

*Slow-adapting students:* Most of the techniques for helping students with initial-with-drawal temperaments just described also apply to these students.

*High-intensity reactions:*

1. Warn students in advance that something will occur that may displease them, and remind them that they tend to overreact to such situations. You might say something like, "I know you don't like achievement tests because you think they are difficult for you. However, everyone will have to take the test on Thursday. And you will see it will be just as easy for you as the one you took last time."

2. Give students practice in thinking before acting, counting to ten before saying anything, saying how they feel rather than acting out their feelings, and toning down the emotional content of the words they choose.

3. If you believe techniques such as these won't work, you can wait until the other students have left the room or else ask intense reactors to step out into the hall before you give them upsetting news so their reactions don't disrupt the class. If you can't do these things, try to postpone the communication until you can.

4. When, despite your best efforts, students overreact, don't let the intensity of their responses fool you into thinking they really are disgusted, petrified, furious, or in some other extreme state. Remind yourself that their intense reactions are only temporary and don't reflect their true feelings. This realization should help you avoid taking comments such as, "I hate your class" or "You're the most boring teacher I have ever had" personally.

5. After the students have calmed down, find a convenient time and place to discuss their overreaction so they, too, do not take their overreaction seriously. (See section on self-management.)

*Low-intensity reactions:*

1. Tune in to the subtle ways students with low-intensity reactions express their feelings and attitudes. Especially watch for signals that they need your support and encouragement, they are having difficulty with a task, or they are especially interested in some topic or subject.

2. Explain to them how their low-intensity reactions affect others. For example, teach them that weak hellos and unenthusiastic responses to peers lead others to think they are unfriendly. You can also point out that their low-intensity reactions to things that bother them may encourage students to take advantage of them because they don't really seem to be angry or annoyed at the way they are being treated. (See section on self-management.)

3. Encourage students to consciously attempt to express their feelings and attitudes more directly.

4. Provide them with opportunities to role play and practice how to express themselves more directly and forcefully.

*High threshold of response:*

1. Make sure you have your students' attention before saying important things, and accentuate what you say strongly enough so they get the message.

2. Give them practice in attending to and interpreting body language, gestures, and the subtle, polite, and indirect ways people often express themselves by having them read stories that contain such material, observing and interpreting the interactions of others, and role playing.

3. Encourage students to ask questions when they are uncertain or confused about what others are communicating.

4. Give them the extra instruction and practice they need to be able to distinguish important information from less essential peripheral material, especially before important lessons and examinations.

*Negative mood:*

1. One of the most important things you can do when you have temperamentally moody students in your class is to analyze your own reaction to them. Do their negative moods affect yours? Do you find being with students when they are moody exasperating? Do you avoid them, exhort them to behave better, or take their complaints personally? To react in these ways some of the time is unavoidable; every educator has limits. But if you react in these ways often, you may be causing unnecessary problems for your students and yourself.

2. Try not to take your students' moodiness personally. You aren't the cause of it, and you probably can't change it.

3. Avoid moralizing or penalizing students for being moody.

4. If possible, adjust your students' schedules so their moodiness doesn't interfere by postponing what can be delayed until they are in a better mood.

5. Try to kid them into feeling better. Your sense of humor could snap them out of a bad mood. Even if it doesn't, it may help you cope with the problem. See if some personal attention, words of praise, or a favorite activity changes your students' moods.

6. If that doesn't work, remind them that they are in a bad mood, and ask them to do the best they can under the circumstances.

7. Do what you can to ensure that their moodiness doesn't interfere with other students, but be especially tuned to involving them in group activities with others when they are in a good mood.

8. Although there probably aren't any activities, hobbies, or careers for which a negative mood is an advantage, moody students would probably profit from being guided toward activities where they can work alone. Careers that involve meeting the public or putting on a happy, smiling face probably aren't a good fit.

9. Help them understand how their moodiness affects others. Say things both nicely and in a complaining, whining voice and call attention to the difference. Discuss how it feels to be around someone when he is nasty, crabby, or unhappy.

10. Help your students recognize when they are in a bad mood. Teach them to wait, if possible, until the bad mood passes before making important or irrevocable decisions. Teach them to say as little as possible when they are in a bad mood and to tell the people they are involved with not to pay attention to their bad mood. And teach them not to blame others for their moodiness. (See section on self-management.)

*High persistence:*

1. Strike a balance between firmness and flexibility when dealing with persistent students. Stand firm when persistent students pressure you to allow them to do things they shouldn't do or if they don't want to stop when it's necessary in order to keep the group together or when you have a schedule to keep. Giving in because you are too busy to deal with the students' persistence only makes it more likely that they will pester you even more next time. But be flexible when temperamentally persistent students don't want to stop what they are doing if it won't inconvenience the group and if it makes good educational sense. The goal should be to avoid unnecessary arguments when possible while helping persistent students realize that rules and schedules exist, others have rights, and people will not always wait for them. You may have to frustrate these students from time to time, but that is preferable to their developing conduct problems.

2. Suggest that students postpone starting on a project that they won't be able to complete during the time available if you think they will have difficulty stopping.

3. When students are already working on something, give them advance warning that they will soon have to stop even though they won't be finished.

4. Direct students toward activities, hobbies, and careers that allow them to work as long as they wish on tasks that require persistence for success. Activities involving rigid schedules, group effort, or constantly shifting activities may be especially difficult for them.

5. Provide students with the self-insight they need to understand that people aren't unfair or impatient just because they insist that the students stick to an established schedule or won't take "no" for an answer. (See section on self-management.)

*Low persistence:*

1. Encourage students to keep trying when things become difficult.

2. Provide the assistance they need to continue as soon as they seem to be becoming frustrated or anxious.

3. Praise and reward students whenever they persevere.

4. If they quit too soon, let them take a break; then encourage them to start again.

5. If students fail because of lack of perseverance, help them understand the cause was lack of persistence, not lack of ability. This is especially important when students fail tests because they quit before finishing. (See section on self-management.)

---

## Self-Quiz: Temperamental Makeup

What is your temperamental makeup? Review the list of fifteen temperamental characteristics and the four criteria for determining an individual's temperamental characteristics and determine your temperamental makeup.

What kinds of temperamental traits in your students are you most and least able to accept? Review the list of temperamental traits and decide which ones evoke positive and negative reactions in you. What can you do to avoid causing temperamentally different students additional problems? List the self-managing techniques you could use to improve and control your own reactions to your students' temperamental characteristics.

---

# Attention Deficit Disorders

Students with attention deficit disorders have some, but not necessarily all, of the following characteristics: short attention span, poor power of concentration, distractibility, constant motion and restlessness (hyperactivity), and impulsivity (48–50). To understand the physiological nature of attention deficit disorders, it will be helpful to review briefly and in a simplified form how the body's neuroendocrine system works.

The neuroendocrine system is composed of two interrelated units—the nervous system and the endocrine system. The nervous system is like an extremely complex information-transmitting circuitry system. The brain receives and processes information it has received from nerve cells throughout the body; "decides" what various specialized cell groups such as the heart, muscles, and so on should do; then sends commands to them through the spinal cord and the nerves in contact with them. It also influences the way the body functions by affecting the rate at which the endocrine glands secrete hormones into the blood. The following vignette illustrates how the neuroendocrine system works.

Leticia, a teenager, is walking home from school reading a flyer about a rally for the basketball team. As she reads, nerve cells are transmitting various kinds of information to her brain. Her eyes are sending sensations that the brain translates into letters, words, and meanings. The brain is also receiving information about the smells of the nearby pizza parlor, the movement of the people around her, and the sounds of the traffic. The brain keeps most of this information out of her awareness, though, so that she can read without distraction as she strolls along. She is relaxed, so her endocrine glands are secreting their various hormones at levels appropriate for her calm state.

*Students with short attention spans often have difficulty finishing their seat work.*

When she comes to the end of the sidewalk, she steps into the street. Suddenly a horn blasts. Her brain directs her legs to stop and her auditory and visual systems to attend to the traffic. It also directs her endocrine system to adjust the rates of secretion of its various hormones to the potential danger.

Leticia jumps back onto the sidewalk out of the path of an oncoming car that just misses her, waits for the light to change, crosses the street, and continues walking with her newspaper tucked under her arm. After a while, her circulating hormones readjust to a level more typical of a leisurely stroll home in the city during the day, and once again she feels relaxed.

A few minutes later Leticia walks into the house where she sees her mother preparing supper. She greets her mother and is about to ask if she can attend the rally when her brain remembers something. The last time she went to a rally, she had promised to come straight home afterward and finish her homework, but she hadn't done either. "Wait!" her brain tells her: "If you want to go, you better do your homework first, then ask." So she goes up to her room and begins to study. After a few minutes, one of Leticia's friends calls to tell her the latest news. It's already a quarter past four, and she still has to finish a good hour of geometry homework, change clothes, and eat supper before six if she is going to get to the rally on time. So she tells her friend that she will call her back after she finishes her homework. A short while later her older brother comes home and blasts his stereo in the room next to her. Her attention drifts from her assignment to the music, but her brain gets her back on track. She continues working until nothing is sinking in. She takes a short break, goes back to studying, and finishes her work in plenty of time to call her friend. Afterwards she explains to her mother that she has already finished all of her homework, not like last time, and is allowed to attend the rally.

Leticia seems to have the ability to control herself, but when the neuroendocrine system doesn't function correctly, people may lose the ability to control their impulses, attend to their environments, talk, understand spoken or written language, and so on. Until a few years ago, children and adolescents with neuroendocrine dysfunctions that cause attention problems (lack of concentration, distractibility, and short attention span), constant motion and restlessness, and impulsivity were labeled hyperactive. Now they are said to have an attention deficit disorder.

## Attention Problems

Attention problems can result when the brain doesn't do an adequate job of censoring out irrelevant information sent to it. This is one of the reasons why some students are easily distracted while doing seatwork. A problem like this would have interfered with Leticia's ability to concentrate on the flyer in the busy street or on her homework in the noisy house.

Students experience another kind of attention problem when they try to read but their minds wander or when they are unable to concentrate on desk work, homework, or even their favorite television programs for as long as they should. If Leticia had this problem, she wouldn't have been able to concentrate long enough to complete her homework even without distractions at home.

## Constant Motion and Restlessness

One way children and adolescents show hyperactivity—or constant motion and restlessness—is by being unable to remain still in situations that require prolonged periods of sitting such as working on seat assignments, watching audiovisual materials, or attending to lectures in class or to long programs in the auditorium. If Leticia had been hyperactive, she might not have been able to sit still long enough to complete her homework.

## Impulsivity

Youngsters act impulsively when they don't stop to think about the possible consequences of their actions before they act. Another expression of this quality is that they begin things without planning or organizing ahead of time. If Leticia had been impulsive, she may not have been able to wait before asking her mother for permission to go to the rally or to hear the latest news from her friend until after she had completed her homework.

# *Identification*

In order to manage students with attention deficit disorders in the classroom, you need to know if they do indeed have such a disorder or if some other cause explains their behavior. Identifying such students is the first step in helping them manage their behavior.

*Informal Assessment*    The discussion below describes behaviors characteristic of children and adolescents with attention deficit disorders. A student could have an attention deficit disorder if she or he behaves in a number of these ways *more often* and *more consistently* than other youngsters and does so in *most* situations both in and out of school.

*Attention span:* Youngsters with attention deficit disorders are often unable to stick to one thing very long. At school they often fail to complete tasks that require sustained attention. At home they get bored with their games and toys easily and even stop watching television programs they like before they end. In addition, although they seem to enjoy great amounts of physical activity, mental work tires them easily, and the results of their mental efforts deteriorate rapidly after a short period of time.

*Distractibility:* These students commonly stop doing what they are involved in to do something else that catches their eye. Thus, they shift from one activity to another within a short period of time. They also have difficulty distinguishing the relevant from the irrelevant.

*Constant motion and restlessness:* Youngsters with this disorder are often on the go—running, jumping, climbing, or moving about in some way. They have difficulty sitting quietly for prolonged periods of time in school and elsewhere. Even when they do sit, they are very fidgety. They also break things, often without meaning to, because of their high energy level.

*Impulsivity:* Such students do things on the spur of the moment, act before thinking, seldom plan ahead, and rarely stop to organize their work. Characteristically, they don't wait their turn. In school they call out answers or raise their hands to answer, but when called on, they often don't know the answer. At home they grab and push ahead.

*Formal Assessment*    Conners and his associates (53–55) have developed two rating scales that teachers and parents can use to evaluate the hyperactive behavior of students. Although these scales don't give a definitive conclusion about what causes students' attention and activity problems, they do provide valuable information that can be used in conjunction with information from professionals to decide how to deal with students' behavior problems.

If you believe a student may have an attention deficit disorder, you should refer her to the appropriate school personnel who can initiate a process to determine what actually causes the student's behavior problems. There are three reasons why you shouldn't attempt to arrive at this decision on your own. First, educators generally tend to overestimate the number of students who have attention and activity problems (51, 56, 57). Second, many of the behaviors that students with attention deficit disorders exhibit can also have non-physiological causes (51). For example, the distractible, fidgety, tense behavior of anxious students sometimes closely parallels the behavior of students with attention problems. Next, three of the temperamental factors identified by Thomas, Chess, and Birch (18)—high activity level, short attention span, and distractibility—are highly similar to some of the symptoms of attention deficit disorder (52). Finally, only a physician is qualified to determine whether a student's behavior problems are caused by physiological factors.

## Self-Quiz: Response to Attention Deficits

What problems of students with attention deficits are you most and least able to accept? Describe how you typically react to the atten-

tion problems, constant motion and restlessness, and impulsivity of students with attention deficit disorders. *What could you do to improve the way you react to these problems?* Describe the specific techniques you could use to manage your reactions to these problems.

## Managing Attention Deficit Disorders

Physicians themselves are often unable to determine whether students' attention problems (short attention span and distractibility) and activity problems (restlessness and fidgetiness) are due to temperamental factors or hyperactivity (52). Research studies regarding the effectiveness of techniques for dealing with these problems don't differentiate between temperamentally different students and those with attention deficit disorders. Thus, the techniques for dealing with the problems of temperamentally different students already discussed should apply equally to students with either condition.

*Self-Managing Techniques*   You can teach students with attention deficit disorders to use the self-managing techniques described in Chapters 7 and 10 and in the previous section of this chapter. The following are examples of how you can teach these students to manage their impulsivity, attention problems, and activity problems.

*Impulsivity:* Impulsive students can learn to slow themselves down a little and look before they leap. While there is no sure-fire, certain way of doing this every time, the following process can help.

1. *Help students see the problem.* You can do this by explaining how their impulsive behavior causes them to make mistakes, gets them into trouble, or makes them do things they are sorry for later. Teaching students to monitor their own behavior can help them appreciate how often they act impulsively by saying things they later wished they hadn't said, calling out without being called on, volunteering to answer a question without being sure they know the answer, and answering a question on a test or starting a seat assignment before either reading the directions or allowing teachers to complete their instructions.

2. *Teach students to recognize when they are in situations that call for well-thought-out responses and the times they are on the verge of acting impulsively and how to control themselves from acting impulsively in such situations.* Tell younger students the instructions they should give themselves in order to control themselves. For example, you can tell students to first instruct themselves to wait and ask themselves if they have thought through what they are about to do before responding.

3. *Help students to develop a plan of action and follow it.* Teach them to rehearse their answers in order to determine whether they really know the answer before they volunteer. Teach them how to formulate alternative ways of reacting to situations and to weigh the pros and cons of each one. Encourage them to slow themselves down by reminding themselves that they will do a better job if they work slowly and carefully. Train them to ask themselves questions such as Do I really know the answer? Do I know exactly what I'm supposed to do? Have I read all of the directions? Do I have a plan? Am I following my plan? Have I thought things through? What will happen if I do it? How else can I do it? What do I do next?

4. *Teach students to reward themselves when they have controlled their impulsivity.* They can do this by congratulating themselves for their achievements, by feeling good about their newfound self-control, by keeping a record of how well they have done, and other forms of self-acknowledgment. If intrinsic rewards aren't effective, allow them to earn some extrinsic reward that they have chosen themselves.

A number of published systems exist for helping students manage their own impulsive behavior. Palkes, Stewart, and Kahana (85) describe how students can use cards that say stop, listen, or think placed on their desks to remind themselves to *stop* before doing or deciding, to *listen* to everything first, and to *think* before acting. Camp and Bash (63) describe a Think Aloud Program that trains students to ask themselves a series of self-managing questions while they work. Sample questions include: What am I supposed to be doing? How do I do it? What is my plan? Am I sticking to my plan? How well did I do? Fagan (68) and Fagan, Long, and Stevens (69) have published a game- and skill-oriented curriculum designed to teach the self-control skills described above.

*Attention problems:* Argulewicz, Elliot, and Spencer (59) have described a practical three-step procedure—tell, show, and do—for teaching young students to manage their attention problems. In the "tell" step, students are told what is involved in paying attention while the teacher models the appropriate behavior. In this case, appropriate behavior includes such things as facing the person or material, maintaining eye contact, and repeating a series of attention-maintaining self-instructions. In the "show" step, students are shown pictures and asked to identify the ones in which people are paying attention. In the "do" step, students rehearse attending behavior under the teachers' supervision until they have learned the technique.

Students can learn to maintain their attention in class by using a timer that emits a soft sound which doesn't distract other students. When the sound tones, they are to monitor whether they are paying attention. Using this device, students can earn rewards by increasing their on-task time (80). Varni and Henker (89) had students monitor their time on task by using a wrist counter.

Students can also manage their distractibility by instructing themselves to clear their desks of any materials that might divert their attention before they begin. They can also choose to work in a cubicle or in a screened-off area if they feel they cannot continue to concentrate on their work without such aids.

*Activity problems:* The suggestions for helping students manage high activity levels covered earlier in this chapter are also appropriate for restless and fidgety students. You can also find more detailed discussions of these and other self-managing techniques in the literature (70, 74, 75, 76, 77, 81, 82, 86).

*Effectiveness:* Ample evidence shows that certain students can use self-managing techniques to modify their behavior to some degree. Students have demonstrated improvement in attention, activity, and impulse problems after being taught to use various self-managing techniques (59–64, 66, 67, 72, 73, 76, 79, 80, 84, 85, 89). While the results aren't conclusive, it appears that these techniques are more effective in improving students' academic skills than their social skills (72). They are also more effective with younger students when they are given extrinsic rewards for using the procedure they have been taught (62, 71, 95).

Although these techniques are effective with many students (62, 76, 79, 80), this effectiveness doesn't generalize to tasks and situations in which students haven't been specifically trained to apply them (64, 72, 78, 83). As Pressley concluded:

> These studies showed that cognitive strategies could be used by children to affect their self-control, but the studies did not show that children would (could) apply the strategies in new situations. In fact, the available data suggest that subjects do not generalize the strategies to new situations. (87, p. 361–362)

Another limitation of self-managing techniques is the fact that their effectiveness often diminishes or disappears over time, especially when teachers permit students to supervise themselves (66, 87, 89). A final drawback is that educators are unable to predict in advance which students will and which won't profit from training in self-managing techniques. As Rosenbaum and Drabman suggest:

> Methods for identifying children for whom self-control is not an appropriate goal need to be developed. (88, p. 481)

*Teacher-Initiated Techniques*    In addition to helping these students learn self-managing techniques, you can also take action to help modify their behavior.

*Managing without consequences:* Educators can manage some behaviors of students who are unable to manage themselves. They can manage such students' impulsive behaviors by:

1. Requiring students to leave their pencils and pens on the desk until the teacher has finished giving directions.

2. Requiring them to delay answering questions or beginning problems for a few seconds so they can think through their answers and approaches.

3. Reminding them to be careful and to take their time before they begin assignments and while working on them.

To help distractible students:

1. Require students, especially young ones, to keep such things as toys, lunch boxes, and other items in another section of the room until recess or lunchtime.

2. Have students keep their desks free of all materials except those they need for the work at hand.

3. Instruct students to fold their paper or cover part of it up so they only see part of it at a time. Give them place markers to use while reading. Put arithmetic problems in boxes or in folded columns to help them focus attention on just one problem at a time. Don't put too much on one page.

4. Supervise your students closely to keep them on-task.

5. When you tell students to do something, make sure they haven't been too distracted to hear you. Make eye contact if possible. Also have them acknowledge that they heard you so you don't assume they did when they were actually distracted by something else.

*Managing with consequences:* A significant amount of research has been conducted on the effectiveness of using positive and negative consequences to modify the behavior problems of students with attention deficit disorders. Researchers have rewarded students for behavioral improvement (92, 94), ignored students exhibiting undesirable behavior and praised and attended them for desirable behavior (99), rewarded other students who were modeling appropriate behavior (91), used peer pressure by applying group consequences for individual student's behavior (97), and had parents reward students for behavioral improvement in school based on daily reports sent home (96). While all of these researchers reported some success with certain students, the overall effectiveness of these programs was difficult to maintain when the extrinsic reinforcements were ended (90, 93, 98). This problem has led many reviewers of the research to conclude that student self-management procedures are preferable to teacher-initiated management procedures that involve extrinsic consequences (59, 95).

## Accommodating to Attention Deficit Disorders

Because neither self-managing nor teacher-initiated managing techniques are effective with all students who have attention deficit disorders, you will sometimes need to accommodate your classroom management techniques to certain students.

*Short Attention Spans*   Below are examples of the many ways you can accommodate your expectations, classroom routines, instruction, and the like to those aspects of students' attention problems that can't be managed. You can also find more detailed descriptions of these and other techniques in the literature on the education of students with attention deficit disorders (100–115).

1. Shorten the length of students' work sessions to fit their attention spans and allow them extra time to complete their work whenever possible.

2. Select activities that suit students with short attention spans. For example, short stories may work better than books and short chapters may be better than long ones. Or you can have a folder of different, but relevant, activities that students can do in a short period of time. Allow students to use this folder quietly when they need a change.

3. Allow students to get up quietly when they feel it's necessary. A short break in the classroom or out in the hall may help these students get ready for another work session.

4. If students do poorly on activities that require sustained attention, determine whether the cause is lack of ability, motivation, effort, or another cause or a short attention span. This is especially important if students do poorly on standardized tests.

*Distractibility*    In addition to techniques listed earlier for distractible students, you can accommodate to their needs by using the following techniques.

1. Provide students with an environment as free from distracting stimuli as possible.

2. Seat students in the front of the room so they are less likely to be distracted by the actions of other students.

3. Place display materials as far away from students as possible.

4. Assign students to work in cubicles when they can't concentrate.

5. Use filmstrip viewers, computers, recordings, and earphones to cut down on auditory and visual distractions.

6. If necessary, allow more time for students to complete things that are likely to involve distractions. If you can plan more time for such activities, you won't have to remind them to get back on task so often.

7. Don't attribute students' inattention to boredom, lack of motivation, or inability if it is caused by distractibility.

# *Summary*

Educators or other professionals are limited in what they can do to modify a student's physiological makeup. They can't, for example, hurry the maturational process of a student who is developmentally delayed, change the temperament of a low-active-level student, or completely control the short attention span, distractibility, and fidgety behavior of students with attention deficit disorders. Thus, with most students whose behavior problems are caused by physiological factors, changing is not a feasible strategy. Teachers can, however, teach students to manage their biological makeup to some degree, manage some of the behavior their students can't manage themselves, and finally, accommodate their expectations and demands to aspects of their students' personalities that neither they nor their students can manage. Doing this will enable students to make the most of their physiological makeup, help teachers avoid unnecessary and fruitless conflicts with students, and reduce the chances that their students will develop additional problems.

# *Activities*

For each of the following behavior problems, state the kind of physiological factors that might be causing the behavior (developmental delay, temperament, or attention deficit disorder), and describe the additional information you would need before deciding that the cause of the problem is indeed physiological.

1. Carlos, a 6-year-old, seldom spends more than four or five minutes at any task before his attention begins to wander. This is especially true when the class is seated on the floor in front of the teacher while she is reading aloud to them.

2. Beth, an 8-year-old who is a slow worker in comparison to other students, typically refuses to stop working on seat assignments that she has not completed when it is time to change activities. She also tends to reject her teacher's suggestions that she try another approach when her way of doing something isn't working.

3. Sheila, a fourth grader, usually avoids or reacts negatively to new situations and tasks. When coaxed or pressured to become involved, she will dig her heels in and stubbornly refuse.

4. A 12-year-old, Jimmy, doesn't spend more than six or seven minutes doing seatwork before looking around the room or playing with something in his desk. Whenever someone says something to someone else or there is some movement in the room, he is the first to lift his head from his work to see what is going on.

5. Consuela, a 16-year-old who has been in the United States for a year and a half, spends very little time with her peers, especially boys. She seems unconcerned about her future, at least so far as school is concerned, and is not at all interested in her schoolwork.

# *References*

DEVELOPMENTAL LAG

1. Ames, L., & Ilg, F. (1965). *School Readiness*. New York: Harper & Row.

2. Spollen, J. C., & Ballif, B. L. (1971). Effectiveness of individualized instruction for kindergarten children with a developmental lag. *Exceptional Children*, 28 (3), 205–209.

TEMPERAMENTAL DIFFERENCES

The references below discuss various theories of temperament.

3. Brown, G. W. (1973). Temperament and child development. *Journal of Learning Disabilities*, 6 (9), 557–561.

4. Buss, A. H. (1984). *Temperament: Early Developing Personality Traits.* Hillsdale, NJ: Erlbaum.

5. Buss, A. H., & Plomin, R. (1975). *A Temperament Theory of Personality Development.* New York: John Wiley & Sons.

6. Diamond, S. (1957). *Personality and Temperament.* New York: Harper & Brothers.

7. Plomin, R., & Dunn, J. (eds.). (1986). *The Study of Temperament: Changes, Continuities and Challenges.* Hillsdale, NJ: Erlbaum.

These citations describe the New York Longitudinal Study.

8. Chess, S. (1968). Temperament and learning ability in school children. *American Journal of Public Health, 58* (12), 231–239.

9. Chess, S. (1971). *Preschool Behavior Style and Later Academic Achievement—Final Report.* ERIC ED 054 511.

10. Chess, S., Thomas, A., & Cameron, M. (1976). Temperament: Its significance for early schooling. *New York University Educational Quarterly, Spring,* 24–29.

11. Chess, S., & Thomas, A. (1986). *Temperament in Clinical Practice.* New York: Guilford Press.

12. Kagan, J. (1982). The construct of difficult temperament: A reply to Thomas, Chess, and Korn. *Merrill-Palmer Quarterly, 28,* 21–24.

13. Lerner, J. V., Chess, S., & Lenerz, K. (1986). Early temperament and later educational outcome. In National Institute of Education, *Temperament and School Learning.* ERIC ED 267 078.

14. Lerner, J. V., & Vicary, J. R. (1984). Difficult temperament and drug use: Analysis from the New York Longitudinal Study. *Journal of Drug Education, 14* (1), 1–8.

15. Thomas, A., & Chess, C. (1976). Evolution of behavior disorders into adolescents. *American Journal of Psychiatry, 133* (5), 339–542.

16. Thomas, A., & Chess, S. (1977). *Temperament and Development.* New York: Brunner/Mazel.

17. Thomas, A., & Chess, S. (1984). Genesis and evolution of behavior disorders: From infancy to early adult life. *American Journal of Psychiatry, III,* 1–9.

18. Thomas, A., Chess, S., & Birch, H. G. (1968). *Temperament and Behavior Disorders.* New York: New York University Press.

19. Thomas, A., Chess, S., & Birch, H. G. (1972). *Your Child Is A Person.* New York: Viking Press.

20. Thomas, A., Chess, S., & Korn, S. J. (1982). The reality of difficult temperament. *Merrill-Palmer Quarterly, 28,* 1–20.

21. Thomas, A., Chess, S., Sillen, J., & Mendez, O. (1974). Cross-cultural study of behavior in children with special vulnerabilities to stress. In D. F. Ricks, A. Thomas,

& M. Roff (Eds.), *Life History Research in Psychopathology, Vol. III*. Minneapolis, MN: Minnesota Press.

The listings below discuss specific assessment instruments.

22. Behavior Style Questionnaire: McDevitt, S. C., & Carey, W. B. (1978). The measurement of temperament in 3–7 year old children. *Journal of Child Psychology and Psychiatry and Allied Professions, 19*, 245–253.

23. The Dimensions of Temperament Survey: Lerner, R. M., Palermo, M., Spiro, A., III, & Nesselrode, J. R. (1982). Assessing the dimensions of temperamental individuality across the life span: The Dimensions of Temperament Survey. *Child Development, 53* (1), 149–159.

24. The Preschool Temperament Inventory: Billman, J. (1981). *The Preschool Temperament Inventory: Construction and Standardization of a Teacher-Rated Instrument for Assessing Temperament of Three- to Six-Year-Old Children*. ERIC ED 224, 592.

25. Teacher Temperament Questionnaire. Sobesky, W. E., List, K. R., Holden, D. L., & Braucht, W. G. (1981). *Dimensions of Child Temperament in School Settings*. ERIC ED 200 315.

26. Thomas, A., & Chess, S. (1977). *Temperament and Development*. New York: Brunner/Mazel.

The references that follow discuss the validity of temperament assessment instruments.

27. Billman, J., & McDevitt, S. C. (1980). Convergence of parent and observer ratings of temperament with observations of peer interactions in nursery school. *Child Development, 51* (2), 395–400.

28. Corsini, D. A., & Doyle, K. (1979). *Temperamental Traits of Preschool Children: Across Setting Consistency*. ERIC ED 183 265.

29. Hubert, N. C., Wachs, T. D., Peters-Martin, P., & Gandour, M. J. (1982). The study of early temperament measurement and conceptual issues. *Child Development, 53* (3), 571–600.

30. Lyon, M. E., & Plomiss, R. (1981). The measurement of temperament using parent ratings. *Journal of Child Psychology and Psychiatry and Allied Disciplines, 22* (1), 47–53.

31. Pfeffer, J., & Martin, R. P. (1983). Comparison of mothers' and fathers' temperament ratings of referred and non-referred preschool children. *Journal of Clinical Psychology, 39* (6), 1013–1020.

The references below discuss additional problems that can result when temperamentally different youngsters aren't handled properly.

32. Barron, A. P., & Earls, F. (1984). The relation of temperament and social factors to behavior problems in three-year-old children. *Journal of Child Psychology and Psychiatry and Related Disciplines, 25* (1), 23–33.

33. Cameron, J. R. (1977). Parental treatment, children's temperament and the risk of childhood behavior problems: Relationship between parental characteristics and changes in children's temperament over time. *American Journal of Orthopsychiatry, 47* (4), 568–576.

34. Nelson, J. A. N. (1985). *Toward Quality of Match: Relationship between Children's Temperament and Specific Aspects of Parent Behavior.* ERIC ED 260 817.

35. Nelson, J. A. N., & Simmer, N. J. (1984). Correlational study of children's temperament and parent behavior. *Early Childhood Development and Care, 16* (3), 230–250.

The following references deal with the problems temperamentally different students experience in school.

36. Barclay, L. K. (1985). *Skill Development and Temperament in Kindergarten Children: A Cross-Cultural Study.* ERIC ED 262 878.

37. Barclay, J. R. (1978). *Temperamental Clusters and Individual Differences in the Elementary Classroom: A Summary.* ERIC ED 160 202, ED 157 600.

38. Carey, W. B., Fox, M., & McDevitt, S. C. (1977). Temperament as a factor in early school adjustment. *Pediatrics, 60,* 621–624.

39. Garside, R., Birch, H., Scott, D., Chamber, S., Kolvin, I., Tweddle, N., & Barber, L. (1975). Dimensions of temperament in infant school children. *Journal of Child Psychology and Allied Disciplines, 13,* 219–231.

40. Keogh, B. K. (1986). Temperament and schooling: Meaning of "goodness of fit." *New Directions for Child Development, 31,* 89–108.

41. Keogh, B. K., & Pullis, M. (1980). Temperament influences on the development of exceptional children. In B. K. Keogh (Ed.), *Advances in Special Education.* Greenwich, CT: JAI Press.

42. Klein, H. A. (1983). The relationship between children's temperament and adjustment to kindergarten and headstart settings. *Journal of Psychology, 112* (2), 259–268.

43. National Institute of Education. (1985). *Temperament and School Learning.* ERIC ED 267 078.

44. Nelson, J. A. N., & Simmerer, N. J. (1983). *Individuality and the Development of Social Competence among Preschool Children.* ERIC ED 246 994.

45. Palsin, H. (1986). Preschool temperament and performance on achievement tests. *Developmental Psychology, 22* (6), 766–770.

46. Pullis, M., & Caldwell, J. (1982). The influence of children's temperament characteristics on teachers' decision strategies. *American Educational Research Journal, 19,* 165–181.

47. Soderman, H. K. (1985). Dealing with difficult young children: Strategies for teachers and parents. *Young Children, 4* (5), 15–20.

ATTENTION DEFICIT DISORDERS

References below provide a definition of attention deficit disorders.

48. American Psychiatric Association. (1981). *Diagnostic and Statistical Manual of Mental Disorders* (3rd ed.). Washington, DC: American Psychiatric Association.

49. Barkley, R. A. (1982). Guidelines for defining hyperactivity in children: Attention deficit disorders with hyperactivity. In B. Lahey & A. E. Kazdin (Eds.), *Advances in Clinical Child Psychology, Vol. 5.* New York: Plenum.

50. Whalen, C. K. (1983). Hyperactivity, learning problems and the attention deficit disorders. In T. H. Ollendick & M. Herson (Eds.), *Handbook of Child Psychopathology.* New York: Plenum.

The following citations describe the identification process with these students.

51. Bax, J. (1978). The active and overactive school child. *Developmental Medicine and Neurology, 14,* 83–86.

52. Carey, W. B., McDevitt, S. C., & Baker, D. (1979). Differentiating minimal brain dysfunction and temperament. *Developmental Medicine and Child Neurology, 21* (6), 765–772.

53. Conners, C. K. (1969). A teacher's rating scale for use in drug studies with children. *American Journal of Psychiatry, 126,* 152–156.

54. Conners, C. K. (1973). Rating scales for use in drug studies with children [Special issue, Pharmacology of Children]. *Psychopharmacology Bulletin,* 24–84.

55. Goyette, C. H., Conners, C. K., & Ulrich, R. F. (1978). Normative data on Revised Conners Parent and Teaching Rating Scales. *Journal of Abnormal Child Psychology, 6,* 221–236.

56. Rich, H. L. (1978). Teachers' perception of motor activity and related behaviors. *Exceptional Children, 45,* 210–211.

57. Rich, H. L. (1979). The syndrome of hyperactivity among elementary resource students. *Education and Treatment of Children, 2,* 91–100.

58. Victor, J. B., & Halverson, C. F. (1976). Distractibility and hypersensitivity: Two behavior factors in elementary school children. *Journal of Abnormal Child Psychology, 3,* 83–94.


SELF-MANAGING TECHNIQUES

59. Argulewicz, E. N., Elliot, S. N., & Spencer, D. (1982). Application of a cognitive-behavioral intervention for improving classroom attention. *School Psychology Review, 11* (1), 90–95.

60. Bender, N. N. (1976). Self-verbalization versus tutor verbalization in modifying impulsivity. *Journal of Educational Psychology, 68,* 347–354.

61. Bolstad, O., & Johnson, S. (1972). Self-regulation in the modification of disruptive classroom behavior. *Journal of Applied Behavior Analysis, 5,* 443–454.

62. Bornstein, P. H., & Quevillon, R. P. (1976). The effects of a self-instructional package on overactive preschool boys. *Journal of Applied Behavior Analysis, 9,* 179–188.

63. Camp, B. W., & Bash, M. A. (1981). *Think Aloud: Increasing Social and Cognitive Skill, A Problem-Solving Program for Children.* Champaign, IL: Research Press.

64. Camp, B. W., Blom, G. E., Hebert, F., & van Doorninck, W. F. (1977). Think aloud: A program for developing self-control in young aggressive boys. *Journal of Abnormal Child Psychology, 5,* 157–169.

65. Cole, P. M., & Hartley, D. G. (1978). The effects of reinforcement and strategy training on impulsive responding. *Child Development, 49,* 381–384.

66. Cullinan, D., Epstein, M. H., & Silver, L. (1977). Modification of impulsive tempo in learning-disabled pupils. *Journal of Abnormal Child Psychology, 5,* 437–444.

67. Douglas, V. I., Parry, P., Maiton, P., & Garson, C. (1976). Assessment of cognitive training program for hyperactive children. *Journal of Abnormal Child Psychology, 4* (4), 389–410.

68. Fagan, S. (1979). Psychoeducational management and self-control. In D. Cullinan & M. Epstein (Eds.), *Special Education for Adolescents: Issues and Perspectives.* Columbus, OH: Charles E. Merrill.

69. Fagan, S., Long, N., & Stevens, D. (1975). *Teaching Children Self-Control.* Columbus, OH: Charles E. Merrill.

70. Finch, A. J., & Spirito, A. (1980). Use of cognitive training to train cognitive processes. *Exceptional Education Quarterly, 1* (1), 31–39.

71. Friedling, C., & O'Leary, S. G. (1979). Effects of self-instructional training on second and third grade hyperactive students: A failure to replicate. *Journal of Applied Behavior Analysis, 12,* 211–219.

72. Glenwick, U. S., & Barocas, R. (1979). Training impulsive children in verbal self-control by use of natural change agents. *Journal of Special Education, 13* (4), 387–397.

73. Glynn, E. L., Thomas, J. E., & Shee, S. M. (1973). Behavioral self-control of on-task behavior in an elementary classroom. *Journal of Applied Behavior Analysis, 6,* 105–113.

74. Hallahan, D. P. (Ed.). (1980). Teaching exceptional children to use cognitive strategies. *Exceptional Education Quarterly, 1.*

75. Hallahan, D. P., Lloyd, J. W., Kauffman, J. M., & Lopez, A. B. (1983). Academic problems. In R. J. Morris & T. R. Kratochwill (Eds.), *The Practice of Child Therapy.* New York: Pergamon.

76. Hallahan, D. P., Lloyd, J., Kosiewicz, M. M., Kauffman, J. M., & Graves, A. W. (1979). Self-monitoring of attention as a treatment for a learning disabled boy's off-task behavior. *Learning Disabilities Quarterly, 2,* 24–32.

77. Hallahan, D. P., Lloyd, J. W., & Stoller, L. (1982). *Improving Attention with Self-Monitoring: A Manual for Teachers.* Charlottesville, VA: Learning Disabilities Institute, University of Virginia.

78. Kagen, R. M. (1976). Generalization of verbal self-instructional training in cognitive impulsive children. *Dissertation Abstracts International, 37,* 4148B. (University Microfilms No. 77-3926).

79. Kendall, P. C., Zupan, B. A., & Braswell, L. (1981). Self-control in children: Further analysis of the self-control rating scale. *Behavior Therapy, 12,* 667–681.

80. Kneedler, R. D., & Hallahan, D. P. (1984). Self-monitoring as an attentional strategy for academic tasks with learning disabled children. In B. Gholson and T. Rosenthal (Eds.), *Applications of Cognitive Development Theory.* New York: Academic Press.

81. Meichenbaum, D. H. (1979). Teaching children self-control. In B. B. Lahey & A. E. Kazdin (Eds.), *Advances in Clinical Child Psychology, Vol. 2.* New York: Plenum.

82. Meichenbaum, D. H. (1980). Cognitive behavior modification: A promise yet unfulfilled. *Exceptional Education Quarterly, 1* (1), 83–88.

83. Meichenbaum, D. H., & Goodman, J. (1971). Training impulsive children to talk to themselves. *Journal of Abnormal Psychology, 77,* 115–126.

84. Palkes, H., Stewart, M., & Freedman, J. (1971). Improvement in maze performance of hyperactive boys as a function of verbal training procedures. *Journal of Special Education, 5,* 337–342.

85. Palkes, H., Stewart, M., & Kahana, B. (1968). Porteus maze performance of hyperactive boys after training in self-directed verbal commands. *Child Development, 39,* 817–826.

86. Polsgrove, L. (1979). Self-control: Methods for child training. *Behavior Disorders, 4,* 116–130.

87. Pressley, M. (1979). Increasing children's self-control through cognitive interventions. *Review of Educational Research, 49* (2), 319–370.

88. Rosenbaum, M. S., & Drabman, R. S. (1979). Self-control training in the classroom: A review and critique.

89. Varni, J. W., & Henker, B. (1979). A self-regulation approach to the treatment of three hyperactive boys. *Child Behavior Therapy, 1,* 171–191.

TEACHER-INITIATED TECHNIQUES WITH CONSEQUENCES

90. Anderson, A., Foder, I., & Alpert, M. A. (1976). A comparison of methods for training self-control. *Behavior Therapy, 7,* 649–658.

91. Broden, M., Bruce, C., Mitchell, M. A., Carter, V., & Hall, R. V. (1970). Effects of teacher attention on attending behavior of two boys at adjacent desks. *Journal of Applied Behavior Analysis, 3,* 199–204.

92.  Coleman, R. A. (1970). A conditioning technique applicable to elementary school classrooms. *Journal of Applied Behavior Analysis, 3,* 293–297.

93.  Drabman, R. S., Spitalnik, R. S., & O'Leary, K. D. (1973). Teaching self-control to disruptive children. *Journal of Abnormal Psychology, 82,* 10–16.

94.  Hallahan, D. P., & Kauffman, J. M. (1975). Research on the education of distractible and hyperactive children. In W. M. Cruickshank & D. P. Hallahan (Eds.), *Perceptual and Learning Disabilities in Children, Vol. 2: Research and Theory.* Syracuse, NY: Syracuse University Press.

95.  O'Leary, S. G., & Dubey, D. R. (1979). Application of self-control procedures by children: A review. *Journal of Applied Behavior Analysis, 12,* 449–465.

96.  O'Leary, K. D., Pelham, W. E., Rosenbaum, A., & Price, G. H. (1976). Behavioral treatment of hyperkinetic children: An experimental evaluation of its usefulness. *Clinical Pediatrics, 15,* 510–575.

97.  Rosenbaum, A., O'Leary, K. D., & Jacob, R. G. (1975). Behavioral intervention with hyperactive children: Group consequences as a supplement to individual contingencies. *Behavior Therapy, 6,* 315–322.

98.  Turkewitz, H., O'Leary, K. D., & Ironsmith, M. (1975). Generalization and maintenance of appropriate behavior through self-control. *Journal of Consulting and Clinical Psychiatry, 43,* 577–583.

99.  Walker, H. M., & Buckley, N. K. (1968). The use of positive reinforcement in conditioning attending behavior. *Journal of Applied Behavior Analysis, 1,* 245–250.

TEACHER-INITIATED TECHNIQUES WITHOUT CONSEQUENCES

100.  Conners, C. K., & Wells, K. C. (1986). *Hyperkinetic Children: A Neuropsychosocial Approach.* Beverly Hills, CA: Sage.

101.  Connors, J. P. (1974). *Classroom Activities for Helping Hyperactive Children.* New York: Center for Applied Research in Education.

102.  Cruickshank, W. M. (1975). The learning environment. In W. M. Cruickshank & D. P. Hallahan (Eds.), *Perceptual and Learning Disabilities in Children, Vol. 1: Psychoeducational Practices.* Syracuse, NY: Syracuse University Press.

103.  Cruickshank, W. M., Bentzen, F., Retzeburg, F., & Tannhauser, M. A. (1961). *A Teaching Method for Brain-Injured and Hyperactive Children.* Syracuse, NY: Syracuse University Press.

104.  Cruickshank, W. M., & Hallahan, D. P. (Eds.). (1975). *Perceptual and Learning Disabilities in Children, Vol. 2: Research and Theory.* Syracuse, NY: Syracuse University Press.

105.  Digate, G., Epstein, M. H., Cullinan, D., & Switzky, H. N. (1978). Modification of impulsivity: Implications for improved efficiency in learning for exceptional children. *Journal of Special Education, 12,* 459–468.

106. Fairchild, T. N. (1975). *Managing the Hyperactive Child in the Classroom.* Austin, TX: Learning Concepts.

107. Fine, M. J. (Ed.). (1977). *Principles and Techniques of Intervention with Hyperactive Children.* Springfield, IL: CC Thomas.

108. Fontenelle, D. (1983). *A Guide for Parents and Teachers.* Englewood Cliffs, NJ: Prentice-Hall.

109. Jacob, R. G., O'Leary, K. D., & Rosenblad, C. (1978). Formal and informal classroom settings: Effects on hyperactivity. *Journal of Abnormal Child Psychology, 6,* 47–59.

110. Kauffman, J. M., & Hallahan, D. P. (1979). Learning disabilities and hyperactivity (with comments on minimal brain dysfunction). In B. B. Lahey & A. E. Kazdin (Eds.), *Advances in Clinical Child Psychology.* New York: Plenum.

111. Lahey, B. B. (Ed.). (1979). *Behavior Therapy with Hyperactive and Learning Disabled Children.* New York: Oxford University Press.

112. Margolis, H., Brannigan, G. G., & Poston, M. A. (1977). Modification of impulsivity: Implications for teaching. *Elementary School Journal, 77,* 231–237.

113. Pick, A. D., Cristy, M. D., & Frankel, G. W. (1972). A developmental study of visual selective attention. *Journal of Experimental Child Psychology, 14,* 165–175.

114. Strauss, A. A., & Lehtinen, L. E. (1946). *Psychopathology and Education of the Brain-Injured Child.* New York: Grune & Stratton.

115. Vallet, R. E. (1974). *The Psychoeducational Treatment of Hyperactive Children.* Belmont, CA: Fearon.

# *CULTURAL DIFFERENCES*

This chapter is concerned with the relationship between cultural differences and classroom behavior problems. It describes the difficulties immigrant students and other students of varying cultures experience in school. The chapter also explores the kinds of behavior problems such experiences can cause. It concludes by offering suggestions for avoiding many of these problems and handling those that do arise.

## *Extent of the Problem*

While it is still true that most Americans and most students are white, the ethnic makeup of the population in the United States has changed drastically in recent years. In 1980, 50 million or 21 percent of Americans were nonwhite. By the year 2000, nonwhites are expected to comprise one-third of the population. Between the 1970 census and 1980 census, the white population increased by 6 percent, with corresponding increases for Blacks and Hispanics at 18 and 61 percent, respectively. In 1980, 27 percent of the student population was nonwhite. By the year 2000, nonwhite students will represent well over a third of all students. Nonwhite students are currently in the majority in the 25 largest school districts in the United States (1).

Foreign Born Population Living in the United States in June 1986

| COUNTRIES OF ORIGIN | ENTERED 1970o1986 | ENTERED 1980o1986 |
|---|---|---|
| All Countries | 13,069,000 | 4,967,000 |
| Mexico | 3,852,000 | 1,375,000 |
| Other North American Countries | 2,650,000 | 934,000 |
| South America | 668,000 | 219,000 |
| Europe | 1,949,000 | 528,000 |
| Asia | 3,721,000 | 1,784,000 |
| Africa and Oceania | 229,000 | 127,000 |

Note: From *Measuring Net Immigration to the United States: The Emigrant Population and Recent Emigration Flows* by K. A. Woodrow, 1988, paper presented at the annual meeting of the Population Association of America, New Orleans.

Many of these minority students are not yet proficient in English (limited-English-proficient). This means their command of English isn't enough for them to profit from instruction in English. Their numbers in the classroom are also growing at an extremely

*In some states, minority students are in the majority.*

rapid rate. Estimates of how many limited-English-proficient children and adolescents are now in the schools vary depending on the criteria and definition. But, as the table on their numbers indicates, in 1985 almost 8 million American youngsters had a non-English background either because they were born elsewhere or they grew up in the United States in a home where another language was spoken. Over 3½ million of these students scored in the lowest 20 percent on tests of English proficiency, and over 5 million scored in the lower 40 percent. Whatever criteria one uses, it's clear that millions of these youngsters don't yet know English well enough to function in English-only classes without considerable difficulty (2).

Numbers of Limited-English-Proficient Minority Students Aged 5 to 17 in the United States by English Proficiency Test Scores

| | |
|---|---|
| Students with non-English language background | 7,887,000 |
| Students who score in the lowest 40 percent | 5,284,000 |
| Students who score in the lowest 20 percent | 3,549,000 |

Clearly, to be effective, teachers will have to be able to deal with the ever-increasing numbers of minority students in their classes. They will also have to be able to help the millions of limited-English-proficient students cope with schools that use languages and teaching styles dissimilar to their native culture.

## Immigrant Students

When people have to adjust to a culture that is significantly different from their own, they often become confused, anxious, and frustrated because they don't know what is expected of them in different situations. They often cannot solve interpersonal problems and do not know what is and isn't acceptable behavior in the new culture. They may become angry at people whose behavior they can't understand. They can also feel anxious and fearful about not being able to function adequately in the new culture or sad and depressed over the loss of their familiar way of life (5). All of this disorientation and confusion is called *culture shock*.

## Culture Shock

Students who immigrate to the United States from other countries can suffer culture shock in school. They may become angry, anxious, sad, or depressed. Some students may withdraw from their teachers and the other students or act aggressively toward them. If these students also have to endure the added frustration of learning new material taught in a language they don't understand and in ways that don't suit their culturally determined learning styles, the resulting anxiety, anger, resentment, and shame can also cause serious behavior problems in the classroom. (Even students who move from rural areas to large cities, or from middle America to the coasts, from the South to the North or vice versa, or students who are bused from one ethnic neighborhood to another can suffer culture shock, albeit to a lesser degree.)

The following excerpt from an interview with a Japanese teacher studying in the United States provides examples of the differences that can cause immigrant students to experience culture shock in American schools.

Q. "What do you think a teacher should know about the background of a recently arrived Japanese student?"

A. "They may not ask questions unless the teacher encourages them to speak up. They tend to be very quiet . . . There is a lot of memorization. For instance, I have been teaching at a senior high school, and I force my students to memorize most of the sentences . . . Most students would expect a teacher to teach them rather than ask them questions or raise discussions. When I first came here, I expected all the professors to be lecturing us rather than asking us questions. At first, I was very embarrassed; it was hard for me to follow."

Q. "Sometimes a problem is created when a teacher picks out a student and corrects him."

A. "I think it might cause the student to react in a negative way. He might try to keep to himself. If the teacher corrects mistakes in class, the student might be very embarrassed."

Q. "What kinds of other adjustment problems would a Japanese student face?

A. "The small daughter of a friend of mine from Japan was having difficulties when she entered school here. When she started to go to school, she used to come back every day, crying. It appears that in her math class, she was doing the math according to the Japanese way. An American student corrected her by saying, 'This is not the way.' And every time she wrote something, the American boy erased it. Since she could not speak any word of English, she had no way of indicating that she was doing it the Japanese way, she had no way but to cry. The teacher thought that the child was kind of nervous and somewhat strange. The child apparently had a hard time for the first two months; now she is doing fine." (3, p. 24–27)

## Language and Teaching Style

Wei (9) describes some of the difficulties Vietnamese students often experience in American schools where they are taught in a language foreign to them and in an unfamiliar teaching style.

There are three categories of educational difficulties that the Vietnamese child must face: (1) different learning styles and classroom activities; (2) a change in the student-teacher relationship; and most of all (3) the language barrier.

*Differences in learning style and classroom activities.* The Vietnamese educational system promotes a passive type of learning where the students learn by listening, watching, and imitating their teachers. The open type of classroom common in many American schools is perceived by the Vietnamese as confusing and disorganized. Since Vietnamese students are used to a lecture method, team teaching and active class participation are uncommon and strange to many of them. They are not used to group activities and do not know how to react. Independent projects or library research are foreign to them, and they need to be guided with patience.

*The student-teacher relationship.* The American teachers' friendliness and informality are shocking to the Vietnamese students and hard for them to accept. The absence of honorific terms in the English language compounds the problem and makes the Vietnamese students feel uneasy and uncomfortable when talking with their teachers. They are reluctant to ask questions in class because such behavior seems aggressive and disrespectful to them. Their confusion is increased when, to their surprise, their teachers reward such behavior in class.

Since they are not accustomed to talking in front of the class, they are shy and uncomfortable when asked to do so in the American classroom. They do not volunteer answers because they have been taught to be modest. If they need help, they probably will not ask for it.

*The language barrier.* The language problem can be very acute when there is only one or very few Vietnamese students in the school. The lack of communication or understanding between the child and the school authority can cause a small misunderstanding to grow into a large emotional or discipline problem. I remember a woman principal who asked me if a little boy in a kindergarten class knew Kung Fu because of his uncontrolled strength. Being the only Vietnamese in the school, he was totally confused and bewildered with no one to turn to for help. His tension had built to an explosive limit. Once explanations were given to him in Vietnamese, he was a changed child.

The language barrier also limits the child's social contacts with American peers. A high school teacher was concerned when a Vietnamese boy changed from being friendly and cooperative to being antisocial. A talk with the boy revealed that he did not know enough English to communicate with his peers, and as a result, he was slowly withdrawing from them. He was frustrated because he could not say "maybe later" or "not at this time" when he was asked to join in an activity. His abrupt responses seemed rude to his classmates, further frustrating him, and in effect, discouraging other social interaction.

Many of the directions and explanations in the American classroom are verbal . . . You can imagine the tremendous amount of self-control and self-discipline that a non-English-speaking child must maintain in order to keep quiet and not disturb others. He can rely only on visual clues. These are not always dependable and mean that the child will always be one step behind the others. This causes his/her reactions and behavior to be out of place. (9, p. 13–14)

## Identity Conflicts

While they are acculturating, immigrant students may experience identity conflicts. These arise if they are pressured at home and in their community to maintain the traditional values of their culture while at the same time they are pressured at school to accept new cultural values. Students sometimes adopt the culture of the school and try to abandon the traditions of their families. If they do this, they may be punished by their parents and suffer from feelings of guilt and shame. Other students may reject the pressures of school and so satisfy their parents, but by doing so, they risk getting into trouble with their teachers and school administrators (7).

Certain minority students born in the United States are brought up by parents who want them to acculturate totally to the culture of the school. Many other students, though, are caught between conflicting messages and pressures regarding the right and wrong ways to live their lives. The schools' role in exacerbating students' identity conflicts is described in the following statements by two Hispanic educators.

> Cultural conflicts between home and school cause youth to either choose one or the other. This causes conflicts in personality, adjustment, etc. He needs to act one way at school and when he gets home, uses a different language and a different set of cultural values. If the school allowed him to be himself, he wouldn't have the problem. (4, p. 122)

> Schools are encouraging us to lose our cultural identity. Ask any high school student to name a Mexican-American actor—he can't. Ask him to sing a complete Spanish song—he can't. Ask an elementary child why he brings his lunch to school on Mexican food day at the cafeteria—he doesn't like Mexican food! Acculturation! (4, p. 75)

## *Refugees*

Students who have fled war, famine, and other forms of suffering in their native lands can also bring the added problems these experiences caused with them to school. Below is a description of the problems such experiences can create for, among others, Southeast Asian students:

> Vietnamese students came to the United States not only as immigrants to this new land, but also as refugees. Immigrants leave their homeland on their own volition, with many possibilities of motivation for the move, whereas refugees have "no choice but to leave or to suffer." Refugees are in fact "driven away from their homeland"—they are "pushed out." Studies have shown that this type of forced migration and the experience of being uprooted causes more psychological problems to refugees than to immigrants. With this in mind, an educator must be concerned about the mental well-being of students who have lived in conditions of violence and sociopolitical turmoil before coming to this country. Such students have been exposed to loss, extended violence, prolonged threat, and terrorization. They may have witnessed violence inflicted to members of their family or to close friends. Their exodus to this country has been paved with dangers and life-threatening situations such as poverty, starvation, drowning at sea, rape, murder, piracy, life in a refugee camp, and the possibility of the separation of the family. (6, p. 1)

## *Identification*

It takes immigrant students who have spent the first four, five, or more years of their lives somewhere else a number of years to acculturate to the way things are done in the United States even if they and their parents want to learn the new ways as quickly as possible. Thus, if a student from another country hasn't been here at least for a few years, you can assume that her classroom behavior will be influenced by the student's original culture. If the student has recently arrived and is just beginning to attend school, you can also anticipate that she will experience some degree of culture shock.

A student's cumulative folder should include the information you need to determine where he was born and how long he has been in this country. The folder may also contain information about whether the student attended school prior to coming here and, if so, the kind of school experiences the student had. This is extremely important for Southeast Asian students who may have spent two, three, four, or more years in refugee camps where there were no schools and for students from rural areas in developing countries where schooling may not have been compulsory or even available. If the cumulative folder doesn't contain this information, you should be able to obtain it from the student if he is old enough. If not, you must get it from his parents.

## Helping Immigrant Students

Imposing the school's culture on immigrant students without regard to the culture they bring with them can cause them to experience even greater degrees of culture shock than they already do. Such insensitivity can result in students acting out this shock in the ways described above. But building bridges between their home culture and the culture of the classroom can help manage the severity of the culture shock they are going through. If you have an immigrant student in your classroom, he or she will feel less culture shock if an assistant teacher, a paraprofessional, or a parent volunteer from the student's culture is available to help the student learn about the new culture. Another approach is to assign another student from the same culture who is knowledgeable about both cultures to be your student's "buddy." You can also include aspects of the student's home culture in the classroom by putting up pictures of her native country, arranging for classroom demonstrations of the cooking, music, or dancing of the student's place of birth, and discussing the student's country of origin. This makes the classroom environment a little less strange and helps smooth the student's transition.

Tolerating symptoms of culture shock in the classroom when they occur, so long as they aren't too disruptive, will avoid putting extra pressure on your student to adjust faster than she is able to. Providing alternatives when the activity of the moment isn't appropriate can sometimes prevent her from having unpleasant experiences. For example, some students may not be ready for coed recreational activities, competitive games, or showering nude in front of others. You can make other options available to them. Or providing alternative foods and snacks to replace what the student's religion prohibits her from eating or is unaccustomed to eating can show both your concern and respect for the student and her customs. Such sensitivity avoids placing the student in a conflict situation.

*Language and Teaching Style*    Research indicates that instructing students for part of the day in their native languages while they are learning a second language helps them adjust better to attending schools where almost every transaction is in English (8). The Bilingual Education Act of 1988 provides that limited-English-proficient students may be instructed bilingually for three years and up to five years if needed in order to bridge the transition from their native language to English. Adapting your instructional

*Teaching others about their cultures can increase students' pride in themselves.*

and classroom management techniques to the learning styles of these students while they acquire the skills necessary to learn in American classrooms can also reduce the likelihood that they will be frustrated, angry, anxious, or resentful in class.

*Readiness Skills*    Before they begin school, some immigrant students are exposed to their own rich culture instead of the cultural experiences that most mainstream educators and school administrators expect and value. As a result, they may begin school already behind because they don't know what their teachers expect them to know about the alphabet, numbers, colors, and places, even though they know a great deal about other areas not included in the traditional curriculum. If their teachers don't capitalize on what these students do know, they may soon fall even further behind. Then, frustrated by trying to produce at the level of the other students, they may act out their anger by behaving in ways that are disruptive to other students. Or they may give up trying, withdraw, and tune out their teachers.

If you have an immigrant student whose academic readiness skills and knowledge vary from those of most students in the class, you can prevent him from feeling frustrated and like a failure by individualizing your curriculum for that student. By starting at the student's current level of functioning, including the concepts and readiness skills the student has acquired, and using teaching techniques that complement the student's learning styles, you could reduce or even eliminate behavior problems you might otherwise have to cope with.

*Identity Conflicts*   You can avoid having your students develop identity conflicts by not pressuring them to do things the way you are used to having them done. Examples of such pressure could include calling on students who don't volunteer or feel comfortable speaking up in class, asking students to state publicly whether they agree with the previous speaker, or requiring students to admit their mistakes and apologize for them verbally when their culturally determined ways are just as effective.

The techniques for reducing culture shock described above and suggestions for adapting educational techniques to students' learning styles that follow will also reduce pressure on students to adopt the school's culture and reject the culture of their families and neighborhoods. Ramirez and Castañeda (7) suggest that educators include aspects of the language, heritage, cultural values, and teaching styles students are accustomed to at home in the school and classroom environments so their students will experience less pressure to either acculturate completely at the expense of the students' original cultures or reject the school's culture in order to maintain their own.

As one person, your influence on your students' identity conflicts is limited; a school-wide approach initiated and encouraged by school administrators can accomplish much more. Still, it would certainly benefit your students for you to do whatever you personally can to help them avoid identity conflicts.

# Culturally Different Students

Although America has been called a melting pot, many descendants of the various groups of people who have immigrated here tend to maintain aspects of their original cultures. As a result, students in schools represent and reflect many different cultural groups. These cultural differences that exist between teachers and school administrators and minority students in the school can contribute to behavior problems in numerous ways.

## Learning and Behavioral Styles

Culture influences how people perceive, think, relate, and learn. Some of the many learning or behavioral style differences observed among people of different cultures are:

Whether people rely more on internal clues—their own feelings, ideas, values, and the like—to understand the world around them (field independent) or on information from their surroundings (field dependent/sensitive).

Whether they prefer solitary activities, personal time, and more distant aloof relationships (field independent) or are sociable, gregarious, and interested in helping people (field dependent/sensitive).

Whether they work better individually (field independent) or in groups (field dependent/sensitive).

Whether they are relatively indifferent to the feelings, ideas, opinions, attitudes, and so on of others when they decide what to do or how to do it (field independent) or are sensitive to and responsive to what others feel and think and how their actions might affect others (field dependent/sensitive).

Whether they prefer to maintain considerable physical distance when they talk with others (field independent) or to be in close proximity to them (field dependent/sensitive).

Whether they are indifferent to praise and criticism from others (field independent) or react intensely to being praised and criticized (field dependent/sensitive).

Whether they function better in competitive situations (field independent) or under cooperative conditions (field dependent/sensitive).

Whether they prefer to work independently (field independent) or seek feedback, guidance, and approval from others (field dependent/sensitive).

Whether they prefer abstract, theoretical tasks such as math computational problems (field independent) or tasks that involve human issues and concerns such as math word problems (field dependent/sensitive).

Whether they respond better to impersonal rewards like money, toys, candy, time off, and so on (field independent) or personal rewards such as praise, smiles, pats on the back, and the like (field dependent/sensitive) (7, 13, 14, 18–20, 27–33, 35, 41, 42)

While research indicates that these field-sensitive and field-independent learning and behavioral style differences exist among people, it's clear that no individual is completely field independent or field sensitive. People—and even an entire culture—may function in a predominantly field-sensitive or field-independent way, but aspects of the opposite learning and behavioral styles also function in their personalities.

Depending on the learning or behavioral style that predominates in their culture, some students may have learning styles that clash with their teachers' teaching styles. For example, research indicates that Black students tend to be field-dependent/sensitive learners. Ramirez and Price-Williams (35), Triandis (40), and Valentine (41) attribute this to their African roots. Blacks tend to rely on external cues and information when forming judgments, opinions, and so forth (11, 22, 34, 36, 38). They also tend to be more people oriented, sensitive to others' feelings, gregarious, sociable, and interested in helping others (23, 26, 39). As an expression of this, they maintain less physical distance between them-

| *FIELD INDEPENDENT* | *FIELD DEPENDENT* |
| --- | --- |
| Internal cues | External cues |
| Solitary activities | Group activities |
| Indifferent to others' feelings and opinions | Sensitive to others' feelings and opinions |
| Considerable physical distance | Close proximity |
| Indifferent to praise and criticism | Responsive to praise and criticism |
| Competitive | Cooperative |
| Self-motivated | Seek feedback and guidance |
| Abstract, theoretical tasks | Humanized problems |
| Impersonal rewards | Personalized rewards |

selves and others (10, 12). In addition, they are more sensitive to both praise and criticism than field-independent people (15, 21). Blacks also tend to learn better when material is presented in an oral/aural rather than visual manner (24, 37).

Black Student

Is highly affective

Uses language requiring a wide use of many coined interjections (sometimes profanity)

Expresses herself or himself through considerable body language

Relies on words that depend upon context for meaning and that have little meaning in themselves

Prefers using expressions that have several connotations

Adopts a systematic use of nuances of intonation and body language such as eye movement and positioning

Prefers oral-aural modalities for learning communication

Is highly sensitive to others' nonverbal cues

Seeks to be people oriented

Is sociocentric

Uses internal cues for problem solving

Feels highly empathetic

Likes spontaneity

Adapts rapidly to novel stimuli (25, p. 38)

Is there a black learning style, a learning style especially suited to innercity students? I believe there is. Use of such a style does not mean lowering standards or expectations, however. It does mean recognizing the students' strengths and utilizing them. (16, p. 755)

*It's extremely difficult to succeed with students without understanding something about their cultural backgrounds.*

Afro-Americans apparently attend to different facial cues, different emotional overtones, and receive different sets of information from people or words. This apparent greater people sensitivity suggests that field-dependency is the cognitive style orientation most often in use. (39, p. 10–11)

Because many—if not most—teachers employ a field-independent teaching style and use primarily visual materials to teach, they unknowingly condemn many of their Black students to have learning and behavioral problems in school. (As we will see later in this chapter, the same applies to large numbers of Hispanic students.) When students with one learning or behavioral style are taught by teachers who use a different teaching style, the students often have difficulty learning the material in the way it's presented and in conforming to their teachers' behavioral expectations. Like many students who aren't succeeding in school, they may feel stupid and lose their motivation to succeed in school and to conform to the classroom rules and regulations. This may help explain why teachers like and relate better to students whose learning styles match their teaching styles (17). Since the predominant teaching style in American schools is field independent, Black, Hispanic, and other field-dependent/sensitive students are the ones most at risk for problems resulting from a mismatch.

---

*Self-Quiz: Evaluating Your Teaching Style*

Ask a colleague to evaluate your teaching style with the Ramirez and Castañeda Behavior Rating Scale and compare your teaching style to the learning styles of your students.

---

## Cultural Misperceptions

Educators can actually misperceive and misunderstand students' behaviors when they see and interpret them from their own cultural perspective. This means they can perceive behavior problems that don't exist, not notice problems that do exist, misunderstand the causes of students' behaviors, and use culturally inappropriate responses to deal with students' behavior problems.

*Nonexistent Problems*    Students who come from different racial, ethnic, or socioeconomic backgrounds than their teachers and the school administrators may have values, goals, and interests that are highly acceptable to their families and communities but not to the school community. For example, teachers may incorrectly think that students brought up not to be assertive or to volunteer their opinions unless encouraged by adults are shy or insecure. And students who are encouraged at home to work independently rather than with others and to judge their accomplishments for themselves rather than rely on the opinions of others may seem like they don't care about others. As a result, educators may not be able to accept behavior that the students and their parents find completely appropriate. Let's look at how two Black professionals see this problem. Gay (46) reports:

> Blacks are accustomed to integrating mental, emotional, and physical activities. Schools tend to encourage compartmentalizing these areas. The Black child's involvement in cognitive classroom activities is likely to be signaled by vocal responses, exuberance, and physical movement. Teachers consider this behavior disruptive because they expect that one can be highly stimulated to intellectual activities without involving affective or psychomotor dimensions. . . .

> What teachers view as total chaos and noise may be structured activity to Blacks. What teachers consider planned activities may be perceived by Black students as prohibiting constraints. The problem of perception stems from different sets of expectations and cultural sensibilities. (47, p. 32, 33)

Elaborating on the way Blacks respond to others when they are reciting, performing, and so on, Gay states:

> There is more total interaction involved; all those in the social environment must play some active response role if it is only through such responses as "right on brother" . . . The Black child in performing looks for verbal and kinesic support from his peers. The

teacher hears noise and is threatened. The child's success is measured by his peers by the extent to which he stimulates the others to provide responses. When this behavior is manifested, teachers see an undisciplined and discourteous group of Blacks.

This situation arises because contrarily in white, middle-class culture the relationship between a performer and his audience demands a show of passivity on the part of the latter . . . When Black children's classroom behavior is assessed using this frame of reference, the conclusions are foreordained. The culturally determined Black ways of demonstrating interest and involvement are interpreted as restlessness, inattentiveness, and sometimes hostility. (46, p. 38)

Dent (45) advises:

Most teachers are unprepared to accept the active, aggressive behavior of Black boys. The aggressive behavior of a Black child is immediately interpreted as hostile. The teacher's expectation is that the student should be compliant, docile, and responsive to authority. The student is expected to conform to a standard of behavior that the teacher is familiar with, the compliant child standard that was indicative of the teacher's upbringing. It is as though the teacher makes an unwritten contract with the student, "If you don't behave, I won't (or can't) teach you." (45, p. 78)

*Unnecessary Problems*   These cultural misperceptions can cause problems where none existed. To quote Dent again:

The next step in the process is that the teacher will make futile attempts to control the aggressive, active behavior, but abandon those efforts very quickly and conclude that the child is unmanageable. The child resists the teacher's efforts to control the behavior. More often than not, the behavior becomes more unmanageable. As the disruptive behavior increases, the amount of time and effort available to devote to attending to the instructions and acquiring academic skills decreases. In all likelihood the student prefers to avoid the academic work. Within a short period of time it becomes apparent that this unmanageable student is not functioning at grade level. This then can be interpreted, depending on the tolerance level of the teachers, as a learning problem and a justification for referral for special placement. The longer the time span involved, the greater the learning problem. (45, p. 78–79)

---

## THEORY FOCUS: DENT ON BLACK STUDENTS

Harold Dent has contributed much to our understanding of the reasons why traditional educational methods are often inappropriate for Black students. He coauthored the Black Psychological Association's position paper that explains how standardized tests can be biased against Black students, describes the kinds of abuses that often result from their use, and calls for a moratorium on their use with Blacks. In other published articles, he has focused attention on how and why non-Black educators often misunderstand the behavior of Black students and so use culturally inappropriate classroom management techniques with them. Dent currently serves as the director of a project designed to pilot and evaluate alternative assessment models for Black students.

This kind of mismatch between the teacher's way of working and the student's way of learning or being is not reserved for only Black or Hispanic students. The following quotation provides insight into the kinds of cultural misperceptions educators can make with Chinese students.

> The child does not volunteer to answer. He just sits and waits for his teacher to call upon him. So in the eyes of the American teacher, Asian children, as compared to the American students, are dull, passive, unresponsive, and lack initiative. Most of the time, Chinese (Asian) students are ignored because of their absolute silence in class. (56, p. 11)

Examples of the kinds of cultural misperceptions educators can make with Southeast Asian students are illustrated in the quotations that follow.

> American straightforwardness is considered at best impolite, if not brutal. In Indochina, one does not come directly to the point. To do so is, for an American, a mark of honesty and forthrightness while a person from Indochina sees it as a lack of intelligence or courtesy. Falsehood carries no moral structure for a Cambodian, Laotian, or Vietnamese. The essential question is not whether a statement is true or false, but what the intention of the statement is. Does it facilitate interpersonal harmony? Does it indicate a wish to change the subject? Hence, one must learn the "heart" of the speaker through his/her words.

> In Indochina, one thinks very carefully before speaking. The American style of "speaking one's mind" is thus misunderstood.

> The Vietnamese literal equivalent of the English word "Yes" is "Da" (pronounced "Ya" in the Southern Vietnamese dialect). However, whereas the English "Yes" means unequivocally "Yes," the Vietnamese "Da" means a variety of things. In the final analysis, it can mean "Yes," but in general usage it merely means "I am politely listening to you," and it does not at all mean that "I agree with you." The listener may disagree with what he hears, but due to his politeness, cannot say no. His English "Yes" for him conveys the polite and noncommittal Vietnamese "Da," but to the American it can carry only its English meaning. Thus, the Vietnamese may appear insincere, or even stupid, to the American. (53, p. 6, 7, 19)

It's easy to understand how educators who do not know these facts could misinterpret their students' responses. For example, they may think their students have just agreed to do what they have been asked to do and so become angry and frustrated when the students don't follow through after saying "yes."

*Unnoticed Problems* Educators who are not tuned to the ways students from other cultures communicate can miss a request for help or assistance. They may not even realize that their students have problems. This is brought out clearly in the following description of one Hispanic cultural characteristic.

> Hispanics are expected to be sensitive to the needs, feelings, and desires of others so that it is unnecessary for others to be embarrassed by asking for help or understanding or to be left alone. Males especially may rely on the sensitivity of others and express their needs only in indirect and subtle ways . . . Therefore educators should be tuned into

these subtle expressions of need. They should not assume that because Hispanic students have not expressed a need for help or understanding in a direct and forthright manner, they do not need special attention or consideration. (4, p. 96)

*Incorrect Causes*   Educators may mistakenly attribute behavior problems that are culturally determined to other causes. For example, educators who are unaware of their students' identity conflicts may attribute their behavior to other causes such as lack of interest and motivation to succeed in school, lack of respect for teachers, poor parenting, and other reasons. Then, instead of responding with understanding to their students' identity conflicts or helping them resolve these conflicts, they are likely to use inappropriate techniques to squash the objectionable behavior. Some of the ways white teachers can misunderstand the causes of Black students' behavior are revealed in the following quotation.

The Black children displayed unfamiliar behavior that teachers found difficult to adjust to and cope with. At one time or another teachers commented:

"There's so much pent-up anger in them."

"They talk so loud."

"When he came here he was totally nonverbal."

"Did you ever see such antsyness?"

Teachers called attention to kids who used "foul" language ("I'll never get used to that"), to children who spoke out in class, to antisocial behavior (fighting, spitting at other children, stealing), to short attention spans, to immaturity (e.g., thumb sucking). Each of these behaviors made the job of teaching much more difficult than it had been prior to desegregation . . .

The first and most basic teacher response to the number of problems presented by the Black children was to devise some personal explanation for the unfamiliar behavior. While these explanations varied somewhat from teacher to teacher, a common theme emerged. On several occasions unfamiliar and disturbing behavior (whether antisocial actions or difficulty mastering classroom work) was attributed to problems in a child's environment. Comments such as "I think Ben is brutalized at home" were offered as explanations for children's actions or attitudes. To a lesser extent I heard references made to children's previous schools not having demanded enough of them. Whether these explanations accurately represented fact or not, they made the problems understandable and to some extent served to legitimize the approach taken by the teachers to ameliorate the problems. (50, p. 21)

Another specific example of how whites can misinterpret the behavior of Blacks occurs in the different ways in which eye contact between individuals is interpreted in the two cultures. Blacks tend to avoid direct eye contact with authority figures or elders as a sign of respect and submission; they maintain eye contact with authority figures when they wish to communicate disrespect and rebellion (44, 48, 49). Whites, in contrast, tend to interpret eye contact as an indication of trustworthiness, sincerity, and positive feelings; averting one's eyes indicates insincerity, guilt, or lack of positive feelings (48, 49, 52). The expression "Look me in the eye and tell me the truth" expresses the white perception of what eye contact means. Thus, when Black students avert their eyes while being confronted about their behavior, their teachers may misinterpret their lack of eye contact as indicating insincerity, guilt, lack of positive feelings, and so on rather than respect and submission.

Johnson describes the problem this way:

> Avoidance of eye contact by a Black person communicates "I am in a subordinate role and I respect your authority over me," while the dominant culture member may interpret avoidance of eye contact as "Here is a shifty, unreliable person I'm dealing with." (49, p. 18)

Differing interpretations about what eye contact means is only one small example of how cultural differences can quickly generate misunderstandings. An example of one way non-Hispanic teachers can misinterpret Hispanic students' reticence to voluntarily participate in classroom discussions is explained by Burger.

> Anglo education emphasizes verbal inquisitiveness, an argumentative discourse that is termed "forensics." In the Anglo-dominated school system, the child is encouraged, even pressured, both to ask and analyze questions . . . There is consequently a built-in clash between the ethnic (Raza) home tradition and the Anglo school tradition of constant and formal questioning. The WASP "inquisition" would be highly hostile to the Mexican-American attitude of tolerance. In South Texas, for example, it is inexcusable to try to change views. (43, p. 64)

The tendency of Hispanic students to avoid openly disagreeing with another or to appear to challenge another's point of view has been observed by other authors as well (4, 51). Educators unaware of this culturally determined tendency to avoid expressing personal opinions especially about controversial issues can easily misinterpret their Hispanic students' lack of participation.

*Inappropriate Techniques*    Even educators who perceive certain students' behavior problems as being culturally determined may still respond with techniques that are inappropriate. Unless educators have the knowledge needed to adapt their approaches to the cultural realities of their students, this is a possibility.

*Hispanics:* An educator who wishes to communicate effectively with Hispanic students benefits from understanding the differences between the cultures and how these impact the classroom.

> Hispanic parents tend to speak more politely and indirectly when they criticize or discipline their children. In the United States educators are much more gruff and direct with students . . . Some Hispanic students, especially males, may interpret the gruff or more direct manner of Anglos as an indication that educators do not consider them worthy or deserving of a proper relationship. When educators speak to them in a matter-of-fact or authoritarian manner, they may feel insulted, angry, or resentful and lose respect for these educators and the desire to cooperate or conform. (4, p. 102)

*Blacks:* The following quotation exemplifies the view of many Black educators that using extrinsic consequences to modify Black students' behavior does them more harm than good.

Perhaps one of the most overriding criticisms of externally oriented management techniques is the tendency of teachers to use these approaches as control tactics rather than teaching students to become self-directing individuals . . . Many otherwise promising teachers resort to interpreting and utilizing traditional management approaches as control tactics, which often results in making students behaviorally stifled, docile, overcompliant, and further doubt their abilities. Additionally, the use of these approaches in this vein has the tendency to foster impulsive conformity in students and often turns them off to school and learning . . . Many behaviorally disordered Black children have histories of failure and have developed predispositions to expect failure and, thus, are often unwilling to take chances in learning situations . . . Given this reality, management approaches which result in these students doubting their abilities further exacerbate an already regressive situation for the life progression of exceptional Black children. (54, p. 1–4)

*Hawaiians:* At times the very techniques teachers choose to motivate individual students backfire because of different cultural values.

There is evidence that Hawaiians are seldom concerned with the pursuit of success for the purely personal satisfaction involved . . . Hawaiians apparently derive little personal pleasure from competing successfully against others and, in fact, avoid individual competition. . . . As an illustration, many children in our school refused to accept material rewards (e.g., cokes or candy) for high grades or successful competition unless the rewards could be shared with their friends. (55, p. 146)

## Unequal Cross-Cultural Relationships

The history of the relationship between the students' cultural groups and the group the teacher represents—usually the dominant culture—can affect a student's classroom behavior. A student who has personally experienced prejudice, oppression, rejection, or abuse by members of the white dominant culture or who has been brought up to anticipate and be wary of such treatment may be suspicious of the teacher's motives. Thus, the student may reject the teacher's friendship, act provocatively and disrespectfully, or rebel against the teacher's authority.

The following quotations from a Black educator represent how some Blacks view the educational system in the United States. Whether one agrees or disagrees with these opinions, one can imagine how they might affect the classroom behavior of students who share them.

The educational system's overt practices of segregation and discrimination, reckless foisting of programs upon entire populations without so much as a cursory consideration of their culture, values, and heritage, and its dehumanization of students through corporal punishment and rejection simply because they do not present themselves as "ideal clients," have resulted in oppression of its Black students . . . It is obvious that Black people cannot sit idly by and watch white conceptions of normality and abnormality or appropriateness and inappropriateness of school behavior be foisted upon their children . . . Black self-determination, Black pride, and Black consciousness are the values which inner-city schools must teach . . . Until the establishment adopts a positive perspective of Blacks and builds educational programs which are special for Blacks, determined by Blacks, then Blacks have little alternative except to reject what is offered as racist, stigmatizing, and helping to maintain a vast number of children in good and bad "nigger roles." Education must support our culture as we determine it, as it can do in a multi-social, pluralistic, technological, and humanistic society. (58, p. 241, 246, 247, 249)

In a similar vein, when discussing the fact that Black students tend to be suspended from school at a much higher rate than white students, Bennett and Harris state:

The exact causes of disproportionality among Black students are difficult to establish. However, our broader findings show that these causes are related to an overall orientation of white predominance which includes institutional and individual racism. Sources of racism are difficult to pinpoint because they originate in a social context beyond the school, but this does not relieve the school from taking action to mediate racism . . .

Many of the teachers would not live in a desegregated neighborhood, did not favor mandatory school desegregation, felt the civil rights movement had done more harm than good, and felt that the problems of prejudice were exaggerated. One-third believed that Blacks and whites should not be allowed to intermarry. Furthermore, the majority of the teachers perceived their white students to be superior intellectually, socially, and in other characteristics related to school achievement. Given what we know about the power of teacher expectations, the picture is grim for many Black students. (57, p. 420–421)

In discussing the attitudes of Black students toward white educators, Gay and Abrahams report:

The most important dimension of the Black stereotype of whites is that Black children are taught early to be suspicious of whites. In its overt form this attitude comes out, "I don't trust any white person because I know they don't like me." More covertly, this attitude emerges as a continuing skepticism of whites. (47, p. 332)

Black students aren't the only ones who are hostile toward or suspicious of white teachers. Speaking of the current attitude of some Hispanic students toward their teachers, a Hispanic educator states:

Chicanos are intolerant of, and hostile toward, whites who approach them with the usual racist stance in terms of language, attitudes, and behavior. Because of their new self-perception, they are apt to cause whites, particularly those who harbor residuals of racism, a great deal of anxiety. Therefore, the educator who is unable or unwilling to acknowledge the new concept of this group is apt to be ineffectual in relating to them. (4, p. 121)

Another Hispanic educator states:

The Anglo image of Latin Americans is very similar to that of Chicanos. Both are seen as foreign and inferior. When our children start school, they are made to feel inferior merely because they are different from the Anglos. (4, p. 151)

Writing about the attitudes of Hispanic immigrant parents toward school, a third Hispanic educator writes:

> I have found that many Mexican immigrants who do not have legal documentation to be in this country often are unwilling to question any educational practice, are afraid and/or unable to come to school . . . are reluctant to answer questions about their family or give any information they think could lead to deportation. (4, p. 152)

An individual teacher may not merit such feelings on the part of his or her students, but their existence in the students' attitudes can adversely affect how they function in class and in school.

Students from different cultures who are alienated, hostile, and suspicious of the dominant society and its institutions and organizations can bring this hostility to school. They may disbelieve and reject out of hand much of what they are taught in class. For example, even at a young age, they may already disbelieve the concept "your friend, the police officer." As they progress through the grades, they may reject both their teachers' and the textbooks' interpretations of American and world history as well as the standard explanations of how the American economic and political systems function. In addition, their opinions about the best way to solve the current issues facing America and the world may be at odds with those of their teachers. They may believe, sometimes with justification, that their teachers are insensitive to their cultural needs and indifferent—or even prejudiced—toward them. As a result, they may be suspicious of their teachers' motives.

Although some students keep their feelings to themselves in class, many others—especially the older ones—act them out. In doing so, they may repeatedly challenge their teachers' statements and demonstrate a lack of respect and disregard for their teachers' authority by not following rules, acting bored, making sarcastic and provocative comments, and purposely disrupting the class. Some students may withdraw from what they consider to be an irrelevant and prejudicial education by tuning their teachers out, arriving late, and cutting class. These students may behave the same way in your class regardless of whether you merit their reactions because of what you represent to them, at least until they get to know and trust you.

## Identification

Ramirez and Castañeda (7) have pointed out that minority students have three options for resolving their cultural identity conflicts. They can maintain the values, beliefs, and practices of the home and reject the mainstream culture (traditional); they can reject the culture of the homeland and adopt the mainstream culture (acculturated); or they can identify with and accept both cultural systems and use each in appropriate situations (bicultural). Each choice has implications for classroom behavior and teaching.

Students who are acculturated or bicultural are minority students, but their learning and behavioral styles may parallel majority students. Thus, merely knowing a student's surname, ethnic background, skin color, and so on isn't enough to determine whether she or he should be considered culturally different. The following process can assist you determine whether cultural differences may be contributing to minority students' behavior problems.

*Informal Assessment*   Observe the students' behavior. Comparing your problem students' behavior to the typical ways nonassimilated youngsters of their cultures behave can help you pinpoint whether their problems are characteristic of students with their cultural backgrounds or are likely to be caused by other factors. If you aren't sure, answer the following questions about their behavior.

1. Do students socialize only with students from their same ethnic or social backgrounds, only with students from the mainstream culture, or with all types of students?

2. What language do bilingual students prefer to use when they aren't in class (at lunch, recess, after school): English only, another language, or a mixture of both?

3. Do students dress like mainstream students or in ways that identify them as members of a different group?

4. What do the statements students make about the mainstream culture and the culture of their homes reflect about their cultural identity? Do they express pride in their ethnic or racial background or reject it? Do they comment positively or negatively about the mainsteam culture?

5. Do students' reactions to national and ethnic holidays indicate a bicultural identity or a preference for one type of holiday over the other?

6. Are the students' behavior problems typical of students with their cultural background?

*Interview the student*: Ask students if any of the classroom procedures, routines, rules, or social patterns conflict with how they are used to doing things at home or in school. You can also ask students if they ever feel pressured in school to behave in ways that make them uncomfortable because they behave differently at home or in their neighborhoods.

*Consult with colleagues*: If you aren't knowledgeable about your students' cultures, ask colleagues (other teachers, paraprofessionals, and so on) who are, to observe the students and tell you whether they think cultural differences could be contributing to their behavior problems.

*Formal Assessment*   A number of instruments for evaluating the acculturation of minority students exists (59–62). Among those currently available for assessing learning and teaching styles, the one that appears to be especially useful for minority students who may be field dependent or sensitive is the Ramirez and Castañeda Behavior Rating Scales. (See Chapter 8 for examples of items from these scales and other learning-style assessment instruments.) By applying the rating scales both to your students and yourself, you can determine if a match or mismatch exists between their individual learning styles and your teaching style.

Acculturation Scales

| | AGES/LEVEL | NUMBER OF ITEMS |
|---|---|---|
| Children's Hispanic Background Scale | 9–16 years | 30 |
| Children's Acculturation Scale | 1–6 grade | 10 |
| Bicultural Involvement Questionnaire | High School | 33 |
| School Situation Picture Stories Technique | 9–11 years | 7 |

## *Developing a Cultural Guide for Culturally Appropriate Classroom Management*

When a student's culturally determined behavior isn't acceptable in school, it is a mistake to maintain that the school's way is best or to require your student to choose between how his family and neighborhood expect him to behave and the way school officials expect him to behave. Instead, explain to the student that the way he is behaving may be perfectly okay for his home or neighborhood, but in school it's necessary to do some things differently. For example, explain that using tough, aggressive street language or calling someone *gordo* (fatso) or *flaco* (skinny) is fine for situations where people talk that way, but in school he has to learn to speak to people another way. State clearly that this is not because the school's way is better, but because a student needs to be able to function in both worlds. Or in other circumstances, explain that while you understand and approve of students' desires to help each other, whispering the correct answers to those called on to recite doesn't really help them learn. Or when students fight on school grounds, make it clear that you aren't criticizing them for the way they settle their disagreements but rather that school rules prohibit students from fighting on school grounds. When correcting your student, don't evaluate her behavior in terms of concepts such as good and bad or right and wrong. Instead use concepts such as appropriate and inappropriate for a particular setting or situation. Approaching your students in these ways may keep any resentment they may feel about having to behave differently in school to a manageable level.

Certain behavior of students from other cultures is acceptable, but it interferes with their ability to function as well as they could in school. For example, students who work at a slow pace, request a great deal of feedback and direction, express their needs only in extremely subtle indirect ways, or resist admitting they don't know or understand something are not prepared to function in the typical classroom. But their behavior isn't disruptive; it doesn't interfere with the rights of others and in other situations it would be fine. Teachers can help students who function in ways that limit their ability to succeed in mainstream classrooms by adapting *both* their classroom management and instructional techniques to their students' cultural characteristics. In addition, they can assist them in functioning biculturally in school.

The following is a list of questions you can ask about a student's culture so you can develop a guide to that culture. This, in turn, will help you adapt your classroom management techniques to characteristics of your student's culture. One of the best sources for answers to these questions is a colleague whose cultural background is similar to the student's.

## Interpersonal Relationships

We tend to take something as everyday as child-adult relationships very much for granted. This, however, can be a major area for differences between cultures.

### Relationships with Adults

*Formal versus informal relationships:* Do parents function more as aloof authority figures or do they maintain a warm, close personal relationship with their youngsters? Would your student be more comfortable in class if you maintained a formal relationship with her or acted in a warm, personal, informal manner? Although most authors encourage teachers to develop warm relationships with students, students from certain cultures may prefer a more formal relationship.

*Dependent versus independent:* Are youngsters trained to accomplish things on their own and to arrive at their own independent opinions and decisions, or are they brought up to be dependent on the aid, support, opinions, and feedback of their parents? Is your student prepared to be relatively self-reliant and independent in class, or will he require a great deal of support and assistance from you? Preparing students to function independently is a worthwhile goal, but field-dependent/sensitive students may require more time and assistance than others to adapt to field-independent teaching styles.

*Perception of authority:* Are youngsters expected not to speak unless spoken to, not ask questions, and to obey their elders just because they are the authorities? Or can they disagree with adults and ask their elders to justify why they are requiring them to do certain things or punishing them? Should you expect your student to accept your opinions, rules, and consequences simply because you are in charge, or will you be expected to justify yourself to the student? Although many experts advise teachers to be authoritative rather than authoritarian (Chapter 3), students from other cultures may require help in adjusting to an adult who is authoritative and not authoritarian. These students may also have difficulty participating in democratic classrooms in which the students are actively involved in establishing rules, procedures, and consequences.

Are the authority roles of male and female adults the same? Is one gender the authority figure and the other the nurturer? Does each gender express and enforce its authority in the same or different ways? Is your student prepared to accept you as an authority figure regardless of your gender? Does he or she expect you to use techniques to enforce your expectations that are appropriate for your gender?

*Perception of educators:* Are educators seen as fountains of information that students passively absorb, or are they expected to function more as guides who lead and stimulate students' active learning? Which types of relationship will make your student most comfortable? Active participatory learning is more effective than passive learning, but until some students from other cultures learn how to function in this environment, they may require additional direct education and supervision during self-directed activities.

*Role of adolescents:* Is the relationship between adolescents and adult authority figures more like that between children and adults or between adult and adult? What special rights and privileges do adolescents enjoy that are denied to children? What special classroom management techniques should you use with your student because she is a teenager? Which techniques that are appropriate with younger students are inappropriate with adolescents?

**The Individual Vis-à-Vis the Group**    Different cultures have different values about group loyalty and the importance of the individual.

*Identification with the group:* What groups are youngsters taught to identify with: the immediate family, extended family, friends, peers, strangers? Can you expect your student to experience a sense of loyalty to her or his friends in the class or to other students with whom the student is not particularly friendly?

Fostering group cohesiveness is recommended as a way of avoiding behavior problems. In American schools, students are encouraged to feel that they are a part of the class as a whole. Thus, minority students taught to be loyal only to a small circle of friends may require special help in identifying with and cooperating with students outside of this circle. You may also have to encourage them to select students beyond this circle when it's their turn to choose committee or team members.

*Individual versus group rights:* Does the student's culture stress the rights of individuals, or does it emphasize the individual's duties and obligations to the group? Are youngsters encouraged to establish their own goals and strive for individual excellence, or are they expected to be sensitive to the needs and desires of the group? Are they taught to behave cooperatively rather than compete with others? Is it appropriate to strive for individual recognition, or is anonymity stressed? Is the student likely to sacrifice her desires for the benefit of others in the class? Will she be motivated by competitive games and individual rewards? Should you recognize your student for her accomplishments in front of others? Would it be a good idea or a bad idea to try to motivate your student by comparing her to others? Field-dependent/sensitive students may have difficulty in classrooms that stress individual goals, individual recognition, and competition.

*Conflict resolution:* Are conflicts faced and dealt with or swept under the table? Should you attempt to bring the student's conflicts with others into the open to resolve them, or should you allow your student to avoid them? Students brought up not to disagree with others in public and to make sure everyone "saves face" may react negatively if you require them to discuss their disagreements with others openly and frankly.

Are youngsters who disagree permitted to argue and/or fight it out, or are they required to settle their disagreements peacefully and shake hands and make up? Is it better to intervene when your student is involved in a conflict with others, or should you permit him to settle it any way he wants? Should you require the student to shake hands and "make friends"?

*Gender patterns:* How do boys and girls relate at various ages? Should you require your student to engage in coed activities? In recent years an increased emphasis on nonsexist coeducational activities in the schools has been required by Title IX and supported by the courts (see Chapter 13). Yet, some minority students may both overtly and covertly resist being required to engage in activities that are reserved for the opposite sex in their cultures. They may also balk at being made to engage in coed activities that are usually carried out in sexually segregated groups in their home culture.

# Communication Style

The way people express themselves is such an inherent part of their culture that a keen observer can learn much from everyday communications. Because of language barriers, you may also have to ask direct questions of people who know your students' culture well.

*Direct Versus Indirect*    Do people express themselves directly, openly, and frankly, or is their primary goal to maintain smooth interpersonal relationships? Are people expected to say when they are unwilling or unable to do something? Are they likely to express disagreement? When people say they feel a certain way or will do a certain thing, do they mean it or is this just their way of avoiding disagreement? Should you be indirect rather than frank if you have something critical to say? Can you believe your student if she tells you something? Can you count on her if your student commits herself to do something? If your student doesn't tell you the truth or doesn't fulfill a contract, does she think of it as lying or as appropriate behavior? Students who are brought up to believe that not following through on promises and saying something that isn't so are acceptable behavior don't have conduct problems and shouldn't be handled as if they do.

*Themes Discussed*    All cultures have unwritten rules about what should or shouldn't be talked about and with whom. Thus, you and your culturally different students may have different expectations about what they should be willing to discuss with you.

*Needs:* Do individuals express their needs openly, or are people expected to be sensitive to the feelings and problems of others without needing to have them expressed? Can you assume that because your student hasn't said he has a problem that he doesn't need your help, understanding, or tolerance? Would encouraging students to discuss their problems by using "active listening" (Chapter 3) be helpful, or would this approach be too confronting to some students?

*Facts versus feelings:* Are people equally comfortable discussing facts and feelings? Can you expect your student to discuss her feelings of resentment, anger, shame, guilt, and the like, or is this not an accepted topic?

*Admission of error, mistakes, lack of understanding:* Do people admit when they are wrong or have made a mistake? Should you require your student to admit that he made a mistake or to apologize to you or another student for something he did? Would that make your student lose face?

Students should learn to accept both responsibility for and the consequences of their behavior. But some minority students may be willing to accept the consequences of their behavior while resisting admitting their responsibility to others. Until such students can function biculturally in this respect, it may be more effective to permit them to avoid having to admit their errors, mistakes, and misunderstandings.

*Sensitive Issues*    How well do individuals have to know each other, and what kind of a relationship do they have to have before they can discuss sensitive or intimate things? When will your student be willing to discuss certain things with you and with peers?

*Affection*    Do people demonstrate affection easily? Do they do so verbally or physically? Would your student welcome or reject your displays of affection? What are the acceptable ways you may demonstrate affection for your student? Although many students might welcome physical touching such as a pat on the back or an arm on the shoulder, this is "taboo" behavior in some cultures.

*Group Processes*    How do groups arrive at decisions and resolve disagreements? Do groups usually have leaders? If so, do the leaders make the decisions, or do they abide by the will of the group? Are differences of opinion aired in open discussion, or are they side-stepped or squashed? Does your student expect to have an equal say with you in the decision-making process? Will she be comfortable expressing opinions and feelings that may differ from other members of the group? Minority students who have been trained to avoid public conflicts and disagreements may be unable to participate in discussions of controversial issues, express opinions that are different from a previous speaker, or even vote on what the group should or shouldn't do.

## Time

Because time is primary to our functioning and is even measured by instruments, it is easy to assume that all cultures share a similar relationship to time. This is not, however, the case.

*Present Versus Future*    Do people live for the present, or do they tend to sacrifice present satisfactions for future goals? Can you expect your student to work toward the attainment of long-term goals and rewards, or would your student be attracted to short-term goals and immediate gratification?

Students should learn to work toward achieving long-term goals and to work on long-term projects. Some minority students, though, come from cultural backgrounds that stress living for the moment and letting the future take care of itself. Such students may put off working on long-term projects such as term papers until it's almost too late to complete them. You may have to divide long-term projects into units that have to be completed step by step. These students may also require immediate positive reinforcement with something tangible like candy, free time, and the like rather than points or tokens that they can turn in later for tangible rewards. Students who behave in these ways for cultural reasons may appear immature, but they aren't.

*Pace*    How fast or slowly do people work and play? Do they attempt to accomplish as much as they can in as short a time as possible, or do they prefer to do things at a relaxed, steady pace? Is your student able to keep up with the other students in the class, or does he fall behind? Students who are accustomed to doing things at a slow pace may profit from the techniques described in Chapter 11 for working with low-activity-level students until they can function biculturally.

*Punctuality*    Do people keep to rigid schedules, or are beginning and ending times flexible? Is your student accustomed to arriving on time, starting things when she is supposed to, and completing them within a specified time period? If not, it may be necessary to help the student learn to function biculturally in this respect.

# Discipline

The ways in which people from different cultures train their young vary tremendously.

*Consequences*   How much praise and reward do students receive from adults? Although rewarding and praising students unnecessarily and excessively can cause learned helplessness, what are unnecessary or excessive rewards for mainstream students may be just what some field-dependent/sensitive students need until they can function in a more bicultural way.

Is the student accustomed to receiving personal or impersonal rewards? Should you use personal reinforcements such as statements of approval, smiles, pats on the back, and the like or impersonal rewards such as check marks, gold stars, tokens, toys, or sweets to motivate your students?

Is the student accustomed to individual rewards? Would he respond better if the group as a whole were rewarded for his individual achievements and contributions?

What kinds of negative consequences do adults use to discipline youngsters—physical punishments (spankings, slaps), loss of affection and attention (statements of anger and disappointment, removal from the presence of others, being sent to their rooms), loss of privileges (no watching television or playing with friends), loss of material things (sweets, toys, allowances)? What consequences work best with your student?

*Public or Private Feedback*   Are children and teenagers given feedback about their behavior in public or only in private? Is it all right to compliment your students in front of the class and place her work on display, or would that be too embarrassing? Can you write the student's name on the blackboard when she misbehaves and comment about the student's inappropriate behavior before the class, or should you only correct your student in private to make sure she doesn't "lose face"?

*Tone of Voice*   What tone of voice do adults use when they discipline and criticize children and teenagers? Are they gruff, emotional, and direct or gentle and indirect?

*Adult Authority or Reasonable Rules*   Are youngsters expected to obey adults because they are the authorities, or do adults often explain and justify their orders and demands? Which of these approaches should you use with your student, assuming you are comfortable with it?

# Unequal Cross-Cultural Relationships

If you have an alienated student in your class and you are the recipient of his anger, resentment, and distrust of the system, you can do a number of things to help the situation.

1. Tell your student that you understand how he feels but explain how things are different in your classroom.

2. Earn your student's trust and confidence by including his culture in the classroom, adapting your instructional and classroom management techniques to your student's cultural background, and advocating for the rights of minority students with your colleagues and superiors.

3. If your student acts out his anger or resentment in class, tolerate behavior problems that don't seriously disrupt the class. But make it clear that although you understand how he feels, you won't permit your student to interfere with the other students' rights to an education.

4. If your student withdraws from class—tunes out, comes late, cuts classes, or does other things to avoid class—explain that there are better ways of solving the problem than denying oneself the value of an education.

# Hispanic Students

Space doesn't permit discussing all the various cultures represented in American schools today. The discussion that follows of the Hispanic culture is offered as an example of how information about students' cultures can help educators do a better job of adapting techniques to their students' cultural characteristics. Keeping in mind that not all Hispanic students are alike and that what is true for some Hispanic students isn't true of all Hispanic students, this section includes suggestions for helping Hispanic students whose behavior problems are caused by culture shock, the frustration of being taught in a foreign language in an unfamiliar teaching style, culturally determined differences in readiness skills, identity conflicts, and a history of unequal cross-cultural relationships. The section lists cultural traits that research indicates are more likely to characterize Hispanic students than non-Hispanic students and makes suggestions for when and how to adapt classroom management techniques to these cultural differences. It also describes some typical ways educators misperceive the behavior of their Hispanic students.

The material included in this section is based on a variety of published sources (7, 10, 13, 18, 27, 30, 31, 33, 35, 51, 63–99). The quotations included here are edited statements from the literature about the education of Hispanic students. In a national survey approximately 400 Hispanic educators, counselors, and psychologists as well as non-Hispanic professionals with considerable experience in working with Hispanic students agreed with both these quotations about Hispanic cultural characteristics and the suggestions that follow them for helping Hispanic students cope with the acculturation process in school (4).

## Culture Shock

Since Hispanic students are used to foods, music, holidays, language, and customs which are very different from what Anglos are accustomed to, Hispanic students may have difficulty relating to the Anglo-oriented classroom. Students from families with low incomes may suffer cultural shock in school because of the differences between what is available to them at home, where they may have to wear out, make do, or do without, and what is provided by the school system. These differences may do harm to these students' self-concepts and make it difficult for these students to adjust to school. (4, p. 69, 70, 74)

Educators should take pains to reduce or eliminate those aspects of their classroom environment, teaching materials, and teaching techniques which might cause cultural shock. They should make the classroom culturally relevant to these students so as to ease their entrance into the world of school. (4, p. 70)

## Language and Teaching Style

The two quotations below relate to language—how Hispanic students relate to their native language and what they need to do well in schools.

Many Hispanic parents have considerable pride in being both Latin and belonging to "La Raza." This pride is often expressed in attempts to maintain the use of the Spanish language at home and in the community even after many years of residence in the United States. Some Hispanic parents may have not acquired enough English to speak to their children in English because of not having lived in the United States for enough time or because of having lived in a neighborhood-barrio where English fluency was unnecessary. As a result, some Hispanic students are not fluent enough in English when they start school to profit from instruction in arithmetic, science, social studies, etc.,

*Research indicates that bilingual education helps students learn a second language more efficiently.*

when the language of instruction is English. Immersing them in a completely English program may cause them to fall behind their English-speaking peers in these subject areas and make it difficult for them to adjust to school. (4, p. 59–60)

Therefore, such limited English proficient students should receive a bilingual education. They should be taught such subjects as math, science, etc. in Spanish while they are being helped to become proficient enough in English to profit from English language instruction in these subject areas. (4, p. 61)

Cultures, through their members, have characteristic ways of passing on information and skill. Educators who know about and use a teaching style that "speaks to" how their minority students usually learn in their home culture are likely to be successful with these students.

The Hispanic culture emphasizes learning by doing. As a result, some Hispanic students learn more by touching, seeing, manipulating, and experiencing concrete objects than by discussing or reading about ideas. Therefore, educators should deemphasize the lecture approach and emphasize direct experiences with these Hispanic students. (4, p. 57)

## Readiness Skills

Prior to their entrance into school, Hispanic students may be exposed to the richness of the Hispanic culture at home rather than to the many cultural concepts that are expected and valued by the Anglo school system. Therefore, educators should adapt their curriculum and instruction techniques to the knowledge and experiences Hispanic students bring to school. This will prevent them from being educationally behind as soon as they enter the school system. (4, p. 67)

## Unequal Cross-Cultural Relationships

History, geography, social roles, etc. are often studied exclusively in terms of the Anglo point of view. Too often, students are taught that Columbus rather than the Native Americans discovered America, that Ponce de Leon was a fool who was looking for a fountain of youth, and that Latin Americans are lazy procrastinators who live in small underdeveloped pueblos . . . When their foods are not mentioned during discussions of what are good foods to eat in order to have a balanced diet, their music is not played during assemblies and music appreciation classes, etc., Hispanic students may feel that they and their culture are inferior in the eyes of their teachers. (4, p. 73–74)

Therefore, educators should include the Hispanic contribution in the curriculum, correct inaccurate and prejudicial stereotypes of Hispanics, and include as much of the Hispanic foods, music, language, values, etc. as possible in the daily curriculum. And they should act as advocates for Hispanic students when they are confronted by discrimination. (4, p. 75)

The following sections provide descriptions of the differences between the Hispanic and mainstream cultures. Included are suggestions for how to take these differences into account when working with Hispanic students.

# *Interpersonal Relationships*

Each culture has characteristic patterns for all relationships that set the tone and possibly content. Information about these patterns will help you realize "where your students are coming from." The following quotes describe children's usual relationship with adults in Hispanic cultures.

> Hispanic children tend to have formal respectful relationships with adults. As a result, they may be uncomfortable with the less formal relationships usually observed between Anglo teachers and Anglo students. Therefore, educators should not attempt to develop informal relationships with their Hispanic students who are not comfortable with such relationships. However, they should also explain to them that although formal relationships may be appropriate at home, a less formal relationship is more typical of the classroom. (4, p. 98–100)

> Hispanic children are brought up to look up to their elders, especially their parents, and respect their wishes, opinions, attitudes, and advice and to model themselves after adults whom they like. As a result, they may function better when adults are involved and supportive and provide encouragement and feedback about how they are doing. Hispanic parents tend to discourage their children from showing too much initiative or independence or expressing their own ideas and opinions without consulting their elders first. They are much more likely than Anglo children to ask their parents and other adults for their advice and suggestions when they have to make important decisions. As a result some Hispanic students may have difficulty when educators want them to form their own opinions and make their own decisions independently of their teachers. Therefore, educators should try to encourage these students to be less dependent on the opinions and approval of adults so that they can begin to learn to function more independently. However, until they are able to do so, educators should provide these students with the guidance and approval they need in order to make decisions in the classroom and the encouragement and feedback about how they are doing they require in order to work effectively. (4, p. 45–48)

> Because the Hispanic culture tends to be patriarchal, some Hispanic male students, especially adolescents, may have difficulty complying with female authority figures. Therefore, female educators should stress nonauthoritarian methods such as requesting rather than ordering for managing the classroom behavior of these Hispanic male students. (4, p. 104–105)

How does the individual relate to a group? This is a key question because the answer will explain and even help predict students' classroom behavior.

> Hispanic children are brought up to believe in the importance of the extended family; to sacrifice their own desires for the good of the family; and to expect that the family will support and aid them when they are in need. This upbringing tends to make Hispanic students more cooperative and group oriented than other students. As a result, Hispanic students may allow other students to copy their homework or their answers on examinations in order to show their helpfulness, brotherhood, and generosity. They may not consider this to be bad behavior. (4, p. 80–81)

> Educators should explain that while working on homework assignments together and helping each other when they are being evaluated may be acceptable in some cultures, it is not acceptable in the school system they are attending. (4, p. 83)

Hispanics tend to believe that it is bad manners to try to excel over others in the group or to attempt to be recognized for their individual achievement. As a result, many Hispanic students will avoid competing with their peers for fear of being criticized or rejected by them. Because of their belief that it is bad manners to try to excel over others, some Hispanic students may not volunteer answers or they may even pretend not to know the correct answer when called upon. (4, p. 84–86)

Educators should deemphasize competition and stress cooperation when attempting to motivate some Hispanic students. They should praise and reward students for cooperative behavior as much as for individual achievement. They should also be sensitive to the needs of those Hispanic students who prefer not to be singled out in front of the group and recognize their achievements in a less public manner. One way of doing this would be to communicate their praise to their students' families. (4, p. 85–86)

Hispanic boys are taught to be protective of their sisters and other girls, escorting them to and from school, protecting them from other boys, handling their money, etc.; Hispanic girls are encouraged to assume a submissive role toward brothers and other boys. As a result, both sexes may feel uncomfortable when they are required to work and play together as equals. They may prefer to work in school in groups of their own sex and feel uncomfortable when well-meaning egalitarian nonsexist Anglo educators require that the sexes work or engage in athletic activities together. However, despite their discomfort, educators should require that the sexes work and play together in class. (4, p. 111–112)

## Communication Style

Our usual way of communicating seems so natural that it's hard to realize that, in fact, it has particular rules and values that are not shared by all cultures. Americans tend to be direct and straightforward and to value this approach. Other cultures favor indirectness.

Anglos are taught to value openness, frankness, and directness. They are much more likely to express themselves simply, briefly, and frequently bluntly. The traditional Hispanic approach requires the use of much diplomacy and tactfulness when communicating with another individual. Hispanics often find themselves in difficulty if they disagree with an Anglo's point of view. To them, direct argument or contradiction appears rude and disrespectful. On the surface they may seem agreeable, manners dictating that they do not reveal their genuine opinion openly unless they can take time to tactfully differ. Hispanics are less likely to state their unwillingness to do what others ask or expect from them. This is especially true of children and adolescents who are taught to respect their elders. Therefore, educators should not assume that because Hispanic students have verbally acquiesced to their expectations or demands, they either agree with them or plan to carry them out. Instead, educators should take into consideration the vast array of nonverbal communications that some Hispanic students use to express their disinclination or disagreement. (4, p. 91, 93, 131)

What does one express or keep to oneself? The answer very much depends on where one is born and grows up.

Hispanics are less likely to verbally acknowledge responsibility for mistakes and errors or to apologize when they have wronged someone. Instead of blaming themselves for errors, they frequently attribute it to adverse circumstances. Educators should not assume that Hispanic students who do not "own up" to their errors, mistakes, and wrongdoings are either unaware of them or too rebellious and recalcitrant to admit them and apologize for them. They should not shame Hispanic students by requiring them to make verbal acknowledgements of their mistakes and wrongdoings in ways which are culturally unacceptable to them. (4, p. 114–116)

Hispanics, especially males, also tend not to admit to not knowing something or being unable to do something. Therefore, educators should not assume that Hispanic students who have not said that they do not understand something or cannot do something or have not asked for help actually understand their lessons and can do their assignments without help. Rather, educators should be sensitive to the subtle clues which indicate that they are in need. (4, p. 115–116)

Warmth, affection, and touching are more acceptable in some cultures than others.

Hispanics tend to show affection and acceptance through touching. Friends are likely to kiss when they meet. Males are likely to hug each other or pat each other on the back as well as shake hands. And it is not unusual for people to hold others by the arm or place their hands on their shoulders when conversing. Therefore, educators should utilize physical contact when expressing approval and acceptance of their Hispanic students, especially the young ones. (4, p. 97)

How do people usually act in groups? What are the ways in which groups function? The answers to these questions will help you understand why your students behave as they do.

In the Hispanic culture it is not impolite for more than one person to speak at a time during group discussions. Multiple conversations may be carried out simultaneously without anyone being considered rude or discourteous. However, despite this, educators should explain to Hispanic speakers that while it may be all right for more than one person to speak at a time at home, in school students are expected to wait their turn before speaking. (4, p. 100)

When a group of Hispanics disagree, they may resolve the issue by continuing to discuss it until it becomes apparent that a consensus has been reached without polling the group or calling for a vote. Therefore, when working with groups of Hispanic students, educators should allow them to arrive at a consensus in whatever manner is most comfortable for them. Educators should not insist that decisions be made by voting. (4, p. 100–101)

## Time

Does the student's home culture stress the present or the future? Emphasis on either has an effect on school, which tends to be future-oriented.

Hispanics tend to be more present time oriented. Finishing a conversation now may be more important than keeping an appointment later. Living to the fullest now and enjoying what the present has to offer may be more important than saving, planning, and striving for future satisfactions and security. The anticipation of a large reward or satisfaction in the future may be much less motivating than a smaller satisfaction in the here and now. Therefore, educators should provide immediate feedback, approval, recognition, and reward to Hispanic students. (4, p. 50–52)

The pace at which people work is also influenced by culture and even by location.

Hispanics tend to be more concerned with doing a job well, regardless of the amount of time required, than they are in finishing rapidly so they will have more time for the next task. They tend to prefer to work at a relaxed pace even if it means taking longer to finish something. At home, Hispanic children are permitted to do things at their own pace without adhering to strict time schedules. As a result, Hispanic students may not complete classroom work as fast as their Anglo peers. When required to rush or stop working before they have finished in order to begin the next task with their peers, they may become anxious, nervous, rebellious, etc. Therefore, educators should not rush Hispanic students when they are called on to answer questions in class. However, they should not allow Hispanic students to spend as much time as necessary to complete class assignments. Instead they should help such students adjust to the time orientation which they encounter in school and which will govern their lives in the dominant culture. This should include helping them to adjust to the pressures of time limits. (4, p. 52–54)

Ideas about time include being on time and what being "on time" means. This simple-sounding concept can have quite different meanings.

The Hispanic concept of punctuality is different than the Anglo concept. If a meeting is called for two o'clock, people are expected to arrive sometime after that. If a party or dance is set for nine o'clock, people may be expected to arrive at eleven or even later. An agreement to repair a TV for Wednesday means that it will probably be ready sometime after Wednesday. Because of this, educators should inform Hispanic students that although the Hispanic concept of punctuality is fine for their homes and community, in school and other similar situations it would be best if they adapted to the dominant culture's expectations of punctuality. (4, p. 54–55)

## Discipline

Children are taught and disciplined according to patterns in their culture. An effective form of discipline for some youngsters, therefore, may backfire with students from another culture.

Some Hispanic parents tend to use physical punishment rather than deprivation of love and affection when disciplining their children. Moreover, once they have punished their children, they tend to forgive them rather than to remain angry, resentful, or to hold a grudge. Therefore, educators should not use deprivation of affection to manage Hispanic students. (4, p. 101–102)

Hispanics tend to be more interested in and dependent on the approval of others than Anglos who are more likely to be receptive to more impersonal and materialistic forms of recognition. Therefore, educators should stress the fact that Hispanic students' families will be proud of them and share the honor of their accomplishments. And they should use praise, hugs, pats on the back, and other personal rewards with Hispanic students more than checks, gold stars, and materialistic forms of reinforcement such as sweets and toys. (4, p. 37, 40)

Hispanic students may be much more willing and able to accept criticism, direction, and discipline from educators with whom they have a close personal relationship. Therefore, educators should not maintain an impersonal, objective, aloof, or distant relationship with Hispanic students. (4, p. 94)

## Role of Education

Hispanics place a high value on education. However, Hispanic children also have a very active role to play in the family. They may be responsible for helping to take care of the younger children and may have many chores to do. When their parents do not speak English, they may be required to serve as translators when the adults have to meet with doctors, agencies, businessmen, etc. When these responsibilities interfere with the students' attendance at school or homework and study time, Hispanics tend to view the students' responsibilities to the family as more important than their responsibility to the school. Therefore, when Hispanic students miss school or come unprepared, educators should determine when conflicting family responsibilities are the cause and accommodate their expectations and teaching methods to the students' and parents' realities. They should not lower course grades or punish Hispanic students in other ways when family responsibilities prevent them from completing assignments, arriving on time, or attending class. Nor should they pressure students to choose between their responsibilities to their families and the school by insisting that they attend school and complete assignments even when family responsibilities interfere. However, they should talk with the Hispanic parents and try to help them to shift their priorities somewhat so that the students' responsibilities at home do not interfere with their success in school. (4, p. 105–107)

## Cultural Misperceptions

Because of the cultural differences between the Hispanic and Anglo cultures, educators who teach Hispanic students but know little or nothing about the Hispanic culture may have some misperceptions. For example, the Hispanic culture requires good students to be passive learners—to sit quietly at their desks, pay attention, learn what they are taught, and speak only when called upon. In contrast, Anglo educational methods often call on students to be active learners—to show initiative and leadership, to volunteer questions and answers, and to question the opinion of others. As a result, teachers may incorrectly perceive Hispanic students who can't assume this more active role as insecure, shy, or excessively passive.

In another example, Hispanic students who are trained to be dependent on the opinions, values, and decisions of adults may seem to be overly dependent, immature, or even slow. Or Hispanic students who are brought up to be cooperative rather than competitive in their relationships with their peers may be seen as too passive and nonassertive in school activities. In addition, Hispanics who are not necessarily expected to admit responsibility or apologize when they have made a mistake or wronged another person may resist doing so, especially in front of their peers. Educators can misperceive this unwillingness as recalcitrance, stubbornness, or defiant behavior. Another potential area for mistaken perception is in doing schoolwork. Hispanic students who help each other when they are called on, during examinations, or with their homework may seem to be cheating rather than cooperating to a teacher unfamiliar with the Hispanic culture.

Cultural conflicts between Hispanic and Anglo expectations for children and adolescents may cause identity problems for Hispanic youth. Some resolve these identity crises by adopting rebellious, exaggerated behavior patterns designed to express their individuality. When students demonstrate these behaviors in school, they may threaten educators who may think that these Hispanic youth have emotional or behavioral problems.

Hispanic students who are made to compete against their will, criticized in front of their peers, denied the dependent relationship they are accustomed to having with adults, and coerced into other behaviors that are culturally at odds with theirs may feel rejected, abused, or picked on by their teachers. They may become insecure and anxious, they may rebel against such treatment, or they may withdraw from further attempts to succeed in school or relate to their teachers. Educators can misperceive such situational, emotional, and behavioral problems as personality problems. Teachers can believe that students who do not complete assignments or attend school when family responsibilities prevent them from doing so are unmotivated or irresponsible. They can also see students who work at the slower, more relaxed Hispanic pace in school as lazy or slow, instead of as working in what to these students is "the right way."

---

## Self-Quiz: Cross-Cultural Exercises

List the various cultural groups that exist in your community. Evaluate your knowledge of their cultural characteristics especially as they relate to classroom management.

Answer the questions in the section on "Developing a Cultural Guide" about your own ethnic or cultural characteristics. Compare these to characteristics of the Hispanic culture and identify possible differences that might exist between you and some Hispanic students.

Prepare a "culture guide" for one of the minority groups in your community, addressing the topics covered in the discussion of the Hispanic culture. Compare their cultural characteristics to your own.

Engage a colleague whose cultural background is different than your own in a conversation about the ways each of you perceives the other's culture and the history of the relationships between your two cultural groups.

---

# A Controversial Issue

Although cultural differences can create behavior problems in the classroom, cause educators to misperceive and misunderstand their students' behavior, and lead them to select culturally inappropriate techniques to solve behavior problems, some educators are against taking cultural factors into consideration when working with students from other cultures. Three reasons are often cited by these educators. First, they feel that culturally different students and their families should adapt to the mainstream culture in the school and not vice versa. This idea is embodied in the following statements.

> People who want to live in the United States should adapt to the American culture and not expect the American system to adapt to them. If they want to continue to live their lifestyles, they should stay where their lifestyles are acceptable. (4, p. 14)

> We cannot survive as a culture with different laws for different people. Everyone must pay taxes, serve in the army, respect private property and the rights of others regardless of where they were born or what religion they profess. (4, p. 13)

> The role of schooling traditionally has been one of acculturation. To change the role of schooling now would be to court disaster. (4, p. 14)

These three quotations are in turn based on two assumptions: that a multicultural educational approach in the classroom necessarily leads to having different laws for different cultural groups; and that the United States has a single culture which must be preserved in order for the nation to continue to prosper.

The first assumption is not correct. Permitting students to work at their own pace, developing the kinds of interpersonal relationships with them that make them feel comfortable, and allowing them to choose whether to compete or not does not necessarily lead to adopting two or more sets of laws for citizens. The second assumption is also false. While a dominant culture does exist in the United States, so many subcultural differences also exist that we are truly a pluralistic society.

To illustrate this, let's take a look at some differences in child-rearing practices. Some parents take Lamaze classes and are active participants in their child's birth. Other mothers are sedated while the doctor delivers the children and later shows them to the proud parents. Some children are breast-fed; others are given formula. When infants begin to crawl, some parents place any dangerous or breakable things out of reach so the children can explore without restrictions. Other infants have no such freedom. Believing that children have to learn self-control from the beginning, their parents teach them what they are allowed and are not allowed to do or touch, or they are confined in a playpen. When some children misbehave, they are spanked, sent to their rooms, or deprived of one or another privilege. Other children are made to feel guilty, ashamed, or disapproved of but are not spanked and seldom lose privileges.

During their early school years, some children have paper routes and are paid money for doing various jobs around the house. Others receive allowances regardless of how they behave. When they are a little older, some youngsters are closely supervised to make sure they have completed all their homework assignments before they watch television or go out to play, while others are only reminded occasionally to do their homework. As teenagers, some are allowed to have a little wine, beer, and maybe even hard liquor once in a while, but others are protected as much as possible from developing what their parents consider to be bad habits. Finally, some are encouraged to study hard because a good education can lead to a good job, while others are encouraged to study in order to become well-educated, well-rounded people.

These are just a few examples of the many different lifestyles that coexist in the United States. And while each individual may feel that his particular way of life is the best, many others would disagree. The important point here is that Americans don't share a single way of life. Many different yet acceptable subcultures exist simultaneously outside the class-room. It is therefore entirely feasible and even appropriate that the classroom should reflect this multicultural reality.

The second reason some give for not taking cultural factors into consideration in the classroom is that it is impossible to accommodate educational approaches to the cultural needs of the many culturally different students found in any particular school system or often within one classroom. These people find it difficult to believe that educators can accommodate their methods and techniques to a variety of cultural groups at the same time. The following quotations give voice to this viewpoint.

> My school district, the Los Angeles County School District, has over one hundred dif-ferent language/culture groups.

> How can anyone be expected to know about all these different cultures, and how can anyone be expected to apply what they do know? From what I have been told during in-service training, what are appropriate teaching techniques for one group are inappropri-ate for another. How can I teach my Anglo students one way, my Latino students a second way, my Vietnamese students a third, my Korean students a fourth way, my Hmong, my Portuguese, etc. at the same time? Impossible! (4, p. 15–16)

> The idea of teaching all students in the style to which they are accustomed is a good one, but where will you find all those people who can walk on water? (4, p. 16)

On the surface this line of reasoning has considerable merit. Yet it is also based on the false assumption that it would be impossible to provide a culturally relevant education to stu-dents from different cultures simultaneously because their cultural needs are so different. Not every culture requires a unique educational approach. Only so many alternative meth-ods of instructing students, organizing classrooms, and counseling parents exist to choose from. For example, educators can require their students to work individually or in groups; they can motivate them through the use of competitive games or cooperative settings; they can allow them to work at their own pace or encourage them to work as quickly as possible; they can attempt to develop close personal relationships with them or maintain a "profes-sional distance"; they can correct and criticize them in front of their peers or in private; they can encourage them to discuss controversial issues and express differences of opinion or emphasize similarities of experience and opinion. Since counselors, educators, and psy-chologists are always choosing among a limited set of alternatives like those listed above, it would be entirely possible for them to satisfy the needs of many students from different cultures by means of the same alternative.

The final argument is that it is better to emphasize the similarities among people than to stress their differences. The following quotations express this point of view.

> When people focus on the differences among themselves, they engender conflict and hostility. Jew vs. Moslem, Moslem vs. Hindu, Catholic vs. Protestant, Missionary vs. native heathen. Religious differences have caused the human race more misery than all the solace and comfort religions have given to their adherents. (4, p. 17)

> We are all Americans and as Americans we would do well to be blind to the differences that divide us. (4, p. 17)

> Teachers should teach to the commonalities among their students which are much more important than any superficial differences. (4, p. 17)

In essential respects, human beings are basically the same. They all prefer success to failure, praise and recognition to criticism or condemnation, and acceptance and attention to rejection and inattention. Nevertheless, their perceptions of and reactions to what these situations mean are influenced by their cultures. For example, they have different criteria for success. They find different forms of praise and recognition rewarding. They differ in terms of when, where, why, and how they are willing to accept criticism or condemnation and express acceptance and rejection in their own culturally determined ways.

Expecting all individuals to behave the same way, or interpreting everyone's behavior from a single culturally determined point of view can engender hostility and conflict. People like to be accepted as they are and respected for that. At least as much risk occurs in treating everyone the same as in relating to individuals as members of different cultural groups.

---

### *Self-Quiz: Adapting to Cultural Differences*

Ask yourself whether you believe educators should or should not adapt their classroom management techniques to the cultural differences among their students. Give the reasons for your opinion.

---

## *Summary*

While some educators don't think it is necessary to take cultural differences into account when trying to help culturally different students with behavior problems, others believe that it is desirable to do so. Culture shock, the frustration of being taught in a foreign language and in an unfamiliar teaching style, cultural differences in readiness skills, identity conflicts, different norms of acceptable behavior, and unequal cross-cultural relationships can all cause classroom behavior problems. These problems require an understanding of the role of cultural differences to be dealt with effectively. Even when a student's problems are caused by educational, conduct, emotional, or physiological factors, if the student is from a minority culture, it's advisable to adapt one's techniques to the student's cultural background.

## *Activities*

Which of the behavior problems described below could be caused by cultural factors? What cultural factors could be contributing to these behaviors?

Martín is an almost-seven-year-old student whose parents immigrated to the United States when he was three. His first-grade teacher described him as having the following problems.

1. He works so fast when writing letters and numerals that his work is often almost illegible.

2. He often miscounts when he uses his fingers to do simple addition and subtraction problems.

3. He constantly asks me to check over his work to see if he is doing it correctly even though he is almost always on track.

4. He almost never volunteers questions, answers, or comments in class. But when I call on Juan or Carlos, his two best friends, he will whisper the correct answers to them.

5. He often enters the room noisily and roughhouses with his friends before taking his seat.

6. He often asks to go to the bathroom when his attention wanes or the work is difficult.

7. He will not check out books from the library in English or Spanish unless I encourage him and help him select the books I think he will enjoy.

8. He sometimes takes things from his peers' cubbies.

9. He has difficulty sharing toys and materials with other students and resists relinquishing materials when it is another student's turn to use them.

10. He hits his peers when he is angry and teases the weaker children in the class.

# *References*

EXTENT OF THE PROBLEM

1. National Information Center for Children and Youth with Handicaps. (1988). *Minority Issues in Special Education: A Portrait of the Future.* Washington, DC.

2. Woodrow, K. A. (1988). *Measuring Net Immigration to the United States: The Emigrant Population and Recent Emigration Flows.* Paper presented at the annual meeting of the Population Association of America, New Orleans.

IMMIGRANT STUDENTS

3. Geschwind, N. (1974). *Cross-Cultural Contrastive Analysis: An Exploratory Study.* Unpublished masters thesis, University of Hawaii, Honolulu.

4. Grossman, H. (1984). *Educating Hispanic Students: Cultural Implications for Instruction, Classroom Management, Counseling, and Assessment.* Springfield, IL: CC Thomas.

5. Juffer, K. A. (1983). Culture shock: A theoretical framework for understanding adaptation. In J. Bransford (Ed.), *Monograh Series: BUENO Center for Multicultural Education, 4,* 136–149.

6. Nguyen, T. P. (1987). Positive self-concept in the Vietnamese bilingual child. In M. Dao, *From Vietnamese to Vietnamese American: Selected Articles.* San Jose, CA: Division of Special Education and Rehabilitative Services, San Jose State University.

7. Ramirez, M., & Castañeda, A. (1974). *Cultural Democracy, Bicognitive Development and Education.* New York: Academic Press.

8. Troike, R. C. (1978). *Research Evidence for the Effectiveness of Bilingual Education.* Rosslyn, VA: National Clearinghouse for Bilingual Education.

9. Wei, T. T. D. (1980). *Vietnamese Refugee Students: A Handbook for School Personnel* (2nd ed.). ERIC ED 208 109.

## CULTURALLY DIFFERENT STUDENTS

The references below deal with culturally influenced learning and behavioral styles.

10. Aiello, J. R., & Jones, S. E. (1971). Field study of the proxemic behavior of young school children in three subcultural groups. *Journal of Personality and Social Psychology, 19,* 351–356.

11. Barclay, A., & Cusumano, D. R. (1967). Father absence, cross-sex identity, and field-dependent behavior in male adolescents. *Child Development, 38,* 243–250.

12. Bauer, E. (1973). Personal space: A study of blacks and whites. *Sociometry, 36,* 402–408.

13. Buriel, R. (1975). Cognitive styles among three generations of Mexican-American children. *Journal of Cross-Cultural Psychology, 6* (4), 417–429.

14. Canavan, D. (1969). *Field Dependence in Children as a Function of Grade, Sex, and Ethnic Group Membership.* Paper presented at annual meeting of the American Psychological Association, Washington, DC.

15. Cooperman, M. L. (1975). Field-dependence and children's problem-solving under varying contingencies of predetermined feedback. *Dissertation Abstracts International, 35,* 2040–2041.

16. Cureton, G. O. (1978). Using a Black learning style. *The Reading Teacher, 31* (7), 751–756.

17. DiStefano, J. J. (1970). Interpersonal perceptions of field-independent and field-dependent teachers and students. *Dissertation Abstracts International, 31,* 463A–464A.

18. Dixon, C. N. (1977). *Matching Reading Instruction to Cognitive Style for Mexican-American Children*. ERIC ED 158 269.

19. Dunn, R. V., & Dunn, K. (1978). *Teaching Students Through Their Individual Learning Styles: A Practical Approach*. Reston, VA: Reston Publishing.

20. Dunn, R. V., & Dunn, K. (1979). Learning styles/teaching styles: Should they?—can they?—be matched? *Educational Leadership, 36,* 238–244.

21. Ferrell, J. G. (1971). The differential performance of lower class, preschool, Negro children as a function of sex of E, sex of S, reinforcement condition, and the level of field dependency. *Dissertation Abstracts International, 32,* 3028B–3029B.

22. Gill, N. T., Hertner, T., & Lough, L. (1968). Perceptual and socioeconomic variables, instruction in body part orientation and predicted academic success in young children. *Perceptual Motor Skills, 26,* 1175–1184.

23. Gitter, A. G., Black, H., & Mostofsky, D. (1972). Race and sex in the perception of emotion. *Journal of Social Issues, 28,* 63–78.

24. Goldstein, R. (Ed.). (1971). *Black Life and Culture in the United States*. New York: Thomas Crowell.

25. Hale, J. E. (1981). Black children: Their roots, culture, and learning styles. *Young Children, 36* (2), 37–50.

26. Hilliard, A. (1976). *Alternatives to I.Q. Testing: An Approach to the Identification of Gifted Minority Children*. Sacramento, CA: Final report to the California State Department of Education.

27. Holtzman, E. H., Goldsmith, R. P., & Barrera, C. (1979). *Field-Dependence/Field-Independence: Educational Implications for Bilingual Educators*. Austin, TX: Dissemination and Assessment Center for Bilingual Education.

28. Hsi, V., & Lim, V. (1977). *A Summary of Selected Research on Cognitive and Perceptual Variables*. ERIC ED 145 003.

29. Hwang, B. (1978). Examplars of instructional units for cultural diversity. In L. Morris, G. Sather, & S. Scull (Eds.), *Extracting Learning Styles from Social/Cultural Diversity*. Southwest Teach Corps Network.

30. Kagan, S. (1974). Field dependence and conformity of rural Mexican and Anglo American Children. *Child Development, 45,* 765–771.

31. Kagan, S., & Zahn, L. C. (1975). Field dependence and the school achievement gap between Anglo-American and Mexican-American children. *Journal of Educational Psychology, 67* (5).

32. Knight, G. P., Kagan, S., Nelson, W., & Gumbiner, J. (1978). Acculturation of second- and third-generation Mexican-American children: Field independence, locus of control, self-esteem and school achievement. *Journal of Cross-Cultural Psychology, 9* (1), 87–97.

33. Kogan, N. (1971). Educational implications of cognitive style. In G. S. Lesser (Ed.), *Psychology and Educational Practice*. Chicago: Scott, Foresman.

34. Perney, V. (1976). Effects of race and sex on field dependence-independence in children. *Perceptual and Motor Skills, 42*, 975–980.

35. Ramirez, M., & Price-Williams, D. (1974). Cognitive styles of children of three ethnic groups in the United States. *Journal of Cross-Cultural Psychology, 5*, 212–219.

36. Ritzinger, C. F. (1971). *Psychological and Physiological Differentiation in Children Six to Eleven Years of Age.* Unpublished doctoral dissertation, East Texas State University, Commerce, TX.

37. Robbins, H. A. (1976). *A Comparison Study of Cognitive Styles Across Educational Levels, Race and Sex.* Unpublished doctoral dissertation, East Texas State University, Commerce, TX.

38. Schratz, M. (1976). *A Developmental Investigation of Sex Differences in Perceptual Differentiation and Mathematic Reasoning in Two Ethnic Groups.* Unpublished doctoral dissertation, Fordham University, New York, NY.

39. Shade, B. J. (1979). *Racial Preferences in Psychological Differentiation: An Alternative Explanation to Group Differences.* ERIC ED 179 672.

40. Triandis, H. C. (Ed.). (1976). *Variations in Black and White Perceptions of the Social Environment.* Urbana, IL: University of Illinois Press.

41. Valentine, C. (1971). Deficit difference and bicultural model of Afro-American behavior. *Harvard Educational Review, 41*, 137–157.

42. Witkins, H., Moore, C. A., Goodenough, D. R., & Cox, P. W. (1978). Field-dependent and field-independent cognitive styles and their educational implications. *Review of Educational Research, 47* (1), 1–64.

CULTURAL MISPERCEPTIONS

43. Burger, H. G. (1972). Ethno-lematics: Evoking "shy" Spanish-American pupils by cross-cultural mediation. *Adolescence, 6* (25), 61–76.

44. Byers, P., & Byers, H. (1972). Nonverbal communication and the education of children. In C. G. Cazden, V. P. John, & D. Hymes (Eds.), *Functions of Language in the Classroom.* New York: Academic Press.

45. Dent, H. L. (1976). Assessing black children for mainstream placement. In R. L. Jones (Ed.), *Mainstreaming and the Minority Child.* Reston, VA: Council for Exceptional Children.

46. Gay, G. (1975). Cultural differences important in the education of Black children. *Momentum*, October, 30–33.

47. Gay, G., & Abrahams, R. D. (1973). Does the pot melt, boil, or brew?: Black children and white assessment procedures. *Journal of School Psychology, 11* (4), 330–340.

48. Gilliam, H. V. B., & Van Den Berg, S. (1980). Different levels of eye contact: Effects on black and white college students. *Urban Education, 15* (1), 83–92.

49. Johnson, K. R. (1971). Black kinetics: Some nonverbal communication patterns in the Black culture. *Florida Reporter*, Spring/Fall, 17–20, 57.

50. Kritek, W. J. (1979). Teachers' concerns in a desegregated school in Milwaukee. *Integrated Education*, 17, 19–24.

51. Madsen, W. (1964). *Mexican-Americans of South Texas*. New York: Holt.

52. Mehrabian, A. (1969). Significance of posture and position in the communication of attitude and status relationships. *Psychology Bulletin*, 71, 359–372.

53. Nguyen, L. D. (1986). Indochinese cross-cultural adjustment and communication. In M. Dao & H. Grossman (Eds.), *Identifying, Instructing and Rehabilitating Southeast Asian Students With Special Needs and Counseling Their Parents*. ERIC ED 273 068.

54. Patton, J. M. (1981). *A Critique of Externally Oriented Behavior Management Approaches as Applied to Exceptional Black Children*. ERIC ED 204 902.

55. Slogett, B. B. (1971). Use of group activities and team rewards to increase individual classroom productivity. *Teaching Exceptional Children*, 3 (2), 54–66.

56. Wong, M. K. (1978). Traditional Chinese culture and the behavior patterns of Chinese students in American classrooms. In *Second Annual Forum on Transcultural Adaptation (Proceedings): Asian Students in American Classrooms*. Chicago: Illinois Office of Education.

UNEQUAL CROSS-CULTURAL RELATIONSHIPS

57. Bennett, C., & Harris, J. J. (1982). Suspension and expulsion of male and black students: A case study of the causes of disproportionality. *Urban Education*, 16 (4), 399–423.

58. Johnson, J. L. (1969). Special education and the inner-city: A challenge for the future or another means for cooling out the mark? *Journal of Special Education*, 3, 241–251.

The references cited below relate to formal assessment.  59.

Franco, J. N. (1983). An acculturation scale for Mexican-American children. *Journal of General Psychology*, 108, 175–181.

60. Martinez, R., Norman, R. D., & Delaney, H. D. (1984). A Children's Hispanic Background Scale. *Hispanic Journal of Behavioral Sciences*, 6 (2), 103–112.

61. Ramirez, M., & Castañeda, A. (1974). *Bicultural Democracy, Bicognitive Development and Education*. New York: Academic Press.

62. Szapocznik, J., Kurtines, W. M., & Fernandez, T. (1979). *Bicultural Involvement and Adjustment in Hispanic American Youth*. ERIC ED 193 374.

HISPANIC STUDENTS

63. Aragon, J., & Marquez, L. (1973). *Spanish American: Language and Culture*. Reston, VA: Council for Exceptional Children.

64. Aramoni, A. (1972, January). Machismo. *Psychology Today*, 69–72.

65. Baca, L., & Lane, K. (1974). A dialogue on cultural implications for learning. *Exceptional Children*, 40 (8), 552–563.

66. Bryant, B., & Meadow, A. (1979). School-related problems of Mexican-American adolescents. *Journal of School Psychology*, 14 (2), 139–150.

67. Casavantes, E. J. (1969). *A New Look at the Attributes of the Mexican American*. ERIC ED 028 010.

68. Caskey, O. L. (1967). *Guidance Needs of Mexican-American Youth*. ERIC ED 036 374.

69. Condon, E. C., Peters, J. Y., & Sutero-Ross, C. (1979). *Special Education and the Hispanic Child: Cultural Perspectives*. Philadelphia: Teacher Corps. Mid-Atlantic Network, Temple University.

70. Cross, W. C., & Maldanado, B. (1971). The counselor, the Mexican-American and the stereotype. *Elementary School Guidance and Counseling*, 6 (1), 27–31.

71. De Blaisse, R. R. (1976). *Counseling With Mexican-American Youth*. Austin, TX: Learning Concepts.

72. Demos, G. D. (1962). Attitudes of Mexican-American and Anglo-American groups toward education. *Journal of Social Psychology*, 67, 249–256.

73. Felder, D. (1970). The education of Mexican-Americans: Fallacies of the mono-cultural approach. *Social Education*, 34 (6), 639–647.

74. Flores, J. M. (1980). *Chicano Education: Clearer Objectives and Better Results*. ERIC ED 198 968.

75. Henkin, C. S., & Henkin, A. B. (1977). Culture, poverty and educational problems of Mexican-Americans. *Clearing House*, 50, 316–319.

76. Hepner, E. M. (1970). *Self-Concepts, Values and Needs of Mexican-American Underachievers or Must the Mexican-American Child Adopt a Self-Concept that Fits the American Schools?* ERIC ED 048 954.

77. Hernandez, L. (1967). The culturally disadvantaged Mexican-American student. Part II. *Journal of Secondary Education*, 42 (2), 59–65.

78. Hernandez, L. (1967). The culturally disadvantaged Mexican-American student. Part II. *Journal of Secondary Education*, 42 (3), 123–128.

79. Hosford, R. E., & Bowles, S. A. (1974). Determining culturally appropriate reinforcers for Anglo and Chicano students. *Elementary School Guidance and Counseling*, 8 (4), 240–300.

80. Jarimillo, M. (1973). *Cautions When Working with the Culturally Different Child*. ERIC ED 115 622.

81. Kagan, S., & Madsen, M. C. (1971). Cooperation and competition of Mexican, Mexican-American and Anglo-American children at two ages under four instructional sets. *Developmental Psychology*, 5 (1), 32–39.

82. Keller, G. D. (1974). *The Systematic Exclusion of the Language and Culture of Boricuas, Chicanos and Other U.S. Hispanos in Elementary Spanish Grammar Textbooks Published in the United States.* Ypsilante, MI: Bilingual Press. Editorial Bilingue, Department of Foreign Languages and Bilingual Studies, Eastern Michigan University.

83. Knapp, R. R. (1960). The effects of time limits on the intelligence test performance of Mexican and American subjects. *Journal of Educational Psychology, 51* (1), 14–19.

84. LeVine, E. S., & Bartz, K. W. (1979). Comparative child rearing attitudes among Chicano, Anglo and Black parents. *Hispanic Journal of Behavioral Sciences, 1* (2), 165–178.

85. Masden, M. C. (1971). Developmental and cross-cultural differences in the cooperative and competitive behavior of young children. *Journal of Cross-Cultural Psychology, 2* (4), 365–371.

86. Maes, W. R., & Rinaldi, J. R. (1979). Counseling the Chicano child. *Elementary School Guidance and Counseling, 8* (4), 279–284.

87. Martinez, J. L. (Ed.). (1977). *Chicano Psychology.* New York: Academic Press.

88. Martinez, J. L., & Mendoza, R. H. (Eds.). (1984). *Chicano Psychology* (2nd ed.). New York: Academic Press.

89. Mendiville, M. (1979). A Hispanic perspective on curriculum reform and design. *Social Education,* February 108–110.

90. Moses Lake Intermediate School District. (1969). *Mexican-American Cultural Differences: A Brief Survey to Enhance Teacher-Pupil Understanding.* ERIC ED 041 665.

91. Ortiz, F. I., & Morelan, S. J. (1974). *The Effects of Personal and Impersonal Rewards on the Learning Performance of Field Independent-dependent Mexican-American Children.* Paper presented at the annual meeting of the American Educational Research Association, Chicago, IL.

92. Padilla, A. M., et al. (1985). *Acculturative Stress in Immigrant Students: Three Papers.* Los Angeles: Spanish Speaking Mental Health Research Center.

93. Prago, A. (1973). *Strangers in Their Own Land: A History of Mexican-Americans.* New York: Four Winds.

94. Ramirez, M. (1967). Identification with Mexican family values and authoritarianism in Mexican-Americans. *Journal of Social Psychology, 73,* 3–11.

95. Roberts, A. H., & Greene, J. E. (1971). Cross-cultural study of relationships among four dimensions of time perspective. *Perceptual and Motor Skills, 33,* 163–173.

96. Smith, G. W., & Caskey, O. L. (Eds.). (1972). *Promising School Practices for Mexican-Americans.* ERIC ED 064 003.

97. Stewart, I. S. (1976). Cultural differences between Anglos and Chicanos. *Education Digest, 41*, 29–31.

98. Wagner, H. A. (1977). A comparison of selected differences in adolescence in Mexico and the United States. *Adolescence, 12* (47), 381–384.

99. Vigil, D. (1979). Adaptation strategies and cultural lifestyles of Mexican-American adolescents. *Hispanic Journal of Sciences, 1* (41), 375–392.

# *SEX-ROLE DIFFERENCES*

Many of the effects of ethnic differences noted in Chapter 12 apply to gender differences as well. Authors who have written about or studied male-female behavior have agreed that while the behavior of both genders is similar in most respects, males and females do behave differently in a number of ways. Much less agreement exists about what roles biology versus social learning plays in causing and maintaining these differences.

## *Gender Differences*

By the time boys and girls begin school, many striking differences exist between the sexes. During preschool, kindergarten, and early elementary school years, boys and girls engage in different play activities (1–6). Boys prefer to play with airplanes, blocks, water and sand, trucks and cars. Girls prefer dolls, beads, makeup, cradles, and kitchen toys. During their free time, boys engage in more physical rough-and-tumble play. They also tend to select loosely structured activities with few externally imposed rules or guidelines that are self-initiated and self-organized. Girls are more likely to engage in highly structured activities.

As they get older, girls outdistance boys in verbal ability, but they trail behind in visual, spatial, and math ability. Girls demonstrate less interest than boys in math, computers, and science (7–11). Girls are less competitive and more polite than boys, also more altruistic and helpful. They are more likely to share and to express their support for their classmates. They tend to avoid conflicts rather than deal with them openly (12–24).

Girls use a somewhat different moral approach to solving ethical questions than boys do (25–30). They tell the truth more consistently and do what they say they are going to more than boys and are more likely to empathize with others. Boys are more prone to maintain a double standard. They espouse higher standards for others than for themselves, and they are less self-critical than girls are. Boys also acquire a moral sense later than girls (25–30).

Boys are more assertive, aggressive, and dominant than girls (31–39). They behave in ways their teachers consider unacceptable more often and are punished and suspended from school more often (40–41). Girls react less positively than boys to difficult and challenging situations and are less likely to take risks (42–43). Each gender also has somewhat different learning styles (44–52).

Girls and boys appear to have different emotional styles (53–55). Girls are more likely to experience themselves as sad, depressed, or afraid than boys, who are angry more often than girls. Girls are also more willing to express weakness, fear, and anxiety. But when males do express their emotions, they do so more intensely than females. When young, females tend to be more anxious and timid in school than boys. As adults, they tend to be less comfortable with success (56–59). Girls tend to seek the attention, proximity, and assistance of adults more than boys do, and women tend to use helplessness as a way of influencing others more than men do (60–61).

In school, boys are motivated more by intrinsic motivation than girls. They are also less motivated to behave in socially acceptable ways in order to obtain their teachers' approval (62).

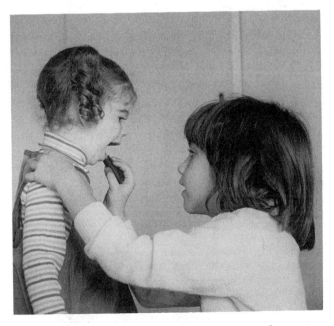
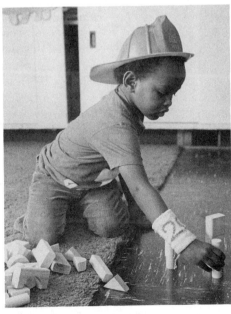

*The play of many young children fulfills current sex-role stereotypes.*

Males and females have different communication styles. Girls' language is more polite, contains fewer four-letter words, and fewer forceful words (63–65). Girls are also more sensitive than boys to nonverbal cues (66–67). In their relationships with males, females tend to allow males to dominate the conversation by permitting them to choose the topics of conversation, to interrupt, and to hold the floor more often.

## Desirability of Sex-Role Differences

A broad range of opinion exists about whether these sex-role differences are natural and desirable. Below are examples of statements from each camp—claiming that such role differences are harmful to males and females or that these role differences are natural and desirable.

### Pro

Certain commentators assert that women and men are most happy and fulfilled when acting out different roles. Woodward claims that:

> Mothers who don't want to be mothers and "liberated" women who feel their daughters ought not to learn feminine ways . . . are robbing their daughters of their sexual identities . . . The forces arrayed against sexual roles in general seem formidable: the more militant women's liberationists for whom mothering is a form of indentured servitude; overachieving fathers for whom inflation is a goad to still longer hours at work; and an increasingly androgynous youth culture that seeks psychological security by deliberately blurring sexual distinctions. (71, p. 28)

Schlafly believes:

> The overriding psychological need of a woman is to love something alive. A baby fulfills this need in the lives of most women. If a baby is not available to fill that need, women search for a baby-substitute. This is the reason why women have traditionally gone into teaching and nursing careers. They are doing what comes naturally to the female psyche. The schoolchild or the patient of any age provides an outlet for a woman to express her natural maternal need. (70, p. 50–51)

### Con

> In American society, men are supposed to be masculine, women are supposed to be feminine, and neither sex is supposed to be much like the other. If men are independent, tough, and assertive, women should be dependent, sweet, and retiring. A womanly woman may be tender and nurturant, but no manly man may be so . . .

> I have come to believe that we need a new standard of psychological health for the sexes, one that removes the burden of stereotype and allows people to feel free to express the best traits of men and women . . . In fact, there is already considerable evidence that

## THEORY FOCUS: SCHLAFLY ON BOY'S EDUCATION

No stranger to controversy, Phyllis Schlafly has spoken and written on a wide variety of issues facing women, including sex-role differences, women's liberation, and abortion. Many of her twelve books express her views on these subjects. Her impact on women's issues has also resulted from her membership and service on such committees and organizations as Stop ERA, Illinois Commission on the Status of Women, and former President Reagan's Defense Policy Advisory Group.

Though most authors have written about the effects of sex roles on female students, Schlafly is equally concerned that males should receive an appropriate education. According to her,

at the age that formal schooling begins for most Americans, little boys lag at least a year behind little girls in maturity. Yet no provision is made for this gender difference either in our compulsory school attendance laws or in the curriculum of kindergarten and first and second grades. It is unnatural for little boys of that age to be expected to sit quietly at a desk and do neat pencil-and-paper work as little girls can so easily do.

This equality of treatment is grievously unfair to the boys, and often causes a deep sense of failure and frustration. When boys cannot compete successfully with girls at their assigned tasks, they seek other (perhaps antisocial) ways of using their excess energies. The result is that boys outnumber girls 13 to 1 in learning failure classes and 8 to 1 among the emotionally disturbed.

Early school entry is harmful to both boys and girls because it makes them peer dependent, but it is twice as harmful to boys. This is only the beginning of the regulations, curricula, and customs of public schools which try to teach a gender neutrality that is contrary to human experience. Coed sports and coed sex classes that pretend a gender neutrality are harmful both physically and psychologically. School materials that induce role reversals, such as showing men as househusbands and women as construction workers, teach false notions far from reality.

Teachers used to believe they were doing a good thing by trying to make left-handed children right-handed. We now know that is unwise. Likewise, it is unwise to ignore gender identity and try to teach gender neutrality. Gender differences cannot be eradicated, and mixed-up children are the results of those who try.

(Phyllis Schlafly, personal communication, May 16, 1989)

---

traditional sex typing is unhealthy. For example, high femininity in females consistently correlates with high anxiety, low self-esteem, and low self-acceptance. And although high masculinity in males has been related to better psychological adjustment during adolescence, it is often accompanied during adulthood by high anxiety, high neuroticism, and low self-acceptance.

Traditional sex typing necessarily restricts behavior. Because people learn, during their formative years, to suppress any behavior that might be considered undesirable or inappropriate for their sex, men are afraid to do "women's work," and women are afraid to enter "man's world." Men are reluctant to be gentle, and women to be assertive. In contrast, androgynous people are not limited by labels. They are able to do whatever they want, both in their behavior and their feelings. (68, p. 32)

The masculine imperative, the pressure and compulsion to perform, to prove himself, to dominate, to live up to the "masculine ideal"—in short, to "be a man"—supersedes the instinct to survive . . .

A man's psychological energy is used to defend *against*, rather than to express, what he really is. His efforts are directed at proving to himself and others what *he is not*: femi-

---

## Self-Quiz: Sex-Role Differences

What is your opinion about the observed differences in the sex roles of students in school? For each of the differences listed below, state whether you think it's innate or learned, desirable or undesirable. Indicate whether you believe it should be encouraged, accepted, or discouraged.

### Interpersonal Relationships

Males are more competitive and less cooperative.

Males share less.

Males are less polite.

Males express less support for their classmates.

Females are less likely to deal openly with conflicts.

Females are less assertive.

Males' moral development proceeds at a slower pace.

Females are more honest, trustworthy, and empathic.

Males tend to be less critical of themselves and to use a double standard when judging their behavior.

In their relationships with males, females are less competitive, more submissive, and allow them to dominate the conversation.

### Dependency-Independency

Males are less compliant toward adults.

Females are more anxious and insecure.

Females are more likely to seek the attention and assistance of adults.

Females are more extrinsically motivated.

Males are less motivated to behave appropriately in order to obtain approval.

Females use helplessness to influence others more often.

### Communication Style

Females are more willing to express weakness, fear, and anxiety.

Females are more sensitive to nonverbal cues.

Males use less polite and more forceful language.

### Reactions of Challenging Situations

Females react less positively to challenging situations.

Males are more willing to take risks.

### Interests in School

Females are less interested in math, science, and computer courses.

Females engage more often in play activities that involve dolls, beads, makeup, cradles, and kitchen toys and less often in activities that involve airplanes, trucks, cars, blocks, water, and sand.

Females tend to select highly structured free-play activities.

Females are less likely to engage in contact sports or those that involve strenuous activity.

nine, dependent, emotional, passive, afraid, helpless, a loser, a failure, impotent and so on . . . The repression of emotion, the denial and suppression of vulnerability, the compulsive competitiveness, the fear of losing, the anxiety over touching or any other form of sensual display, the controlled intellectualizing, and the general lack of spontaneity and unself-conscious playfulness serve to make the companionship of most men unsatisfying and highly limited. Men are at their best when a task has to be completed, a problem solved, or an enemy battled. (69, p. 91, 93)

### Third Position

Many people are not completely in favor of either of the positions described above. They react to sex-role differences on an individual basis, believing that some are natural and healthy, and others are unnatural and harmful.

# School's Role

Because school is a major influence on how people behave, it is important to look at what role the school plays in issues of gender.

## Fostering Differences

Despite the requirement of Title IX that students should not be treated differently on the basis of gender, considerable research evidence shows that schools accommodate to and encourage sex-role differences in school in many ways (87). For example, classroom procedures often involve the separation of students by sex. Teachers also encourage male and female students to enroll in different courses and to engage in different physical activities. The textbooks students read reflect sex-role stereotypes. In addition, teachers respond differently to boys and girls when they ask questions or volunteer answers. Teachers also attribute the poor performance of boys and girls to different causal factors, and they encourage male and female students to behave differently. They also use different management techniques with the two sexes.

*Classroom Procedures*    Roberts (95), Guttentag and Bray (88), and others have reported that some teachers assign different chores to boys and girls, separate them when assigning seats or forming groups, and have separate areas for each sex to hang their clothes. Roberts summarizes why some educators follow such practices in the following statement.

> The physical separation of boys and girls can be interpreted in a variety of ways. At one level, teachers continue this practice because of their belief that a certain degree of mischief and teasing will be avoided. Also, some teachers feel that girls need this kind of protection and insulation from supposedly aggressive boys who might take advantage of and dominate the girls. Another explanation of teacher and school policy that separates the sexes is the fear that boys and girls will become involved in sexual games together.

For many teachers, this very terrifying possibility is avoided by turning girls and boys into "natural" rivals, and by accentuating stereotypical behavior differences. This process helps to prevent girls and boys from developing open, healthy friendships with one another. (95, p. 156–157)

*Courses and Activities*   Tavris and Wade (101), Schaffer (96), and Roberts (95), among others, have described how educators and the educational system reinforce societal stereotypes regarding the courses of study and physical activities that are appropriate for males and females.

As children get older, teachers and other school personnel can directly influence their academic attitudes and ambitions. For example, a recent review of the literature on math achievement found that teachers, counselors, and parents all reward boys more than girls for learning math, and encourage boys more to enter math-related careers. (In one study, counselors unapologetically admitted *discouraging* girls from taking math courses) . . . In math and science courses, teachers tend to interact with and praise boys more, especially when teaching students who are mathematically talented. It is hardly surprising that by high school girls have more negative attitudes toward math and are less likely than boys to appreciate its usefulness. (30, p. 226–227)

Many elementary schools have separate physical education classes for girls and boys, with distinct physical activities for each sex. Girls are often denied access to the traditionally "male" sports and generally given less encouragement in this whole area. Similarly, boys are not encouraged to participate in such "female" activities as dancing, skipping rope, or using the balance beams. When children are interested or determined enough to pursue activities not seen as suitable for their gender, they are labeled "tomboy" and "sissy" . . . Furthermore, by creating artificial barriers to experience, schools perpetuate the myths that all boys are athletically inclined and that all girls are not— thereby severely limiting the potential of both sexes. (95, p. 157)

The educational system has traditionally reinforced existing sex-role stereotypes and has exerted pressures on boys and girls to conform to appropriate roles. Teachers and guidance counselors have tended to reinforce conformity and to encourage the students to pursue different goals and engage in separate activities. Girls have often been discouraged from taking advanced courses such as physics or calculus and, until recently, were completely excluded from the more strenuous and prestigious sports activities and athletic competition. Boys, on the other hand, have been expected to participate in sports and to take science and math courses but to avoid "feminine" courses such as languages, home economics, or typing. (96, p. 83)

As these authors point out, educators who reinforce such sex-role stereotypes can discourage students from fulfilling their true potential. They can also create problems for certain students if they pressure them or require them to get involved in activities that don't interest them or don't fit their self-concepts.

*Textbooks*   Textbooks often reflect societies' sex-role stereotypes (91, 95, 104, 105). Stories about males greatly outnumber stories about females in students' readers and the biographies found in school libraries. In most, males and females tend to be portrayed as fulfilling stereotypical roles at home and in the workplace. Even in math books, boys learn to count by driving cars, flying planes, and engineering trains, while girls learn to count by jumping rope, measuring cloth, and following cooking recipes.

*Teacher Attention*    Teachers are more attentive to boys than girls (72, 75, 78, 83, 84, 86, 92, 97, 98). They are more likely to respond to boys' solicitations. They talk to, listen to, and call on boys more frequently than girls and respond to boys in more helpful ways. As Boudreau states:

> The idea conveyed to girls is, although subtle, quite clear. What boys do matters more to teachers than what girls do. (73, p. 68)

*Teacher Feedback*    Teachers praise boys more than girls for high levels of achievement (85). Teachers also tend to attribute girls' poor performance to lack of ability and boys' poor performance to lack of motivation (80). Teachers praise boys more than girls for *successful* performance of tasks and girls more than boys for neatness, following instructions exactly, and speaking clearly. Even when girls give the wrong answer, they are often praised for raising their hands and volunteering (80). The different types of feedback teachers provide male and female students may contribute to the fact that girls are more likely than boys to attribute their poor performance to lack of ability rather than to lack of effort or motivation (82, 93). It may also help to explain why girls are less persistent and perform less adequately on tasks than boys following failure or the threat of failure (76, 79, 81, 93, 103).

Teachers praise boys more than girls for creative behavior (102) and girls more than boys for conforming behavior (97, 98). In addition, teachers are more accepting of dependent behavior in girls and aggressive behavior in boys (89). In describing the possible results of such differences, Boudreau warns:

> The patterns of reinforcement that young girls receive may lead them to stake their sense of self-worth more on conforming than on personal competency. (73, p. 87)

Levy puts it this way:

> Elementary schools reinforce girls' training for obedience, social and emotional dependence, and docility . . . at the secondary school level, passive learning continues to be rewarded or no intellectual demands are made on girls; and it is expected that girls' education is chiefly a preparation for marriage and child-rearing. (90, p. 53)

*Management Techniques*    Boys get into trouble with their teachers more frequently than girls. Two reasons for this are that boys are less prepared to behave in the ways their teachers desire (73), and teachers react more often to the misbehavior of males than of females (98).

Boudreau (73) points out that girls and boys come to school with different behavior styles, and this is likely to cause them to have different kinds of problems.

> Girls, on the average, enter school better equipped to play the student role than boys. The nonassertive, nonaggressive behavior that is part of girls' socialization fits right in with the structured routine of the classroom. The competitive, self-assertive behavior for which boys have been rewarded outside the classroom creates greater adjustment problems for them. Boys are more likely to "get into trouble" than girls. Paradoxically, the very behavior that allows girls to fit into school more easily also functions to make them less visible, inhibits their learning process, and leads to differences in self-expectancies for success. (73, p. 98)

Moreover, when teachers reprimand students for misbehaving, they tend to speak briefly, softly, and privately to girls and publicly and harshly to boys (92, 98, 100). This is unfortunate since public and harsh reprimands are often counterproductive. (See Chapter 7.)

## Different Opinions

While no evidence as yet directly supports the following suppositions, it seems probable that few educators would disagree that teachers should:

1. Choose readers, biographies, and textbooks that are equally representative of males and females.

2. Pay equal attention to boys and girls who volunteer answers or ask questions.

3. Provide the same amount and kind of help to students regardless of their gender.

4. Praise male and female students equally for high achievement and creativity.

5. Attribute the cause of students' poor performance accurately.

6. Be equally attentive to the misbehavior of boys and girls.

7. Avoid using public and harsh reprimands with all students.

8. Discourage dependent, helpless, and overconforming behavior in all students.

Less agreement exists among educators about whether they should:

Separate boys and girls during certain activities.

Permit males and females to choose to work and play in homogeneous groups.

Encourage, permit, or discourage boys and girls from enrolling in courses and engaging in activities that reflect societal sex-role stereotypes.

Encourage, permit, or discourage sex-role differences in cooperative versus competitive behavior, assertive versus passive behavior, risk-taking, politeness, emotional expressiveness, conformity, and docility.

The controversy about sex-role differences in society at large is reflected in people's attitudes regarding what, if anything, educators should do about sex-role differences in the schools despite Title IX, which requires the elimination of differential treatment in schools based on gender. Individuals who feel that the sex-role differences listed at the beginning of this chapter are natural basically favor leaving things as they were twenty, thirty, or forty years ago. Individuals who don't approve of sex-role differences, at least to the extent that they currently exist in our society, criticize educators whom they believe help to maintain a sexist society.

Some authors, for example, believe that educators should permit and even encourage sex-role differences in school (94, 99). Their point of view is exemplified in the following statement.

*There are many exceptions to sex-role stereotypes.*

Countless teachers, the overwhelming majority of whom are women, expect boys to behave, react, and learn like girls. Even though frequently unaware of it, many of these women value neatness and cleanliness above individual initiative. They prefer conformity, mental passivity, and gentle obedience—at which girls excel—to the aggressive drive and originality of many boys. (94, p. 22)

As noted earlier in this chapter, many others feel that the schools should discourage such sex-role differences. For example, Brooks-Gunn and Mathews argue:

If docility, obedience, and conformity are undesirable traits for boys, surely they are undesirable for girls as well. (74, p. 188)

Tavris and Wade conclude:

If children can learn sex roles in school, they should be able to unlearn them there, too. Even one math teacher can inspire a girl to be interested in math if the teacher gives sincere praise for good work and explicit advice about the usefulness of math in high-paying, high-status jobs. And nothing about children's classroom behavior is impervious to change. Using praise and attention as rewards, preschool teachers can get girls to be more independent and both sexes to play more with each other and select both boys' and girls' toys. The effects are surprisingly rapid; simply by moving into a particular area and giving attention to a particular type of play, a teacher, within minutes, can eliminate sex differences in play patterns that were "obvious" all semester. When the teacher withdraws attention or praise, children tend to revert rapidly to their previous sex-typed behavior. Still, the fact that such behavior can be eliminated quickly shows the enormous impact of the environment—including the teacher—on children's day-to-day conformity to sex roles. (101, p. 226–227)

Carson and Carson further suggest:

It is senseless to expect boys to misbehave simply because they are boys or to expect girls to behave simply because they are girls . . . Such sexual stereotyped thinking often causes problems for everyone . . . Viewing a child's behavior on the basis of his or her sex is unfair to the uniqueness of the child. Furthermore, labeling the child as "sweet, good, little girl" or "all boy" rather than describing the specific behavior is a judgment that serves no important purpose other than establishing sexist and confining behavioral expectations. (77, p. 125)

*Accommodation*   Educators who believe that boys should be allowed to be boys and girls allowed to be girls may avoid some disagreements and conflicts with their students by not trying to change their behavior. For example, educators who permit boys to behave less

*Schools can discourage sex-role differences.*

politely, less compliantly, and more aggressively than girls don't need to scold and discipline them as much as educators who require the same compliant, nonassertive behavior from both genders. Educators who permit girls to feign helplessness and act dependently may avoid the battles of wills that could result from attempts to get them to change their behavior. And educators who allow girls and boys to maintain the kinds of relationships with each other that they have outside of school, even though it means looking the other way when girls submit to male domination, may avoid the hassles that could come with trying to change their relationships. But going along with the prevailing gender stereotypes can also be detrimental to students if it results in allowing and encouraging females to submit to male domination or if it confirms female students' beliefs that it is appropriate for them to be dependent and helpless.

*Changing*   Changing sexual stereotypes can help students. For example, convincing girls that they can do well in math, science, and computer courses or convincing boys that it's okay for them to express their anxieties and fears can be beneficial. But pressuring girls to take courses they feel they can't do well in or to engage in rough sports that they think are unfeminine or pressuring boys to take home economics or to expose their feelings to others when they feel they shouldn't can create, not solve, problems.

---

## Self-Quiz: Gender Differences

What is your opinion about the ways in which educators maintain sex-role differences? State whether you think educators should or shouldn't treat male and female students differently in the following ways.

Speaking briefly, softly, and privately to females and harshly and publicly to males when they misbehave.

Punishing males more often then females.

Separating students by sexes for some physical activities and sports.

Encouraging males and females to enroll in different courses such as math, science, computers, home economics, and typing.

Assigning different classroom chores to males and females.

Seating males and females at different tables.

Assigning males and females different areas for hanging up their clothing.

Responding more often to males when they volunteer answers or comments.

Praising males more often for their accomplishments and creativity and females more often for conformity.

Attributing females' poor performance to lack of ability and males' poor performance to lack of motivation.

Being more accepting of dependent behavior in females and assertive and aggressive behavior in males.

Reacting more often to males than to females when they misbehave.

Ask a colleague to help you observe whether you relate to male and female students differently by keeping track of classroom interactions. Review the results of your observations and decide whether you should modify any of your instructional and classroom management techniques.

## General Principles

When dealing with sex-role differences in school, it's worthwhile keeping the following things in mind. First, only a fine line separates *encouraging* students to change and *pressuring* them to do so. What an educator thinks is encouragement, students can experience as pressure. Second, by encouraging students to behave in ways that their families and friends think is totally inappropriate, well-meaning educators may place students in conflict situations between the school on one side and the home and community on the other. This can cause students to experience the same kinds of identity conflicts as culturally different students. Third, while it is clear that some of the observed differences in behavior between female and male students are learned, unnecessary, and harmful, considerable controversy still exists over the origin of other differences. For example, after reviewing the available research, Maccoby and Jacklin (21) suggest that the observed differences between males and females in verbal, visual-spatial and math ability, and aggressiveness may be biologically determined; many other authors, however, reject this possibility. Basically we do not at present know for sure which, if any, sex-role behaviors are biologically based and which are socially learned.

---

### THEORY FOCUS: MACCOBY STUDIES GENDER ROLES

In addition to serving as the codirector of the Maccoby-Jacklin longitudinal study of behavioral differences among males and females, Eleanor Maccoby has brought together the research in the area of sex or gender role differences in her pioneering works *The Development of Sex Differences* and *The Psy-chology of Sex Differences*. Through these and other publications, she has contributed significantly to our objective knowledge about what sex role differences actually exist and to our ability to begin to apportion the origins of these differences between genetic and environmental causes.

---

Even if some of the observed differences do have a biological basis, it's still unclear whether these biological factors *require* people to behave in certain ways or merely incline people to behave in these ways unless they are taught to behave differently. Until we know more about which gender differences are biologically based and which are learned and the extent to which even biologically based behavior patterns are modifiable, educators' decisions to accommodate to or change sex-role differences in behavior will continue to be based on their preferences, values, and biases rather than on a body of proven scientific fact.

Finally, virtually no research has been done to determine the most effective techniques to help students change behavior that fits a particular sex-role stereotype, to deal with identity conflicts, or to prepare students' classmates, friends, and families to accept and welcome their new behavior. Until we have more reliable information, a cautious, sensitive approach seems the wisest course.

## Self-Quiz: Modeling

Since research indicates that students' behavior is sometimes influenced more by what teachers do than by what they say, you may want to learn about the kind of model you present to your students. If so, ask a colleague to observe and rate you in terms of the behavioral differences typically observed among males and females.

## Summary

Significant differences show up in the ways boys and girls behave in school. Many, but not all, people believe this is a reflection of sex-role stereotypes that exist in society at large. These individuals claim that educators either knowingly or unknowingly contribute to maintaining such stereotypes, and they offer specific suggestions for overcoming and eliminating them in school. Accepting and accommodating to gender differences can help educators avoid some behavior problems, but it can also cause other problems. But then, attempting to eliminate sex-role differences can help students, yet it can cause problems for them as well.

It seems reasonable to assume that the more educators are aware of the relationship between sex-role stereotypes and behavior problems, the more they can help their students. Yet to date little scientific knowledge shows which gender differences are natural and which are learned, when and how to accommodate to necessary sex-role differences, and when and how to eliminate unnecessary ones. Much of what goes on in classrooms behind closed doors regarding the encouragement and discouragement of sex roles is based on the preferences and values of individual educators. Therefore it is imperative that educators become aware of their preferences and values regarding sex roles and do what is best for their students, not what makes them personally most comfortable.

## References

GENDER DIFFERENCES

The references cited below discuss gender differences in play activities.

1. Cameron, E., Eisenberg, N., & Kelly, T. (1985). The relations between sex-type play and preschoolers' social behavior. *Sex Roles, 12* (5), 601–615.

2. Carpenter, C. J. (1979). *Relation of Children's Sex-Typed Behavior to Classroom and Activity Structure.* ERIC ED 178 173.

3. Johnson, J. E., & Ershler, J. (1981). Developmental trends in preschool play as a function of classroom program and child gender. *Child Development, 52* (3), 995–1004.

4. Pellegrini, A. D. (1983). *Children's Social Cognitive Play Behavior: The Effects of Age, Gender, and Activity Centers.* ERIC ED 245 814.

5. Smith, P. K., & Connolly, K. (1972). Patterns of play and social interactions in preschool children. In Burton-Jones (Ed.), *Ethological Studies of Child Behavior.* Cambridge, England: Cambridge University Press.

6. Varma, M. (1980, July). Sex-stereotyping in block play of preschool children. *Indiana Educational Review,* 32–37.

The following references focus on gender differences in academic interests.

7. Allen, R. H., & Chambers, D. L. (1977). *A Comparison of the Mathematics Achievement of Males and Females.* ERIC ED 159 076.

8. Chen, M. (1986). Gender and computers: The beneficial effects of experience on attitudes. *Journal of Educational Computing Research, 2* (3), 265–282.

9. Haertel, G. D., Walberg, H. J., Junker, L. S., & Pascarella, E. T. (1981). Early adolescent sex differences in science learning: Evidence from the National Assessment of Educational Progress. *American Education Research Journal, 18* (3), 329–341.

10. Klinzing, D. G. (1985). *A Study of the Behavior of Children in a Preschool Equipped with Computers.* ERIC ED 255 320.

11. Parsons, J. E. (1982). Sex differences in attributions and learned helplessness. *Sex Roles, 8* (4), 421–432.

Gender differences in politeness, altruism, supportiveness, sharing, and conflict resolution are discussed in the references below.

12. Barnett, M. A. (1978). *Situational Influences and Sex Differences in Children's Reward Allocation Behavior.* ERIC ED 172 081.

13. Becker, J. A., & Smenner, P. C. (1986). The spontaneous use of "thank you" by preschoolers as a function of sex, socioeconomic status, and listener status. *Language in Society, 15* (4), 37–45.

14. Dederick, W. F., et al. (1977). *Interpersonal Values of Intellectually Gifted Adolescent Females: Single-Sex Co-Education.* ERIC ED 140 523.

15. King, L. A., & Barnett, M. A. (1980). *The Effects of Age and Sex on Preschoolers' Helpfulness.* ERIC ED 188 779.

16. Miller, P. M., Danaher, D. L., & Forbes, D. (1986). Sex-related strategies for coping with interpersonal conflict in children aged five and seven. *Developmental Psychology, 22* (4), 543–548.

17. Skarin, K., & Moely, B. E. (1976). Altruistic behavior: An analysis of age and sex differences. *Child Development, 47* (4), 1159–1165.

18. Weissbrod, C. S. (1980). The impact of warmth and instructions on donation. *Child Development*, 51 (1), 279–281.

19. Zarbatany, L., Hartmann, D. P., Gelfand, D. M., & Vinciguerra, P. (1985). Gender differences in altruistic reputations: Are they artifactual? *Developmental Psychology*, 21 (1), 97–101.

20. Zeldin, R. S., Small, S. A., & Savin-Williams, R. S. (1982). Prosocial interactions in two mixed-sex adolescent groups. *Child Development*, 53 (6), 1492–1498.

The references listed below focus on gender differences in the area of competitiveness.

21. Maccoby, E. E., & Jacklin, C. N. (1974). *The Psychology of Sex Differences*. Stanford, CA: Stanford University Press.

22. Moely, B. E., Skarin, K., & Weil, S. (1979). Sex differences in competition—cooperation behavior of children at two age levels. *Sex Roles*, 5 (31), 329–342.

23. Pepitone, E. A. (1973). *Patterns of Interdependence in Cooperative Work of Elementary School Children*. ERIC ED 091 047.

24. Skarin, K., & Moely, B. E. (1974). *Sex Differences in Competition—Cooperation Behavior of Eight-Year-Old Children*. ERIC ED 096 015.

These references discuss the topic of gender differences in moral judgments.

25. Brockman, J., Anderson, T., & Armstrong, S. (1978). *The Developmental Relationship Among Moral Judgment, Moral Conduct and a Rationale for Appropriate Behavior*. ERIC ED 165 051.

26. Gibbs, J. C., Arnold, K. D., & Burkhart, J. E. (1984). Sex differences in the expression of moral judgment. *Child Development*, 55 (3), 1040–1043.

27. Gilligan, C. (1982). *In a Different Voice. Psychological Theory and Women's Development*. Cambridge, MA: Harvard University Press.

28. Jordan, V. B., & Watte, D. (1979). *Effects of Self-Oriented and Other-Oriented Questions on Moral Reasoning*. ERIC ED 181 367.

29. Piaget, J. (1965). *The Moral Judgment of Children*. New York: Free Press.

30. Tavris, C., & Wade, C. (1984). *The Longest War: Sex Differences in Perspective* (2nd ed.). New York: Harcourt Brace Jovanovich.

These articles discuss assertiveness and gender differences.

31. Bender, D. S. (1976). *Psychosocial Dimensions of Sex Differences in the Academic Competence of Adolescents*. ERIC ED 128 695.

32. Cook, S. A., Fritz, J. J., MacCornack, B. L., & Visperas, C. (1985). Early gender differences in the functional use of language. *Sex Roles*, 12 (9), 909–915.

33. Fagot, B. L., & Hagan, R. (1985). Aggression in toddlers: Responses to the assertive acts of boys and girls. *Sex Roles*, 12 (3), 341–351.

The articles below focus on the topic of gender differences in terms of aggression.

34. Ankeney, M. A., & Goodman, G. (1976). Passive aggression versus active aggression in preschool children. *Child Study Journal, 6* (4), 235–244.

35. Barrett, D. E. (1979). A naturalistic study of sex differences in children's aggression. *Merrill-Palmer Quarterly, 25* (3), 193–204.

36. Burdett, K., & Jensen, L. C. (1983). The self-concept and aggressive behavior among elementary school children from two socioeconomic areas and two grade levels. *Psychology in the Schools, 20* (3), 370–375.

37. Eagly, A. H. (1987). *Sex Differences in Social Behavior: A Social Role Interpretation.* Hillsdale, NJ: Erlbaum.

38. Olson, S. L. (1984). The effects of sex-role taking on children's responses to aggressive conflict situations. *Sex Roles, 10* (9), 817–823.

39. Smye, M. D., & Wine, J. D. (1980). A comparison of female and male adolescents' social behaviors and cognitions: A challenge to the assertiveness literature. *Sex Roles, 6* (2), 213–230.

References cited below describe gender differences and misbehavior.

40. Duke, D. L. (1978). Why don't girls misbehave more than boys in school? *Journal of Youth and Adolescence, 7* (2), 141–157.

41. Everton, C. M., Brophy, J. E., Anderson, L. M., Crawford, J., & Baum, M. C. (1975). *Relationship of Grade, Sex and Teacher Rankings to Code Ratings on a Checklist of Student Behavior.* ERIC ED 150 160.

Gender variations in risk taking, challenges, and difficulty are the subject of the following references.

42. Ginsburg, H. J., & Miller, S. M. (1982). Sex differences in children's risk-taking behavior. *Child Development, 53* (2), 426–428.

43. Licht, B. G., Linden, T. A., Brown, D. A., & Sexton, M. (1984). *Sex Differences in Achievement Orientations. An "A" Student Phenomenon.* ERIC ED 252 783.

These references explore gender differences and learning styles.

44. Eagly, A. H. Sex differences in influenceability. *Psychological Bulletin, 85,* 86–116.

45. Eiszler, C. F. (1982). *Perceptual Preference as an Aspect of Adolescent Learning Styles.* ERIC ED 224 769.

46. Hill, K. T., & Dusek, J. B. (1969). Children's achievement expectations as a function of social reinforcement, sex of S, and test anxiety. *Child Development, 40,* 547–557.

47. Hoffman, L. W. (1972). Early childhood experiences and women's achievement motives. *Journal of Social Issues, 28,* 129–155.

48. Horner, M. S. (1972). Toward an understanding of achievement related conflicts in women. *Journal of Social Issues, 28,* 241–253.

49. Lenney, E. (1977). Women's self-confidence in achievement settings. *Psychological Bulletin, 84,* 1–13.

50. Saracho, O. N. (1984). Young children's academic achievement as a function of their cognitive styles. *Journal of Research and Development in Education, 18* (1), 44–50.

51. Van Hecke, M., Tracy, R. J., Cotter, S., & Ribordy, S. C. (1984). Approval versus achievement motives in seventh-grade girls. *Sex Roles, 11* (1–2), 33–41.

52. Wulatin, M. L., & Tracy, R. J. (1978). *Sex Differences in Children's Responses to Achievement and Approval.* Paper presented at the meeting of the Midwestern Psychological Association, Chicago.

The articles below describe the relationship between gender and emotional expression.

53. Baron, P., & Perron, L. M. (1986). Sex differences in the Beck Depression Inventory scores of adolescents. *Journal of Youth and Adolescence, 15* (2), 165–171.

54. Brody, L. R. (1984). Sex and age variation in the quality and intensity of children's emotional attributions to hypothetical situations. *Sex Roles, 11* (1), 51–59.

55. Harlow, L. L., Newcomb, M. D., & Bentler, P. M. (1986). Depression, self-derogation, substance use and suicide ideation: Lack of purpose in life as a mediational factor. *Journal of Clinical Psychology, 42* (1), 5–21.

Gender and discomfort with success is the topic of the following references.

56. Hoffman, L. W. (1974). Fear of success in males and females: 1965–1971. *Journal of Consulting and Clinical Psychology, 42,* 353–358.

57. Horner, M. S. (1972). Toward an understanding of achievement-related conflicts in women. *Journal of Social Issues, 28,* 157–175.

58. Levine, A., & Crumrine, J. (1975). Women and the fear of success: A problem in replication. *American Journal of Sociology, 80,* 964–974.

59. Tresemer, D. (1974). Fear of success: Popular but unproven. *Psychology Today, 7,* 82–85.

Gender differences in the use of helplessness to influence others is the subject of the following articles.

60. Johnson, P. (1976). Women and power: Toward a theory of effectiveness. *Journal of Social Issues, 32* (3), 99–110.

61. Parsons, J. E. (1982). Sex differences in attributions and learned helplessness. *Sex Roles, 8* (4), 421–432.

Gender differences and intrinsic versus extrinsic motivation is discussed in this reference.

62. Harter, S. (1974). Effectance motivation reconsidered: Toward a developmental model. *Human Development, 21,* 34–64.

Gender differences in language, speech, and nonverbal communication are covered in these references.

63. Key, M. R. (1972). Linguistic behavior of male and female. *Linguistics, 88,* 15–31.

64. Lakoff, R. (1974). Language and women's place. *Language in Society, 2,* 45–79.

65. Thorne, B., & Henley, N. (1975). *Language and Sex: Difference and Dominance.* Rowley, MA: Newbury House.

The references below deal with gender differences and sensitivity to nonverbal cues.

66. Hall, J. C. (1978). Gender effects in decoding nonverbal cues. *Psychological Bulletin, 85,* 845–857.

67. Rosenthal, R., Hall, J. A., Di Matteo, M. R., Rogers, P. L., & Archer, D. C. (1979). *Sensitivity to Non-Verbal Communication.* Baltimore: Johns Hopkins University Press.

## DESIRABILITY OF SEX-ROLE DIFFERENCES

68. Bem, S. L. (1983). Traditional sex roles are too restrictive. In B. Leone & M. T. O'Neill, *Male-Female Roles: Opposing Viewpoints.* St. Paul, MN: Greenhaven Press.

69. Goldberg, Herb. (1979). *The New Male: From Self-Destruction to Self-Care.* New York: William Morrow.

70. Schlafly, P. (1977). *The Power of the Positive Woman.* New York: Arlington House.

71. Woodward, K. L. (1983). Children need to learn traditional sex roles. In B. Leone & M. T. O'Neill, *Male-Female Roles: Opposing Viewpoints.* St. Paul, MN: Greenhaven Press.

## SCHOOL'S ROLE

72. Berk, L. E. (1971). Effects of variations in the nursery school setting on environmental constraints and children's mode of adaptation. *Child Development, 42,* 839–869.

73. Boudreau, F. A. (1986). Education. In F. A. Boudreau, R. S. Sennott, & M. Wilson, *Sex Roles and Social Patterns.* New York: Praeger.

74. Brooks-Gunn, J., & Mathews, W. S. (1979). *He & She: How Children Develop Their Sex-Role Identity.* Englewood Cliffs, NJ: Prentice-Hall.

75. Brophy, J. E., & Good, T. L. (1970). Teachers' communications of differential expectations for children's classroom performance: Some behavioral data. *Journal of Educational Psychology, 61* (5), 365–374.

76. Butterfield, E. C. (1970). The role of competence motivation in interrupted task recall and repetition choice. *Journal of Experimental Child Psychology, 2,* 354–370.

77. Carson, J. C., & Carson, P. (1984). *Any Teacher Can: Practical Strategies for Effective Classroom Management.* Springfield, IL: CC Thomas.

78. Cherry, L. (1975). The preschool teacher—child dyad: Sex differences in verbal interaction. *Child Development, 46,* 532–535.

79. Crandall, V. J., & Rabson, A. (1960). Children's repetition choices in an intellectual achievement situation following success and failure. *Journal of Genetic Psychology, 97,* 161–168.

80. Dweck, C. S., Davidson, W., Nelson, S., & Enna, B. (1978). Sex differences in learned helplessness: The contingencies of evaluation feedback in the classroom, an experimental analysis. *Developmental Psychology, 14* (3), 208–276.

81. Dweck, C. S., & Gilliard, D. (1975). Expectancy statements as determinants of reactions to failure: Sex differences in persistence and expectancy change. *Journal of Personality and Social Psychology, 32,* 1077–1084.

82. Dweck, C. S., & Reppucci, N. D. (1973). Learned helplessness and reinforcement responsibility in children. *Journal of Personality and Social Psychology, 25,* 109–116.

83. Fagot, B., & Patterson, G. (1969). An in vivo analysis of reinforcing contingencies for sex role behavior in the preschool child. *Developmental Psychology, 1,* 563–568.

84. Felsenthal, H. (1970). *Sex Differences in Teacher-Pupil Interaction During First Grade Reading Instruction.* Paper presented at the annual meeting of the American Educational Research Association, Minneapolis, MN.

85. Frey, K. S. (1979). *Differential Teaching Methods Used with Girls and Boys of Moderate and High Achievement Levels.* Paper presented at the annual meeting of the Society for Research in Child Development, San Francisco.

86. Good, T. L., Sykes, J., & Brophy, J. E. (1973). Effects of teacher sex and student sex on classroom interaction. *Journal of Educational Psychology, 65* (1), 74–87.

87. Grannis, J. C., Kaminsky, S. W., & Furman, W. W. (1972). *Teachers' and Pupils' Roles in Variously Structured Classroom Settings and Subsettings: A Report from the Columbia Classroom Environments Projects.* Paper presented at the annual meeting of the American Educational Research Association, Chicago.

88. Guttentag, M., & Bray, H. (1977). Teachers as mediators of sex-role standards. In A. Sargent (Ed.), *Beyond Sex Roles.* St. Paul, MN: West.

89. Levitin, T. A., & Chananie, J. D. (1972). Responses of female primary school teachers to sex-typed behaviors in male and female children. *Child Development, 43,* 1309–1316.

90. Levy, B. (1972). The school's role in the sex-role stereotyping of girls: A feminist review of the literature. In D. Gersoni (Ed.), *Sexism and Youth.* New York: Bowker.

91. Lips, H. M., & Colwill, N. L. (1978). *The Psychology of Sex Differences.* Englewood Cliffs, NJ: Prentice-Hall.

92. Meyer, W. J., & Thompson, G. G. (1956). Sex differences in the distribution of teacher approval and disapproval among sixth graders. *Journal of Educational Psychology, 47,* 385–396.

93. Nichols, J. G. (1975). Causal attributions and other achievement-related cognitions: Effects of task outcomes, attainment value, and sex. *Journal of Personality and Social Psychology, 31,* 379–389.

94. Pollack, J. H. (1968). Are teachers fair to boys? *Today's Health, 46* (4), 21–25.

95. Roberts, E. J. (Ed.). (1980). *Childhood Sexual Learning: The Unwritten Curriculum.* Cambridge, MA: Ballinger.

96. Schaffer, K. F. (1981). *Sex Roles and Human Behavior.* Cambridge, MA: Winthrop.

97. Sears, P., & Feldman, D. (1966). Teacher interactions with boys and girls. *National Elementary Principal, 46* (2), 31.

98. Serbin, L. A., O'Leary, D. K., Kent, R. N., & Tonick, J. J. (1973). A comparison of the preacademic and problem behavior of boys and girls. *Child Development, 44,* 796–804.

99. Sexton, P. (1965, June). Are schools emasculating our boys? *Saturday Review,* p. 57.

100. Spalding, R. L. (1963). *Achievement, Creativity, and Self-Concept Correlates of Teacher-Pupil Transactions in Elementary Schools.* Cooperative Research Project No. 1352. Washington, DC: U.S. Department of Health, Education and Welfare, Office of Education.

101. Tavris, C., & Wade, C. (1984). *The Longest War: Sex Differences in Perspective* (2nd ed.). New York: Harcourt Brace Jovanovich.

102. Torrance, E. P. (1965). *Rewarding Creative Behavior: Experiment in Classroom Creativity.* Englewood Cliffs, NJ: Prentice-Hall.

103. Veroff, J. (1969). Social comparison and the development of achievement motivation. In C. P. Smith (Ed.), *Achievement-Related Motives in Children.* New York: Russell Sage Foundation.

104. Weitzman, L. J., & Rizzo, D. (1971). *Sex Role Stereotypes in Elementary School Textbooks.* New York: NOW Legal Defense and Education Fund.

105. Women on Words and Images, Dick and Jane as Victims. (1972). *Sex Stereotyping in Children's Readers.* Princeton: Women on Words and Images.

# INDEX

**Photo Credits** (continued from the copyright page)